THE
FIRST POPULIST

THE DEFIANT LIFE
of ANDREW JACKSON

DAVID S. BROWN

SCRIBNER

New York   London   Toronto   Sydney   New Delhi

Title page illustration: The United States in 1818. The steady admission of new states beyond the
Appalachian Mountains introduced a populist note to the country's politics apparent in the kind
of "common man" democracy that made Andrew Jackson president.

For Bill and Suzanne

Bear me out in it, thou great democratic God! . . . Thou who didst pick up Andrew Jackson from the pebbles; who didst hurl him upon a war-horse; who didst thunder him higher than a throne!

Herman Melville, *Moby-Dick, or, The Whale*, 1851

Contents

Introduction:
The Populist Persuasion

It was the People's day, and the People's President and the People would rule. God grant that one day or other, the People do not pull down all rule and rulers.

Washingtonian Margaret Bayard Smith
on Jackson's first inauguration, 1829

Andrew Jackson, the first president to be born in a log cabin, to live beyond the Appalachians, and to rule, so he swore, in the name of the people, refuses to fade away. Controversial in his own day, he remains unrepentant. Some identify him as the common man's crusader in chief, a defender of farmers and wage earners who, with a single lethal veto, is said to have saved the republic from a rapacious Money Power by quashing a government-chartered national bank catering to economic elites.[1] Others are far less willing to accept as a hero a slaveholder, an architect of Indian removal, and a critic of abolitionism. The epithets "racist," "white nationalist," and "ethnic cleansing," rather, now vie with the Bank War and the Battle of New Orleans in reckoning with Jackson's fluctuating reputation. On one point, however, all sides can perhaps agree—Old Hickory, the first president to come from neither Virginia nor Massachusetts, broke up the long train of coastal executive aristo-crats, embodying in his improbable ascent the promise of western fron-tier peoples negotiating a natal age of expanding political participation.

More precisely, Jackson, a cotton nabob, master to hundreds of enslaved people in multiple states, in fact straddled two sections. As the country's fifth southern president he aligned as well with the interests of

1

an entrenched squirearchy, having sought entry into its environs from an early age. The orphan of impoverished Scots-Irish immigrants, Jackson strove to ape the gentry and become a gentleman among Tennessee's self-anointed blue bloods. Along the way this parvenu acquired a plantation, bought and sold slaves, engaged in land speculations, and bred racehorses. He pushed for military appointment, fought in class-affirming duels, and more generally adopted a distinctly southern notion of honor that elevated landed nobility above mere citizens.

Two reflections of an aged Jackson by British women—the visiting writer Harriet Martineau and the expat actress Fanny Kemble— offer contrasting but retrospectively revealing judgments. The former depicted the General as fundamentally ill-informed and uneducated, a poorly postured eminence betrayed by a trace of depression:

> Jackson is extremely tall and thin, with a slight stoop, betokening more weakness than naturally belongs to his years. He has a profusion of stiff gray hair, which gives to his appearance whatever there is of formidable in it. His countenance bears commonly an expression of melancholy gravity; though, when roused, the fire of passion flashes from his eyes, and his whole person looks then formidable enough. His mode of speech is slow and quiet, and his phraseology sufficiently betokens that his time has not been passed among books.[2]

Kemble, by contrast, more amiably emphasized the courtly, martial side of her subject, whom she described as

> very tall and thin, but erect and dignified in his carriage—a good specimen of a fine old well-battered soldier. . . . His manners are perfectly simple and quiet, therefore very good. . . . Of his measures I know nothing; but firmness, determination, decision, I respect above all things: and if the old General is, as they say, very obstinate, why obstinacy is so far more estimable than weakness, *especially* in a ruler, that I think he sins on the right side of the question.[3]

Jackson, of course, cultivated both impressions. While Martineau stressed the unlettered side of her subject, Kemble, once described by the writer Henry James as having "seen everyone and known everyone . . . in two hemispheres," noted a natural patriarch, an air still more abundantly asserted by a cotton oligarchy committed to the appearance of chivalry in the practice of slavery.[4]

Martineau's musing further underscores the surprising corporal frailty that trailed Jackson through most of his life. The general's cadaverous physique idled in pain and discomfort; his many ink-stained letters are filled with references to internal afflictions, ailing teeth, and weak lungs. Scarcely a hypochondriac, Jackson paid with his body for the chain of military campaigns—from the American Revolution to the War of 1812 to the subduing of the southern Indians—and ritual affairs of honor that secured his redoubtable reputation. He suffered from dysentery, dyspepsia, and bronchiectasis, contracted chronic diarrhea, battled pulmonary infection and malaria, and may have carried intestinal parasites. His body lodged two bullets, one from a duel and the other received in a brawl, thus creating cavities prone to infection; the lead from these missiles leached steadily over the years into his system. Jackson bore the aches and inconveniences of these several infirmities for much of his life, and one cannot help but wonder if they exacerbated an already ingrained tendency toward cross and quick-tempered responses.

This splenetic cast of mood and attitude, "formidable" in Martineau's rendering and "very obstinate" in Kemble's, is perhaps Jackson's defining emotional attribute. He could be a singularly devout and fierce hater, inspiring in turn the devout and fierce hatred of others. A series of pre-presidential episodes—ordering the deaths of deserting militiamen, killing a Tennessee dandy in a duel, and overseeing the executions of two British subjects while commanding a U.S. army sweeping illegally through Spanish Florida in pursuit of Seminoles—prefaced a sequence of equally astonishing presidential actions. These included the violent removal of Indian peoples from their ancestral homes, asserting his right to enforce or ignore Supreme Court decisions, and firing off more executive vetoes than all of his predecessors combined. Cocksure in the extreme, Jackson found both essence and consequence trafficking in a world of enemies—made, cultivated, and over the years assiduously accumulated. This congenital unquiet helps to place a couple of other antecedents in context, for Old Hickory is also the first executive to be targeted by a would-be assassin and the sole occupant of that high office to suffer a senatorial censure.

Drawn to these and other rare episodes of presidential Sturm und Drang, we too casually discount Jackson's real skills as a statesman.

More polished and lawyerly than what the secondary literature suggests, he often read the public far better than Congress did. None of his vetoes were overridden; an unprecedented third term was his for the asking. As if caught between two worlds, a number of Washingtonians were surprised upon first encountering the legendary general, expecting something of a savage from the wild backwoods. A bemused Jackson—like a wry coonskin cap–wearing Benjamin Franklin playing the rustic in Paris—enjoyed the juxtaposition. An underrated politician, he knew well the length and limits of his personal popularity, courted easily the sudden electoral prominence of western constituencies, and managed to combine an aristocratic persona with a less posh public face.

Taken altogether, balancing Jackson's legacy is a problematic exercise, complicated by contradictions. Is he the era's greatest democrat or its elected autocrat? Should he be remembered primarily for the Bank War—the fight against economic privilege—or for his efforts extending white privilege (and slavery) into the Gulf Coast states? And to what extent, if any, should Jackson be evaluated within the conditions of our concerns as opposed to the cultural context that shaped his own? "At one time in the history of the United States," a biographer accurately enough reminds us, "Andrew Jackson . . . was honored above all other living men." It is also true, however, that many of his contemporaries thought the General petty, narrow, and excessively partisan to the prejudices of agrarian and frontier communities. The perceptive French political thinker Alexis de Tocqueville captured some of this criticism in the first volume of his important study *Democracy in America* (1835), when noting that "Jackson is the spokesman of provincial jealousies; it was *decentralizing* passions . . . that brought him to sovereign power." Tocqueville further recognized the reciprocal relationship that linked the seventh president to his supporters—"he yields to its intensions, desires, and half-revealed instincts, or rather he anticipates and forestalls them." On the other side of the social divide, so the Frenchman insisted, "all the enlightened classes are opposed to General Jackson."[5]

Despite these still extant interpretive differences, a shared consensus exists among historians that Jackson, as much as any president, imposed his priorities upon the nation. This makes him an especially relevant figure to revisit today when many people, perhaps not so far removed from Tocqueville's position, see populism as a challenge to liberal democracy. It is often asserted that an organized populist persuasion, as opposed to a mere expression or attitude of the same, first found traction in America during the late nineteenth century, and that the People's Party (circa 1890–1910)—southern and western defenders of agrarianism, railroad regulation, and monetary reform—advanced its most coherent ideological vision.[6] Its champion, three-time Democratic nominee for the presidency William Jennings Bryan (aka the Great Commoner), anticipated, so the narrative goes, future adherents of an anti-elite, culturally conservative, and blue-collar political faith. These included Louisiana senator Huey Long (Depression-era author of a notional Share Our Wealth program), Joseph McCarthy (suspicious of academics and Hollywood types during the Red Scare of the 1950s), and the segregationist Alabama governor George Wallace (a stalwart defender of white rights during the civil rights sixties).

In our own time, populism has entered the mainstream, personified in self-described democratic socialist Bernie Sanders's Bryan-like anger at Wall Street and former president Donald Trump's provocative appeals to working-class voters. But Jackson, the product of an earlier vox populi upheaval, predated all of these pols. He energized a mass movement aimed against an eastern ruling regime, he claimed to speak (so he said in one state paper) for the nation's "farmers, mechanics, and laborers," and he frankly distrusted experts, preferring his informal Kitchen Cabinet of advisors to administration officials.[7] Not above demonizing—this long list included bankers and abolitionists as well as political opponents—he ruled by agitating, confronting, and dividing. One might argue that Jackson, a political celebrity around which a remarkable cult of personality developed, stands as the country's original anti-establishment president.

The script being written today, that economic inequality, liberal elitism, and demographic change in America and elsewhere have encouraged a backlash reflected in the rise of charismatic strongman leadership, is one that applies to Jackson as well. Importantly his several resentments—against the monetary dominance of the National Bank, against a political system that routinely returned quasi aristocrats to the presidency, and against a Supreme Court that disagreed with him on the Indian removal question—were matched by much of the culture. Each antagonist embodied the prerogative of an establishment institution that in practice ministered primarily to an Atlantic Seaboard society even as the Ohio and Mississippi valleys were rapidly growing. These waxing regions, only just coming into their own, were soon to shake the electoral landscape. In the 1828 presidential contest every trans-Appalachian state went for the victorious Jackson over the Harvard-educated incumbent John Quincy Adams of Massachusetts.

In Jackson's relationship to the electorate we again see a number of precedents—the nation's first populist president, the first executive to be selected (in the wake of suffrage extensions in state constitutions) by the franchise of white men from all classes, and the first to practice a politics of resentment against an entrenched gentry. A modern iteration of this latter element might be observed in Ronald Reagan's famous 1981 inaugural address attack on Washington politics—"government is not the solution to our problem; government is the problem. From time to time, we've been tempted to believe that society has become too complex to be managed by self-rule, that government by an elite group is superior to government for, by, and of the people." More recently, in a 2019 rally, Trump told a Grand Rapids, Michigan, crowd, in reference to his critics, "They say they're the elite . . . [but] we got more money, we got more brains, we got better houses and apartments . . . you're the elite, we're the elite."[8] All three of these men, over a span touching three separate centuries, either stated or suggested a return to a polity or an economy premised on popular control.

I hope in this biography to produce a portrait of Jackson that illuminates many of the early republic's questions and controversies. For to trace this polemical general's days is to reckon with the issues of race and revolution, populism and sharpening partisanship that tremored through the young nation during its formative decades and touch us still. Caught by the 1820s in the throes of twin market and transportation revolutions that overturned older notions of community and economy, much of the country seemed eager to experiment with a new political order.[9] Jackson mastered this raucous realignment, feeding off its energy and opportunities. In the process he became the defining figure of his era, variously a hero, a sometime scoundrel, and, to his enemies, a second Caesar. His ability to address both the aspirations and estrangements of emerging constituencies outside the orbit of the eastern mainstream profoundly reconfigured the nation's electoral map. These advancing groups, exemplars of popular politics, seemed prepared in their plainspoken devotion to make him the man-on-horseback idol of their adulation.

Part I

MAN ON THE MAKE

I well recollect when I was left an orphan.
Andrew Jackson, 1830

In youth, the southern-born Jackson resettled across the Appalachians, part of a larger western migration that would one day reshape the map of American politics.

1

Ulster to America

Andrew Jackson's ancestors were part of a long Scottish migration to northern Ireland initiated by a string of English kings and queens in the company of a prolonged Tudor conquest. By the seventeenth century these established Ulster plantations mirrored a broader Elizabethan exodus to assorted Atlantic World entrepôts, including the distant forests and fisheries of North America. Many of those who came to Ulster were poverty-mired Scottish Lowlanders driven by the timeless search for better opportunities overseas. "Amongst these, Divine Providence sent over some worthy persons for birth, education and parts," wrote one contemporary observer, "yet the most part were such as either poverty, scandalous lives, or, at the best, adventurous seeking of better accommodation, set forward that way."[1] Having made their migrations across the narrow North Channel, Jackson's people, now Ulster Scots, lived in County Antrim, perhaps in or at least near the vicinity of Carrickfergus, one of Ireland's oldest towns and about a dozen miles north of Belfast, then a city of some few thousand. Briefly in the 1690s, the satirist, poet, and cleric Jonathan Swift, author of *Gulliver's Travels*, lived in neighboring Kilroot.

Jackson family lore insists that the future president's paternal grandfather, a linen-weaver of some means named Hugh Jackson, served during the Seven Years' War as a company officer at the 1760 Battle of Carrickfergus Castle, an imposing twelfth-century Norman structure situated on a rocky promontory. There, a detail of Ulster men, their ammunition spent, surrendered to a French raiding party of some several hundred led by the notorious privateer François Thurot—who was killed shortly afterward while contesting a stronger British squadron near the Mull of Galloway.

Jackson's maternal side, the Hutchinsons, also resided in County Antrim, where, in about 1737, his mother, Elizabeth (Betty), was born. Little is known of her early years except that in the winter of 1759, in a modest parish church, she married Andrew Jackson Sr., thought to be the same age. Family lore maintains that Jackson, unlike his father, "was very poor" while the Hutchinsons were considered more "thrifty, industrious and capable." Occupying a point on the Irish Enlightenment's outer edge, Carrickfergus, older than Belfast and still somewhat medieval in outlook, long retained a reputation for countering English Anglo-Saxonism's cold arithmetic interest in economic and imperial advancement with a Celtic superiority in matters of imagination, wonder, and folklore. "When Andrew Jackson, the elder, tilled his few hired acres," wrote one nineteenth-century historian, the people of County Antrim "still believed in witches, fairies, brownies, wraiths, evil eyes, charms, and warning spirits. They had only just done trying people for witchcraft."[2]

In 1765 Betty and Andrew Jackson were living in a thatched cottage on a small farm near Castlereagh with their two young sons Hugh and Robert; rising rents and tithes had recently aroused organized resistance by the Hearts of Oak, a regional protest movement made up largely of farmers and weavers in counties Armagh, Londonderry, Fermanagh, and Tyrone. Abandoning their tired lands that year, the Jacksons uprooted and, from Carrickfergus, sailed to America, almost certainly influenced by the earlier migration of Betty's sisters, four of whom, between 1763 and 1766, settled just east of Appalachia along the hazy blue border separating North and South Carolina. Three of the sisters are said to have arrived unmarried but, soon after docking in Philadelphia, acquired northern Irish husbands, perhaps in Pennsylvania, possibly in Virginia, or perchance elsewhere on the primeval route down the mountains.[3]

Though sizable, the Scots-Irish advance into the South Carolina backwoods lagged far behind the contemporaneous (1760–1774) importation into Charleston of some forty-two thousand Africans. On the eve of the American Revolution, blacks constituted a striking 60 percent of the colony's population.[4] Years earlier, a 1731 law had taxed the introduction of newly enslaved people into South Carolina—and used a portion of the funds to encourage, through such emoluments as tools, rations, and rent-reduced lands, the relocation of Europeans. With such inducements did the colony exhibit certain racial fears that informed its course and character over time. Its Anglo founders felt vulnerable to the threat of Spanish invasion from the south, to attack from Native Americans (the recent Cherokee War, 1758–1761, fresh in memory), and to the perpetual possibility of slave insurrection (the 1739 Stono Rebellion constituting the largest ever uprising among black captives in the British mainland colonies). The settlement in which Andrew Jackson would spend his formative years, in other words, idled apprehensively, alive to the suggestion of conspiracy and willing to spill blood to quell its enemies.

The Jacksons were part of a significant circa 1760s exodus out of northern Ireland; one estimate claims that as many as twenty thousand Ulsterites left the province during this crucial decade. In fair weather these voyages might take seven or eight weeks and be attended by a host of discomforts and privations associated with eighteenth-century ocean travel. Just where the Jacksons made landfall is still something of a mystery. The General's first biographers, John Reid and John Henry Eaton, both associates of their subject and perhaps deferring to his supposition, insisted that the family arrived in Charleston. In the 1930s, however, the historian Marquis James dissented, writing, "Had the Jacksons landed at Charleston at any time between 1761 and 1775 their debarkation would have been noted in the records of His Majesty's Council for South Carolina, which are intact in the original manuscript in the office of the Historical Commission of South Carolina at Columbia." James thought Philadelphia, a principal designation of Scots-Irish settlers, a far likelier guess.[5] But in 2001 biographer Hendrik Booraem argued otherwise:

> James's reasoning no longer seems as good as it once did. Part of his argument was that the Crawfords [the family of one of Betty Jackson's sisters] resided in Pennsylvania before coming to the Waxhaws [a region on the North and South Carolina border], and that Andrew and Betty Jackson probably came with them; but . . . current understanding of the Crawfords' migration suggests that they . . . could as easily have come [from Ireland to America] via Charleston as via Pennsylvania. James's other point, that the Jacksons' and Crawfords' names would have appeared in Council Records if they had entered

through Charleston, is based on a misunderstanding. The Council Records list only immigrants who were applying for bounty land; those who intended to buy their own would not have registered with the Council. Accordingly, I have accepted the Reid version.[6]

In a 2017 communication to the author, Booraem added: "My thinking was that Andrew and Betty Jackson knew where they were going, because other kinfolk had arrived in Carolina before them, so it made more sense for them to go directly to Charleston and skip the long overland trek from Philadelphia; and the colony of South Carolina had the welcome mat out for Irish settlers at that time, because they were trying to build up the population of the backcountry." Booraem does allow, however, that "there is no hard evidence where the Jacksons landed in America."[7]

With more certainty we know that the family settled in the Waxhaws region, named after a meandering tributary creek of the Catawba River once home to the Waxhaw tribe, who were defeated in 1716 by the Catawba, who were themselves devastated by smallpox in 1759. Down to perhaps a few hundred, they remained in the area during Jackson's youth, "harmless and friendly," reduced to vying for a living in the woven basket and trinket trades.[8] Betty and Andrew moved onto a large allotment of land, perhaps as much as two hundred acres, adjoining Twelve Mile Creek and in the vicinity of Betty's sisters and their families. The farm, only indifferently surveyed, sat about four miles from the nearest post road; its remoteness proposed an availability born of thin, unpromising soil. It is possible that the Jacksons, at this time apparently without a deed, squatted on the land, a by no means uncommon occurrence. In any case, Betty, Andrew, and their two boys, survivors of the long journey from Ulster to America, set about building a new life.

In the late winter of 1767, the Jacksons appeared to be making progress; the family ate garden crops grown in fields laboriously claimed from the forest, and they sheltered in a small log cabin. Then suddenly, perhaps in early March, Andrew Jackson Sr. died. Legend suggests that he collapsed while attempting to maneuver a particularly heavy log, though it seems just as likely that the incident implicated a broader exhaustion from which his broken body, engaged in constant labor, failed to recover. He took to bed, never to rise again. Conveyed by a primitive wagon to the Waxhaw churchyard, he received burial, with no marker, then or since, to indicate his remains. Part product and part victim of an unforgiving colonial frontier, the senior Jackson later became a small but central piece in the elaborate lore of his rising son. "It is a delightful reflection to the emigrant from the European monarchies," wrote a florid biographer, "that, like the father of Andrew Jackson, he may, under the institutions whose protection he seeks, give a chief magistrate to a great nation, and live in history more honoured than the fathers of kings."[9]

The elder Andrew, whether more honored or not, never saw his third, last, and namesake son, born March 15, 1767. Newly widowed, Betty and her boys eventually stayed with the family of Betty's sister Jane Crawford. The McCamies, the family of yet another Hutchinson sister, Peggy, and her husband, George, were only about a mile away—but in a different colony. Jackson believed that he was born at the Crawford homestead in South Carolina, though there is an oral tradition passed down by Jackson's cousin Sarah Leslie, who insisted that she attended the delivery at the McCamies' in North Carolina. To this day both states claim Jackson's nativity in statues and markers. Though the evidence remains inconclusive, those in the Palmetto State point with pride to an 1824 communication in which Jackson wrote: "I was born in So Carolina, as I have been told, at the plantation whereon James Crawford lived about one mile from the Carolina road." Jackson's will left a legatee "the large silver vase presented to me by the ladies of Charleston, South Carolina, my native State."[10]

Over the next fourteen years, young Andrew lived at the Crawfords' with his mother. As a poor relation Betty took up many of the household chores and, along with caring for her sons, looked over no fewer than eight Crawford children. She eventually sent her eldest, Hugh (Huey), to live with the childless McCamies; the evidence places him under ten at the time. A strong, portly, and pious woman, Betty wanted her youngest boy educated and groomed to become a Presbyterian minister. If not quite cut out for the cloth, Jackson seemed nevertheless eager to keep this maternal presence nearby throughout his life. His wife, Rachel, also a strong, portly, and pious woman, inclined in her later decades to a dry and partial Presbyterianism. In such echoes and linkages it is perhaps permissible to surmise that more than any Jackson, Crawford, or McCamie man, Betty proved to be Andrew's most important influence. Her strong sense of honor apparently anticipated his own. "One of the

last injunctions given me by her," he told a friend, "was never to insti-
tute a suit for assault and battery, or for defamation [as the defamed
should defend their own rights]; never to wound the feelings of others,
nor suffer my own to be outraged; these were her words of admonition
to me; I remember them well, and have never failed to respect them."[11]
Possibly in such stern maternal instruction lie the seeds of several duels
and lesser dustups.

Described by one contemporary as "mischievous" and prone to
pranks, Jackson enjoyed in youth physical activity, competition, and
self-assertion. "He was exceedingly fond of running foot-races, of leap-
ing the bar, and jumping; and in such sports he was excelled by no one
of his years," wrote biographer James Parton, who interviewed many of
Jackson's Waxhaws neighbors:

> To younger boys, who never questioned his mastery, he was a gen-
> erous protector; there was nothing he would not do to defend them.
> His equals and superiors found him self-willed, somewhat over-
> bearing, easily offended, *very* irascible, and, upon the whole, "dif-
> ficult to get along with." One of them said, many years after, in the
> heat of controversy, that of all the boys he had ever known, Andrew
> Jackson was the only bully who was not also a coward.[12]

Unlike his brothers, who attended common schools, Jackson, presumably earmarked for some distant Presbyterian pulpit, received more
formal training. Later in life, when contesting for political power, he
heard repeatedly dismissive references to his shaky education. One 1824
newspaper, touting the supposed virtues of a John Quincy Adams–
Andrew Jackson presidential ticket, played upon the conjectured contrasts in the men, asking readers to imagine a perfect pairing of:

> John Quincy Adams,
> Who can write,
> And Andrew Jackson,
> Who can fight.[13]

Certainly Jackson's rickety syntax (when compared to previous presidents', not to the average American's) gives some surface credibility to
this claim, but on the whole it is a false lead. As an adult Jackson read

with interest a good number of newspapers, journals, letters, and law books; he left behind a sizable library and maintained an extensive correspondence. But it is true, and particularly in youth, that he valued the outdoor life—hunting and riding—and likely found few bookish models among his many cousins. Nothing if not resourceful, Jackson always read *enough* to get by, trusting his instincts above all else.

And yet because of Betty's expectation that her youngest enter the ministry, she and the Crawfords set aside money for Jackson to attend local academies. In these frontier establishments, run by Dr. William Humphries and James White Stephenson, the boy acquired the rudiments of a formal education, learning his letters and how to read. Engaged in practical training, he never developed an interest in either literature or poetry, and with the possible exception of *The Vicar of Wakefield*—a hugely popular moral tale written in the early 1760s by Oliver Goldsmith and featuring comedy, satire, and sentimentalism—novels meant little to Jackson. It is perhaps enough to say that his mind worked quickly, intuitively, and fluently. Singled out by Betty for an education denied his brothers, Jackson possibly evinced a conspicuous mental spark, a persuasive tongue (the sermonizer's imperative instrument), or a spontaneous intelligence. He may have simply struck his mother as special.

Considering Betty's strong presence in her youngest son's life, it would be easy if imprecise to disregard her absent husband's influence. From testimony we know that the junior Andrew, something of a rowdy and a ruffian, could be bossy, oppressive, and high-handed. He exhibited further a tremendous confidence that often bordered on conceit. Bearing in mind his secondary status living in the Crawford household, his lack of a strong paternal figure, and his lowly rank among a scrum of older brothers and cousins, it is possible that the fatherless Jackson dealt with insecurity by both asserting and overasserting himself. He soon learned that a strong personality brought him attention and recognition; he seemed to relish opportunities to compete and proclaim his strength. "I could throw him three times out of four," one classmate reported, "but he would never *stay throwed*. He was dead game, even then, and never *would* give up."[14]

2

Forged in War

Nothing quite impacted Jackson like the American Revolution. It destroyed his patriot family, left him an orphan, and shifted his loyalties decisively and forever from clan to country. Just sixteen when the war concluded, Jackson saw service as a courier in the militia, attended to troops at the Battle of Hanging Rock fought in the chaotic South Carolina interior, and was later captured and held prisoner. He remains the only POW to become president. From these several and traumatic experiences he developed an abiding hate for Great Britain and, more generally, the hereditary underpinnings of monarchical civilization. This hostility Jackson never relinquished, casting peerage as the eternal enemy of the people, a resilient adversary that he recognized in subsequent struggles including the Bank War, in which he denounced the offending national depository as "a dangerous aristocratic influence."[1] For Jackson, that is to say, the Revolution never really ended. Long after independence, it continued to frame his way of reckoning with the world, offering a constant and convenient ideological rival to rail against.

To suggest that Jackson's Anglophobia commenced with the Revolution, however, underestimates the potent weight of history. The Scots and Irish shared a long chronicle of opposition to English domination registered in centuries of rebellions, border skirmishes, and wars for independence. Presumably the Jackson and Hutchinson families identified with this legacy, having just a decade earlier abandoned Ulster, whose gentry charged high rents for land upon which peasants eked out a bare existence. Reid and Eaton, privy to Jackson's reminiscences, wrote that Betty's "opposition to British tyranny" and rule of the wellborn, quite completely biased her boys. "Often would she spend the winter's night, in recounting to them the sufferings of their grandfather, at the siege of Carrickfergus, and the oppression exercised by the nobility of Ireland, over the laboring poor."[2]

Beyond these familiar fireside recitations, Jackson saw more immediate models of martial repute in the activities of the popular Waxhaws militia. Aside from supplementing the regular army, the local guards in the South Carolina upcountry constituted one of the few opportunities for social advancement. Militiamen paraded, carried or wore weapons, exchanged gossip, and were a center of community pride. The more ambitious might compete for rank, give speeches, and maneuver for recognition; the possibility of battle-born glory always lingered lightly in the background. The reputation of the militia grew during the Revolution as Minutemen—famously mustered to meet the British at Lexington and Concord, Bunker Hill, and in Saratoga's thick forests—captured the public's imagination. For a boy in the remote Waxhaws, such storied soldiery must have conjured the very epitome of honor, ambition, and bravery.

In the Revolution's early years, however, the uplanders did little but drill. Not until 1780, following generally unsuccessful British campaigns in New England, New York, and the mid-Atlantic, did the war come to the Waxhaws. Adopting a southern strategy designed to take advantage of the section's presumably large loyalist population, London's imperial policy makers concentrated on capturing shoreline cities. In December 1778 a British army of some three thousand under the command of Lieutenant Colonel Archibald Campbell, a veteran of the Seven Years' War, seized weakly defended Savannah and looked next to Charleston, which it failed to subdue that spring. In connection with this campaign, Jackson's eldest brother, Hugh, perhaps sixteen, died from heat exhaustion and fatigue following the Battle of Stono Ferry, fought just west of South Carolina's coveted capital city. Come winter General Sir Henry Clinton and his second in command, Charles (the Earl) Cornwallis, accompanied a large force consisting of fourteen thousand troops and sailors aboard ninety warships, to Savannah. From there, their army advanced on ill-prepared Charleston, which, after a six-week siege, capitulated in May 1780. This proved to be Britain's greatest victory of the war.

The capture of South Carolina's oldest and largest city opened the state to a long season of savage violence. Redcoats and local Tories penetrated the interior, and in the spring of 1780 the predacious Lieutenant Colonel Banastre Tarleton, "rather below the middle height, and with a face almost femininely beautiful," so one Virginia newspaper said, led a mainly loyalist force into the Waxhaws, where, on May 29, near Lancaster, it defeated a Continental Army force led by Colonel Abraham Buford.[3] Patriot soldiers accused the charging dragoons of ignoring a white flag and attacking the surrendering Americans. This Battle of the Waxhaws, known also and notoriously as the Waxhaw Massacre or Tarleton's Quarter, resulted in more than three hundred Americans killed, wounded, or captured and served as an appalling preface for the fighting that followed. During the entire independence movement, more combat action took place in South Carolina than in any other colony; the deadly patriot versus loyalist dimension made this desperate struggle a civil as well as a revolutionary war.

Directly after the Tarleton massacre, the people of the Waxhaws were expected to offer up a loyalty oath on pain of seeing their farms and fields wasted. This condition, combined with the humiliating mid-August defeat of a large American force at the Battle of Camden some thirty miles east of present-day Columbia, sent a shock of fear (and a flood of wounded soldiers) through patriot settlements in the suddenly war-torn upcountry. Betty Jackson and her two surviving sons fled to the north, joined by the Crawfords and many of their frightened neighbors. Throughout the summer this refugee community moved back and forth, evading British soldiers and loyalists while foraging in the picked-over wilderness. Tarleton himself passed through the Waxhaws on his way to negotiate for the neighboring Catawba people's assistance; Jackson, hiding with a cousin, saw the prettily put together officer in his "breeches of white linen" and polished russet leather boots ride by— "I could have shot him," he later recalled.[4]

If this sounds suspiciously like the vague boast of a boy, it should be noted that earlier that summer Jackson had experienced a battle— his "first field." Only thirteen and perhaps operating in the capacity of a messenger, he accompanied a force led by Colonel William Richardson Davie (later to serve as a delegate to the Constitutional Convention) and charged with harassing British outposts in the area. On August 6, Davie's militia, as part of a larger force operating under General Thomas

Sumter (a South Carolina planter whose name later adorned the famous sea fort in Charleston), attacked one such station at Hanging Rock, south of Heather Springs. The assault initially succeeded—casualties were inflicted, horses and weapons were captured—before loose discipline and British reinforcements turned the tide. As a disappointed Davie later wrote, "A retreat was by this time absolutely necessary—The commissary stores were taken in the center encampment, and numbers of the men were already inebriated, the greatest part were loaded with plunder and those in a condition to fight had exhausted their ammunition."[5]

Briefly sojourning in the Waxhaws following the Battle of Hanging Rock, Jackson soon bolted before the pending threat of Cornwallis's roaming army. Yet again he traveled north, this time to Charlotte, where he stayed for a few months with distant kin. By February he had returned home to be with his mother and brother Robert. Not long after, a cavalry regiment commanded by the Boston-born Tory John Coffin arrived in the Waxhaws to assist local loyalists, only to be opposed by several dozen armed and mounted patriots including Andrew and Robert. In one attack Coffin's invading light dragoons scattered this resistance, taking a handful of prisoners, though Jackson fled into a neighboring swamp. Later that day Jackson and Robert, who had made a separate escape, were reunited and after an evening hiding in the wilderness made their way to a Crawford relative's house where, desperately hungry, they scoured for food. A Tory neighbor, discovering their horses and muskets, reported their presence to nearby British soldiers, who promptly took the boys prisoner.

The house now filled with Redcoats, and one of the haughty officers ordered young Andy to clean his mud-crusted jackboots. What transpired became, in years to come, a crucial part of the Jackson legend. As Reid and Eaton related the story:

> This order [Andy] positively and peremptorily refused to obey; alleging that he looked for such treatment as a prisoner of war had a right to expect. Incensed at his refusal, the officer aimed a blow at his head with a drawn sword, which would, very probably, have terminated his existence, had he not parried its effects by throwing up his left hand, on which he received a severe wound.[6]

Approached retrospectively the episode appears, considering its principal, uncannily anticipatory. Jackson exhibited a characteristic stubbornness in facing the officer down, he managed to evade what could easily have been a very serious if not fatal injury, and he now carried with him physically—and psychically—wounds dispensed by an enemy. This small contest in the Waxhaws would be replayed many times over in succeeding years as Jackson confronted any number of nemeses—on dueling grounds, at New Orleans, in Congress, and so on. Even in his early teens he gave every indication for those willing to notice of communicating a rigid, formidable, and oddly indestructible quality.

Andy and Robert accompanied some dozen prisoners to Camden, a forty-mile march without provisions. There they were incarcerated with more than two hundred men and, as Jackson later recalled, "treated badly & inhumanly." The injured youths (Robert too having received a head wound from the enraged British officer who had assaulted his brother, and for the same transgression) were given no medical care, their shoes and jackets were taken, and they sat in a cramped jail where smallpox circulated. "Many fell victims to it," Jackson later related. "I frequently heard them groaning in the agonies of death and no regard was paid to them." Seeking her sons, Betty arrived in Camden and, arranging their inclusion in a prisoner exchange, took them home. "Having only two horses in our company when we left Camden," Jackson remembered, "and my brother, on account of weakness caused by a severe bowel complaint and the wound he had received . . . being obliged to be held on the horse, and my mother riding the other, I was compelled to walk the whole way. The distance to the nearest house to Camden where we stopped that night was forty five miles and . . . I had to trudge along barefooted."[7]

The journey proved too much for the weakened Robert, who died shortly after arriving home. Jackson, worn to the bone, fell ill but recovered; soon after, Betty accompanied a couple of Waxhaws women to Charleston, where they nursed prisoners, including two Crawford nephews, held on ships in the harbor. There, she contracted typhus (colloquially called ship fever) and subsequently, that autumn of 1781, died. All of Jackson's immediate family were now gone. Betty's clothes, apparently the only things in her possession, were sent to her only surviving son; she was buried just outside of Charleston, in an unmarked grave. Many years later James H. Witherspoon, a Waxhaws man distantly related to Jackson through marriage, wrote to the now famous general, the Hero of New Orleans, after interviewing one Agnes Barton, a Charlestonian who reported that her carpenter husband and two other men had carried out the interment. After more than forty years, she could no longer recollect the burial site's location. Finding his mother's remains, Jackson replied to Witherspoon, "would be great satisfaction, that I might collect her bones," though he seemed to hold no real hope for their recovery; in fact they have never been located.[8]

Betty died just as the military phase of the American Revolution closed with Cornwallis's conclusive October surrender to French and Continental forces at Yorktown, Virginia. Considering the fate of so many in the upland, mere survival undoubtedly constituted Jackson's greatest accomplishment during these dangerous years. Only entering his teens, he had already witnessed arson, killings, and outright butchery. In the Waxhaws "the laws were literally silent, and there were no courts to protect property or punish crime. Men hunted each other like beasts of prey," while the unspoken motives of revenge issued "in cruelties to the living and indignities to the dead."[9] The War of Independence further imbued in Jackson a deep nationalism; with his closest kin now gone, the country became, in a sense, a kind of surrogate to which he swore an undying allegiance. When he believed the republic endangered—by British soldiers at New Orleans, by a too powerful National Bank in Philadelphia, or by South Carolinians eager to nullify federal law—he acted decisively to end their threats.

But these lines of identification formed over time, and a callow Jackson carried more immediate concerns. Filled with ambition he moved forward, in search of a profession, in search of himself.

3

But a Raw Lad

Following Betty's abrupt death, a shaken Jackson, still recuperating from illness, lived briefly at the home of his uncle Thomas Crawford. No firm evidence identifies the reasons why he soon broke from his kin, though a combination of shock, resentment, and perhaps some simmering rage appears to be the principal source of his suffering. Several decades later, for the edification of an interviewer, Jackson recalled his explosive, unyielding conduct during this difficult period. "Captain Galbraith in charge of Comissary Stores, ammunition &c. for the American Army, was then staying with my Uncle," he reported,

> and being of a very proud and haughty disposition, for some reason, I forget now what, he threatened to chastise me. I immediately answered, that "I had arrived at the age to know my rights, and although weak and feeble from disease, I had courage to defend them, and if he attempted anything of that kind I would almost assuredly Send him to the other world."[1]

Perhaps no more than fifteen, but certain of himself, Jackson apparently refused to make amends for his threat and, for this or possibly other reasons, not long after quit the Crawfords—upon whose initiative it is unclear—to board with yet another if more distant blood connection, a Mr. Joseph White, and his family. Within three years he would leave the Waxhaws, never to return. Over the ensuing decades one Crawford cousin or another attempted to rekindle relations with their by-now famous relation, but Jackson, offering only a chilly politeness in return, seemed determined to leave behind his unhappy past.

Possibly he resented occupying among the Crawfords the unwanted position of laboring apprentice. Even at an early age he seemed to believe himself destined for some impending prominence. Though Betty's wish for her youngest to enter the learned clergy never materialized, the boy nevertheless sought a station above the common. There is a story that when the Crawfords were building a new house to replace the burned-out structure left behind by the British, Jackson, expected to contribute, grew frustrated. While sweating over the arduous process of converting rounded logs into flat lumber, he is reported to have flung "down his axe and swore that he was never made to hew logs."[2] Not long after he moved on to the Whites, where, under the auspices of Joseph White's son, he began, with little interest, to learn the saddler's trade. He later remembered this brief interlude for a biographer's aide in detached terms: "I remained there about six months, assisted him as much as the fever and ague with which I was then afflicted would allow me." With what the aide took to be "considerable humor," Jackson, the most celebrated man of his era, concluded with a wink, "I think I would have made a pretty good saddler."[3]

Taking destiny into his own hands, Jackson enrolled in 1782 in the New Acquisition, a primitive school run by one Robert McCulloch; there, he sampled Shakespeare and the Greek historian Plutarch among a "desultory course of studies." Though this decision exhibited both ambition and maturity, it also encumbered the impatient and perhaps bored teen with an education of mere rules and recitations. The following year, the year the Treaty of Paris formally ended the American Revolution, he received a modest inheritance from his paternal Irish grandfather, Hugh. The sum, meant for Betty, came to between three and four hundred pounds sterling, and a more conservative soul might have invested it in land or perhaps a business. But Jackson soon took off for the distant delights of Charleston, recently evacuated by the British. During its occupation (1780–1782) many of its prominent citizens had retreated to the Waxhaws, offering the locals a fugitive glimpse of urban sophistication. No doubt Jackson coveted their manners, refinement, and affluence. For when he arrived in this city of fifteen thousand, long the center of the southern colonies' Atlantic trade, he seemed intent to mimic the master class. While strolling its environs, he spent freely on

clothing, bought a gold watch and pistols, and purchased a fine horse—
a de rigueur sign of respectability among young southern white men.
He soon ran through his inheritance, owing a landlord and unable to
pay his debts. In some desperation he wagered his recent equine acquisition against $200 in a tavern crap game and by the merest chance won.
"My calculation," so he later observed, "was that, if a loser in the game,
I would give the landlord my saddle and bridle, as far as they would go
toward the payment of his bill, ask a credit for the balance, and walk
away from the city; but being successful, I had new spirits infused into
me, left the table, and from that moment to the present time I have
never thrown dice for a wager."[4]

Jackson likely learned several lessons in Charleston. He knew that he
wished to live as a gentleman, that such a vocation required resources
beyond the reach of an artisan or a farmer, and that he had foolishly
thrown money away. He soon returned home, perhaps the small object
of quiet ridicule for his imprudence; this episode almost certainly factored into the apparent ease with which he later left the Waxhaws. Many
years after, in 1817, he sent Andrew Jackson—Jack—Donelson, both a
nephew and one of his several wards, to the U.S. Military Academy at
West Point with the following paternal advice: "My Dear Andrew, you
are now entered on the theatre of the world amonghst stranger, where
it behoves you to be guarded at all points. . . . You must recollect, how
many snares will be laid for the inexperienced youth to draw him into
disapation, vice & folly, against these snares I wish to guard you."[5]

The Charleston misstep may have caused Jackson a bit of embarrassment, but his brush with the city's comparative cosmopolitanism
clarified a desire to advance beyond the backwoods. He returned to
McCulloch's school and, with a smattering of literacy, soon began to
offer instruction himself in the Waxhaws; the work may have disciplined his thinking and steadied his finances, though it held no intrin-
sic interest for the clearly aspiring Jackson. Accordingly, he removed
in December 1784 to Salisbury, North Carolina (seat of rural Rowan
County, forty miles northeast of Charlotte); eager to assume the status
of a gentleman, he chose to study law, the proven path in the Revolutionary era for young men on the make.

Intensely self-conscious, Jackson, all of seventeen, brought to his new
surroundings a bit of Charleston. A handmade long coat accentuated
his lean frame, complementing a pewter-buttoned waistcoat, buckskin

breeches, and silk stockings. He certainly looked the part of a grandee-lawyer and had reason to anticipate a rapid professional ascent. The region's surplus of attorneys had thinned considerably due to the war and its attendant exodus of educated Tories. For reasons unclear, Jackson soon abandoned Salisbury and rode west seventy-five miles to Morganton, expecting to read law with Colonel Waightstill Avery, trained at Yale College and currently serving in the North Carolina House of Commons. But this request, so Avery's son later recalled, could not be accommodated:

He came to Morganton, with a view to study law with my father, prompted by the fact that my father had at that time the best law library in western North Carolina. The country was new. My father's improvements were of the log-cabin order, and want of house-room rendered it inconvenient to receive the young man into his family as a boarder, though he was desirous to do so.[6]

Rebuffed, Jackson returned to Salisbury, where its local eminence, Spruce Macay, Rowan County state's attorney and later a judge, agreed to take him on.

Quartering at the Rowan House tavern, an ancient ramshackle structure featuring several large fireplaces, a primitive un-ceilinged roof, and a landlord's special punch concoction, Jackson proceeded to study law and raise hell. Parton visited Salisbury in the 1850s and interviewed a number of elders who claimed some knowledge of their famous former neighbor. "Salisbury [is replete] with traditions respecting the residence there of Andrew Jackson as a student of law," he wrote. "Their general tenor may be expressed in the language of the first old resident of the town, to whom I applied for information: 'Andrew Jackson was the most roaring, rollicking, game-cocking, horse-racing, card-playing, mischievous fellow, that ever lived in Salisbury.'" Educationally, these reports continue, "he did not trouble the law-books much," while vocationally he dallied "more in the stable than in the office"; a natural leader, he soon came to "the head of all the rowdies hereabouts." Jackson and his friends stole signposts, hid outhouses, and "occasionally indulged in a downright drunken debauch." He never repeated in Salisbury, however, his graver Charleston transgressions. Still under twenty, he enjoyed himself, possessing a certain enveloping charisma that others enjoyed as well. He delighted in hunting, riding, and cockfighting and was, so an enslaved man remembered, "very fond of the ladies." Though sometimes violent—once he and a small celebrating party destroyed a tavern—and occasionally cruel—he callously invited "two women of ill-repute" (a mother and her daughter) to a Christmas ball "to see," so he said, "what would come of it"—Jackson seemed more generally in control of his emotions. Salisbury lore remembers him as essentially a conventional young man, spirited, highly sociable, and eager for amusement. With hindsight, Jackson described himself during these fitful years as admittedly rough, if well intentioned: "I was but a raw lad then, but I did my best."[7]

Physically, Jackson now possessed a long, thin face resting below a high forehead crowned by abundant sandy-red hair that ashened with age and bristled up. Hardly handsome, he exhibited a remarkably slender build, carrying some 140 pounds on a bony frame slightly exceeding six feet. His eyes were a deep blue and mesmeric, and typically conveyed his emotions. He moved with a concentrated grace.

Perhaps having learned all he could from Macay, Jackson left this mentor in late 1786 to complete his studies with Colonel John Stokes, a Revolutionary War veteran who had lost a hand at the Battle of the Waxhaws; in its vacant place he wore a prominent silver knob, an effective instrument to bang upon jury boxes. Approximately a year later, after passing an examination administered by two judges of the state's Superior Court of Law and Equity, Jackson won the right to practice law in North Carolina. For three years, the period of his legal apprenticeship, it appears that he kept afloat financially principally as a sportsman, carefully betting on cards, cockfights, and horse races. He seemed to have no other means of income other than a parental inheritance of two hundred acres in Mecklenburg managed by a Crawford relative, but that could hardly account for his liberal spending. He attended dancing school, managed to keep himself in room and board, and, so one Salisbury resident remembered, made an effort to look like "one of the genteel young men of the place."[8]

In November 1787, only two months after receiving admission to the North Carolina bar, Jackson, along with a group of friends—all attorneys—was arrested in Rowan County, on the vague complaint of trespassing, and charged with damages coming to £500, about $18,000 in current dollars. With no official record of what transpired, it seems almost certain that the case was settled out of court. More prosaically, Jackson began collecting licenses in early 1788 to practice in several central North Carolina counties. This pregnant period in the young esquire's life overlapped almost precisely the many and identical months devoted to the drafting and ratification of the U.S. Constitution. For Jackson, it might be said that both career and country were born together. He rode hundreds of miles during this time, a distinctly endeavoring young man on an extended rural circuit in search of work and eager to earn a reputation, though still uncertain of his future.

4

Western Apprentice

While Jackson read law in Salisbury, a small body of settlers led by the frontiersman John Sevier—"a pioneer," so a biographer has written, "of the most aggressive type"—founded the extra-legal State of Franklin in 1784.[1] Nestled in what is today eastern Tennessee, this presumably autonomous territory actually belonged to North Carolina; in effect Sevier's group casually engaged in a secession movement. The State of Franklin (also known as the Free Republic of Franklin or the State of Frankland) never earned admittance into the Union, of course, and existed a mere four years before an unamused North Carolina reasserted control over the region.[2] In early 1788 John McNairy, Jackson's slightly older friend, mentor, and fellow Macay student, won appointment to serve as Superior Court judge in what was then called the Western District of North Carolina—approximately half of present-day Tennessee. He offered Jackson the post of district attorney, and Jackson, his east-of-the-Appalachians ambitions at bay, promptly agreed. Representing the legal arm of the state in this rising West, he possibly guessed, could make a man for life. Accordingly, Jackson and McNairy joined a party at Morganton that spring and proceeded across the green mountains into a young country.

The group stopped at Jonesborough, Franklin's provisional capital and a modest settlement consisting of several dozen cabins. Nashville, their destination and the principal city of the Mero District (a corruption of "Esteban Rodríguez Miró y Sabater," the Colonial Spanish governor of Louisiana), lay nearly three hundred miles away through thick forest. The suggestion of an Acadian paradise just beyond the high hills

28

had long enticed pioneers, promising an extraordinary abundance of game and crops. "The fertility of the soil and goodness of the range almost surpass belief," one Virginia advertisement fairly rhapsodized in 1775, "and it is at present well stored with buffalo, elk, deer, bear, beaver, &c., and the rivers abound with fish of various kinds. Vast crowds of people are daily flocking to it, and many gentlemen of the first rank and character have bargained for lands in it."[3]

This pleasing notion of the petty potentate claiming his share in a freshly white West must have held immense appeal to Jackson. For the vocation that called to him most clearly was that of gentleman. In the country's older settlements and states, that coveted designation often extended through pedigree, though in the new communities across the mountains a bit of acting and attitude could be opportunely invoked. To adopt the pose, impression, and trappings of a gentleman in a still crude and fluid society proposed a kind of audacious improvisation. Certainly Jackson, his education spotty, his lineage undistinguished, could make no claim of gentry status other than the one he fashioned for himself. With some knowledge of the saddler's business, he frequented racetracks in Jonesborough, perhaps exhibiting his learning as a kind of currency; he also took possession of Nancy, a young enslaved woman maybe in her late teens, given to Jackson for legal services rendered. Over the next eight years he acquired at least fourteen other men and women—George, Molly, Aaron, Peg, Roele, Hannah, Bet, Betty, Hanna, Tom, Mary, Swaney, Charles, and Suck—who worked the properties he acquired in the Cumberland Settlements. In all, Jackson owned slaves for the final fifty-seven years of his life, forming but a single link in a new post-Revolutionary, post-Appalachian plantocracy—and Nancy, in turn, anticipated the coming armies of enslaved who seeded, harvested, and ginned their plundered agricultural wealth.

A gentleman further retained the privilege of challenging another gentleman to an affair of honor. This Jackson did soon after arriving in Jonesborough when embarrassed in a district court case by a more learned attorney, Waightstill Avery—the very man who nearly four years earlier had declined to offer Jackson legal instruction. Avery's son later described the events leading up to their duel:

In the trial of a suit one afternoon, General Jackson and my father were opposing counsel. The General always espoused the cause of

his client warmly, and seemed to make it his own. On this occasion, the cause was going against him, and he became irritable. My
father rather exultingly ridiculed some legal position taken by Jackson; using, as he afterwards admitted, language more sarcastic than
was called for. It stung Jackson, who snatched up a pen, and on the
blank leaf of a law book wrote a peremptory challenge, which he
delivered there and then.[4]

Avery, possibly disinclined to take the confrontation seriously,
ignored the note. But the following day Jackson, in a second communication, made that method all but impossible:

When amans feelings & charector are injured the ought to Seek
aspeedy redress; you recd. a few lines from me yesterday & undoubtedly you understand me. My charector you have Injured; and further
you have Insulted me in the presence of a court and a larg audianc
I therefore call upon you as a gentleman to give me Satisfaction for
the Same; and I further call upon you to give me an answer immediately without Equivocation and I hope you can do without dinner untill the business done; for it is consistant with the charector
of agentleman when he Injures aman to make aspedy reparation;
therefore I hope you will not fail in meeting me this day.[5]

In effect, Jackson informed both Avery and the whole of Jonesborough that he too was due respect and honor. Avery's son observed further the sudden weight the summons carried: "My father was no duelist;
in fact, he was opposed to the principle, but, with his antecedents, in
that age and country, to have declined would have been to have lost
caste." Naturally the senior Avery "promptly accepted" the challenge.[6]
Having secured a second, John Adair, later to represent Kentucky
in both the House and Senate, Avery agreed to meet Jackson the next
evening. At the appointed hour, just north of Jonesborough, on mea-
sured ground, the two men aimed and fired—innocently into a darken-
ing summer sky. Their differences having been carefully ironed out by
dutiful handlers, Jackson's honor was restored (or perhaps recognized
for the first time), while Avery managed to extricate himself from the
surprising anger of a much younger man. The duel terminated with a
ready handshake and friendly words. Had Jackson killed Avery, it might

have injured equally his future prospects. A Revolutionary War veteran, a well-liked lawyer in western Carolina, and, as noted, a seasoned member of the North Carolina General Assembly, Avery enjoyed a modest if real prestige.[7] Jackson, by contrast, lacked a strong patron at this time, and had he, at a careless twenty-one, actually plugged the forty-seven-year-old Avery, he might have courted powerful enemies. Not for the first time did he engage in a reckless action, and not for the last time did he emerge from a rash course with his reputation strengthened.

Several weeks after the Avery duel Jackson and McNairy, along with an assemblage of some sixty families, left Jonesborough on a recently blazed stump-strewn trace, bound for Nashville. Riding a "fine young stallion," Jackson relied on "a stout pack-mare" to carry "my personal effects," including books and blankets, tea and tobacco. Aside from three pistols, he also possessed a new rifle made in Charlotte.[8] Thinly populated with colonizers, the area between the Cumberland Settlements and the Appalachians proved a formidable, even dangerous trek. Traveling this route a few years later, in 1797, the English astronomer Francis Baily wrote:

> The *whole of that distance* is scarcely better than a wilderness . . . for the houses are so far apart from each other, that you seldom see more than two or three in a day. I was determined also in starting so soon, by the idea that I should meet with a plantation on the road, where I should find a pasture, and where I should accordingly stop and refresh my horses; for there is no part of these new settlements but you may take this liberty, if you pay them well for it; the idea of their being hospitable and doing a kindness to strangers for *nothing*, is false. This hospitality is only shown to neighbors, &c, where they expect it will be repaid by the same return, and arises from a want of inns on the road, where travellers may call and do as they please.[9]

Though largely devoid of white settlements, the region teemed with Cherokee. One night Jackson and the colonizing group were nearly attacked by neighboring Indians. Legend has it that Jackson, alerted by the ubiquitous hooting of nocturnal "owls," convinced the company to abandon its camp before daybreak and press on to Nashville. Early that morning a luckless hunting party, said to have occupied their freshly abandoned site, suffered a deadly assault. Thus did Jackson's reputation as a frontier leader take root; though neither guide nor commander of the company, he somewhat imperiously assumed responsibility for its safety and demanded to be at its center.

In thinking about the growing importance of western constituencies in the politics of the early republic, the pilgrimage made by settlers from coastal enclaves into the interior deserves a brief word. For many, this journey (or the remote memory passed down by parents) constituted a common existential experience, traversing the mountains, fearful of roaming wolf packs, and always mindful of Indian populations. In making their exoduses, these people thus adopted an identity sacred to their own.

Jackson's band reached Nashville in late October 1788, though the young district attorney's plans were impermanent. Making a "merely experimental move," he wished before committing himself to be certain of "the advantages that might be disclosed." He soon discovered that Nashville, founded less than a decade earlier and home to fewer than three hundred colonizers, a couple of taverns, and a courthouse, offered sufficient opportunity for a young man on the make. The Treaty of Hopewell, conducted just three years earlier between the old Confederation Congress and a Cherokee delegation, recognized a boundary of American settlement lying mainly in the present-day Mid-Cumberland Region, with Nashville its mini metropole. A nineteenth-century source describes the area as "a gently undulating and most fertile country; a land of hard wood, with the beautiful river Cumberland winding through the midst thereof."[10]

In 1788 a twenty-one-year-old Jackson, alive to the political and economic opportunities of the rising West, crossed from North Carolina into the "Tennessee Country."

Though conflict with the area's Indians continued, so did the steady migration of pioneers from the East. By remaining in this region, Jackson casually adopted the adversaries of his handpicked home. In the Carolinas the Catawba were a peaceful people—the last warfare in the Waxhaws between Native and Euro Americans occurred prior to Jackson's birth. But in the Cumberland Settlements the Cherokee threat, provoked by Anglo encroachments on their lands, remained real and Jackson, assuming the attitude of a westerner, enlarged his list of enemies to include the region's Indians as well as the Spanish colonial regime to the south.[11]

There is, beyond the possibility of professional advancement, yet another compelling reason why Jackson decided to stay in the Cumberland Valley—Rachel Donelson Robards. Among the area's first white settlers, the Donelsons had migrated from Virginia in 1780; Rachel, the eighth of the family's eleven children, turned thirteen at the time. Five years later, with Nashville's meager corn reserves drained by a difficult winter and a sudden influx of pioneers, the Donelsons moved north to Kentucky. They subsequently returned, but Rachel, married in 1787 to Captain Lewis Robards, a land speculator living in Harrodsburg, remained.

The same age as Jackson, Rachel grew up in rural Pittsylvania County, Virginia. Her father, Colonel John Donelson, a member of the House of Burgesses (1769–1774), had taken Rachel to visit the homes of both Washington, whom he had served under during the Revolution, and Jefferson. Though lacking a formal education, she proved otherwise proficient, mastering a number of textile arts, including sewing, spinning, weaving, and embroidery. She liked to play musical instruments, enjoyed horseback riding, and later developed a strong religious streak. Rachel had long black hair, dark eyes, and a permanently tanned complexion—opposite the period's more coveted pale-skinned standard. Contemporaries described her as "bright-eyed" and "sprightly" as well as "stout" and "robust."[12]

Not long before Jackson's arrival in Nashville, Rachel's mother, Rachel Stokely Donelson, was widowed, the colonel having been shot and killed, it is unclear by whom, along the banks of the Barren River while conducting a survey. Seeking protection, she opened her blockhouse to boarders, including Jackson and John Overton, a Virginian eager to establish a legal career in the West. The two men became close and in coming years Overton served Jackson as a loyal friend and advisor.

Rachel and Lewis, their marriage having deteriorated in Kentucky, also lived with Mrs. Donelson. Robards had grown uneasy in Harrodsburg at what he regarded as his wife's too intimate conversations with a certain Mr. Short and insisted, in a letter to his mother-in-law, that she retrieve her daughter. One of Rachel's brothers went to Kentucky and promptly brought her home, though Robards returned for her not long after, then decided instead to stay. A playful, flirtatious young woman, Rachel enjoyed attention, and this Jackson, the new boarder, supplied aplenty. They seemed to have had an immediate and mutual rapport, and there are several stories as to how their illicit courtship tempestuously progressed. One insists that Robards accused Jackson of undue intimacy with his wife, another that Jackson threatened Robards with a knife, and still another that Jackson assured Robards of his wife's loyalty and (on Overton's advice) moved out.[13] All we know for certain is that Jackson left the Donelson blockhouse, decamping for Mansker's Station, one of several small, fortified settlements in Middle Tennessee. But the drama in the Robards' marriage persisted, or perhaps Lewis Robards simply realized that he had lost his wife. Not long after Jackson's removal the captain returned to Kentucky, alone.

Professionally, Jackson's nascent career took off in Nashville. With both a license to practice law and the added sinecure of public prosecutor, he occupied a unique position in the Mero District. Creditors and merchants immediately sought his services to pursue litigation against debtors, which he did energetically, issuing in but a single month more than five dozen writs. In contrast to his later and sharp criticisms of the country's creditors during the Bank War, Jackson proved a willing agent of the district's emerging financial class, aggressively pursuing defaulters. More broadly, he handled a variety of cases ranging from land and merchandise sales to prosecuting violent behavior—mainly assault and battery. The following citations from the West Tennessee court records offer a few examples of the rustic legal arena in which Jackson operated: "John Rains is fined five shillings, paper money, for profane swearing"; "John Barrow . . . Sayeth, [Humphry] Hogan threatened he will kill [John] Kitts' hogs, if he did not keep them from his door, and also whip himself"; "in an affray . . . between Wm. Pillows and Abram Denton, in

fighting, the said Pillows bit off the upper eend of Denton's right ear."
Considering that more than three thousand Tennesseans were black,
many of them chattel, it is unsurprising that Jackson processed slave
sales. "Andrew Jackson, Esq.," one extract notes, "proved a bill of sale
from Hugh McGary to Gasper Mansker, for a negro man."[14]

In the early summer of 1789, only a few months after arriving in
Nashville, Jackson got his first taste of Indian fighting. Two years earlier
General James Robertson, a Virginia-born explorer and onetime companion of the iconic frontiersman Daniel Boone, had led some 130 men
against a contingent of Creek and Cherokee supplied by French trad-
ers at Muscle Shoals in present-day northwestern Alabama. Confiscating guns, ammunition, and other goods, Robertson's victorious troops
proceeded on to Nashville, only to attract retribution as several of the
area's primitive military stations were attacked. Jackson arrived in the
Cumberland Settlements during this active and ongoing phase of frontier warfare. Following a daytime assault by Indians on a nearby fort, a
Captain Sampson Williams raised a small company of twenty men—
including a conscripted Jackson—and pursued the enemy. As one early
nineteenth-century history of the District of East Tennessee notes,
"They overtook the Indians at Duck river, killed one, wounded several
others, and drove them across the river, taking from them sixteen guns,
nineteen shot-pouches, and a quantity of baggage, clothing, &c."[15] The
surprised natives had failed to fire a shot, and Jackson, a mere private,
could now make some slender claim to having a hand in securing the
Cumberland Settlements.

His education in the ways of the backwoods, its careful compromise
among competing Native, Anglo, and European powers, had only just
begun.

5

The Conspiracy Game

To the south of the Cumberland Settlements lay the old Spanish Main's sprawling coastal colony. Americans above the thirty-first parallel (the northern boundary of current-day Tangipahoa Parish, Louisiana) were unable, without Spanish approval, to market their produce in New Orleans or to use its coveted port for purposes of export. These western farmers fumed at their government's inability to negotiate access to the Gulf, along with its failure to provide protection from the area's Creek Indians. Without such admittance to markets or a secure border, the region's prospects remained uncertain. Thomas Jefferson, a great advocate of agrarian interests, referred a little worrisomely in correspondence about this time to "the unsettled state of our dispute with Spain."[1] Thus commenced, in the republic's early years, a steady stream of rumors, schemes, and connivances known collectively as the Spanish Conspiracy, an exercise in enticement designed by a diminishing Spanish empire to coax trans-Appalachian Americans into separating from the East and offering their loyalty to the Madrid government—in effect, to create an improbable buffer between the Anglo and Iberian powers.

The extent and seriousness of the conspiracy remains a matter of some conjecture. Several of Tennessee's early leaders, including James Robertson, John Sevier, and the surveyor-cum-military-colonel Anthony Bledsoe listened patiently to Spanish promises—but to what end? Perhaps they sought, in the spirit of a less than candid negotiation, entrée to the Mississippi or a lessening of Creek assaults on white settlements, without actually giving their loyalty and service to the Spanish Crown. Or possibly they hoped to pressure North Carolina, its focus

Atlantic-facing, into rescinding control of the Cumberland Settlements and thus making themselves sovereigns of a new state—this last eventuality coming, of course, to pass.

Jackson's October 1788 arrival in Nashville anticipated by a few weeks a change in Spanish policy. That December officials in Madrid, eager to draw increased immigration into the empire's sparsely populated Louisiana and West Florida frontiers, offered a financial incentive to Americans in the region: for a 15 percent tax, they would now be allowed to ply the Mississippi to New Orleans; and those who pledged loyalty to the Crown would further receive land grants, commercial concessions, and the right to practice (in private) their Protestant faith. Jackson, eager to operate a trade enterprise, first visited Natchez in early 1789 and found himself sorely tempted to offer up an oath. Through sheer energy and bravado, he quickly acquainted himself with the community's commercial elites, promising—and actually beginning to ship—coffee, sugar, and pork from Nashville. He understood that in order to continue, he would have to sign an affidavit attesting to his allegiance. This he did (along with more than a dozen other men) in Natchez on July 15, 1789. The pledge stated in part: "They would defend it [Spain] and help it with all their might, will, and power, especially obligating them to take up Arms against any Enemy that attempt to attack this Province."[2]

The impact of Jackson's oath—presumably a pragmatic, dissembling gesture and nothing more—proved to be nil. North Carolina's surrender of its former western territories later that same year put an end to many of the Cumberland Settlements' concerns, and within a few years Pinckney's Treaty (1795) both guaranteed the United States navigation rights on the Mississippi and prevented Spain from supplying arms to the Chickasaw and Choctaw nations. Jackson's pledge, in any case, was not uncommon. One historian has estimated that "between ten thousand and twenty thousand Anglo-Americans took the Spanish option in the twenty years after the [Revolution]."[3]

In the spring of 1790, the U.S. Congress organized what it called the Southwest Territory—present-day Tennessee. President Washington appointed William Blount its first governor. A generation older than Jackson, Blount hailed from a prominent colonial family, had sat in the Continental Congress, and served on North Carolina's delegation at the Constitutional Convention. Sensible of appearance, he impressed Nashvillians with "the well-cut coat, the lace, the buckled shoes, the polished phrase and manner." Temperamentally reserved, even secretive, he tended to offer assurances rather than promises. From the territory's capital in Knoxville, Blount, holding large appointment powers, began to build a political dynasty, and emerged as the region's dominant figure. As a frontier politico he had no peer, and ambitious men, eager for advancement, were suddenly dependent upon him. It is unclear how Jackson came to have an audience with the governor in February 1791, though his friendship with Justice McNairy, a Blount protégé, may have proven decisive. At that meeting the governor promptly made Jackson attorney general of the Mero District; approximately a year and a half later he named him "judge advocate for the Davidson County cavalry regiment." This last move facilitated Jackson's relationship with Tennessee's militia, a tie of immense personal importance that lasted into the War of 1812 and laid the foundation for his national reputation.[4]

While Blount himself engaged extravagantly in land speculation (upward of 2.5 million acres), he was obliged to see that illegal squatters in Cherokee territory, as defined by the recently signed Treaty of Holston, were removed, and this task fell upon Jackson. "It will be the Duty of the Attorney of the District Mr. Jackson," Blount wrote General Robertson in January 1792, "to prosecute on Information in all such cases and I have no doubt but that he will readily do it."[5] In fact he did so energetically. When the balance of power later made it possible for the United States to engage in systematic Indian removal, Jackson, of course, played a critical role in this process. In his youth, however, when taking direction from a federal government then preoccupied with the Ohio Indian Wars (1785–1795) and eager for peace on its southern frontier, he promptly organized the expulsion of white settlers encroaching on Cherokee territory.

As in other parts of America, the acquisition of land in Tennessee led to the acquisition of enslaved men and women. Indeed, it is possible that the Spanish Conspiracy appealed to a certain class of white settlers concerned that the U.S. government might act as an agent of abolitionism in the Old Southwest. It should be remembered that the Northwest Ordinance of 1787 had recently prohibited slavery's extension into present-day Ohio, Michigan, Indiana, Illinois, and Wisconsin, and this important compact may have impacted how some southerners reckoned their allegiances. One eighteenth-century observer of migration into the Illinois country noted that with such restrictions to slavery in place, enslavers "have gone to the Spanish side," crossing the Mississippi and extending their loyalty to the viceroyalty of New Spain.[6]

This noxious combination of land fever and slavery quickly became a part of Jackson's conventional equipment. It informed his economic prospects, public attitudes, and sense of identity. Only in his early twenties, but able through effort and connections to claim increasingly the status of a frontier gentleman, he proposed to keep this studied momentum moving. With success beginning to settle in, he now sought a wife.

6

Marriage(s)

When Lewis Robards returned to Kentucky without Rachel, he incautiously reduced their relationship to that of *a mensa et thoro*, which meant, in the day's Latin legalese, no longer sharing a bed or meals. Typically applied by courts in cases of extreme cruelty or desertion, it denotes a de facto separation between parties without actually dissolving the marital bond. Though Robards appeared to have abandoned the marriage, neither the circumstances of his departure from the Donelson blockhouse nor Jackson's role as an admirer (or more) of Rachel are clear. Gone for more than a year, Robards, rumor had it in the fall of 1790, planned to return to Tennessee and claim his wife. Presumably due to this report, Rachel decided to exchange Nashville for friends in Natchez. The journey south may have offered her a pretext for publicly breaking the relationship and assuming, in a fluid frontier environment, an implied single status—though in fact she remained legally espoused.

There is further the possibility that Rachel and Jackson, both twenty-three and very much in love at this point, determined to wed no matter the consequences. If so, they may have come to an understanding that, after joining her on the journey to Natchez as a guardian, he might then cleanly and quietly assume the role of bridegroom. This trip, in other words, conceivably constituted an elaborate elopement. Propriety demanded that Jackson maintain a polite distance, and so Colonel Robert Start, a friend of Rachel's mother, became the official escort, with Jackson tagging along to provide security while the trio moved through Indian country. The younger man's appearance, however, offered every indication of an impending marriage. Would her brothers have allowed this gentleman to assume such a trip otherwise? Did they believe that Robards had obtained a divorce? And if so, how would they have come upon such a fiction? It seems possible, rather, that the interested parties may have brashly gambled on forcing a humiliated husband into giving up his wife.

And so they did—though not in the way that either intended. That December, while Rachel lived in Natchez with two families and Jackson returned to Tennessee, Robards petitioned the Virginia Legislature (Kentucky being more than a year away from statehood) for an enabling act that would allow him to seek a divorce in the District of Kentucky's Supreme Court. He accused Rachel of desertion and of living in adultery with Jackson. The act put into play the possibility of a trial which promised to shame his wife. The writ reads in part:

> A jury shall be summoned, who shall be sworn well and truly to inquire into the allegations contained in the declaration. . . . And if the jury . . . shall find in substance, that the defendant hath deserted the plaintiff, and that she hath lived in adultery with another man since such desertion, the said verdict shall be recorded, and THERE-UPON, the marriage between the said Lewis Robards and Rachel shall be totally dissolved.[1]

But for reasons known only to himself, Robards, despite winning the writ, took no action. He remained a married man.

Word drifted back to Nashville, however, stating otherwise. Several months later—the documentation is sketchy but probably in the summer of 1791—Jackson returned to Natchez and married Rachel. Perhaps. No record, license, or certificate corroborates this story, and it seems unlikely that a priest (only Catholic Church–conducted marriages were legal in Spanish Natchez) would have consented to solemnize the union of a divorced woman. It is possible that Rachel and Andrew married in a Protestant ceremony (illegal in Natchez, but certainly licit in Tennessee), though even so an attendant, all-encompassing difficulty persisted—Rachel remained married to Robards.

That fall, after a brief stay at Bayou Pierre, the couple returned to Nashville, where they lived as a married couple. Two more years passed before Robards sought a divorce decree, which he received in September 1793; it stated plainly: "Rachel Robards, hath deserted the plaintiff, Lewis

Robards, and hath, and doth, still live in adultery with another man."[2] Presumably the arrival of this news came as a rude surprise to Rachel and Jackson. Interestingly, they did nothing immediately to amend the situation. Found by law to have engaged in an adulterous relationship (if not a bigamous one as well), they seemed to have slipped into a brief and possibly embarrassed period of resentful inaction. Finally unable to evade any longer the implications of a Kentucky County court's decision, they were married or remarried in January 1794.

One way to understand Jackson's unconventional courtship of Rachel is to see it as part of a broader personal approach by which he reckoned with the world. Over a long public service career he was occasionally accused of skirting legal niceties in the name of expediency. While president he controversially removed federal deposits from the country's National Bank (thus earning a Senate censure for "assum[ing] upon himself authority and power not conferred by the constitution"), and in another episode he tacitly supported southern postmasters who, in direct opposition to postal law, refused to deliver abolitionist materials.[3] Jackson, and indeed much of the political movement he headed, believed the country too confined by treaties and technicalities, the kind of formalities and piddling points that easterners presumably used to maintain hegemony over westerners. In a similar vein, he believed his marriage to Rachel legal in the only sense meaningful to him, showing little concern for the lack of a contract. In both contexts, in and out of power, he demonstrated a tendency for the intuitive, the immediate, and the practical. This attitude no doubt reveals something about his personality and temperament, though it is almost certainly indicative as well of the frontier's mounting pressure upon older American institutions, practices, and protocols.

In Nashville, Jackson and Rachel occupied a cabin for four years (1792–1796) alongside the Cumberland River in present-day Hadley's Bend. They called their farm Poplar Grove. After leaving this property, they resided for eight years at nearby Hunter's Hill, in a frame plantation home sitting on some 640 largely uncultivated acres, before a poor financial investment forced them to take a smaller plot on adjacent land. Theirs is often considered a special bond, the triumph of love over both Lewis Robards and legal impediments. No doubt such obstacles excited a young Jackson's appreciation of valor and vindication. For in making

Rachel's honor an issue, he quite conspicuously advertised his own. He aspired at an early age to the station of a gentleman, and a spouse complemented this end, offering the young squire the kind of secure home life he had scarcely experienced in the Waxhaws. Possibly he required little more from her. They were often separated by duty and distance, and his conjugal communications frequently indulged in formulaic (if finely recited) promises to remain forever at her side. One such letter reads in part:

> Tho I am absent My heart rests with you. With what pleasing hopes I view the future period when I shall be restored to your arms there to spend My days in Domestic Sweetness with you the Dear Companion of my life, never to be separated from you again during this Transitory and fluctuating life. I mean to retire from the Buss [business] of publick life, and Spend My Time with you alone in Sweet Retirement, which is My only ambition and ultimate wish.[4]

Only twenty-nine when he wrote these sentimental words, Jackson retained at the time a thick portfolio of "publick life" ambitions only to grow in coming years. What is more, he certainly never offered to any observer at any time—correctly laced correspondence aside—the mild face of a retiring type.

On the tangential question of whether Jackson's passions strayed during his marriage, scholars have come up empty. No messy carnal conflicts, no paternity suits, and no confirmed rumors of fathering children with slaves have surfaced. He seemed, rather, cool, even diffident on the question of sex. Uninterested in proving himself with women, he equated manhood with compeer competition, in law, politics, and social positioning. In at least one consociate sense this conformed to a broader pattern in presidential convention—the republican refusal to pass the crown and scepter on to a son. Of the first five presidents only one, John Adams, had male heirs known to voters (the paternity of Sally Hemings's offspring secreted), the eldest of whom, John Quincy Adams, became, to the concern of those dreading precedent, a kind of John II.

7

Nashville Nabob

Jackson's early years in the Cumberland Settlements overlapped the final stage of Chickamauga resistance to white encroachments on their lands. Once part of the Cherokee Nation, the Chickamauga seceded during the Revolution when most of the Cherokee, defeated in the Carolinas by American militia sometimes supplemented by neighboring Catawba, made peace with the patriots in 1777. The unreconciled, under the leadership of the war chief Dragging Canoe, organized themselves as Chickamauga (or Lower) Cherokee and established a presence principally in eastern Tennessee. Treaties between the Cherokee and the United States at Hopewell (1785) and Holston (1791) were designed to define boundaries between Anglos and natives but failed to keep settlers from pushing deeper into the West. Thereupon, sporadic frontier warfare intensified as the Chickamauga, allied with neighboring Creeks, carried off a series of raids along the Cumberland River.

Much to Jackson's disgust, the U.S. Government wished to pursue a cautious policy on its southern border. All but defensive operations were expressly forbidden. But in the late summer of 1794, responding to rumors that small groups of Creeks were about to attack squatters, the old Indian fighter General James Robertson, under his own authority, sent a combined force of regular army, Mero District militia, and Kentucky volunteers to the Five Lower Towns, the Chickamauga's main area of settlement just west of Chattanooga. There, they killed approximately seventy natives and destroyed the villages of Nickajack Town and Running Water Town. This Nickajack Expedition, which continued into the fall, resulted in several treaties favorable to the Americans. Doubtless

Jackson approved of such a course. In May he had complained of the
Chickamauga to one Knoxville man: ·

> I fear that their Peace Talks are only Delusions; and in order to put
> us of[f] our Guard; why Treat with them does not Experience teach
> us that Treaties answer no other Purpose than opening an Easy
> door for the Indians to pass [through to] Butcher our Citizens; what
> [motives Cong]ress are governed by with Res[pect to its] pacific
> Disposition towards [them I] know not.[1]

It appeared that the government knew not either. Though congressional pressure led to Robertson's resignation (so flagrantly did he
ignore his orders), the administration failed to appoint a successor and
the controversial general remained in place, suggesting that after all the
War Department, led by the rotund Bostonian Henry Knox, quietly
accepted his actions.

The campaign against the Chickamauga encouraged Blount to
demand Tennessee's statehood. As a territory it remained under Congress's authority, though admission into the Union promised a greater
independence in treating its Indian trouble. The region, despite white
concerns for security, continued to attract settlers in abundance—its
population trebled in the 1790s, from 35,000 to about 105,000—and
Blount moved in 1795 to alter its status, a novel operation in the young
country. The once independent Vermont Republic had entered the
Union in 1791 and Kentucky, formerly a part of Virginia, which consented to its separation, did so the following year. Now Tennessee proposed to become the first territory to achieve this feat.

In late December a convention met in Knoxville to discuss the path
to statehood; Blount chaired the assemblage and Jackson served as a
Davidson County (Nashville) delegate; he also sat on a select committee that prepared a preliminary constitution. In early February the
convention unanimously accepted the committee's draft, which it subsequently forwarded to Philadelphia to be acted on by the U.S. Congress. Commensurate with his colleagues, Jackson favored universal
suffrage for all free men in Tennessee, including blacks, but thought
office holders should possess property—at least two hundred acres of
land for legislators and five hundred acres for governors. He believed
the document popular in Tennessee, writing Blount shortly after the

convention convened, "The people Generally approve of the Constitution."[2]

Beyond drafting a structure of laws, the delegates also made several high-level appointments. The powerful east Tennessee political leader John Sevier was designated governor while Blount and William Cocke, a pioneer lawyer and statesman, were selected to serve in the U.S. Senate. Upon arriving in Philadelphia, however, they were refused seats. Tennessee's actions came as a surprise to more than a few annoyed congressmen who briefly blocked its efforts. Some contended that only the federal government could trigger the machinery of statehood; others quibbled that Tennessee's constitution lacked polish. More significantly, that autumn's presidential election—pitting the flinty New England Federalist John Adams against the Virginia Republican Thomas Jefferson—promised to be tight, and Tennessee, if in the Union, could conceivably swing the election toward the Republicans, whose southern, agrarian, pro-slavery profile it emulated. Naturally Jeffersonians championed Tennessee's cause and, with a majority in the House, produced a majority in its favor. Every Federalist but three opposed the measure.

The Senate tried to delay admission until after the election, but the House countered by proposing that Tennessee receive immediate statehood with only a single House member (it had asked for two), pending the next federal census in 1800. This meant that instead of possessing four electoral votes in the fall election (for two senators and two congressmen), it would have but three. The Senate accepted this compromise, and in June 1796 Tennessee entered the Union. Jackson, still several months shy of his thirtieth birthday, received Tennessee's single congressional seat, demonstrating his growing strength among the infant state's potentates. In the closely contested presidential race all of Tennessee's electoral votes predictably went for the defeated Jefferson. Four years later, aided by those same votes, Jefferson overcame Adams by a slender eight ballots.

Months before attending Tennessee's constitutional convention, Jackson had traveled to Philadelphia in order to liquidate property and conduct various other transactions. The year before he had formed a partnership in land speculation with his good friend John Overton, and now he hoped to sell some fifty thousand acres of their holdings (much of it legally in Indian hands) as well as, via commission, another smaller parcel owned by the John Rice family. Jackson now actively engaged in a number of economic ventures, including land speculation, running a general store in Nashville (with his brother-in-law Samuel Donelson), operating a farm (Poplar Grove), and trafficking in enslaved people. In March 1795 Overton wrote to the Philadelphia-encamped Jackson: "If you sell Lands and get money that you can spare, it will be best that you purchase, somewhere in the lower part of the eastern States such Negroes we may want for Rice, and also a likely Negroe Boy which I want for a Servant."[3] This communication encapsulates the aspirations of many budding nabobs in the American southwest. Land, money, and slaves formed a distinct and controlling trinity of concerns that teased men like Jackson with a whispering promise of wealth, status, and power.

At times, these ruling passions of frontier authority threatened to ruin their patrons. Jackson, struggling in Philadelphia to sell the property entrusted to him, suddenly found a taker in David Allison, a friend from Tennessee. In certain matters, Allison closely mirrored Jackson. He too hailed from the Carolinas, had arrived at the Cumberland Settlements in 1788, and quickly ingratiated himself to Governor Blount, to whom he served as something of a business agent. Now settled in Philadelphia, he agreed to buy all the land that Jackson proposed to unload—and did so with three promissory notes. Eager to stock his mercantile business, Jackson promptly used these drafts (which he had too eagerly guaranteed) as payment to purchase supplies from two Philadelphia companies.[4] Always generous with his friends and not a little innocent in financial matters, Jackson promptly discovered the danger of his endorsement. Allison's notes were soon protested and Jackson was legally obligated to make payment. One of the firms, Meeker, Cochran & Company, acquainted him of this not inconsiderable detail in an August communication:

> We are sorry so soon after your departure, to follow you the advice, that any notes or acceptances of David Allisons now falling due are not generally or regularly paid, and that there is little reason to expect he will be more punctual hereafter. . . . We take this early oppertunity to make Known to you that . . . we shall have to get our money from you, which we shall expect at maturity.[5]

Three years later, in 1798, Allison died in a Philadelphia debtors' prison, though Jackson remained under the shadow of the "Allison claim" for several years more. He sacrificed much of his property to make good on the authorized notes, and the errant transaction may have decisively informed his hostility to speculation so apparent several years later during the Bank War.

Despite the Allison disaster, Jackson, with the aid of several variously capable friends and advisors, probably managed over the years to make a profit speculating in land. For roughly three decades (1790–1820) he engaged in this erratic enterprise, and it is quite likely that his important political connections and growing martial repute contributed to whatever success he enjoyed. Public position always interested Jackson, however, and a private real estate empire, partnership in a general store, and playing a frontier attorney hardly scratched the surface of his ambitions or, as we might say today, skill set. As one of Jackson's friends carefully observed in the 1840s, the "General . . . was not made for what is usually called a first-rate lawyer."[6] Jackson sought, rather, to supplement his success in the Cumberland Settlements with greater goals than even he perhaps realized. The business trip to Philadelphia—a bigger arena of operation—suggested as much, as did his eagerness to join the Blount faction, which had the power to propel his career, to bring him into the center of Tennessee politics, and to make him a congressman.

8

The Outsider

Mark Mitchell, a Tennessee justice of the peace, took an amused interest in Jackson's virtually uncontested campaign for the United States Congress. In an autumn 1795 communication with the candidate, he raised certain wry doubts about Jackson's slight frame, but otherwise took comfort in his large presence. "Your sise is ganst you," he wrote. "I never Knew a man of a Hundred and forty [lbs.] in Congress if you would get you a [pair] of Cloth over hols, and Ware your Big Coat you might pass you have loud Speach." The following June Tennessee officially entered the Union and that fall Jackson, the Blount-approved front-runner, predictably claimed its only House seat, capturing nearly 99 percent of the vote in drubbing one James Rody 1,113 to 12. "I must beg leave to congratulate you on your interest and popularity in this country," Overton wrote his friend. "Your election is certain and I believe that there is scarcely a man in this part of the Territory that could be elected before you."[1]

Jackson's aspirations exceeded a mere congressional seat, however, and he sought in 1796 to assume the major generalship of the Tennessee militia, a plum post that opened when its incumbent, John Sevier, became the state's first governor. The two men, equally ambitious, grew to cordially hate each other over the years. Though more than two decades older than Jackson, Sevier rightly regarded the younger man as a rival for the few prizes Tennessee could bestow. Noting Jackson's recent appointment to the House, the cagey pol convinced an electorate of field officers and brigadier generals to give the major generalship to another candidate. The young congressman would have to wait on his martial glory.

Arriving in Philadelphia to assume his House seat, Jackson resolved to meet sartorial expectations. With the assistance of a local tailor he matched a traditional black coat and breeches with various cloth and velvet accessories. Some remained skeptical. Pennsylvania Representative Albert Gallatin ridiculed the new congressman as "a tall, lank, uncouth-looking personage, with long locks of hair hanging over his face, and a queue down his back tied in an eel skin; his dress singular, his manners and deportment those of a rough backwoodsman." Perhaps this description is apt, though it is possible that Gallatin, expecting an exotic creature from the queer American hinterland, surmised a semi-savage. A Swiss émigré, Gallatin, soon to begin his long tenure as treasury secretary in the Jefferson and Madison administrations, had emerged from an aristocratic environment in Geneva.[2] He preferred, in America, a culture of social deference to frontier democracy and may have read this affinity into his dismissive report of Jackson.

With a population nearing forty thousand, Philadelphia, the so-called Athens of America, offered a comparatively eclectic, cosmopolitan environment. The country's second largest city after New York, it served concurrently as the nation's political, financial, and cultural capitals. Market Street elites collected around the Delaware River wharves as a surplus of ships brought to shore West Indies sugar and a rich assortment of European goods. Local artisans—a small mob of goldsmiths, clockmakers, saddlemakers, and such—could turn a tidy profit in the center city area, while the majority held working-class jobs as carpenters, candlemakers, stable keepers, and so on. Three open-air markets supplied fresh foods, nearly two hundred taverns nursed the thirsty, and thirty churches were spread throughout a number of neighborhoods. Jackson seemed unmoved, however, by Philadelphia's many amenities. Perhaps he associated the metropolis (and its caveat emptor banking culture) with the endorsed notes disaster he had inherited from Allison, or maybe, as Gallatin would have it, his rustic roots made him subtly inadaptable to Philadelphia and the political class it attracted.

Early in his tenure, in December 1796, Jackson broke with most of his congressional consociates on what many considered a mere matter of etiquette. Three months earlier a sixty-four-year-old George Washington, having just lost his last tooth and about to retire from the presidency, had issued a farewell address to the nation. It seemed to require a suitably generous rejoinder from the House, a statement filled with

ornate praise and appreciation. But Jackson, a little boldly, discour-
teously, and perhaps foolishly, allied with a small minority in voting
against this perfunctory measure of congressional gratitude.

Rather, he quietly condemned both Washington's alleged indiffer-
ence to recurrent Indian attacks on the western frontier and the president's supposed assault on the nation's checks and balances system. "The
Executive of the Union has Ever Since the Commencement of the present Government," he complained to Overton (in words later applied to
his own presidency), "been Grasping after power, and in many instances,
Exercised powers, that he was not Constitutionally invested with." These
sharp words bear evidence of their author's great disdain for the controversial Jay's Treaty, ratified in the Senate the previous year by a bare
two-thirds majority (20–10) and subsequently signed into law by Washington. The compact gave Britain most favored nation trading status,
while saying nothing about the illegal interception of American ships
or the impressment (kidnapping) of their sailors by the Royal Navy. The
treaty, according to its critics, effectively made the neutral United States
an adjunct in monarchical Britain's ongoing global conflict against revolutionary republican France. "What an alarming Situation," Jackson, a
practiced Anglophobe, wrote at the time.[3]

A member of the House for less than a year (December 1796—
September 1797), Jackson left little impress on that body. Predictably
he emerged as a vigorous advocate of national defense, voting in favor
of enlarging (by three frigates) the country's fledgling navy and against
sending payments to those North African Berber pirates and privateers
demanding ransom and tribute from the United States. Closer to home
he argued successfully for the reimbursement of a suspect 1793 expedition headed by General Sevier into Cherokee lands. Jackson asserted in
a House speech that Sevier's force responded to the threat of "the knife
and the tomahawk," and he contradicted Secretary of War Timothy
Pickering's insistence that the militia attacked the Cherokees. Always
sensitive to honor, he now sought vindication as well as compensation.
His proposed act reads in part: "*Resolved*, That General Sevier's expedition into the Cherokee Nation . . . was a just and necessary measure,
and that provision ought to be made by law for paying the expenses
thereof." When a gaggle of congressmen, being congressmen, reacted to
the resolution with varying gradations of deliberation, debate, and disagreement, Jackson fidgeted. A House Report of the discussion impishly

stated, "Mr. Jackson owned he was not very well acquainted with the rules of the House, but from the best idea he could form, it was a very circuitous way of doing business. Why now refer it to the Committee of Claims, when all the facts are stated in this report, he knew not. If this was the usual mode of doing business, he hoped it would not be referred."[4]

Jackson's disdain for the roundabout House had hardly ripened when, in the fall of 1797, he unexpectedly became a United States senator. Again, he owed an important appointment to Blount. The previous year rumors began to spread that Spain, subdued by France in the War of the First Coalition, planned to cede Spanish Louisiana to the French Republic. Such a transfer might threaten America's recently won navigation rights on the Mississippi River—and thus imperil the precarious fortunes of the region's land gamblers. In a response born of desperation, Blount, a U.S. senator and speculator extraordinaire, hoped to reach a secret agreement with Great Britain to support a large-scale filibustering expedition—a private military action—composed of Creeks, Cherokee, and frontiersmen. Combined, this irregular force affected to clear both Louisiana and Florida of French influence, leaving Britain to rule these territories in a new imperial system that gratefully lavished land concessions on its white allies.[5] Blount believed, in other words, that even after joining the Union, Tennessee still retained mastery of its future.

In April 1797 he wrote incautiously to James Carey, a Cherokee interpreter at Tellico Blockhouse along the Little Tennessee River, of his plans. Calling himself "the head of the business on the part of the British," he invited "the Indians [to] act their part" in the plot. Within a matter of weeks the contents of the letter had leaked, and Blount found himself the object of both congressional scrutiny and the tart attack of the new president's wife. "When shall we cease to have Judas's?" a choleric Abigail Adams wrote to her sister Mary Smith Cranch. "Here is a diabolical plot disclosed." Charles Lee, the nation's attorney general, maintained that Blount's letter constituted "evidence of a crime" and began the lengthy process of seeking the senator's impeachment. Blount's peers took a more immediate route, however, and secured his expulsion.[6]

Blount's old Senate seat went unopposed to Joseph Anderson, a former U.S. territorial judge; Tennessee's senior senator, William Cocke, up for reelection, hoped to retain his post, but having voted for Blount's banishment, he attracted the fury of the Blountites, who proposed Jackson in his place.[7] Aside from score settling, the nomination made regional sense as Anderson and Cocke both hailed from eastern Tennessee, and the former Cumberland Settlements now sought their share. With Blount's popularity holding steady, Jackson handily carried the election in the state assembly 20 to 13.

Perhaps unsurprisingly, he proved to be an awful senator. Temperamentally unsuited to thrive in a debating society, he seldom participated in floor discussions, rarely voted with the majority, and introduced only a single bill. In the spring of 1798, tired of being surrounded by distinguished men who judged him by his clothes, his comparatively unpolished manners, and his mangled syntax, he resigned and returned to Tennessee. But if the year or so in Congress constituted a false step, it also concentrated Jackson's attention. He returned home eager for high placement, wanting something commensurate with his ambitions and glad to be again near the land speculations, plantations, and business partnerships that constituted his fortune. In Nashville, rather than Philadelphia, Jackson began his slow ascent to national prominence.

9

Justice Jackson

Pressed by various commercial commitments, Jackson needed to obtain a sinecure to supplement his limited income. An open seat on the Superior Court of Law and Equity—Tennessee's highest tribunal—promised such a prospect, and with the blessing of the Blount faction Jackson became a justice, edging out Bennett Searcy, another Spruce Macay student, 18–13 in the legislature. At $600 a year his salary ran second only to the governor's $750.[1] Since coming to the Cumberland Settlements a decade earlier, Jackson had laid claim to a series of prizes, including attorney general of the Mero District, delegate to Tennessee's constitutional convention, and elevation to the U.S. House and then Senate. The receding western frontier opened a raft of opportunities, which Jackson pursued methodically, confidently employing a combination of assertion, will, and skill. Despite a reputation for impatience, he had a knack for leveraging situations, waiting out opponents, and collecting appointments. As a young superior court judge he stood to make contacts throughout the state while overseeing his various financial interests in the Nashville region and beyond. By any measure the position suggested an attractive stepping-stone to other offices and perhaps larger possibilities.

Jackson served on the superior court for nearly six years; few records exist of his verdicts, though Parton, privy to numerous interviews, offered a positive assessment: "Tradition reports that he maintained the dignity and authority of the bench . . . and that his decisions were short, untechnical, unlearned, sometimes ungrammatical, and generally right."[2] Apparently they also demanded expediency—in one fifteen-day stretch Jackson handled a full fifty cases. An itinerant jurist, he rode an extended circuit, holding court in Nashville, Knoxville, and Jonesborough. Respecting the position's value, he might have held it into retirement; only impeachment stood as an official reason for removal. "I am in Possession of a verry independant office," he crowed to one correspondent three years into the job. This sovereignty included, so he said, in a tangle of legal patois,

> all Pleas, real, personal, and mixt; and also all Suits and Demands relative to Legacies, Filial Portions, and Estates of Intestates; all Pleas of the State, and criminal Matters, of what Nature, Degree, or Denomination soever, whether brought before them by original or mesne Process, or by Certiorari; Writ of Error, Appeal from any Inferior court, or by any other Ways or Means whatsoever.[3]

Most commonly, Jackson oversaw suits seeking payments for rendered services and delivered goods; he also heard cases involving the recovery of personal property (including enslaved men and women) "converted" by another party. On no fewer than ten occasions did Jackson hand down capital sentences, including three in a single session for horse stealing.[4]

Despite the office's real attractions, Jackson remained ever interested in the next main chance, and in the late winter of 1801, said chance arrived in the guise of a more attractive appointment—major general of the Tennessee Militia, the post he had coveted six years earlier. For this commission he faced in John Sevier an opponent both familiar and formidable. Having served three consecutive terms as governor, Sevier, per the state's constitution, now had to relinquish the position for at least one term. Fortunately for Jackson the Blount faction, surviving William Blount's recent death, remained a powerful force in Tennessee politics and had engineered the election of Archibald Roane—a Pennsylvania-born veteran who had taken part in Washington's historic crossing of the Delaware River—to succeed Sevier. And when Jackson and Sevier tied at seventeen in the assembly, Governor Roane obediently cast the deciding ballot in the former's favor. Not without considerable influence of his own, Sevier, the following year, saw that his supporters in the state house pushed through a measure dividing Tennessee into two military districts—and he, not Jackson, received the more powerful post, in the east.

Despite their mutual animosity, Sevier and Jackson, both shaped by the narrow field of frontier politics, shared much, including a tremendous self-pride. Sevier recognized this when, in 1797, amid an earlier contretemps with Jackson regarding cavalry officer commissions, he wrote to his young antagonist, "Any observations I made in [my] letters [regarding you] . . . were not bottomed on malice; they were the language of A man who thought himself highly injured, and if it betrayed a little imprudence, I will here add that like yourself when passion agitates my Breast I cannot view things in the calm light of mild philosophy." As New York proved too small an arena for both Alexander Hamilton and Aaron Burr, whose overlapping interests ended in a duel, so Tennessee could hardly contain the conflicting ambitions of Jackson and Sevier. The latter, eligible for a fresh gubernatorial term, announced in 1803 his candidacy against Roane, who sought reelection. Anticipating this challenge, Roane and Jackson had carefully accumulated materials implicating Sevier in ancient land frauds, namely forging deeds while the state still belonged to North Carolina. Scrambling for the high ground, Jackson wrote in July 1803 to Benjamin J. Bradford, publisher of the *Tennessee Gazette*, that such shenanigans disqualified Sevier from public office: "Can an honest public view the scene and not feel indignant at characters who are endeavoring to place a man guilty of crimes like these in the executive chair of this state?" Apparently an honest public could— and did. The ever-popular Sevier, still regarded warmly by many as a backwoods hero and a founding father of Tennessee, handily defeated Roane in the early August balloting, 6,780 to 4,923.[5]

Several weeks later the Jackson-Sevier dispute, having simmered for some time, erupted in Knoxville. The two men came upon each other in front of the county courthouse, its abrupt gable facade facing the street, and Sevier, infuriated by the accusations of land fraud, verbally went on the attack. Jackson is reported to have replied, perhaps a little pompously, that services to the state required the intrigue's unveiling. This only baited Sevier, who is said to have responded with acid: "Services? . . . I know of no great service you have rendered the country, except taking a trip to Natchez with another man's wife." This comment precipitated a minor melee—shots were fired, at least one unblessed bystander received a grazing, but the principals walked away uninjured. Jackson, in any case, seemed uninterested in merely wounding Sevier; he wished, rather, either to humiliate or to kill him.[6]

The following day the aggrieved superior court justice challenged the wily governor to a duel:

> The ungentlemany Expressions, and gasgonading conduct, of yours relative to me on yesterday was in true charactor of your self, and unmask you to the world, and plainly shews that they were the ebulutions of a base mind goaded with stubborn prooffs of fraud, and flowing from a source devoid of every refined sentiment, or delicate sensation. . . . To the office [of governor] I bear respect, to the Voce of the people who placed it on you I pay respect, and as such I only deign to notice you, and call upon you for that satisfaction and explanation that your ungentlemany conduct & expressions require, for this purpose I request an interview, and my friend who will hand you this will point out the time and place, when and where I shall Expect to see you with your friend and no other person. my friend and myself will be armed with pistols. you cannot mistake me, or my meaning.[7]

There was nothing particularly honorable in Jackson's invitation. At a brisk thirty-six to Sevier's slower fifty-eight, he gave every indication of playing the young cub eager to take down the aging lion. Sevier, the legendary Indian fighter and acclaimed frontiersman, need not prove himself to anyone. But perhaps Jackson did need to prove something. He coveted his opponent's popularity, reputation, and power; he wished all these things for himself and wished to wait no longer.

Sevier replied confidently to Jackson's summons in a communication dated October 2: "I shall wait on you with pleasure at Any time and place not within the State of Tennessee, attended by my friend with pistols presuming you know nothing About the use of Any other Arms." An 1801 statute made dueling in Tennessee a criminal offense, and Sevier's letter, though apparently obliging, began to ease the momentum that Jackson craved. The ruffled justice answered the following day, calling Sevier's unwillingness to duel in Tennessee "a mere subterfuge" and insisted that having "Take[n] the name of a lady into your poluted lips" in Knoxville, he should be willing to make amends in Knoxville. Jackson demanded an immediate showdown—"you must meet me between this and four oclock this afternoon"—on pain of publishing a statement identifying Sevier "as a coward and a paltroon." Sevier, playing for time, began to use the younger man's eagerness against him. "Your letter of this day is before me And I am happy to find you so Accommodating," he wrote right back. "My friend Will agree upon the time and place of rendezvous."[8] Of course Sevier had absolutely no intention of exchanging shots with Jackson.

And then nearly a week went by with apparently no contact between the two. Sevier pled "Committee business," which Jackson, in a furious letter on the ninth, denounced as yet another "mere Subterfuge." He renewed his threat to file a shaming public notice and apprised Sevier of its contents: "To all who Shall See these presents Greeting. Know yea that I Andrew Jackson, do pronounce, publish, and declare to the world, that his Excellency John Sevier Esqr. Captain General and commander in chief of the land and Naval forces within the State of Tennessee—is a base coward and paltroon, He will basely insult, but has not courage to repair." Jackson informed Sevier that he could avoid the open censure only "by meeting me in one or two hours after the receipt of this."[9]

After receiving "this," Sevier seemed almost to delight in sporting with Jackson, authoring in response a lecture on the need to respect the law. "An interview within the State you know I have denied," he wrote. "Anywhere outside you have nothing further to do but name the place, and I will the time. I have some regard to the laws of the State over which I have the honor to preside, Altho you a Judge Appear to have none, it is to be hoped, that if by any strange and unexpected event, you should ever be metamorphosed into an upright and *Virtuous Judge*, you will feel the propriety of being Governed and Guided by the laws of the State, you are Sacredly bound to obey and regard."[10] The following day, on the tenth, the *Knoxville Gazette* published Jackson's "coward and patroon" proclamation.

Over the next several hours, three communications flew between the would-be combatants. Accusations and counter-accusations built up—"You have not named a place" vied with "you have been well advised what part of the Indian boundary line I would go with you." Finally, Jackson believed that he had pinned Sevier down to a date (the twelfth) and location (Southwest Point, Virginia, a day's ride from Knoxville). But the governor, the ever-busy public servant, almost certainly playing yet another card, failed to show until the sixteenth. An angry Jackson and his party had just mounted up to return home when Sevier and his entourage suddenly appeared on the horizon. According to testimony,

Jackson jumped off his horse and produced pistols, causing Sevier to do the same. The two men then proceeded to swear loquaciously at each other and for a moment put their weapons away, though when Jackson advanced on the governor, the latter drew his sword and Jackson again brandished a pistol. At this point a general chaos ensued. Sevier crouched behind a tree while Jackson demanded he "unmark himself"; Sevier's son then leveled his gun at Jackson, and Jackson's second aimed his own gun at Sevier's son. The absurdity of the situation lessened when some among the governor's camp interceded and gestured for calm. After a mist of souring blue oaths filled the air, both groups agreed to end the feud. They casually rode back to Knoxville together, though the principals never reconciled.[11]

Despite never firing a shot, Sevier had actually defeated Jackson. Experienced, shrewder, and shielded by an imposing reputation, he presented a target in Tennessee perhaps too elusive for any man to mark. Sevier had won the governor's seat despite Jackson's accusations of land fraud and then managed a public insult on the perpetrator of that charge which resulted in neither his contrition nor his blood. Jackson, by contrast, lost considerable ground as a result of what appeared to some to be an ugly vendetta against one of the West's leading figures; not until the War of 1812 did he again assume a prominent civic role in Tennessee.[12] The state, it seems clear, lacked the bounty of military appointments and plumages to accommodate both men, even as their paths continued, in one way or another, to uncomfortably cross. It is perhaps fitting that when Sevier died in 1815, he did so while in the Alabama Territory, making a survey of Creek lands recently acquired by Jackson.

In 1803, the year of the Jackson-Sevier scrape, the United States negotiated the Louisiana Purchase. Seeking a more lucrative federal appointment, Jackson hoped to be selected governor of the Territory of Orleans, a piece of the Purchase encompassing most of present-day Louisiana. His inability to win this post bears collateral resemblance to his difficulties with Sevier. Though he secured some congressional support and appealed personally to those close to Jefferson, Jackson seemed innocent of the fact that stronger, more entrenched men queued ahead of him. While traveling to Washington in April 1804 to purchase merchandise for his stores and perhaps to privately solicit the president, then home at Monticello, Jackson, suddenly horrified at the thought of being tagged a sycophant, appears to have lost his nerve. He wrote to John Coffee, his loyal friend and business partner:

> Nothing on the subject of Governor of New orleans the President at Monticello—under present circumstances my feelings could not consent to pay my respects to him least it might be construed into the conduct of a courteor—and my vissit might have created such sensations in his mind—I therefore passed on without calling—of all ideas to me it is the most humiliating to be thought to cringe to power to obtain a favour or an appointment.[13]

That summer Jefferson decided on his fellow Virginian William C. C. Claiborne, formerly a territorial administrator in Mississippi, as governor. "There were characters superior to him whom I wished to appoint," Jefferson later wrote, "but they refused the office: I know no better man who would accept of it."[14] Apparently Jackson stood rather low on his list.

That July, soon after Claiborne's appointment, Jackson resigned from the superior court. Several good reasons informed the decision, including health concerns (circuit riding had proved arduous), inevitable conflicts of interest (Justice Jackson and land speculator Jackson were bound to clash in chancery), and the prodigal jurist's need to improve his pecuniary portfolio. "I sink money," he had written to one correspondent, "the Salary is too low . . . the Judiciary scar[c]ely bears my Expence."[15] In the name of consolidating his outlays, Jackson sold Hunter's Hill and moved with Rachel and their nine slaves to an adjoining tract just east of Nashville. They called their new two-story log farmhouse and grounds the Hermitage. Chasing financial stability, he joined Coffee and a nephew, John Hutchings, in opening a merchant shop that sold Philadelphia-delivered goods for a sharp markup. This Nashville enterprise soon begat branches in nearby Lebanon and at the site of a former unfortified military camp along the southwest bank of the Tennessee River. The business, despite the aspirations of its founders, ultimately failed; as usual, Jackson kept his eye open for the next best break.

10

Befriending Burr

The still shadowy Burr conspiracy (1804–1807) grew out of the circumstances, opportunities, and avarice that had long propelled white settlement across the Gulf frontier. Briefly, former vice president Aaron Burr is alleged to have fostered a treasonous scheme to carve out an independent dominion in the lower Mississippi Valley. Historians remain puzzled, and Burr left an elliptical, self-serving, and incomplete correspondence behind. It seems more certain, however, considering his collection of men, boats, and provisions, that he planned some type of assault on territory either in or adjoining U.S. soil. In doing so he would need to explain himself to some of the more prominent figures in the southwestern states, including Jackson. We know that Burr solicited supplies on his four visits to Nashville, we know that Jackson agreed to provide Burr these materials, and we know that when Jackson, major general of the Western Tennessee Militia, suspected Burr of treason, he informed Jefferson. His actions are, in hindsight, deeply ironic. For in the wake of the War of 1812 Jackson himself led a much disputed invasion into Spanish territory. That he subsequently ascended to the presidency indicates, depending on one's perspective, his superiority to Burr in either timing, electioneering, or luck.

And not many, it must be said, were superior to Burr. Scion to a distinguished colonial family (he counted the noted Congregationalist theologian Jonathan Edwards a grandfather), the Newark-born Burr received a College of New Jersey (Princeton) degree at the age of sixteen. A soldier in the Revolution, he subsequently made his way in New York politics, serving as a U.S. senator before becoming vice president.

Though slight of height and balding, Burr rather easily drew the interest of others. Charismatic, with piercing dark brown eyes, he was a brilliant conversationalist, dressed elegantly, and read widely. Attractive and narcissistic, he cadged thousands of dollars over the years from admirers, is said to have schemed to cheat Jefferson out of the presidency when both claimed the same number of electoral votes in the 1800 election, and, of course, killed Alexander Hamilton in a duel. "He was clearly," two prominent scholars have written, "a deviant type."[1]

Flawed or not, Burr shared certain affinities with Jackson. Both speculated in land, engaged in duels, and championed the interests of a growing West. Importantly, they also resided outside of the prevailing American power structure. Neither, in other words, were Virginians. Jackson's refusal to join his congressional colleagues and laud Washington is on par with Burr's cutting insistence that the great general lacked completely "independence of character" and managed to somehow become a national hero "without talent."[2] Men on the make, they would have to make their own opportunities.

Burr in particular showed few scruples when contemplating a new empire in the southwest. He first thought to ingratiate himself with European powers, perhaps promising to stem the tide of further American expansion. In August 1804 Anthony Merry, the British envoy to the U.S., wrote his London superior, "I have just received an offer from Mr. Burr, the actual Vice-President of the United States . . . to lend his assistance to his Majesty's government in any manner in which they may think fit to employ him . . . in endeavoring to effect a separation of the western part of the United States from that which lies between the Atlantic and the mountains, in its whole extent."[3] And in March of the following year, just after Burr's vice presidential term expired, Merry again informed London of the enterprising American's especial interest in the West:

> Mr. Burr . . . has mentioned to me that the inhabitants of Louisiana seem determined to render themselves independent of the United States, and that the execution of their design is only delayed by the difficulty of obtaining previously an assurance of protection and assistance from some foreign Power, and of concerting and connecting their independence with that of the inhabitants of the western parts of the United States, who must always have a command over

them by the rivers which communicate with the Mississippi. It is clear that Mr. Burr (although he has not as yet confided to me the exact nature and extent of his plan) means to endeavor to be the instrument of effecting such a connection.[4]

Had Jackson, or a good many other western men whose confidences and kindnesses Burr cultivated, known of his English entreaties, they would have denounced his efforts from the beginning. And Burr appreciated this. He played, rather, upon the region's interest in overthrowing Spanish rule in present-day Florida, Texas, and the southern tiers of Alabama and Mississippi. These precious possessions, he suggested, were, in light of Madrid's declining imperial power, ripe for America's picking.

In April 1805 Burr, now a private citizen, left Washington on horseback for Pittsburgh, from which he embarked on an ambitious western trek, eager to sniff out support, contract for supplies, and recruit associates. He sought, in other words, to assess the feasibility of amassing and moving sometime in the near future a force of men down the Mississippi; to do what exactly, again, remains a matter of conjecture. In late May he arrived in Nashville to a hero's welcome. A champion of Tennessee statehood while presiding over the Senate (Jackson once referred to Burr as "always and . . . still a true and trusty friend to Tennessee"), he may have burnished his frontier bona fides by recently dispatching the arch Federalist Hamilton. Dinners and public balls celebrated his brief stay in Tennessee's capital city; the prominent seeking the prominent, Burr lodged at the Hermitage with the Jacksons. "I have been received with much kindness and hospitality," he wrote to his daughter Theodosia, "and could stay a month with pleasure."[5]

From Nashville he traveled some 150 miles west, meeting with General James Wilkinson at Fort Massac along the Ohio River in present-day Illinois. Though governor of the Louisiana Territory and commanding general of the U.S. Army in the lower South, Wilkinson also happened to spy for the Spanish, who knew him as the opportunistic Agent 13. Plump, ruddy complexioned, and resplendent in medals and gold epaulettes, he knew how to perform before power, even while entertaining the air castles of visiting adventurers. Presumably he and Burr discussed the future feasibility of detaching a generous serving of New Spain. In late June the busy Burr, now bearing south, landed in New Orleans, where, as in so many other stops, he happily endured a crowded calendar of banquets, suppers, and receptions. He remained in the city for three weeks before pivoting and, once again, lingering in Nashville with the Jacksons, who, at least on Andrew's part, remained eager for the association. His western tour a success, Burr returned to the East, wintering in Philadelphia.

Jackson appears to have been completely taken in by his new friend's enthusiasm for, so he believed, a government-approved move against the Spanish. Far more deftly did Burr size up Jackson, a militia general in command of some two thousand Tennesseans, as someone in position to advance his plans. He seems further to have genuinely enjoyed his company. While in Nashville, Burr had informed his diary, "For a week I have been lounging at the house of General Jackson, once a lawyer, after a judge, now a planter; a man of intelligence, and one of those prompt, frank, ardent souls whom I love to meet."[6] Jackson liked Burr as well, though he believed him to be operating at the covert behest of the federal government—only under such terms could he possibly count himself a confederate.

In September 1806 Burr, having contracted for several boats from the Anglo-Irish aristocrat Harman Blennerhassett, proprietor of an Ohio River island, once more moved on to Kentucky and then Tennessee. In Nashville, he again met with Jackson, who agreed to construct yet more boats and provide additional supplies for the project—receiving from Burr $3,500 in Kentucky banknotes to cover expenses. Jackson further provided Burr with information on the local military scene and offered up an officers list; all potentially valuable intelligence to be forwarded, so he apparently artlessly believed, to Secretary of War Henry Dearborn.[7]

At this point Burr's half-baked plans began to collapse. Wilkinson, perhaps fearful that the conspiracy or even his own Spanish intrigues were vulnerable to exposure, decided to betray Burr. In a communication dated October 21 and received by Jefferson about a month later, he claimed to have knowledge of an illegal scheme to organize up to ten thousand men from several states who were to descend the Allegheny River and proceed south, picking up reserves in Tennessee on their way to New Orleans, which would serve as a jumping-off point for a February invasion of Veracruz. Wilkinson wrote in a separate dispatch to Jefferson that "should this association be formed, in opposition to the Laws & in defiance of Government, then I have no doubt the revolt of this Territory will be made an auxiliary step to the main design of attacking Mexico, to give it a new master in the place of promised liberty."[8] Wilkinson never mentioned Burr's name in his communications to Jefferson, but considering the former vice president's well publicized western campaigns, he need not. The president and his advisors, along with a growing number of newspapers, were already speculating on Burr's behavior.

Jackson too at this time began to entertain doubts about the shape-shifting man he had just agreed to aid. In early November Captain John Fort, a New York native with business interests in the Gulf, showed up at the Hermitage with a letter of introduction. During a brief stay Fort innocently told his host what he himself had learned from John Swartwout, the brother of Burr's ally Samuel, a New York–based soldier and land speculator: that New Orleans, not Spanish territory, enticed the conspirators. Alarmed and sensing himself vulnerable to accusations of complicity, Jackson quickly fired off several letters. To Orleans governor Claiborne he offered both a warning—"I fear there is something rotten in the State of Denmark . . . you have enemies within your own City, that may try to subvert your Government, and try to separate it from the Union"—and a statement of personal loyalty: "I love my Country and Government, I hate the Dons [the Spanish]—I would delight to see Mexico reduced, but I will die in the last ditch before I would yield a part to the Dons, or see the Union disunited." Most importantly, Jackson assured Jefferson of his integrity in a discreet statement that never cited Burr nor the rumors milling about him. "In the event of insult or aggression made on our Government and country from any quarter," he wrote, while fairly saluting, "I am so well convinced that the publick sentiment . . . within this state, and particularly within my Division, are . . . of such a nature and of such a kind, that I take the liberty of tendering their services, that is, under my command." The letter hit its mark. A few weeks after its arrival, Jefferson informed Wilkinson, "Be assured that Tennessee, and particularly General Jackson, are faithful."[9]

That same unsettled November a Kentucky district attorney named Joe Daviess sought a court order to bring Burr before a grand jury in Frankfurt to have him answer questions regarding his plans and meanderings. The court refused the motion, but Burr voluntarily agreed to discuss his activities. He smartly procured the services of a young lawyer,

Henry Clay, blue-eyed, light-haired, and, so one Virginian maintained, full of "disgusting vanity and inordinate ambition." Only twenty-nine, but just two months shy of joining the U.S. Senate, Clay worked adeptly, and Burr received from the grand jury a written declaration of exoneration in early December. His chief accusers were without hard evidence. Still, Burr attracted increasing and unwanted attention—Ohio senator John Smith warned him of hearing "various reports prejudicial to your character. It is believed by many that your design is to dismember the Union. . . . I must confess, from the mystery and rapidity of your movements, that I have fears . . . [and] that the tranquillity of the country will be interrupted, unless [your object] be candidly disclosed, which I solicit, and to which, I presume, you will have no objection."[10]

Trailing a thick cloud of mystery, Burr again headed south, arriving in Nashville near mid-month, inquiring about his boats and provisions. This time he avoided the Hermitage, apparently on request. Jackson confided to his close friend Congressman George Washington Campbell that after learning from Captain Fort of New Orleans's possible imperilment, "I wrote Colo. Burr in strong terms my suspicions of him, and untill they were cleared from my mind no further intimacy was to exist between us." But while now back in Nashville, Burr, so Jackson reported, "said that he . . . was sanctioned by legal authority, and . . . would produce the Secratary of wars orders that he wanted but young men of talents to go with him."[11] Burr, in other words, told Jackson that he aimed, with the government's assent, to move against New Spain, not New Orleans.

On the strength of the Kentucky grand jury's acquittal, Jackson delivered up to Burr the boats he had promised. Clearly he wished to believe the former vice president a gentleman engaged in a mission to roll back the Spanish empire from the open American frontier. Still, Jackson remained cautious in making any kind of commitment. This mixed-mindedness underscored his decision to allow one of Rachel's nephews to join Burr's expedition, but only after arming the boy with letters of warning to give Governor Claiborne should the youth discover New Orleans itself to be the filibuster's real target. In late December, Burr and a small outfit of volunteers departed from Nashville bearing down the Cumberland River.

Having just entrusted a nephew to Burr's care, Jackson received orders in early January from Jefferson and Dearborn to prepare his militia to move against the former vice president should the need arise. By this time, much of the West seemed alerted to the possibility of a conspiracy. Wilkinson had declared martial law in New Orleans and then, upon learning of Jefferson's late November proclamation to move against those "confederating [to conduct] a military expedition or enterprise against the dominions of Spain," dispatched a force of nearly three hundred to capture Burr and his band near Natchez. The latter shrewdly surrendered. A grand jury impaneled in the Mississippi Territory refused to indict the celebrity adventurer, although, at the behest of Thomas Rodney, one of the judges, Burr was told to remain in the area. Insisting on the jurist's "vindictive temper and unprincipled conduct," and no doubt mindful of Jefferson's still extant arrest order, Burr instead fled. About two weeks later, and more than two hundred miles to the east, a makeshift posse of soldiers captured the fugitive near Wakefield, Alabama. Apparently his "remarkably keen" eyes and "elegantly shaped" boots had alerted a federal land registrar unaccustomed to such quality.[12] On March 5, under a close guard of nine men, Burr began the long ride to Richmond to face his accusers.

Jackson, in a manner, followed him to Virginia, arriving in the capital on May 12, eager to testify on Burr's behalf. For several months, ever since conversing with Captain Fort in November, Jackson had mulled over the conspiracy question and decided, based on a selective interpretation of Fort's testimony, that Burr's intentions were benign while Wilkinson's approached treason. This presumption aligned nicely with Jackson's warm feeling for the charming Burr (shared by many) and his commensurate dislike of Wilkinson. Just three years earlier the latter had humiliated Colonel Thomas Butler, a career army officer, Revolutionary War veteran, and Jackson friend, over the question of a queue. Butler, serving in New Orleans, wore a slender braid down his back, and Wilkinson, defying a long if recently abolished custom among some in the military, charged him with disobedience for refusing to have it clipped. Jackson wrote to Jefferson at the time on Butler's behalf, implying strongly that Wilkinson had ungenerously maneuvered to force his consociate's resignation:

His removal for the disobedience of such an order, would raise unpleasant sensations in the minds of the citizens. It is thought by many that the renewal of the order was bottomed on a plan to drive the Colo. out of the service. It is stated that his well known attachment to his hair, which he had wore both as an ornament and for health untill it had grew gray in the service of his country were such, that nothing but death itself could seperate them from him. It is also thought that such an order approaches too near [to] despotism . . . and [is] better calculated for the dark regions of the east, than for enlightened America.[13]

But neither Jackson's letter to Jefferson nor a petition sent seventeen months later to the U.S. Senate and signed by several dozen prominent Nashvillians did any good. Jefferson refused to arbitrate the affair. A few months after the unavailing Nashville appeal, the twice court-martialed Butler died of yellow fever—and kept his queue in the coffin. He is said to have asked associates to "bore a hole through the bottom of my coffin right under my head, and let my queue hang through it, that the damned old rascal [Wilkinson] may see that, even when dead, I refused to obey his orders."[14] In its connection to the Burr affair, the Butler affair anticipated Jackson's antipathy toward both Wilkinson and Jefferson. In setting off for Richmond he possibly hoped to even a few scores.

In the Virginia capital, however, he played only the most minor of roles. Jackson had a knack for making coastal constituencies nervous; to these populations he seemed to court a brashness of conduct, an ignorance of implications that belied the tone and surface of polite society. Among dozens of other witnesses, the General gave testimony before a grand jury and, in an insolent, imprudent manner, proceeded to conjecture on Wilkinson's many misdeeds. Congressman John Randolph, foreman of the jury and no friend of Jefferson's, remarked to James Monroe on Jackson's capricious testimony: "There are I am told upwards of forty witnesses in town, one of whom [Jackson] does not scruple to say that W[ilkinson] is a pensioner of Spain, to his knowledge, & that he will not dare to show his face here." George Hay, the U.S. attorney for the Virginia District and soon to serve as lead prosecutor in the Burr trial, similarly informed Jefferson, "Gen: Jackson, of Tennessee has been here . . . denouncing Wilkinson in the coarsest terms in every company."[15] And even Burr's company grew apprehensive of Jackson's rash accusations. Accordingly, the defense decided not to call the voluble general to the witness stand.

On September 1, a little more than six months after his arrest, Burr

walked away a free man, acquitted by a jury. Simply put, the government failed to prove that the accused had committed treason. *Intent* to
do so, presiding judge John Marshall contended, came up short—and
no witness testified of Burr having engaged in an overt act of sedition.
The acquittal allowed Jackson to indulge both his loathing of Wilkinson and growing rift with Jefferson. In late November he wrote from
the Hermitage to a correspondent, "I have no doubt nor have I had of
the guilt of Wilkingson from the proofs I see exhibited against him at
Richmond." The president disappointed him greatly: "Notwithstanding
I have loved Mr Jefferson as a man, and adored him as a president, could
I see him attempt to support such a base man with his present knowledge of his corruption and infamy, I would withdraw that confidence
I once reposed in him and regret that I had been deceived in his virtue."[16] That Burr quite obviously trafficked in deception as well seems
not to have troubled Jackson. Certainly the trial had made absolutely
clear that, despite the New Yorker's many promises of federal support,
federal officials were indeed all too blind to his intentions.

But this hardly shook Jackson's regard for the man. Perhaps he saw
more than a little of himself in Burr, a dashing, decisive military figure eager to effect the removal of Spanish power from the Gulf region.
And thus in moving, as a major general in the U.S. Army, against Spanish Florida in 1818 and then recognizing, as president, the Republic of
Texas in 1837, Jackson might be said to have made real Burr's ambitious
vision—if, that is, Burr had intended no treason. But at the time, Jackson's defense of this controversial worthy cost him. Some Jeffersonians
assumed that he angled to embarrass the administration by attacking
Wilkinson; others paused over his involvement with Burr, wondering
if the boats and provisions he supplied might give the lie to his own
loyalty. What we know is that during the War of 1812 President Madison, once Jefferson's chief lieutenant, seemed uninterested in offering
Jackson command of a large federal army. Among such well-placed Virginians, the General's intemperate outbursts in Richmond undoubtedly
raised questions about his judgment and capacity for self-control, as did
his reputation for dueling—the same sin attached, of course, to Burr.

11

The Duelist

It might fairly be asked what Jackson received for his fast friendship with the mercurial Burr. One way to answer is to go back to a late May day in 1806 when the General coolly killed Charles Dickinson in a duel. A young, well-connected attorney once tutored by Justice John Marshall, Dickinson, so a biographer has noted, enjoyed "a large circle of gay friends."[1] By embracing Burr—an admired figure in much of the West—Jackson possibly sought, among other sympathies, to insulate himself from Nashville's sharp criticism. To many observers, the deadly gunfight had revealed a disturbing lack of restraint, wisdom, and self-awareness on his part, a currency of sound qualities one wished to see in, say, a senator, a jurist, or a militia general. So quick off the mark to claim a slew of Tennessee sinecures, Jackson seemed suddenly on the verge of wrecking this solid progress. The Dickinson duel played a role in this near reversal, and it began with a horse race.

In May 1805 Jackson bought Truxton, a five-year-old Virginia-bred bay stallion sired by the English import Diomede, for $1,500 (some $35,000 in current dollars). Though described by one contemporary as a "Horse of Horses," the animal proved to be one of Jackson's typically uneven financial investments. Supposed to be a tremendous distance competitor, Truxton contended in few contests before being retired perhaps a year after Jackson's purchase; cash and cotton stud fees continued, however, until his 1817 retirement to a Mississippi plantation.[2] For Jackson, ownership of a fine horse constituted a gentleman's prerogative, identifying him as one of Nashville's grandees. Apart from privilege, however, Jackson genuinely loved horseracing, which appealed to his competitive spirit and evident need to test himself. In the various arts of land speculation, dueling, and betting on bred horses, he engaged in rough play.

Sometime in 1805 Jackson and Captain Joseph Erwin, a former Revolutionary War officer living at Peach Blossom farm in Nashville, agreed to a late November race between their respective horses with stakes set at $2,000. Erwin subsequently called off the contest, however, after his stallion, Ploughboy, came up lame; he owed Jackson an $800 forfeit. What happened next remains opaque; it appears that some of the currency Erwin offered to Jackson differed from the promissory notes previously agreed upon. This in itself caused no rupture, for Erwin quickly accommodated Jackson, as both later related. The unfortunate intrusion of two younger men, rather, Erwin's son-in-law Charles Dickinson and Dickinson's insecure colleague Thomas Swann, incautiously angled this otherwise nebulous affair in a deadly direction.

A stray, dangerous story circulated around Nashville of Jackson having publicly impugned Erwin's integrity. Dickinson heard the report and asked Swann to approach Jackson, who vindicated Erwin but emphasized the original unacceptability of his notes. This information Swann reported to both Dickinson and Erwin, who then met on December 28 with the General, at which time, so Swann subsequently learned, Jackson denied making any public accusations against either man and denounced Swann as "a damn'd lyar." In a communication to the General dated January 3, Swann imprudently made note that the "harshness of this expression has deeply wounded my feelings"; he seemed intent on making his reputation by provoking Jackson.[3]

The General's reply on January 7 took Swann's meager measure. During the earlier Sevier entanglement, Jackson had failed to best the older man, but now, with the advantages of age and experience, he wrote evenly to his adversary, "I never wantonly sport with the feelings of innocence—nor am I ever awed into measures—if incautiously I inflict a wound, I always hasten to remove it. If offence is taken when non is offerred or intended, it gives me no pain. . . . At all times be assured I hold myself answerable for any of my conduct." Five days later a strutting Swann, refusing, so he said, "to be intimidated by your threats," challenged Jackson to a duel.[4] The next day, on January 13, Jackson, accompanied by John Coffee, met Swann at Winn's Tavern and, refusing to recognize his antagonist as a gentleman, proceeded to lash him repeatedly with a cane before they were separated.

Both men subsequently printed their sides of the feud in the February 15 *Impartial Review and Cumberland Repository*. Jackson's invective-laced piece caused considerably more damage, describing Dickinson, whom he suspected of being Swann's prod, as "a worthless, drunken, blackguard scounderal" and disparaging for good measure several of the young men in his circle. Nathaniel McNairy, brother of Jackson's old friend and mentor Judge John McNairy, found himself ridiculed in the piece as a "valiant squire" with "a natural weakness of memory" and went on the offensive. In his own *Review* report McNairy denigrated Jackson as "the braggadocio General" and abused Coffee as well, who immediately challenged the younger man to a duel. They met two weeks later in Kentucky, where an anxious McNairy fired early ("about the word 'two,'" related one witness), wounding an infuriated Coffee in the thigh.[5]

Having humbled Swann, Jackson now turned his attention to Dickinson for reasons not entirely clear. One of the General's earliest biographers, working off of interviews, maintained that even before Swann's ill-advised interference, Dickinson had publicly "uttered offensive words respecting Mrs. Jackson" on at least two occasions. Presumably a mixture of ignorance and arrogance rather than malice prompted these alleged remarks, which were said to have come in a drunken state. A skilled shot, Dickinson may have imagined himself immune from the consequences of his actions, which, in any event, he could blame on alcohol, and apparently did. Following the first public performance, Dickinson, when confronted by Jackson, is said to have pled a combination of confusion and inebriation. After a second exhibition (in a Nashville tavern) Jackson, so local gossip has it, warned Captain Erwin to control his son-in-law—"I wish no quarrel with him, he is *used* by my enemies in Nashville, who are urging him on to pick a quarrel with me. Advise him to stop in time."[6]

But the subsequent exchanges between Swann and Jackson invariably and disastrously drew a clearly reckless Dickinson again into the affair. Perhaps he had sought all along an excuse to humiliate the General. Three days before Swann's caning, Dickinson wrote to Jackson, "Do you pretend to call a Man [Swann] a *tale bearer* for telling that which is and can be proven to be the truth?" And closed trailing abuse—"As [to] the word *Coward, I think it as* [appli]cable to yourself as any one I [know]."[7] Dickinson then left immediately for Natchez and New Orleans to sell a number of slaves, practicing, legend has it, his marksmanship along the route. Jackson later latched on to this rumor as vindication for killing his adversary.

In the meantime, the rescheduled contest between Truxton and Ploughboy finally transpired. A public notice dated March 1 promised onlookers "the greatest and most interesting match race ever run in the Western country." A little over a month later, in a steady rain, Truxton defeated Ploughboy in a pair of two-mile races. Shortly thereafter Jackson confided to Rachel's nephew John Hutchings that the horse gamely ran lame: "Truxton had on Tuesday evening before got a serious hurt in his thigh, which occasioned it to swell verry much, and had it not have been for myself, would have occasioned the forfeight to have been paid—but this I was determined not to permit."[8] Apparently neither Truxton's health nor Jackson's own financial investment in the animal much mattered. A conspicuous show of strength and mastery, rather, crowded out other considerations for the General—and continued to do so upon Dickinson's return to Nashville.

Following months of maneuvering, the principals now proceeded toward a quick and violent conclusion. Plainly preparing to duel, Dickinson publicly assailed Jackson in the May 24 *Review*. After quoting the General's February insults to him in the same paper—"worthless, drunken, blackguard scounderal"—Dickinson issued his own: "Should Andrew Jackson have extended these epithets for me, I declare him . . . to be a worthless scoundrel 'a poltroon and a coward.'" As expected the General returned fire, writing immediately to Dickinson, "I hope sir . . . that I will obtain speedily that satisfaction due me for the insults offered—and in the way my friend [Thomas Overton], who hands you this, will point out—He waits upon you, for that purpose, and with your friend, will enter into immediate arrangements for this purpose."[9] The parties agreed to meet in six days some forty miles to the north, at Harrison's Mill in Logan County, Kentucky.

While traveling to the dueling grounds with a small entourage, Dickinson is said to have put on an exhibition of shooting skills, saying to one tavern keeper, after splitting a string from a distance of several feet, "If General Jackson comes along this road, show him *that*!" Such a display of high emotion, whether literal or not, perhaps captures something of the moment's intensity on the eve of what promised to be a deadly affair. Jackson, by contrast, quietly arrived the night before the contest with a party of seven or eight at the tavern of David Miller; apparently he discussed strategy with the dependable Overton, who acted as his second. The combatants had agreed to stand eight paces (twenty-four feet) apart, they were to hold their long-barreled, 70-caliber pistols down until commanded to draw. Assuming Dickinson to be the quicker and better shot, Jackson determined not to let fly first. He expected, in other words, to be wounded, to withstand the blow, and to then return fire. "I should have hit him," he later insisted, "if he had shot me through the brain."[10]

The following day, shunning breakfast, the General and his entourage rode to the dueling site. There they dispersed, with only Jackson, Overton, and a surgeon dismounting, while the others tarried a short distance away. With the group now joined by Dickinson's party, the two sides listened as details were swiftly worked out. Dickinson won choice of position; Overton would give the call, and the principals assumed their places. Assured that both men were ready, Overton wasted no time

THE DUEL.

An 1834 illustration of Jackson's (notorious) 1806 duel with Charles Dickinson. Dickinson shot first, drilling Jackson in the upper chest (where the bullet remained lodged for the rest of his life). Jackson then shot and killed Dickinson. The duel became a strong feature of the Jackson legend: the man whom neither the British nor duelists could kill.

in shouting "FIRE!" (likely pronounced "FERE!" on the field). As expected, Dickinson volleyed first, scraping Jackson's breastbone and shattering perhaps two ribs, but missing his target's heart by about an inch. Having positioned his thin frame exceedingly sideways to limit exposure, the General stayed erect. Dickinson is reported to have wavered in surprise, taking a step or two back and shouting, "Great God!, have I missed him?" Ordered by Overton to resume his position, Dickinson then awaited Jackson's shot. The General slowly took aim, pulled the trigger, and . . . nothing happened. His pistol had locked at half cock. Returning the hammer to its original place, he again aimed, and this time the weapon fired, catching Dickinson flush in the lower abdomen. After checking on the hemorrhaging man, now in the care of his shocked coterie, Overton stated to Jackson, "He won't want anything more of you, General," and they left the grounds.[11] Only then did Overton notice the blood collecting in one of Jackson's shoes.

Dickinson's aim appears to have been true—he directed the shot precisely where he believed his target's heart to be. But as one chronicler acquainted with the witnesses of that fateful morning later wrote, "the thinness of [Jackson's] body and the looseness of his coat combin[ed] to deceive Dickinson." Returning to David Miller's tavern, the General requested a cup of buttermilk. He subsequently allowed a surgeon to peruse his painful but not life-threatening wound and directed one of his men to check on Dickinson. Upon learning that the young man's "case was past surgery," Jackson sent his now former adversary a bottle of wine.[12] Dickinson died that evening.

Some dozen years later, Jackson offered a former aide advice on surviving a duel against a superior shot. He spoke, of course, from personal experience. "Charge your friend to preserve his fire, keeping his *teeth firmly* clenched, and *his fingers* in a position that if fired on and *hit*, his fire may not be extorted." Being merely quick off the shot, after all, guaranteed nothing. For if a duelist "fires and does not kill his antagonist, he leaves himself fully in his [opponent's] power."[13]

Young Dickinson's violent demise brought Jackson no peace. At the behest of more than seventy Nashvillians, the city's two newspapers, the *Review* and the *Tennessee Gazette*, adorned their June 7 editions with black mourning borders "as a tribute to respect for the memory, and regret for the untimely death of Charles Dickinson." Incensed at what

amounted to a civic rebuke, Jackson demanded that the editor of the
Review publish the names of those behind the accolade. "Your paper is
the public vehicle, and is always taken to be the public will," he wrote,
"unless the contrary appears." Deciding for all concerned that the contrary had indeed appeared, he imperiously and a little incoherently
declared "the PUBLIC IS NOT IN MOURNING at this event," meaning
that some other incentive had spurred the signatories. Searching for a
conspiracy, he claimed the print memorial to be "so novel, that the names
ought to appear that the public might judge [whether] the true motives
of the signers 'were a tribute of respect for the deceased,' or something
else, that at first sight does not appear." Presumably that something else
involved a direct attack on Jackson's actions and character. More than
twenty quite possibly panicked signatories quickly recalled their names
after learning of Jackson's high-handed request; but more than forty,
including several of Nashville's propertied elite, did not.[14]

Jackson, being Jackson, went on the offensive. He knew that some
believed the duel should have ended after his pistol snapped and failed
to fire. In reply, he hastily acquired statements from the seconds indicating that the affair "was conducted agreeably to what was agreed upon,
so far as any agreements were made." But this lawyerly maneuver hardly
satisfied those who thought Jackson a butcher rather than a gentleman for his decision to recock his weapon before a defenseless man.
Nor could it have pleased Dickinson's partisans when Jackson brashly
drafted a public letter that ungraciously attacked his late opponent. "It is
truly unpleasant at all times to disturb the ashes of the dead," he opined,
and then proceeded to do just that. Citing the willingness of Nashville's
"intermedling mourners" to interfere in a "private dispute" as justification, he denounced Dickinson as a slave trader, "making a fortune
of speculating on human flesh." Jackson too, of course, engaged in the
domestic trade of enslaved men and women, a point he neglected to
mention. He insisted instead on Dickinson's intent to eliminate him,
having browbeat a sketchy statement from a witness to the effect that
Erwin had goaded his son-in-law the previous Christmas Day to murder the General: "By God Sir, I think you can kill him." "Is it Possible,"
Jackson asked, tossing yet more dirt on the dead man's grave, "that Mr.
Dickason, can be thus seriously regretted?"[15]

Over the summer, tensions relating to the interview at Harrison's
Mill continued to cook. In September an agitated John Overton wrote

to Jackson, prompted by a (probably baseless) rumor that Swann now looked to challenge the General. Even if he survived another duel, Overton asserted, Jackson risked destroying his reputation: "If you were to kill this Swann, or some such lad, what would be the consequence? why it would be said that you delighted in human blood." Stroking Jackson's ego—"No[t] . . . even your worst enemies doubts your personal courage"—he also affirmed that "many judicious men of honor" in the area wished to see this feral and drawn-out episode ended.[16]

Combined, the caning of Swann and the killing of Dickinson, with their accompanying scenarios of intimidation, counterclaims, and unseemly public appeals, did Jackson little credit. These months of, as many believed, senseless violence, overlapped the General's deepening relations with the soon to be sullied Aaron Burr and, together, called into question his impressive momentum since coming to Tennessee nearly two decades earlier. As he turned forty in the late winter of 1807, Jackson's public career appeared to have stalled. A now *former* congressman, senator, and justice, he protectively embraced his role and high rank in the militia as a sign of station, respect, and possibility. At this point it appeared his only opportunity for advancement. He needed a war.

Part II

HERO FOR AN AGE

Now to Orleans, emporium of the west,
Jackson repairs with thunder on his breast.
To Carolina South, his birth was given –
There the bold chief inhal'd the air of heaven.

Richard Emmons, 1827

The Creek War and Battle of New Orleans made Jackson a national hero.
Here, in military dress, he sits astride Sam Patch, a gift from the people
of Pennsylvania.

12

Erratic Rehabilitation

In the aftermath of the Burr trial, Jackson gave every indication of having peaked as a public figure. Tennessee, though agreeable to the aspirations of frontier sovereigns in the old Blount/Sevier mold, provided only a limited arena of opportunity, while the country at large appeared reluctant to award westerners high office. Between 1788 and 1828 all of the nation's presidents came from Virginia or Massachusetts; not until 1825 did Kentucky's Henry Clay become the first trans-Appalachian to serve as secretary of state in more than an acting capacity; only in 1837 did a candidate hailing from outside one of the original thirteen colonies, Richard Mentor Johnson, also from Kentucky, claim the vice presidency. Geography, once on a young Jackson's side, now seemed to work against him.

For six years, 1807–1812, the General's ambitions lay in abeyance. A friendly biography published in the wake of the Battle of New Orleans, offered only a glancing report of this period. "Determined now to spend his life in tranquility and retirement," it read, "he settled himself on an elegant farm, ten miles from Nashville, on the Cumberland river; where . . . he enjoyed all the comforts of domestic and social intercourse."[1] The Jacksons occupied a solid preexisting two-story log house hewn from neighboring elm, red oak, and tulip poplar timbers. A large room dominated the first floor while matching private bedchambers were located on the second; a cramped attic loft capped the structure. On this site Jackson served as the guardian for several children—including Jack Donelson (Rachel's nephew) and Andrew Jackson Hutchings (grandson of Rachel's sister Catherine)—typically the offspring of relatives or men known to the General. Apart from these and several other wards, the Jacksons adopted an infant twin of Rachel's brother Severn Donelson, naming him Andrew Jackson, Jr. The couple had no children of their own.

Though a force within his own state, Jackson remained aloof from national politics in the years preceding the War of 1812. Reflecting irritably on Burr's arrest and trial, he grew coldly hostile to Jefferson and Madison, suspicious that these men harbored the "traitor" Wilkinson from public scrutiny. In 1808 he quietly backed James Monroe, the candidate of more states' rights–oriented southern Republicans, for the party's nomination over the ultimately victorious Madison. "Some of our old republican friends," he complained about this time, "have either lost their usual good Judgt. or their political principle."[2] Without these allies, however, Jackson stood, like Burr, on the other side of power.

To place him on power's proper side required a desperate country, one willing to look beyond the General's pride and insecurity, his high-handedness and questionable judgment. Such circumstances arrived gradually over a handful of restless years as the United States struggled to defend its neutrality during the widening Napoleonic Wars. British confiscation of U.S. shipping, impressment of seamen on American ships, and armed support for an Indian presence in the Old Northwest eventually pulled a hitherto reluctant Madison administration into the broader global conflict. Until that day Jackson brooded at the Hermitage for word of war, entreating Tennessee congressman Felix Grundy for his impression. "Shall we have War?" Grundy replied in early February 1812. "That is the question you want answered—*So do I.*" Later that month Congress offered an affirmative retort of sorts, authorizing the enlistment of fifty thousand volunteers. Jackson, in his capacity as major general of the western Tennessee militia, promptly issued an order to its 2nd Division requesting soldiers. "The hour of national vengeance is now at hand," he declared and called upon these "free born sons of america" to defend their rights. Perhaps invoking his own latent ambition for martial glory, he supposed them "burning with impatience to illustrate their names by some signal exploit."[3]

Notwithstanding such lofty expectations, Jackson suffered a summer of quiet humiliation. On June 18 Congress approved an act declaring war "to exist between the United Kingdom of Great Britain and Ireland and the dependencies thereof, and the United States of America and their territories," thus prompting the positioning of various armies in North America. But not Jackson's. He remained edgy and eager for combat, writing to Governor Willie Blount (William Blount's younger half brother) in early July, "we are ready," and informing his Tennessee volunteers later that month, "I know your impatience . . . you burn with anxiety to learn on what theatre your arms will find employment." In September, following the disastrous surrender of a large American army in Detroit to a combined British-Indian-Canadian force, he somewhat wildly informed Blount, "it will give me pleasure . . . to march to the relief of that quarter without delay."[4] Still out of official favor, however, he waited.

Jackson's emancipatory moment arrived in October when the government required soldiers for a southern campaign. Blount received word from Washington to send fifteen hundred volunteers to New Orleans and gave the command to Jackson. And so in early December two divisions, numbering a little over two thousand soldiers, including mounted infantry, were readied and, amid a deep snowfall, left Nashville on January 10, 1813. Nearly six weeks later the bulk of the volunteers encamped in Natchez, Jackson's friend Coffee, commanding cavalry, having arrived earlier. Why remote Natchez?—because the commander at New Orleans, the irrepressible Wilkinson, wanted to keep Jackson as far away as possible. "Understanding casually that you are approaching Natchez with a body of Dragoons, Infantry and mounted Gun Men, destined to this city," he had written to his adversary, "it becomes my duty to request you to halt in that vicinity." Wilkinson proceeded in the communication to list for a no doubt infuriated Jackson the "several reasons which will prevent my calling you lower down the river"; lack of provisions for extra horses, troop health, and the desire to maintain a separate force able to protect American settlements in the area of Mobile were among the motives. In turn, a tetchy Jackson, blocked from going any farther, slipped into a resentful silence. Recognizing the General's passive-aggressive feint, Wilkinson, from the safety of distance and power, chastised Jackson in yet another letter for practicing secrecy. "Without knowing what may be your orders, instructions or the extent of your command," he fairly purred, "I must regret, that you have not done me the honor to communicate with me; because . . . you can find no man more zealously disposed to cherish the band of patriots, whom you lead, than myself."[5]

Not wishing to share the "extent" of his command, or anything else, with Wilkinson, Jackson sat irritably, impatiently in Natchez—as several weeks passed. In the middle of March and much to his astonishment, he received a directive written the previous month from secretary of war John Armstrong. It was brutally brief, saying in the main: "The causes for embodying & marching to New Orleans the Corps under your command having ceased to exist, you will on receipt of this Letter, consider it as dismissed from public service, & take measures to have delivered over to Major General Wilkinson, all articles of public property which may have been put into its possession." Jackson described the order to Grundy as "extraordinary" and complained to Rachel of his soldiers having "been but illy rewarded."[6] He reserved for Armstrong a more insolent and condescending critique, writing sarcastically, perhaps even a little hysterically, to his superior on the 15th:

> If it was intended by this order that we should be dismissed eight hundred miles from home, deprived of arms, tents and supplies for the sick—of our arms and supplies for the well, it appears that these brave men, who certainly deserve better fate and return from their government was intended by this order to be sacrificed—Those that could escape from the insalubrious climate, are to be deprived of the necessary support and meet death by famine The remaining few to be deprived of their arms pass through the savage land, where our women children and defenceless citizens are daily murdered—Yet thro. that barbarous clime, must our band of citizen soldiers wander and fall a sacrafice to the Tomahawk and scalping knife of the wilderness our sick left naked in the open field and remain without supplies without nourishment or an earthly comfort.[7]

As for disbanding his forces, Jackson simply refused. Undoubtedly some among his discharged volunteers, hundreds of miles from home, would, if no other option presented itself, end up augmenting Wilkinson's army in nearer New Orleans; this deplorable prospect Jackson determined to prevent at all cost. "I mean to commence my march to Nashville in a few days," he informed Armstrong, "at which place I expect the troops to be paid and the necessary supplies furnished by the agents of Government while payment is making, after which I will dismiss them to their homes and their families."[8]

And so the volunteers began the difficult one-month march back to Nashville, fighting the elements, a swelling sick list, and a lack of horses and wagons. Jackson and his officers gave up their mounts to convey the incapacitated, an action that, mingled with other signs of stoicism on the journey, earned the General the respectful sobriquet "Hickory," evoking the toughness of the man and to evolve later into the inevitably affectionate Old Hickory. The worn but intact army arrived in Nashville on April 22; two days later Jackson wrote a strong letter to Armstrong, complaining of the "heart burnings occasioned by the apparent neglect of the Government towards this detachment" and insisting with great feeling if little evidence that unnamed Washington officials had planned to make his men—"reduced by want"—desperate to join Wilkinson's force. Then, noting the fighting in the war's northern theater, he suddenly pivoted, dubiously informing Armstrong that if ordered, his infantry, which he had just declared all but incapacitated, could easily "have marched . . . on to Malden," an enemy-occupied fort on the Canadian side of the Detroit River some six hundred miles from Nashville.[9] But Armstrong had no intention of moving Jackson's army anywhere for the time being. Five months passed, rather, before the 2nd Division received orders to muster again.

Though Jackson had stewed all the way back to Nashville, musing along every mile how the government sought to diminish his force and undermine his command, the expedition proved privately beneficial. Known locally as the man who killed Dickinson and in a few Washington circles as Burr's abettor, Jackson now assumed an altogether more paternal air as the devoted general who cared for his men, shared their deprivations, and returned them safely home. His reputation appeared to be altogether strengthened and his tenacity respected until, in a single violent encounter that summer, he nearly lost everything.

Viewed from any attitude, the infamous Jackson-Benton brawl edified neither of its principals. In brief, Jackson, only weeks after returning his troops to Nashville, agreed to serve as second for William (Billy) Carroll in a duel with Jesse Benton, the younger, excitable, and indiscreet brother of Lieutenant Colonel Thomas Hart Benton, formerly Jackson's aide-de-camp and now representing the General's military interests— chiefly squaring accounts and expenses—in Washington. Carroll, a Pittsburgh native said by one biographer to bear "an expression of delicacy in his smooth, fair countenance that found small favor in the eyes of the rougher pioneers," received Jackson's indulgence as a brigade inspector during the difficult march from Natchez to Nashville. This stirred up some petty enmity among a few of the junior officers, including Benton, who, following a string of assumed grievances, challenged Carroll. The latter promptly asked Jackson to serve as his friend and second. The forty-six-year-old general apparently attempted to beg off, citing age, but the twenty-five-year-old Carroll appealed to his patron's vanity and sense of paternalism, explaining that the great man's attentions had aroused jealousy in the ranks. Jackson agreed to look into the affair.[10]

He discussed the situation with Benton, seeking to diffuse the quarrel, though ultimately to no effect, and thus he consented to stand as Carroll's second. The duel proved to be a fiasco. The opponents stood back-to-back a mere ten feet apart (to compensate for Carroll's poor shooting), and Jesse Benton turned on the signal, shot first, and then quickly crouched so as to provide his opposite (suffering a wounded thumb) only a truncated target. Carroll fired in return, hitting Benton's prominently exposed bottom; the wound proved decidedly embarrassing if not exactly life-threatening. Shortly thereafter Thomas Hart Benton returned from Washington and learned of his now convalescing brother's shame. Though possessed of more self-control than Jesse, the senior Benton immediately inserted himself into the Carroll controversy, writing to Jackson directly on July 25. He outlined four points of "error" in Jackson's "agency in that affair."

1. That it was very poor business in a man of your age and standing to be conducting a duel about nothing between young men who had no harm against each; and that you would have done yourself more honor by advising them to reserve their courage for the public enemy.

2. That it was mean in you to draw a challenge from my brother by carrying him a bullying note from Mr. C. dictated by yourself [Carroll said years later that he himself had authored the note], and which left him no alternative but a duel or disgrace.

3. That if you could not have prevented a duel you ought at least to have conducted it in the usual mode, and on terms equal to both parties.

4. That on the contrary you conducted it in a savage, unequal, unfair, and base manner.

The cadence of accusations—"savage," "unequal," "unfair," and "base"—amounted to a relentless attack on Jackson's conduct. Benton, however, pulled up just short of resorting to an outright challenge. "I shall," he closed, "neither seek, nor decline, a duel with you."[11]

Benton's broad point, that Jackson should have recused himself from a scrape between two younger men, is well considered, though his own questionable intervention in the affair only exacerbated matters. On August 4, Jackson replied to Benton's note with a predictably studied indignation, reviewing his efforts to keep the young men apart and defending the duel's probity. He concluded, as had Benton, by neither asking for nor backing away from a challenge: "Thus sir I have fully [and] frankly explained the circumstances of th[is affair] to you. If satisfactory I shall be gratified, [but if] otherwise . . . I am always ame[nable] to the process of honorable men."[12] One month later said honorable men were scuffling like bandits with guns and knives in a Nashville hotel.

After sending his rejoinder, Jackson learned that Benton, obviously dissatisfied with the dispatch, had on several occasions publicly attacked the conducting of the duel. Anxious as always to defend his reputation and honor, Jackson let it be known that he planned to horsewhip Thomas Benton the next time their paths crossed. Jackson remained, in other words, a prisoner of his passions. Both Bentons arrived in Nashville on September 3 and, apparently intending to avoid Jackson, stayed at the City Hotel, which the General never frequented. That evening Jackson and Coffee, apprised of the Bentons' arrival, also rode into town, merely, so Coffee claimed, to pick up their respective mail. They put up, as was the General's custom, at the Nashville Inn. The following morning Jackson, with whip in hand and a small gentleman's sword on his hip, walked to the post office with Coffee, passing at an angle the City Hotel, where the senior Benton, tall, thickly built, and well proportioned, stood defiantly in the doorway. Having collected their mail, Jackson and Coffee then used the sidewalk route back to the inn—which led them directly to Benton. Nearing his nemesis, Jackson is reported to have got his whip at the ready, saying, "Now, you damned rascal, I am going to punish you. Defend yourself." Benton appeared to be grasping for a firearm, enough provocation for Jackson to produce a pistol and methodically back his opponent into the hotel. The two men had almost reached the rear of the building when Jesse Benton suddenly appeared from behind the pair and fired a slug that shattered Jackson's left shoulder; a second ball entered his left arm. Hearing the shots, Coffee raced inside to see Jackson on the ground bleeding. He raised his pistol and fired on Thomas but missed, the latter having inadvertently stumbled down a flight of steps to safety. Jesse escaped serious injury as well; though attacked outside the hotel by a dagger-wielding nephew of Rachel's, he survived when the two were separated by bystanders.[13]

Taken back to the Nashville Inn, Jackson, legend has it, bled through two mattresses and talked a caucus of doctors out of severing his severely wounded arm. The ball, lodged near the bone, stayed in his limb for years, being extracted in 1832. Thomas Benton, marching up from the basement, proceeded to loudly condemn Jackson as an "assassin" and snapped his assailant's abandoned sword in the pubic square.

The Benton boys appeared to have carried the contest, but in the following days they began to fear for their lives. On the 10th Thomas issued a broadside presenting the brothers' side of the fracas. He emphasized their efforts taking "lodgings in a different house" to avoid Jackson; he stated that the General came to their hotel and "commenced the attack by levelling a pistol at me"—this justified, he maintained, Jesse's firing on Jackson. "These facts are sufficient to fix the public opinion," he concluded, and certainly they were, though not in the way he wished. An uncomfortable number of Nashvillians, rather, wanted Benton's blood. "I am literally in hell here . . . all the puppies of Jackson are at work on me," he wrote with concern a few days after the brawl, and sensing the threatening public mood, he returned home to Franklin, Tennessee.[14] Following the War of 1812 Benton decided to move to Missouri.

13

The Creek War

Though the celebrated American victory at the Battle of New Orleans solidified Jackson's reputation as a national hero, his earlier actions in the Creek War (1813–1814) were arguably more consequential. For in joining with Choctaw, Cherokee, and Lower Creeks to defeat the Upper Creeks (also known as Red Sticks for their red-painted war clubs), Jackson's army created the circumstances in which millions of acres of Indian territory in present-day Georgia and Alabama were soon ceded to the United States. In effect, Jackson took advantage of a civil war between those Creeks living closer to white settlers and their more traditional, less mixed-raced Red Stick brethren. Only with the conquest of the Red Sticks and only with the quieting of the southwestern frontier could Jackson direct his attention to the Gulf Coast. His army's subsequent invasion of Spanish Florida (November 1814) and thwarting of British forces at New Orleans (January 1815) were predicated on the longer, deadlier, and more crucial Creek campaign.

Throughout the southwest lived approximately sixty thousand native peoples—mainly Cherokee, Choctaw, Chickasaw, Chickamauga, Seminole, and Creek—typically bound by treaties with the United States. During the War of 1812 some Indian nations, concerned with uninterrupted encroachments on their lands, allied with Great Britain; these included the Lower Great Lakes Indians (led by the famous Shawnee warrior Tecumseh), the Mohawks in Quebec and Ontario, and the Red Sticks.[1] Though part of a larger pan-Indian movement, the latter engaged in the Creek War over issues relating to divisions within the Creek Confederation. Heightened in the atmosphere of war, this factionalization drew the interest of outside parties—the Spanish, the British, and eventually Jackson—who used it for their own ends. Violence first broke out between the Upper Creeks and the United States in late July 1813 when a territorial militia in southern Alabama clashed with Red Sticks returning from Spanish Florida with arms. This Battle of Burnt Corn concluded with perhaps two dozen combined casualties in a Red Stick victory.

One month later a far deadlier confrontation occurred at Fort Mims, forty miles north of Mobile (then part of the Mississippi Territory). Peter McQueen and William Weatherford, two mixed-race chiefs, gathered as many as a thousand warriors from nearly a dozen Creek towns along the lower Alabama River. This force descended on Fort Mims, a primitive stockade defended by 120 militia and peopled by 300 whites, slaves, and multiracial Indians. On August 30, at midday, the Red Sticks stormed the fort through a partially opened gate, only to encounter a separate inner enclosure. A second assault three hours later overwhelmed the garrison, and, despite Weatherford's efforts, a massacre ensued in which more than two hundred scalps were taken.

News of the carnage spread quickly, and two weeks later President James Madison called into service the region's various militias. With the Tennessee legislature's blessing, Governor Willie Blount mustered five thousand soldiers (a blend of regulars and volunteers) and called upon Jackson, still convalescing from the wounds he'd received less than two weeks earlier in the bloody Benton dispute, to command half of them. Desperate to take the field and eager to erase the previous year's humiliating dispersal of his soldiers in Natchez, Jackson, his arm painfully propped in a sling, swung gingerly into action. Addressing the Tennessee Volunteers on September 24, he employed the language of frontier fear—"savage foe," "scalping knifes," "butcher your wives"—in rallying his men. No doubt seeking to disprove rumors of his unfitness, he wrote, as if divinely healed, "The health of your General is restored—he will command in person." And so a visibly fragile Jackson moved his western Tennessee force south, from Fayetteville to Huntsville to Fort Deposit. In this last locale, arrived at on October 24, he established, as the name suggested, a supply storehouse. The journey into northern Alabama, he wrote one officer, proved arduous as his army "encountered every difficulty that can possibly arise from the want of Supplies, & from ruggedness of mountains."[2]

The first week of November saw Jackson on the move again. After establishing Fort Strother along the Coosa River—about ninety miles south of Huntsville—he ordered John Coffee's cavalry and mounted riflemen to assault Tallushatchee, a Red Stick village just to the east and said to be housing two hundred warriors. This attack (on November 3) turned into a massacre. One enlistee, Richard Call, a Virginian later to serve as territorial governor of Florida, remembered the slaughter with a grim precision:

> We found as many as eight or ten dead bodies in a single cabin. Sometimes the dead mother clasped the dead child to her breast, and to add another appalling horror to the bloody catalogue—some of the cabins had taken fire, and half consumed human bodies were seen amidst the smoking ruins. In other instances dogs had torn and feasted on the mangled bodies of their masters. Heart sick I turned from the revolting scene.[3]

Another soldier, the frontiersman and American folk hero Davy Crockett, then serving under Coffee in the 2nd Regiment of Volunteer Mounted Riflemen and later to die at the Alamo, wrote of confronting dozens of Indians in a single dwelling: "We now shot them like dogs; and then set the house on fire, and burned it up with the forty-six warriors in it." Returning the next day, some of the soldiers found potatoes in the basement of the house which, shy of supplies, they abruptly devoured despite the fact, as Crockett noted, "the oil of the Indians we had burned up . . . had run down on them."[4]

The day after the battle Jackson informed Rachel that Coffee had destroyed Tallushatchee "in elegant stile." He noted further of having sent "a little Indian boy" north to be raised at the Hermitage—superintendency being a not uncommon occurrence among men fighting, trading, and treating with Indians. This particular child, called Lyncoya and orphaned in the late campaign, was one of at least two Creek wards in the Jackson family (another, named Theodore, died in infancy). Though expected to be a companion for Andrew Jackson, Jr., Lyncoya also received some education, and Jackson seemed to entertain hopes that he might attend West Point. Rather, the boy ran away several times and was eventually apprenticed to a Nashville saddler. He died of tuberculosis in 1828 while still in his teens. Lyncoya may have emblematized for Jackson the white frontier's self-serving coupling of benevolence and victory, virtues of civility and sword that displayed the conquering race's presumptive humanity amid a violent process of reduction and removal.[5]

Six days after the battle of Tallushatchee, Jackson's army engaged in yet another clash with the Weatherford-led Red Sticks at Talladega, about thirty miles to the south. With a numerical advantage of two thousand (combined infantry and cavalry) to seven hundred, the Americans earned a qualified victory as hundreds of Indians managed to bolt through a gap in Jackson's line. As General Coffee recalled:

> We had nearly surrounded the Indians when they broke through an opening . . . that had not been closed, through which many of them escaped. We pursued them three or four miles, killing and wounding as they ran. We have counted two hundred and ninety-nine Indians dead on the ground, and it is believed that many have not been found that were killed dead; but the battle ground was so very large we had not time to hunt them up.[6]

If less than definitive, the Battle of Talladega nevertheless capped an impressive fall campaign for Jackson's forces in the heart of Creek country. That December his army returned to Fort Strother, awaiting reinforcements and provisions. He now planned, so he told a Scotsman licensed to trade with the Creeks, to assemble enough supplies "to enable me to carry a war of destruction through every part of the Creek nation that remains unfriendly."[7] In fact, as winter neared, his army threatened to melt away.

To Jackson's immense frustration, the enlistments of hundreds of men under his command neared expiration. A February 1812 law defined the term of service for volunteers as twelve months, unless dismissed earlier. When informed on December 4 by Colonel William Martin that in six days his Regiment of Volunteers intended to "claim their discharge as a matter of right" and return to Tennessee, Jackson blanched. Replying at length and in a somewhat obfuscating fashion two days later, he denied that the terms of service were actually up and mixed paternalism—"a father never deceives his children"—with the promise of violence—"Mutiny & desertion *shall* be put down, so long as I retain the power of quelling them." Thus ensued a brief, tense stand-off. On the evening of the 9th General William Hall informed Jackson that his 1st Brigade, Tennessee Volunteer Infantry, had determined to march secretly out of camp. Jackson responded by employing troops along the road to avert the brigade's dispatch and threatening, via positioned artillery pieces, to destroy any who tried to head home. He then, so one observer recalled, rode along the line "and addressed [the evacuating troops] by companies, in a strain of impassioned eloquence. He feelingly expatiated on their former good conduct, and the esteem and applause it had secured them; and pointed to the disgrace which they must heap upon themselves, their families, and country, by persisting, even if they could succeed, in their present mutiny. But he told them they should not succeed, but by passing over his body."[8]

The expected-at-any-time arrival of Major General John Cocke's East Tennessee Volunteers constituted the carrot in this anxious conversation. Upon their arrival, Jackson promised, those claiming their service to have expired would be free to leave. Three days later Cocke turned up at Fort Strother with fifteen hundred men—on short three-month enlistments soon to end, in but a few weeks; at this time Hall's brigade promptly departed. A frustrated Jackson wrote to Rachel at the end of the month, "I have been much pestered and vexed with the shamefull retrograde of the Volunteers . . . and with the still more shamefull indolence of the contractors, in not supplying us with provisions."[9] Such blame and belittling, however, could not disguise the fact that Jackson had overplayed his hand. By ignoring the enlistment terms of his men and penetrating too deeply into remote territory difficult for merchants to reach, he invariably raised eyebrows in a skeptical War Department.

Jackson reacted to his predicament predictably—he took action. Leaving Fort Strother with a small force of sixty-day enlistees in mid-January, he proceeded a little desperately to make war on the Creeks at Emuckfaw and Enotachopo. These engagements were indecisive, and Jackson's army, numerically outnumbered, withdrew back to Fort Strother with just under one hundred casualties. He need not have been so rash. For the general progress of the Creek campaign since Tallushatchee's destruction, generously reported in newspapers, had boosted recruiting in the West. By February Jackson suddenly found himself commanding a large force of roughly four thousand, which included several hundred U.S. Army regulars, thus adding much-needed tone to the militia. During this late winter period, however, he seemed on edge, perhaps still brittle over losing enlistees and eager to assert his command. In February and March, he ordered a handful of court-martials and flew into a rage upon hearing rumors that Major General Cocke had told his men that he, Jackson, had knowingly ignored the legal enrollment terms of his soldiers. Claiming that Cocke had spurred desertion among Tennessee's volunteers, Jackson requested that Governor Blount "have him immediately arrested under the act of congress, making it penal, for any individual to entice or persuade soldiers in the service of the united States to desert." Though Blount smartly refused to insert himself in this ugly affair, Jackson himself saw to Cocke's arrest, leading to his court-martial and trial in Nashville. There the major general won acquittal despite, so he later wrote, facing a tribunal "composed of my bitterest enemies and General Jackson's most devoted personal friends."[10]

The Cocke affair, run on rumor, scuttlebutt, and gossip, constituted a minor contretemps between posturing officers. It paled beside the repercussions of the Wood case. In early March Jackson refused to halt the execution of John Woods, a volunteer said to be not yet eighteen. Returning from night duty Woods had received an order from an officer to take breakfast, only to be questioned by a second officer when he did. Cold, exhausted, and hungry, he answered abusively and, when ordered back on duty, refused, apparently waving his rifle around for emphasis. Subsequently taken into custody, he was quickly convicted of a number of charges, including mutiny. After the war, and particularly when Jackson became a candidate for the presidency, critics looked back on his decision to permit Woods's execution as an indication of an underlying authoritarianism. He had wished, some argued, to make an example of the young soldier in light of the recent enlistment controversy among his troops. Calling Woods's insubordination "an important crisis," he had refused to suspend the sentence and approved the teenager's death, which occurred by firing squad in front of the entire army on March 14, only two days after conviction and thus leaving no time for an appeal.[11] Other than for desertion, no American soldier had been executed since the Revolution.

The same day that Woods died, Jackson, with a replenished army that included hundreds of friendly Creek and Cherokee, left Fort Strother, determined to end the Creek War. His opponents could martial perhaps a thousand warriors. Moving south, Jackson established

Fort Williams as a supply depot for the coming campaign. From this new station his army tramped through the forest to within a few miles of a Red Stick camp by a curve in the Tallapoosa River. The ensuing Battle of Horseshoe Bend occurred on March 27 and resulted in the great victory Jackson sought. The outnumbered Red Sticks occupied a poor strategic location; their Tohopeka village sat on a tiny peninsula, nearly encircled by the Tallapoosa. Jackson positioned artillery on high ground and bunched his main line, which included the disciplined 39th U.S. Infantry, a regiment of the regular army, on the peninsula's neck. Coffee established main and reserve lines on the other side of the river. The Red Sticks were, in effect, surrounded. Following a two-hour artillery barrage in the late morning, Jackson ordered a bayonet charge against his opponents' breastworks, commencing a brutal few hours of hand-to-hand combat that lasted until dark. More than eight hundred Red Sticks were killed, against perhaps seventy of the combined American/ Native American force; the results of this awful slaughter Jackson conveyed to Rachel: "The *carnage* was *dreadfull* . . . and it was dark before we finished killing them." More generally, he expressed hope in this note that the battle might constitute the end of Red Stick resistance. "Having destroyed at To'hope'ka, three of their principl prophets leaving but two in their nation—having tread their holy ground as the[y] termed it, and destroyed all their chiefs & warriors on the Tallapoosee river above the big bend, it is probable they may now sue for peace."[12]

And sue they did. Moving still farther south, Jackson's army took over Fort Toulouse, erected by the French in 1735, on April 18. Renamed Fort Jackson, it became the meeting ground where Red Stick chiefs, including Weatherford, surrendered.

The Creek War culminated at the precise moment the Treaty of Paris all but ended Europe's protracted Napoleonic Wars. Britain, now free to focus on the United States, commenced that summer on a major Chesapeake campaign, resulting in the humbling August invasion of the nation's capital. Jackson's generalship against the Red Sticks in 1814—a year in which Britain raided coastal New England communities, repulsed an American invasion of Canada at the bloody Battle of Lundy's Lane, and occupied Mackinac Island in Lake Huron, between Michigan's Upper and Lower peninsulas—made him a national figure, months before contesting the British at New Orleans.

While the Creek War raged, a dispirited Rachel wrote to her husband complaining, "all can come home but you." She hoped for the campaign's swift culmination and his safe return to the Hermitage. "You have now don more than aney other man Ever did before you have served your Country Long Enough."[13] When read today these heartfelt and kindly words appear, despite their obvious sincerity, abstract, untimely, and incomplete; through the uncertain fortunes of war, rather, Jackson's sudden star had only begun to rise.

14

Sharp Knife

On April 22, less than a month after the Battle of Horseshoe Bend, Major General Thomas Pinckney, commander of the Sixth Military District (Department of the South), ordered Jackson's West Tennessee troops discharged. Six days later Jackson, in a printed address, offered his soldiers "thanks, & . . . admiration" while proclaiming "Our vengeance . . . gluted." He then marched his triumphant army back to Nashville, where a throng of well-wishers turned out to celebrate the returning campaigners. Escorted to the courthouse, Jackson listened as Congressman Felix Grundy grandly homilized in the conquerors' favor; later the Bell Tavern hosted a banquet at which the General accepted a ceremonial sword. About this time Jackson received a congratulatory communication from John Overton ruminating on Old Hickory's instant popularity. "I can but imperfectly communicate to you the feeling of the people here," he wrote from a distant Rogersville, in the northeastern corner of the state. "Already General, it is the common theme of conversation that you must be our next governor . . . your standing . . . is now as high as any man in America."[1] This compliment no doubt pleased its recipient, though considering Jackson's frustrating stints in Congress, it seems unlikely that the promise of a governor's seat held much appeal. Other and better options, in any case, beckoned. For rather than capping his martial career, the Creek War—and fortuitous timing—brought Jackson to the focal point of American military power.

It began with a resignation. In late 1813 the wealthy South Carolina planter-politician General Wade Hampton, having led a numerically superior American force to a humiliating defeat at the Battle of the Chateauguay just south of Montreal, gave up his appointment. The Madison administration, aware that it owed something to the hero of Horseshoe Bend, offered Jackson a brigadier generalship in the regular U.S. Army, in charge of the Seventh Military District, which included Tennessee and much of the southwest. A major general in the militia, Jackson thought the proposal somewhat disappointing—brigadier constituting a lower grade—but he accepted on June 8. In communicating the offer, Secretary of War Armstrong wrote, almost apologetically, that the rank represented "all . . . that can be done at present." But the next few days revealed otherwise. Armstrong, a divisive figure who, so the historian Henry Adams once wrote, "always created distrust," had been engaged in a quiet conflict with the Virginia-born William Henry Harrison, longtime governor of the Indiana Territory, victorious commander at the Battle of the Thames (October 1813), and later ninth president of the United States. Scrutinizing Harrison's exercise of resources, Armstrong discovered that the General "frequently used troops and funds in excess of the limits stipulated by the War Department, purchased supplies at inflated prices, and employed his own private supply agents rather than the contractors designated for the army." One could interpret such activities as entirely innocuous. Armstrong, however, chose to confront

An officer in the Tennessee militia, Jackson was commissioned a major general in the U.S. Army in 1814 following the Battle of Horseshoe Bend.

Harrison, who, feeling insulted, angrily resigned his commission on May 11. Understanding it to be Madison's intent to tender Jackson the first unfilled major generalship, Armstrong offered the post to Old Hickory, who accepted on June 18.[2]

A few days later Jackson removed from Nashville, heading south to arrange, as per the president's instructions, a formal peace with the Creek Nation. His orders appeared to be ironclad. In March Madison had sanctioned peace on four principal conditions: the yielding up of pro-war prophets, the termination of unapproved trade with Spanish Florida, recognition of the United States' right to build roads and forts on Creek lands, and, most important, the transfer of territory equal to the cost of the war. Nothing in the conditions specifically authorized Jackson to pursue a hard peace and claim both Red Stick territory *and* the lands belonging to the U.S.'s Indian allies. We know from Madison's correspondence, however, that the president remained open to such a possibility. In a May 20, 1814, note to Armstrong, he seemed eager to allow his negotiators maximum leeway in the field:

> Whether the friendly Indians ought to be a party to the arrangement with the hostile ones, is a question it may be best to leave to the Commissioners, who can best appreciate the considerations on which it depends. It seems most suitable that altho' the terms of the peace will be dictated to the hostile Indians, their pride should not be irritated by excluding even the form of consent on their part; especially as it is possible that a foreign enemy of the United States may still make experiments on their character, if the future circumstances of the war should suggest them. Even this question however may be left with the Commissioners, if they see in the other course the surest precaution against revolt.[3]

In the course of negotiations, Jackson permitted "precaution against revolt" to dominate all else. Indeed, two days before Madison wrote Armstrong, the General had informed Horseshoe Bend veteran Colonel John Williams of his own views on the land question. These marked him as a vigorous proponent of Indian removal, an opinion certainly unremarkable among many trans-Appalachian whites. Early in the communication he seemed open to the idea of preserving those Indian nations who fought on the United States' side. While "the hostile Creeks have forfeited all right to the Territory we have conquered," he argued, "Justice to the friendly part of the Nation require[s] that they should be left in the peaceable enjoyment of their towns and villages with a sufficient appendage of woodland." But then he added a caveat: "Still the grand policy of the government ought to be, to connect the settlements of Georgia with that of the Territory of Tennessee, which at once forms a bulwark against foreign [European] invasion, and prevents the introduction of foreign influence to corrupt the minds of the

Indians." Invariably, he argued, "we must . . . extend our settlements to the Mississippi to cut off all communication of the Southern tribes with that of the North, and give to our citizens perfect safety in passing through their country." He concluded by predicting Indian removal's likely impact on race and regionalism in America: "This then will give strength to the southern section of the United States."[4]

Which is precisely what happened. Following the admissions of Mississippi (1817) and Alabama (1819) into the Union, the old Virginia dynasty of slaveholding presidents (Washington, Jefferson, Madison, and Monroe) evolved into a southwestern style of southern republicanism, energized, in part, by advancing into former Indian lands. Between 1820 and 1844 the Democracy, the party most closely associated with the protection and extension of black bondage, captured five of seven national elections; southern enslavers claimed four of those contests.

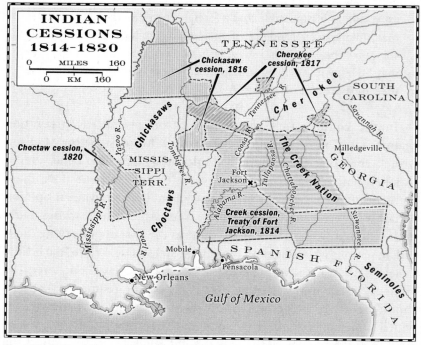

The 1814 Treaty of Fort Jackson resulted in the surrender of more than twenty million acres of Creek territory to the U.S.; the Treaty further set in motion a series of subsequent land cessions that culminated in the removal of the southern Indians. Jackson, as both a military officer and a negotiator, played a critical role in this process.

Negotiations began at Fort Jackson on August 1, though only in a ceremonial sense. In reality Jackson, sole representative of the United States, essentially dictated terms under which the Creek Nation ceded some twenty-two million acres—most of present-day Alabama and the lower fifth of Georgia. Much of this territory belonged to Creeks allied to Jackson's forces. Their failure to control the Red Sticks, he claimed, validated the land grab. A preamble to the Treaty of Fort Jackson drafted on the 5th and outlining his view of the situation concluded with a definitive "The terms of Peace will be read to you." Four days later nearly three-dozen exasperated chiefs signed the accord. The following day Jackson confided to Coffee of having offered the Creek Nation, "many [who had] fought by my side," no options other than removal or war: "I told them at last . . . those who was our friends would sign it— and those who were not might go to the British—that I would furnish them with provisions to take them there and then I would persue and drive them and the British into the sea."[5] The honorific "Old Hickory" denoted a sturdy, paternal presence; following the Treaty of Fort Jackson, the Creeks referred to the lean, bullying general as Sharp Knife.

In 1948 the Creek Nation of Oklahoma filed a claim to obtain payment for the millions of acres lost in 1814. In 1952 the Creek Nation East of the Mississippi received authorization to join this case as "petitioners by intervention."[6] A decade later, in 1962, the Indian Claims Commission awarded the Creeks nearly $4 million (roughly $34 million in current dollars).

15

Optional Invasion

The Treaty of Fort Jackson prefaced Andrew Jackson's desire to expand America's war into the Gulf region. Having gathered information that Creeks along the Georgia border were receiving aid from both Spain and Great Britain, he requested permission to enter Florida in order to discover the truth. "Whether these rumours are founded in fact, or not," he wrote Armstrong that summer, "we ought at least to be prepared for the worst." He planned to march on Fort San Carlos de Barrancas, a citadel constructed in 1797 to protect Pensacola, the capital of Spanish West Florida. Armstrong's equivocal reply hardly clarified matters. "The case you put is a very strong one," he wrote Jackson, "& if all the circumstances stated by you unite, the conclusion is inevitable. It becomes our duty to carry our arms where we find our enemies." But he also cautioned the General: "It is believed, and I am so directed by the President to say, that there is a disposition on the part of the Spanish Government not to break with the U.S. nor to encourage any conduct on the part of her subordinate Agents, having a tendency to such rupture. We must therefore in this case be careful to ascertain facts." Armstrong acknowledged the grounds upon which Jackson's army might march—"If they admit, feed, arm and cooperate with the British and hostile Indians, we must strike on the broad principle of self-preservation"—but then closed on a less assertive note: "Under other & different circumstances, we must forbear."[1] Inexplicably, this vital letter remained in Washington, unsent for several months.

About the time that Armstrong wrote Jackson, the latter, though interested primarily in Pensacola, began as well to formulate a plan to protect New Orleans. He sent a late July communication to Louisiana governor Claiborne reporting rumors of "a considerable British force" said to have unloaded a large cache "of arms and other munitions of war" at Apalachicola Bay, 175 miles east of Pensacola. He warned that Mobile and New Orleans, "of such importance," were certain to be targeted by the British, who were capable, he supposed, of "exciting the black population to insurrection & massacre." He then called on Claiborne to organize a militia of fifteen hundred men, "officered and equiped in the best possible manner."[2] Jackson presumed that Spain, with British aid, planned to recoup Louisiana, which it had lost in 1800 to an ambitious, militarizing France. Already in the summer of 1814 a grand Gulf strategy—subduing Pensacola, securing Mobile, and defending New Orleans—had begun to shape Jackson's thinking.

The quickening pace of events that drove the General forced Britain to introduce a note of improvisation as well. Hitherto focused on the European theater of conflict, it had for two years conducted a largely defensive war in North America. But the end of Napoleon's rule as emperor of France and master of much of Europe now presented the British with other options. American control of Lake Erie, combined with the collapse of Creek power in the southern interior, contributed to the Royal Navy's decision to concentrate on coastal attacks occasionally backed by raiding Royal Marines. The most notorious marauding occurred in the August 24 invasion of Washington in which several government buildings, including the Capitol and the Presidential Mansion, were set ablaze. Madison described the assault in a public proclamation as "a deliberate disregard of the principles of humanity and the rules of civilized warfare."[3] Three weeks later Britain's sea and land assault on Baltimore met with considerably less success as American forces fended off the attackers. A young Maryland lawyer, Francis Scott Key, observed the twenty-five-hour bombardment of Fort McHenry while negotiating a prisoner exchange aboard the British ship HMS *Tonnant* and, under its telling spell, wrote "The Star Spangled Banner." Shortly thereafter Admiral Sir Alexander Cochrane, involved as commander in chief of the North American Station in the Washington and Baltimore operations, counseled his London superiors to prepare for an occupation of the Gulf region around New Orleans. Their acquiescence put his forces on a collision course with Jackson's.

In the middle of August British troops under General Edward

Nicolls, invited by Spanish governor Don Mateo González Manrique, had landed at Pensacola. About the same time Jackson moved his army nearly two hundred miles to Mobile, seized the previous year by Wilkinson's forces. He then sent a small contingent to occupy Fort Bowyer, an earthen stockade fortification meant to command the bay and thus protect Mobile from British ships. "I can but regret that permission had not been given by the government to have seized on Pensacola," he wrote Armstrong on the 27th, "had this been done the american Eagle would now have soared above the fangs of the British lyon."[4] Instead, a congeries of red-clad paladins remained, if somewhat ineffectually, on the move. Using Pensacola as a base, a small British force consisting of four ships, marines, and Indians failed the following month to dislodge the Americans from Fort Bowyer.

Even before this attack Jackson had decided, without direct orders, to invade West Florida and take Pensacola. On September 5, he informed Armstrong that Manrique's summons of Nicolls's forces violated Spain's claim to neutrality. "As [it] has become our enemy covertly if not openly," he wrote, "and is secretly carrying on a war with Great Britain, by means of their Indians from Pensacola against the united States—Why will not the government order the British to be expelled from Pensacola [and] seize and garrison it with their troops." But Armstrong, criticized for failing to defend Washington, had tendered his resignation to Madison the previous day. James Monroe, serving already as secretary of state, agreed to head the War Department as well. On October 21, Monroe, having reviewed Jackson's correspondence with Armstrong, wrote to the hard-charging general, "I hasten to communicate to you, the directions of the President, that you should at present take no measures, which would involve this Government in a contest with Spain."[5] Seventeen days later, on November 7, Jackson's forces seized Pensacola. Monroe's distant letter lingered in transit.

The Battle of Pensacola lasted but two days and resulted in fewer than forty combined casualties. Facing an American army of four thousand, an Anglo–Red Sticks–Spanish force of perhaps six hundred quickly capitulated. The British prudently withdrew from the field, leaving Governor Manrique to surrender the small settlement city of a thousand. Jackson self-servingly portrayed his army's actions as emancipatory—"I came not as the Enemy of Spain," he maintained, but rather "to prevent a repetition of those acts [the occupation of Spanish

forts by Britain] . . . so inconsistent with the neutral character of Spain."[6]
In fact, the recent American annexations of Spanish West Florida in
1810 and 1813 (encompassing an area extending roughly from Baton
Rouge to the Perdido River just west of Pensacola, which the Madison
administration unilaterally claimed as part of the Louisiana Purchase)
had played an important role in prompting Spain's embrace of Britain.

Having taken Pensacola, and observed the reduction of its nearby
forts and the withdrawal of British troops, Jackson returned to Mobile,
leaving Manrique in nominal control of the city. Quickly on the move
again, he slipped out of Mobile on November 22, arriving in New Orleans
nine days later. Several weeks passed before he read Monroe's December
7 communication, an official caution against campaigning in Pensacola:

> I hope that my letter to you of the 21st. of October had reached you
> in time to prevent the attack which you then contemplated mak-
> ing on the British at Pensacola. Altho' the conduct of the Spanish
> authorities there may justify the measure; the President desires that
> it may be avoided, in the hope that the new efforts, which he is now
> making to obtain justice and preserve amity with that power, may
> be successful. Should you have made the proposed attack, you will
> on the receipt of this letter, withdraw your troops from the Spanish
> territory, declaring that you had entered it, for the sole purpose of
> freeing it from British violation.[7]

One wonders if Monroe began about this time to have certain doubts
about Jackson's deference to the "desires" of civilian officials.

There is inferential evidence that the General supposed the coming campaign might be his last. A week before leaving Mobile he wrote
Rachel, requesting that she "and my little son" meet him in New Orleans.
"Before I set out from here I was taken verry ill," he wrote to her, "the
Doctor gave me a dose of Jallap & calemel, which salavated me, and
there was Eight days on the march that I never broke bread—my health
is restored but I am still verry weak."[8] Worn, overworked, and wasting
away, he nevertheless emanated a remarkable inner intensity that fairly
glowed. One Creole woman described Jackson as

> a tall, gaunt man, very erect, . . . with a countenance furrowed by
> care and anxiety. His dress was simple and nearly threadbare. A

small leather cap protected his head, and a short blue Spanish cloak his body, whilst his . . . high dragoon boots [were] long innocent of polish or blacking. . . . His complexion was sallow and unhealthy; his hair iron grey, and his body thin and emaciated like that of one who had just recovered from a lingering sickness. . . . But . . . [a] fierce glare . . . [lit] his bright and hawk-like eye.[9]

Did Jackson believe, with the war winding down, that he might have freely given his health in exchange for military glory? In summoning Rachel, he perhaps anticipated a final, great victory at New Orleans, one that kindled the warrior's resolve and validated the hero's death.

16

To New Orleans

More than the British military brought Jackson to New Orleans. A series of unrelated events, decisions, and a death worked uncannily, rather, to elevate his status in the southern theater. First, Wilkinson was transferred from New Orleans to the St. Lawrence River Campaign in Canada, where U.S. forces had proven ineffective; this move was followed, as noted, by Hampton and Harrison's resignations, which had made Jackson that June a major general in the regular army. Two months later, on September 13, General Thomas Flournoy, a practiced duelist, Georgia planter, and Wilkinson's successor, resigned when passed over for promotion—five days later *his* successor, General Benjamin Howard of Kentucky, died. With Major General Edmund P. Gaines, a career officer from the South, seriously wounded by artillery fire that late summer, in the siege of Fort Erie during the protracted Niagara operations, Jackson's position only solidified.[1] A year and a half earlier, his Tennessee volunteers had departed for New Orleans only to be discharged en route by an order of the secretary of war. Now Jackson arrived to defend the vital city, sent by an administration impressed with his efforts in the Creek campaign, perhaps concerned by his invasion of Pensacola, and almost certainly wary of his strongman mien.

In the last days of November, a large British armada carrying fourteen thousand soldiers crossed the Gulf to New Orleans, where Louisiana, the youngest state in the Union, admitted to divided loyalties. Significant Catholic and formerly colonial French, Spanish, and Creole populations were now part of a conspicuously Protestant republic, self-interested privateers congregated in the paludal bayous of Barataria

Bay, and fears of racial unrest resonated palpably in the region. Only four years earlier, in January 1811, the largest slave revolt in U.S. history, estimated at between two hundred and five hundred rebels, had occurred on the German Coast, above New Orleans in present-day St. John the Baptist and St. Charles parishes. In putting the insurrection down, anxious authorities killed or executed nearly one hundred of the insurgents.[2]

Eager to augment his army, Jackson pragmatically made common cause with both the privateers and many of the city's free blacks, two battalions of which served during this unfolding campaign. Writing to a perhaps doubtful Governor Claiborne, Jackson advanced a concise argument for arming black men: "Our country has been invaded, and threatned with destruction. She wants Soldiers to fight her battles. The free men of colour in your city are inured to the Southern climate and would make excellent Soldiers. They will not remain quiet spect[at]ors of the interesting contest."[3]

Concerned for the city's security, Jackson had considered suspending civilian rule upon entering New Orleans, much to the Louisiana legislature's annoyance. The Royal Navy's December 14 capture of American gunboats on nearby Lake Borgne promptly settled the matter, and Jackson declared martial law on the 16th. Accordingly, no one could enter or leave the city without permission, and a curfew went into effect. "The street lamps shall be extinguished at the hour of nine at night," Jackson's "General Orders" announced, "after which period, persons of every description found in the streets, or not at their respective homes without permission in writing as aforesaid and not having the countersign shall be apprehended as spies."[4]

While the city bowed a little irritably to martial law, Jackson waited anxiously for John Coffee's approach. "I am astonished that the T.[ennessee] & Kentucky Troops are not up," he wrote Coffee on the 16th, and was no doubt relieved when his friend appeared with three thousand volunteers (accompanied by dragoons from Mississippi) four days later.[5] Following the action at Lake Borgne, British general John Keane's advance column could conceivably have taken the lightly defended New Orleans by surprise had it proceeded quickly and decisively. But Keane believed, having listened to the dissembling of captured American soldiers, that a much larger force than his own eighteen hundred shielded the city. So he waited perhaps too patiently for the main body of his command. Finally taking action on the 23rd, his advance force moved stealthily through unobstructed bayous, capturing Jackson's pickets along the way as well as a number of militiamen at the plantation house of Jacques Villeré, about five miles downriver from New Orleans. In return, Jackson aggressively made a night attack that very evening, delaying but not destroying the British advance before falling back to the Rodriguez Canal, a former millrace connecting an all but impenetrable cypress swamp with the Mississippi River. He immediately began to fortify this position, ordering it both deepened and widened while studding its exterior with ramparts and artillery pieces.

If not exactly victorious, Jackson's gritty counterattack managed to impede British progress, hitherto largely uncontested since the action at Lake Borgne. And in the wake of this taut night assault, with noses bloodied all around, a brief stasis ensued. "Both armies have remained, since the action, near the battle-ground," Jackson wrote Mississippi Territory governor David Holmes on a desultory Christmas Day, "making arrangements for something more decisive."[6] That very afternoon, in the pale winter light, decisiveness itself showed up in the glittering visage of Major General Edward Pakenham, the Anglo-Irish commander of British forces in North America. "He was," so one nineteenth-century historian has written:

> in the prime of life and strength, thirty-eight years of age, while Jackson, nearly ten years older, was broken in health and weak in strength. Pakenham had learned the art of war from Wellington [whose army later defeated Napoleon at Waterloo], in the best school in Europe. He was supported by an efficient staff and a military system as perfect as experience and expenditure could make it, and he commanded as fine an army as England could produce.[7]

A decorated veteran, Pakenham, gallant and self-willed, supremely confident and a bit reckless, came with orders to carry out offensive operations, even as peace appeared to be in the offing. Indeed, though no one in North America knew it, a small cadre of American ministers in the Belgian city of Ghent had already signed, along with their British coequals, a treaty on the 24th—Christmas Eve.

On the 28th Pakenham tested Jackson's position, ordering an advance that, after sweeping aside scattered observation corps, withered before American ship and artillery fire. His army retired to lick its wounds. That same day, in response to baseless rumors that the Louisiana legislature planned to surrender the city, a flustered Governor Claiborne, advised by Jackson to monitor the activities of the assembly, had the statehouse locked up. Forty-eight hours later the displaced officials organized a committee to demand from Jackson the reason for their sudden exile. He casually admitted that he "gave no order to the governor to interfere with the legislature" other than "to desire the governor to make strict enquiry into [any plans of forfeiting New Orleans]; and if true, to blow them up."[8] No doubt some of these men, civil leaders now feeling perhaps more than a little scrutinized, stigmatized, and distrusted, saw Jackson as the author of both martial law and the shuttering of their capital. They may have wondered as well if, like Pakenham, he too presented a certain threat to their fair city.

On the first morning of the new year, British batteries opened fire on the main American position. Vincent Nolte, born in Italy to German parents and now representing a Dutch commercial house in New Orleans, fought on the American side at this engagement, which he recalled in a memoir:

> On this day, which saw our whole line, except the batteries, exposed to the fire from 8 o'clock A. M. to 3 o'clock P. M., my worthy friend, Major Carmick, who commanded the volunteer battalion, and was near the pirates' battery, was struck by a Congreve [stick-guided artillery] rocket on the forehead, knocked off his horse, and both his arms injured. I asked leave to accompany him to the guardhouse, and as we reached the low garden-wall behind Jackson's headquarters [at the Macarté house], I saw to my great amazement two of the General's volunteer adjutants . . . lying flat on the ground to escape the British balls. . . . The General, during this five hours cannonade, was constantly riding from one wing to the other, accompanied by his usual military aids."[9]

Repelled, and obviously in need of additional troops, Pakenham awaited daily expected reinforcements. One officer on Pakenham's staff later wrote, "Poor Sir Edward was much mortified at being obliged to retire the army from a second demonstration and disposition to attack, but there was nothing for it."[10] Jackson used the respite to fortify his lines. He took up the French privateer Jean Lafitte's prompting to lengthen his shaky left to the swamp, raised his mud bank redoubts, and deepened the ditches that lay before them. And then he waited.

17

A Victory More Complete

Months before the Battle of New Orleans, Madison had mused anxiously over America's sinking odds against England. A May 1814 communication from Albert Gallatin and James Bayard, two of the appointed peace commissioners who eventually negotiated the war's end, warned the president that with Napoleon exiled in Elba, an island off the Tuscan coast, Britain could now position "all its forces" against the United States. A whipping of its former colonies, they continued, might be in the cards. If so, then America's right to fish in the Grand Banks off Newfoundland, its Great Lakes trade, and its northern boundary with Canada were all in question. As if such grim prospects were insufficiently dire, Gallatin and Bayard further informed the president that Britain might attempt to return Louisiana to Spain, its pre-Napoleonic occupier.[1] As the months passed and British naval power moved from the Chesapeake to the Gulf, the fate of New Orleans looked increasingly uncertain.

On January 4, three days after dueling with Pakenham's batteries, Jackson's forces were increased by the arrival of some two thousand Kentucky militiamen. In all, his front line now included about four thousand soldiers, with another thousand in reserve. Coffee's cavalry, supplemented by a number of Choctaw, held down the left side of Jackson's line running into the swamp, and across the river, on his right flank, a lightly manned position of some seven hundred ill-trained militia and several cannons commanded by Major General David Morgan invited a British assault. Occupation of this vulnerable point would allow a destructive enfilading of the main American force, and Jackson seemed unaware of this danger. Pakenham, with a strength of some eight thousand, planned to attack at a number of spots, sending twenty-two hundred against the center-left of the imposing Rodriguez Canal (Major General Samuel Gibbs's attack), another twelve hundred against the side of the Canal abutting the Mississippi (Major General John Keane's attack), and directing a West Indian regiment to engage with American forces in the swamp; he held fifteen hundred in reserve. Hoping to take Jackson's weakly defended right flank across the Mississippi, Pakenham, early on the morning of January 8, sent a further force of nearly eight hundred under Colonel William Thornton to cross the dark river and capture the American batteries. The water's swift current overwhelmed these plans, however, and Thornton's men were obliged to land farther below the American line than intended. Struggling through marshy terrain in the dim of daybreak, they would be unable to support the main British attack on the east bank.

At about 5 a.m. the battle began when Gibbs's troops advanced; Jackson responded by reinforcing his line with soldiers formerly in the rear. A loud cheer went up on the American side when the British came within firing range—several days of boredom and unease suddenly burst into violent excitement; a regimental band played "Hail Columbia," one of the nation's unofficial national anthems, while Creoles on the line were said to favor "La Marseillaise." The first American line fired, followed, as it reloaded, by a second, and then a third line. One British soldier later recalled that "a rush of our troops was met by the most murderous and destructive fire of all arms ever poured upon column." During the fighting, so another soldier observed, Jackson shouted at his men, "Stand to your guns, don't waste your ammunition—see that every shot tells," as volley after volley penetrated into sequent waves of exposed men. At one point British troops threatened a redoubt on Jackson's right, before being cut down by batteries at close range. "Some few . . . by mounting one upon another's shoulders, succeeded in entering the works," a Scottish soldier later remembered, "but these were speedily overpowered, most of them killed, and the rest taken; whilst as many as stood without were exposed to a sweeping fire, which cut them down by whole companies." In response to this particular horror and a more extensive and "most galling fire . . . from every part of [the American] line," as one British general reported, a mass of frightened men, their momentum and psychology broken, began to fall back in retreat.[2]

Aside from Thornton's errant mission, the British suffered as well from the inexplicable absence of the fascines (bundles of brushwood) and ladders necessary to scale the ramparts mounted behind the canal. One scholar has conjectured that the officer of a presumably expendable Irish unit "felt his men were being sacrificed on a suicidal mission" and neglected his duty.[3] We know with more certainty that the elimination of several senior officers compromised the British assault. Generals Gibbs and Keane were wounded and removed to the rear, while Pakenham died on the field of battle, as grapeshot ripped into his chest. The chief command devolved that day on General John Lambert, who, in a January 19 communication, informed the prominent Tory Lord Bathurst, secretary of state for war and the colonies, of his army's sickening defeat and of Pakenham's precipitous demise:

> He had made the signal for the troops to advance, galloped on to the front to animate them by his presence, and he was seen with his hat off encouraging them on the crest of the glacis; it was there (almost at the same time) that he received two wounds, one in his knee, and another, which was almost instantly fatal, in his body. . . . The effect of this in the sight of the troops, together with major-general Gibbs and major-general Keane being both borne off wounded at the same time . . . and further, the preparations made to aid in crossing the ditch not being so forward as they ought to have been, from, perhaps, the men being wounded who were carrying them, caused a wavering in the column, which in such a situation became irreparable; and as I advanced with the reserve, at about two hundred and fifty yards from the line, I had the mortification to observe the whole falling back upon me in the greatest confusion.[4]

This disastrous attack and retreat before the canal took but thirty minutes.

Another battle, the aforementioned maneuvering on the Mississippi's west bank, ended embarrassingly for the Americans. Though too late to affect the contest's outcome, it demonstrated certain errors in Jackson's judgment. With the Kentucky militia only recently arrived, he had neglected to provide regular army reinforcements to discipline its line; perhaps this is why he kept no boats on hand in case men needed to be ferried across the river. When Thornton's troops—supplemented by three gun barges—finally appeared, the Kentuckians, as Jackson wrote with some shame to Monroe, "ingloriously fled."[5] Now in possession of the west bank, Thornton, in control of cannons, occupied an ideal position to rake Jackson's command behind the canal. Lambert, however, his army decimated, had called off the assault a couple of hours earlier and ordered Thornton's men to rejoin the main group.[6]

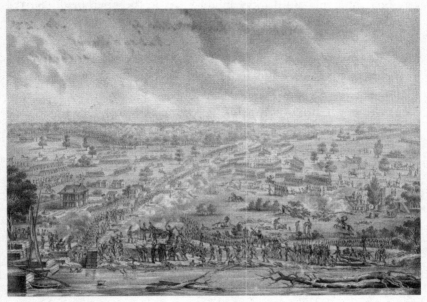

A bird's-eye view of the thirty-minute Battle of New Orleans, with the Mississippi River in the foreground. The American line (on the left, behind barricades) decimated an advancing British force, making Jackson the nation's most popular general since George Washington.

In the heat of the moment a victorious Jackson petulantly criticized the officers on the right bank, thus detaching himself of responsibility for what he called "the abandonment of your lines." In a printed address to these soldiers dated the day of the battle, he complained that "no words can express the mortification I felt at witnessing" the collapse of the Kentuckians. Careful to avoid castigating "the valour of the troops," he confined his censure to those who led them. "How then Could brave men abandon the post committed to their care," he asked—and then answered: "The want of Dicipline, the want of Order . . . appears to be the cause which led to the disaster."[7] With a keen lawyerly attention, Jackson wanted to have his version of the battle on record. As with earlier contests—the duel with Dickinson, the brawl with the Benton brothers, and the extraction of Creek land—he demanded the upper hand, intensely interested in shaping the narrative and reserving right for himself.

In declining to counterattack the British, Jackson undoubtedly made his wisest move of the day. Outnumbered but safely ensconced behind a rampart, his makeshift force might have, in the open field, courted defeat before a large professional army. Once the British abandoned the west bank taken from the Kentuckians, Jackson ordered it reoccupied and made no other major troop movements. The fighting done by morning, he devoted much of the 8th to organizing, through correspondence with General Lambert, an armistice to provide for the care of casualties and return of the dead and wounded. British losses along the east bank were appalling. An estimated 285 soldiers were killed, some 1,265 were wounded, and nearly 500 were captured or went missing. By contrast, only 13 American soldiers died, with fewer than 50 wounded, captured, or missing in the main engagement.[8] The staggering discrepancy in casualties gave Jackson's army the aura of invincibility; some, no doubt, detected Providence's benign hand behind its stunning achievement.

One Kentucky rifleman recalled the desolation of the battleground shortly after the fighting ended:

> When the smoke had cleared away and we could obtain a fair view of the field, it looked, at the first glance, like a sea of blood. It was not blood itself which gave it this appearance, but the red coats in which the British soldiers were dressed. Straight out before our position, for about the width of space which we supposed had been occupied by the British column, the field was entirely covered with prostrate bodies. In some places they were laying in piles of several, one on the top of the other. On either side there was an interval more thinly sprinkled with the slain; and then two other dense rows, one near the levee and the other towards the swamp. About two hundred yards off, directly in front of our position, lay a dark dapple grey horse, which we understood to have been Pakenham's.[9]

In a letter written two days after the battle, Jackson put the question of carnage more simply: "On the morning of the 8h. [the enemy] made a bold attempt to carry my works by storm; but was recd. with the utmost firmness by my troops, and repelled with great loss." Shortly thereafter he offered Monroe a welcome gift: "I believe you will not think me too sanguine in the belief that Louisiana is now clear of its enemy."[10]

Lambert proved Jackson prophetic. The British fleet sailed from New Orleans on the 27th, its ships laden with wounded men. Two weeks later, however, Cochrane's armada captured Fort Bowyer, an irksome reverse, Jackson wrote, which "gave me great pain" and threatened to make Mobile vulnerable to capture in a concentrated campaign.[11] But there would be no more campaigning. In mid-February the Senate ratified the Treaty of Ghent—the war was over.

In a matter of a few momentous weeks, the nation's prospects changed dramatically if not permanently. In December 1814 a group of disaffected New Englanders—their economy in tatters, their coastlines unprotected, and their opportunities for national political leadership compromised by the apparent perpetuity of Virginia presidents— assembled for three weeks to discuss common grievances and propose changes to the Constitution. Though not a secessionist movement, this Hartford Convention suffered from disastrous timing. Shortly after it adjourned, news of both the Treaty of Ghent and the American victory at New Orleans relegated New England Federalism to history's ash heap. Jackson's reputation, on the other hand, skyrocketed. Suddenly a national figure, the Hero, many Americans agreed, had defeated the nation's greatest enemies, preserved (in the sobering wake of the capital's burning) its intense pride, and secured the reputation of republican government in the New World. "GLORIOUS FROM NEW ORLEANS," roared the *Niles Weekly Register*, one of the country's more important magazines, with the news of Britain's stunning humiliation before the bloody Rodriguez Canal. "Glory be to God, that the barbarians have been defeated."[12]

The battle's significance is further increased when considering the possible implications of a British victory. Though the fighting occurred after the signing of the peace pact, that accord remained ineffectual until ratified by the U.S. Senate, more than a month later. Had Pakenham's army prevailed, the return of Louisiana to Spain and perhaps Mobile as well may have been in play. Instead, American power now ruled much of the Gulf region. Spain lost West Florida, the Creeks were forced to cede much of their land, and neither presented any longer a shield against U.S. expansion.

In 1835, two important observers wondered at Jackson's firm hold on the nation's imagination. A skeptical Alexis de Tocqueville described the General in *Democracy in America* as "a man of violent character and middling capacities" whose claim to the public's affections "is all due to the memory of a victory he won twenty years ago under the walls of New Orleans." John Quincy Adams similarly described the battle as "a victory more complete over the people of the U.S. than over the soldiers of Great Britain."[13] Though born the same year as Jackson, Adams, a representative of New England, a former Federalist, and a highly educated son of a past president, remained forever immune to the General's magic. In Jackson he saw decidedly more Caesar than Cincinnatus, the legendary Roman consul who led the Republic's forces to victory over neighboring invaders and then quietly returned to his farm. Many Americans, by contrast, regarded the battle as a triumphal referendum on their blossoming democracy, an indication that rule by citizens—the common man—now rested secure.

18

Defend or Endanger

The newly anointed Hero of New Orleans seemed almost eager to endanger his sudden rise in public esteem. Two days after the battle, with rumors and jittery reports of tall British ships cannonading in the area, Jackson ordered an officer on the west bank to solidify his defenses by demolishing private property—never a popular move among property owners. "Set fire to and destroy every house," he commanded. "Altho I feel great pain at the . . . infliction of individual injury, yet when the imperious dictates of public duty require the sacrafice I am not allowed to hesitate."[1] Governor Claiborne, the state legislators, and a good many living and working in the city grew concerned that Jackson might soon sacrifice all of New Orleans rather than permit enemy troops to pass through its gates. No doubt the high tensions brought about by weeks of gossip, military preparations, and martial law produced a sharp uncertainty only imperfectly punctured by the recent British defeat. The city badly needed a cooling-off period, but what it got was Andrew Jackson.

When word circulated in February of the Ghent Treaty, which brought peace, a general restlessness began to agitate New Orleans. The state militia demanded its release from service while citizens insisted on the restoration of their rights. On the 27th some of these residents sent a communication to Jackson asking that he pardon two soldiers sentenced to death a few days earlier for "disobedience of orders, mutiny, desertion, and using contemptuous and abusive language to their captain." The "undersigned" argued that "the late news leaving no doubt but that peace will put an end to the calamities of war, examples have become less necessary." Jackson, in agreement, set the executions aside.

On the trickier question of relaxing martial law, however, Old Hickory proved unwilling to bend without official word from Washington. That he believed Britain remained a threat is not altogether credible. "Whether it is the purpose of the enemy to abandon the expedition . . . or renew his efforts at some other point, I do not pretend to determine with possitiveness," he had written to Monroe several weeks earlier. "In my own mind however there is but little doubt that his last exertions have been made in this quarter, at any rate, for the present season."[2] Jackson seemed, rather, somewhat reflexively driven by a narrowly defined sense of duty and unable to gauge accurately public sentiment. He bristled when anyone suggested otherwise.

The General stiffened appreciably on February 28 when a group of Creole soldiers, claiming French citizenship, demanded the right to demobilize. Infuriated, he reacted punitively by ordering *all* French subjects out of New Orleans until notification of peace arrived. The French consul in the city, after having processed their applications, was also banished. In reply, *Le Courrier de la Louisiane* carried an appeal on March 3 by "A Citizen of Louisiana of French Origin" demanding the end of martial law. "It is high time," the author maintained, "the laws should resume their empire; that the citizens of this State should return to the full enjoyment of their rights; that, in acknowledging that we are indebted to General Jackson for the preservation of our city and the defeat of the British, we do not feel much inclined, through gratitude, to sacrifice any of our privileges, and, less than any other, that of expressing our opinion of the acts of his administration."[3]

Jackson reacted by ordering *Le Courrier's* unlucky editor to his headquarters, and applying a bit of pressure, he quickly learned that Louis Louaillier, a respected member of the legislature concerned about the stigmatization of the city's French citizens, had authored the appeal. On the 5th a column of soldiers under Jackson's directive arrested Louaillier; that act took place in a busy area of the city, and Louaillier, "astonished and indignant," cried out for assistance.[4] From the steps of a coffeehouse Pierre Louis Morel, a lawyer (and officer in a volunteer battalion), witnessed the apprehension and quickly received the prisoner's consent to serve as his counselor. Morel immediately went to the home of U.S. federal district judge Dominic Augustin Hall (a Madison appointee) seeking—and receiving—a writ of habeas corpus for Louaillier. Hall ordered the incarcerated petitioner to be brought before the court the following morning.

That did not happen. Jackson, rather, upon receiving the writ, incredibly ordered Judge Hall arrested. Things went poorly for the Hero from this point on. A letter from the country's postmaster general (but not from the secretary of war) arrived on the 6th informing New Orleans of peace. A stickler for official notice when it suited his purposes, Jackson maintained martial law, though he could feel his position slipping by the day. On the 11th Louaillier won acquittal before a military court when that body flatly rejected the idea that he operated as a mutineer or a spy. In a long and convoluted "Opinion" of the decision drafted by Jackson's friend Major John Reid and published in several local and national papers, the General petulantly set aside the court's ruling, keeping Louaillier in prison for writing "a wilful & corrupt Libel against the Comg general."[5] With no hope of a court convicting Judge Hall either, Jackson, veering dangerously in the direction of a military chieftain, banished the magistrate from the city on the 12th until peace formally arrived.

And it arrived the following day. With martial law now ended, a number of civilians confined for military crimes were pardoned, and Judge Hall, back in the city, filed an order on the 22nd demanding that Jackson show cause for failing to follow the writ of habeas corpus issued by his court in the Louaillier case. In *United States v. Major General Andrew Jackson*, the General mulishly refused to give Hall any satisfaction, attempting to have the trial conducted without his presence. Claiming an ill wife—Rachel had arrived in New Orleans the previous month—Jackson submitted an extended statement in his defense on the 27th. Broadly condemning what he called "the illegal, unconstitutional and informal nature of the proceedings," he blamed just about everybody but himself for the Louaillier fiasco, including "a portion of the inhabitants of the state . . . the legislature . . . [and] foreign emissaries." He further insisted that desperate circumstances had left him little choice but to curtail civilian rights: "A powerful, disciplined, and royally appointed army was on our coast . . . [and] the physical force of every individual, his moral faculties his property and the energy of his example were to be called into action and into instant action. No delay, no hesitation, no enquiry about Rights."[6] That such a dire military emergency existed in early March, two months after the Battle of New Orleans (and nearly two months after Jackson himself had told Monroe he had "little doubt" but that the British were done for the season), is hardly credible. Hall declared Jackson's account inadmissible and ruled that he must answer in court for his actions. But when this occurred, and the district attorney proceeded to put a series of questions to Jackson—"Did you not arrest Louaillier?" "Did you not arrest the judge of this court?"—the proud General responded dismissively that "under these circumstances, I appear before you to receive the sentence of the court, having nothing further in my defense to offer." Hall then fined Jackson $1,000 ($17,600 in current dollars) for contempt. "The only question," he neatly observed, "was whether the Law should bend to the General or the General to the Law."[7]

With no other option, Jackson paid the fine—and then, seeking a public airing for what he considered a grave injustice, promptly published his response, "To the United States District Court, Louisiana," in several newspapers. Many years later, in 1843, a partisan Congress remitted Jackson's penalty with interest, the old General being long retired and in some financial difficulty. In early 1815, however, the government seemed uncertain of what to do with its Hero. An April 12 communication to Jackson from acting secretary of war Alexander Dallas broached the question of Louaillier's imprisonment and Hall's banishment carefully—"representations have been recently made to the President, respecting certain acts of military opposition to the civil magistrate, that require immediate attention." Dallas proceeded to reference a roster of documents, statements, and general orders attesting to Jackson's robust curtailment of civil liberties in the weeks after the British defeat. "From these representations," he wrote, "it would appear, that the judicial power of the United States has been resisted, the liberty of the press has been suspended, and the consul and subjects of a friendly government have been exposed to great inconvenience, by an exercise of Military force and command." Citing Madison's "surprize," he delicately observed that the president "abstains from any decision, or even the expression of an Opinion" at this time. However, he continued, "in the meantime, it is presumed, that every extraordinary exertion of military authority has ceased . . . [and] the President instructs me to take this opportunity of requesting, that a conciliatory deportment may be observed towards the state authorities, and the citizens of New Orleans."[8] Though officially taking no sides, and no doubt grateful for Jackson's perfect repulse of Pakenham's army, the administration must have reflected dubiously on his casual disregard for civilian rule.

That winter's martial law entanglement overlapped the General's controversial decision in February to allow the executions of six soldiers. Rooted in earlier disputes over service terms for militia, this new controversy had broken out in the late summer of 1814 when, with Jackson in Mobile, troops in the 1st Regiment of Tennessee militia—approximately three months from their muster date—mutinied at Forts Jackson, Williams, and Strother and, with provisions pilfered from the commissary, headed for home. Over the next several weeks about two hundred of the mutineers either returned of their own will or were arrested. In late November Jackson ordered that they be tried at Mobile. Most simply lost pay and were made to complete their time of service, though six unfortunates, presumed to have encouraged the revolt, were subsequently shot.

In early April, the Jacksons departed New Orleans for Nashville, arriving in mid May after being earnestly fêted along the way. At the Hermitage the General replied to Dallas's letter questioning his actions in the Louaillier-cum-Hall controversy. Never one to let things go, Jackson, as though about to engage in a private war, asked that the president "furnish me with the names of those persons who transmitted to him the communications & complaints to which you allude."[9] Dallas refused this request. He did, however, reply at some length on July 1, informing Jackson that Madison understood "the patriotic motives which actuated your conduct at New Orleans." He then politely but firmly reminded the General that he lived in a republic:

> In the United States there exists no authority to declare and impose martial law, beyond the positive sanction of the Acts of Congress. To enforce the discipline and to ensure the safety, of his garrison, or his camp, an American Commander possesses indeed, high and necessary powers; but all his powers are compatible with the rights of the citizens, and the independence of the judicial authority. If, therefore, he undertake to suspend the writ of Habeas Corpus, to restrain the liberty of the Press, to inflict military punishments, upon citizens who are not military men, and generally to supersede the functions of the civil magistrate, he may be justified by the law of necessity, while he has the merit of saving his country, but he cannot resort to the established law of the land, for the means of vindication.[10]

Two months later Jackson responded from Nashville. He gave not an inch. "It is very true that 'no authority exists in the U States to declare or impose martial law beyond the possitive acts of Congress,'" he quoted back Dallas's argument, only to discard it: "but an occassion may nevertheless occur of such pressing emergency as will render such a measure indispensable, & as will admit of no delay; & then the officer who takes upon himself such high authority must do it at his own risk & on his own responsibility."[11] At this point, Dallas dropped the correspondence.

In the late spring of 1863, a few weeks before the Battle of Gettysburg, Abraham Lincoln wrote to a group of New York men critical, so they had informed him, of his administration's "unconstitutional action, such as the making of military arrests." Playing a little loose with the past, Lincoln defended his civil liberties record by referencing Jackson's suspension of the writ of habeas corpus in New Orleans:

> It may be remarked: First, that we had the same Constitution then as now; secondly, that we then had a case of invasion, and now we have a case of rebellion; and, thirdly, that the permanent right of the People to Public Discussion, the Liberty of Speech and the Press, the Trial by Jury, the Law of Evidence, and the Habeas Corpus, suffered no detriment whatever by that conduct of Gen. Jackson, or its subsequent approval by the American Congress.[12]

These remarks lack precision. The "case of invasion" had clearly passed by the time Jackson had Louaillier and Judge Hall arrested, while many living in New Orleans in March 1815, including *Le Courrier*'s imprisoned editor, might dispute the contention that their liberties and freedoms "suffered no detriment whatever." It might be more accurate to say that by the time of the Civil War Jackson's legend had grown so large as to be useful to any number of constituencies. A remarkable half hour atop the Rodriguez Canal had made this public servant a kind of king.

Part III

WARRIOR POLITICS

Jackson made law, Adams quoted it.
        Henry A. Wise, former Virginia governor, 1872

A charcoal drawing of Jackson by Thomas Sully, circa 1824, about the time he lost the presidency in a contingent election in the House of Representatives but became the centerpiece of a new political movement.

19

Removal by Another Name

Perhaps no single individual benefitted more from Spain's sustained decay in the Western Hemisphere than Andrew Jackson. That empire's inability to effectively police its porous frontier invited increasingly loud calls from land-hungry Americans eager to see both Spanish authority and the Gulf region's Native Americans removed and replaced. A concentrated boom in population only increased such pressure. Present-day Alabama and Mississippi counted about sixteen thousand whites in 1810, though that number soared to nearly half a million in 1830 and to almost one million just a decade later.[1] Circumstances far larger than Jackson initiated this in-migration, of course, though he served adeptly as its instrument. In turn a rising plantocracy encouraged his political ascent as a newly developing Deep South and its Atlantic-facing southern coastal antecedents formed the hard core of the General's popular appeal.

Access to Indian lands in the southwest promised a sweeping expansion of white settlements. The Treaty of Fort Jackson (1814) abetted this process, though a number of further cessions negotiated by the General—appointed commander of the army's Southern Division in 1815—bought additional territory formerly home to Choctaws, Chickasaws, and Cherokees. Much of this expansion defied the Treaty of Ghent, in which the United States had agreed "forthwith to restore to such Tribes or Nations respectively, all the possessions, rights, and privileges which they may have enjoyed or been entitled to ... previous to ... hostilities." How, then, did it transpire? Following the war, Secretary Dallas informed the General that the massive Creek cession was now null and void—"Inclosed you will receive copies of communications from the commissioners appointed to make overtures of peace to the hostile Indians in pursuance of the stipulations of the 9th article of the treaty of Ghent"—and reminded Jackson of his obligation "to conciliate the Indians, upon the principles of our agreement with Great Britain." But Jackson simply chose to do otherwise. He ignored both his orders and the Creek chiefs who protested the removal of their peoples with the drawing of new boundaries. Addressing these leaders directly, Jackson left no doubt of his contempt for Article Nine: "Brothers Listen did I ever tell you a lie. Listen I now tell you that line must and will be run, and the least opposition brings down instant destruction on the heads of the opposers." Despite Dallas's strong epistolary stance (and plea that "The President . . . is confident . . . you will cooperate"), the government let Jackson have his way.[2]

Certainly Britain was in no mind to put up resistance. It negotiated settlements with the United States in 1817 and 1818 that demilitarized the Great Lakes and marked the U.S.–Canadian boundary at the 49th parallel north. The king's government could scarcely have pursued a southern strategy at this time designed to maintain as well the integrity of Indian lands. It chose Canada.

The Madison and (by early 1817) Monroe administrations appeared to appreciate London's narrow North American options. Assuming a free hand for itself while nevertheless recognizing the need to address the complaints of its late Indian allies, the government appointed three commissioners—including Jackson—to make new treaties. In September 1816, the General opened deliberations with Cherokee and Chickasaw representatives. Bribery-inspired parleys—laden with presents for the main actors—produced a treaty on the 14th yielding Indian territory south of the Tennessee River. Less than a week later, for a consideration of $200,000 (nearly $3.9 million in current dollars), Jackson purchased Chickasaw lands in southwestern Tennessee, present-day northeastern Alabama, and eastern Mississippi. He wrote resentfully to Rachel of having to conduct such sessions, their object being, in his opinion, to "regain by tribute, what I fairly . . . purchased with the sword."[3] The following month he agreed to apply $330,000 in merchandise and annual payments to facilitate a Choctaw grant of land east of the Tombigbee River, a navigable tributary emptying in Mobile Bay. Additional treaties involving the major tribes followed over the next four years, giving the

United States vast tracts in Georgia, Tennessee, Alabama, and Mississippi.

Hardly a southern phenomenon, momentum for reducing Indian autonomy picked up appreciably in other parts of the country with the continental decline of British and Spanish power. The virtual removal of the Europeans sped up the literal removal of the natives. To the north, much of the former Indian Territory (present-day Indiana) already belonged to the United States through a series of recent treaties—Vincennes, Grouseland, and Fort Wayne—negotiated prior to the War of 1812 by William Henry Harrison. One might say that Jackson's brutal treatment of the southern nations in the late 1810s (wielding, so he wrote Monroe, the "sufficiently strong ... Arm of the Government"), underscored a shared attitude among federal and state officers who, observing a seemingly endless surge of whites into Indian lands, moved steadily toward a policy of dispossession.[4]

In time, questions arose as to whether Jackson or those close to him may have benefitted directly from the treaties. In the late autumn of 1817, a few months before the General entered Spanish Florida and illegally occupied Pensacola in the name of subduing marauding Seminoles, several of his relatives and friends formed the Pensacola Land Company. Some saw collusion, and a defensive Jackson subsequently insisted to secretary of state John Quincy Adams that despite appearances the two acts were unrelated. Another land company—Cyprus—established by Jackson's friend John Coffee in northern Alabama, obtained approximately forty-five thousand acres from the Cherokee in a treaty replete with allegations of fraud. Monroe had appointed Coffee surveyor general of the public lands in early 1817. The following year, with no one bidding against him, Jackson, who held shares in the Cyprus Company, purchased some of this ground. In one communication the General counseled Coffee that in regard to boundary drawing, "the object of the Govt. is to bring into markett this land & have it populated," and should any questions arise on where to run lines, "your own Judgt is your guide."[5] Perhaps having conquered the Creeks, Jackson looked upon the supine Tennessee Valley as a kind of feudal fiefdom, a New World iteration on the old seize-and-fleece banditry practiced by victors upon vanquished.

20

The Chieftain

Having just settled into the presidency, Monroe found himself unhappily drawn into an exasperating confrontation between Jackson and the War Department. The spat began in January 1817 when the General learned of topographical engineer Major Stephen Long's temporary reassignment from the southern command in Nashville to a northern post. Acting secretary of war George Graham had ordered the perfectly innocent move without informing Jackson. Ever prickly on points of courtesy, Old Hickory not so quietly seethed. Believing that division officers (such as Long) owed obedience to division headquarters *and then* the War Department, he immediately confronted Graham. In a courteous February 1 response, the acting secretary assured Jackson that Long, after having completed an engineering study in New York, "will . . . be ordered to report himself to you at Nashville." He concluded by reminding Jackson that "it is distinctly to be understood, that this department at all times exercises the right of assigning officers to the performance of Special duties, at its discretion." Unhappy with this report, Jackson went over Graham's head, taking his complaint ("I cannot forbear") to Monroe in a communication dated March 4—the very day the incoming president assumed office. He insisted that the acting secretary displayed in his interpretation of War Department prerogatives "an inexperienced head, perfectly unskilled in military matters."[1] How, he huffed, did Monroe see matters?

Monroe, of course, wanted to see as little of such matters as possible. Inundated with a tediously long queue of requests, entreaties, and office-seekers, this latest Virginian to occupy the executive mansion directed his initial hours and energies to more immediate concerns. On the question of taking sides in the *affaire de Long*, Monroe deliberated perhaps a little uncomfortably. Jackson's view of the proper chain of command seemed to inch in the direction of lessening civilian control over the American military—a potentially disastrous path for a people's republic to take. And yet Monroe, eager to see a sizable cession of Cherokee lands in Georgia, Alabama, and Tennessee that summer, clearly wished to retain Jackson's services in the southern theater. Hoping to avoid a conflict with a popular if potentially insubordinate subordinate, the president demurred.

Receiving no satisfaction, Jackson, in a typically truculent move, went public. His April 22 Division Order, appearing in several newspapers, amounted to a loud and frustrated whine. "The commanding General considers it due to the principles of subordination, which ought and must exist in an army," he declared, "to prohibit the obedience of any order emanating from the Department of War, to officers of this Division . . . unless coming through him as the proper organ of communication." Not content to merely assert his right, Jackson included in the order an indelicate airing of dirty laundry, selectively reviewing the etiquette eliding circumstances "which removed an important officer from [my] division" and prompted this open appeal.[2]

And still for several more months Monroe let the issue sit. Finally, on August 4, he tendered a careful, conciliatory letter to Jackson ("I intended to have written you long before this"), perhaps hoping his correspondent's temper had cooled. Having, so he observed, read "statements" provided by both Jackson and the War Department on the assignment controversy, he ventured a polite, gently placed reproach— "it appears that a misunderstanding existed on your part, as to a matter of fact, which might have led to a different course on your part, had you been correctly informed." Warming to his duty, Monroe then more plainly addressed the commander of the Southern Division: "The principle is clear, that every order from the dept. of war, to whomever directed, must be obeyed." He then closed cautiously on an affirming note, assuring Jackson of his value: "My wish is that things remain as they are, till we communicate further and fully on this subject, for you may be well satisfied, that it [is] one of my strongest wishes to support your honor and fame."[3]

On September 2 Jackson responded aggressively to the president.

Refusing to respect Monroe's "every order ... must be obeyed" insistence, he based his future loyalty to the administration on the degree to which it *agreed with him*: "Permit me to assure you that I will continue to support the Government in all respects where the orders of the War Dept. do not, in my opinion, go to infringe all law and strike at the very root of subordination & the discipline of the Army." Jackson then played his trump cards. As the Hero of New Orleans, as the nation's most popular military figure since Washington, and as an effective instrument for American aggrandizement in the southwest, he knew his worth. Monroe could have his principles, he shrugged, or he could have Jackson. "Should it, ultimately, be found that my opinion of subordination & legal authority, as exercised by the Dept. of War, does not coincide with yours," he reduced a rather serious question of constitutional power to a matter of impression, "be assured that on my part it will be viewed as an honest differrence of opinion, and in my retirement, will, with that zeal for your welfare and the public good, as heretofore, continue to lend my feeble aid to the administration of the Government under your Presidency."[4] Jackson promised to go away, humbly, loyally, as quiet as a lamb.

One month later, on October 5, Monroe replied in a communication both considerate and firm. "I need not mention that this is a painful office for me to enter on," he opened, "for united as we have been on principle, and connected in operations, in which you rendered the most important services to your country, and acquird for yourself an imperishable fame, nothing could be more distressing to me, than that a difference of opinion should have arisen between us, on a point, involving such serious consequences." After lightly reviewing the implications of Jackson's April directive ("Your order ... makes the issue"), he unpacked his position: the War Department conveys the executive's commands. Thus to ignore or nullify a War Department order is to "disobey ... an order from the President." In such a scenario, Monroe continued, a real threat to republicanism existed, for "if any officer of the army, can disobey [the president's] order ... the government is suspended, and put aside." Offering his highly sensitive correspondent sufficient wiggle room, he concluded that, in regard to the seditious pith and drift of Jackson's position, "I confidently believe nothing is more remote from your views."[5]

Jackson countered on the 22nd, determined to maneuver the president into an exhausted acquiescence. Commencing somewhat

sanctimoniously—"I can never abandon principle, be the personal consequences what they may"—he proceeded to put all in the wrong who
questioned his controversial April order. Though understandably and
not unjustly cast by both contemporaries and historians as a deeply
impulsive operator, Jackson also and frequently performed as a cagey
rhetorician, able to prevail upon the lawyerly arts of obfuscation to get
what he wanted. The strategy worked to the extent that he often wore
down lesser constitutions, simply bullyragging his way to success. With
Monroe, he appealed to a tangle of precedents, policies, and protocols
to assert the essential correctness of his spring directive. He accused the
War Department of a host of ill-defined sins ranging from "improper
interferrence" to "open violation of the regulations" which, quite naturally, he reasoned, "compeled me to resist."[6] In other words, he refused
to budge.

Meanwhile, the public nature of Jackson's Division Order ensured
the interest of any number of army officers, not all of whom sympathized with the General's position. In early September, while Jackson
and Monroe discussed their differences, the former received an anony-
mous letter postmarked the previous month from New York. "Your late
order has been the subject of much private and some public remark,"
it began. "The war office gentry and their adherents, pensioners, and
expectants, have all been busy" determining whether "to call the order
in question an act of mutiny." The note then identified ("I am credibly
informed") thirty-one-year-old Brevet Major General Winfield Scott,
on his way to a distinguished military career and the 1852 Whig Party
presidential nomination, as the author of an article published in the
August 2 *New York Columbiana* attacking Jackson. The mischief-maker
enclosed the article. Signed "A Querist," it maliciously claimed that Jackson sought to bypass the War Department on Southern Division chain-
of-command decisions in order, in this particular case, to advance the
career of a protégé.[7]

Days later Jackson wrote to Scott, whom he had never met, and
enclosed a copy of A Querist's missive. His probing if considerate introduction, "I have not permitted myself for a moment to believe that the
conduct ascribed to you is correct," only raised the question of why,
then, he had written at all. "Candor" was the answer, that and the desire
to give the presumably innocent Scott the opportunity "to say . . . if my
order has been the subject of your animadversion." Scott's October 4

reply opened unequivocally—"I am not the author of the miserable and unmeaning article copied from 'The Columbian'"—and had he ended there so too might the correspondence. But he unwisely persisted. Perhaps feeling vulnerable, he acknowledged that while "conversing with some two or three private gentlemen . . . on the subject of the Division Order . . . it is true, that I gave it as my opinion that the paper was . . . mutinous in its character and tendency." He then proceeded to lecture Jackson—"I must take leave to illustrate my meaning a little"— criticizing both the Division Order and the General's incautious "appeal to the army of the public," which, he editorialized, "seems to have been a greater irregularity than the measure complained of."[8] One could fairly see war clouds forming.

Two months passed before Jackson replied, and his opening sentence—"I have been absent from this place [Nashville] a considerable time"—explained his delay in responding to the "approbrious & insolent language" of his "too contemptible" correspondent. Though not the Querist, Scott, Jackson argued, "preserved a similar course." More, the younger man condescended to lecture to his superior, futilely, as Jackson took pains to convey: "I think too highly of myself to suppose that I stand at all in need of your admonitions, & to light of you to appreciate them as useful." He closed by chiding Scott for "the absurdity of your Tinsel Rhetoric" and, while not offering a challenge, intimating that he would accept one, "if you feel yourself aggrieved at what is here said."[9]

The following month, in a letter dated January 2, Scott refused to duel the fifty-year-old hero of New Orleans, as the fifty-year-old hero had probably calculated. Describing himself as both "restrained . . . by a sense of religion" and sensitive to "*patriotic scruples*," he declined what he called "*your* invitation." Instead, he defended his actions. Noting that Jackson's unusual Division Order appeared "in almost every paper in the union" and thus begged the attention of all officers, he emphasized his freedom "to give my opinion on this *public act* as any body else." There the correspondence ended, but not Jackson's sense of superiority. Writing that summer to his nephew Jack Donelson, he called Scott's recourse to "religion & morallity" a "humble, & extraordinary" tactic that "has shielded this, vain, pompous nullity from any personal conflict with me." The pompous nullity knew how to nurse a grudge as well. In an 1864 memoir, Scott sarcastically described the General, "in all his glory," as displaying throughout the silly Division Order incident a noxious combination of "bad temper, bad writing, and bad logic."[10]

As the last letters between Jackson and Scott were exchanged, Monroe, disappointed with the General's autumn emphasis on individual principle over executive orders, took up the command question once again. Hoping, so he wrote Jackson in early December, "to terminate this unpleasant affair," he offered a wobbly compromise. "As a general rule," he wrote, carefully unveiling a new policy, future orders on the shuffling of personnel "should go to the Commander of the division"—Jackson, that is. However, he continued, the president reserved the right to enumerate exceptions, though in such cases he promised to immediately notify the commander. Jackson, having badgered, complained, and threatened resignation over the Order issue now played the gallant—"The plan proposed," he said, bowing to Monroe, "fully meets my approbation." Accepting the president's "magnanimity of conduct," he extended his own. "I had determined to retire from service, the moment I could with propriety & honor. But I have determined, since the receipt of your letter not to resign." He promised, rather, that "as long as I can be really serviceable to my country and there remains any prospect of my services being wanted I will not retire."[11] Vindication lay at the heart of Jackson's generosity. Never one to be in the wrong and ever sensitive to a slight, he reacted to the self-inflicted Division Order entanglement as a personal insult rather than as a matter of public policy. This strong impression of persecution never lessened over the years. Enemies, from Alabama Creeks to War Department bureaucrats to fellow officers like Scott, were legion.

One might say that in Jackson, Monroe found a kindred spirit of sorts. Not temperamentally, of course, but rather in their shared commitment to American expansion. Perhaps this goes some way in explaining the president's willingness to indulge his difficult general. Whereas Jefferson and Madison appeared reluctant to employ Jackson, Monroe found him to be, in the altered circumstances of the post–War of 1812 southwest, an altogether effective tool for seizing Indian lands and threatening Spanish Florida. It is possible to see Jackson's actions as a continuation of his superior's. In the 1790s, while serving in Paris, Monroe secured French backing for U.S. navigation rights on the Mississippi (then controlled by Spain), and in 1803 he returned to Paris, assisting the old New York chancellor Robert R. Livingston in negotiating the

Louisiana Purchase; later, during his presidency, came conventions and treaties that enlarged U.S. territory in both the North and the South. With perhaps just a tad of embellishment John Quincy Adams once proclaimed that young America's striking territorial growth "was the work of James Monroe . . . more than of any other man."[12]

Jefferson had his Monroe and Monroe had his Jackson.

21

Phantom Letter, Full Invasion

In December 1817, while the Division Order controversy quieted down, newly appointed secretary of war John Calhoun of South Carolina authorized General Edmund P. Gaines to hunt down Seminole Indians who, in defending their lands from American outlaws and squatters, raided as well white frontier settlements in Georgia. "It is the wish of the President that you consider yourself at liberty to march across the Florida line," Calhoun wrote, "and to attack [the Seminoles] within its limits, should it be found necessary, unless," he wrote, inserting a critical caveat, "they should shelter themselves under a Spanish post."[1] The Monroe administration wished not to war over Florida, though it appreciated entirely Spain's ebbing influence in North America. The flood of Anglo pioneers descending upon the Gulf region, it knew further, looked askance at the polite politics of international boundaries and demanded that their government provide protection. This pressure in turn offered the administration an excuse to employ U.S. military power once again in Florida. As noted, Jackson had stormed the territory in the autumn of 1814, briefly seizing Pensacola; more recently, in the summer of 1816, Gaines's forces had destroyed the Negro Fort, a stronghold built along the east shore of the Apalachicola River by the British during the War of 1812 and offering refuge to nearly three hundred runaway slaves and Native Americans. Monroe now called for yet another limited invasion, one that might finally convince Spain of its impossible position.

The disputed Treaty of Fort Jackson proved to be the catalyst for conflict along the Georgia-Florida line. Southern Georgia Seminoles refused to recognize the right of whites to remove them from their land after the Creek defeat. Gaines's orders followed a few weeks of scattered frontier violence that included the burning of an Indian village—Fowltown—and, in its revenge, the massacre of several dozen white settlers on an open boat plying the Apalachicola River. So commenced the first Seminole War. In late December it became Jackson's war when the General was suddenly ordered to Fort Scott on the west bank of the Flint River in southwest Georgia. He, not Gaines, would lead the expedition against the Seminoles for an administration clearly sensing the moment ripe to seize a tottering colony. Calhoun acquainted Jackson with Gaines's orders "to penetrate to the Seminole Towns, through the Floridas," but he did not authorize Jackson to attack Spanish installations. He did, however, end on a provocatively opaque note, directing the General "to adopt the necessary measures to terminate [the] conflict." Calhoun subsequently informed former Georgia senator William Bibb that, commensurate to policing the Florida frontier, "Jackson is vested with full powers to conduct the war, in the manner which he may judge best."[2]

More ambiguity arrived when Monroe wrote to Jackson directly, reminding him, in regard to the looming Seminole campaign, that "great interests are at issue, and until our course is carried through triumphantly & every species of danger to which it is exposed is settled on the most solid foundation, you ought not to withdraw your active support from it." "Every species of danger"—might that include Spanish forts sheltering Seminoles? Perhaps Monroe meant nothing more than to encourage his general before a campaign, or possibly the president wished to see Spain supplanted in Florida without having given Jackson an actual order to do so. In 1810 then President Madison had sent general and former Georgia governor George Mathews to foment a filibuster in East Florida; Secretary of State Monroe further encouraged Mathews to pursue annexation, "especially," he wrote at the time, "if you entertain any reasonable hope of success there."[3] But when it became clear that "success" would require significant and thus open support from the United States, the government, fearing war with Spain and Britain, backed off. Madison disclaimed the operation, though perhaps its overtones informed Monroe's later decision to set Jackson on the Seminoles in Florida.

Whatever Monroe's intentions, Jackson wanted something concrete—an order, a letter, or at least an understanding—authorizing an attack on

Spanish forts if necessary. In a January 6 communication marked "*Confidential*," he pressed the president to make such an agreement explicit. "The arms of the United States," he argued, "must be carried to any point within the limits of East Florida, where an Enemy is permitted & protected or disgrace attends." He then astonishingly advised "The Executive Government" to order "the whole of East Florida seized & held as an indemnity for the outrages of Spain upon the property of our citizens: this done, it puts all opposition down, secures to our Citizens a compleat indemnity, & saves us from a War with Great Britain, or some of the Continental Powers combined with Spain." He dubiously assured Monroe of plausible deniability—"this can be done without implicating the Government"—and promised a timely resolution—"in sixty days it will be accomplished." All Monroe had to do, Jackson wrote, measuring the moment, was signal his agreement "through any channel."[4] Leaving nothing to chance, he recommended Tennessee congressman John Rhea as a convenient conduit.

There is no doubt that Monroe received Jackson's communication, for he acknowledged as much, though, pleading illness, he claimed to have put it aside and forgotten its presence until after the General's Florida invasion. There is instead a January 30 letter from Monroe to Calhoun in which the president directed the secretary to formally limit Jackson's options: "Instruct him not to attack any post occupied by Spanish troops, from the possibility, that it might bring the allied powers on us." Calhoun, however, never sent this order. Possibly he thought the note merely replicated instructions not to touch Spanish fortifications already sent to Gaines and subsequently relayed to Jackson. In any case, no reply from Monroe on the subject of Rhea's services has ever been discovered, though Jackson alleged differently, maintaining (in 1827 as a presidential candidate) that he received a note from Rhea affirming the administration's support. This assertion, however, appears problematic, as both Jackson's critics and defenders agree. Monroe biographer Harry Ammon has written, "The story of the Rhea letter seems to have been nothing more than a fabrication on Jackson's part, for Monroe certainly never authorized the general to seize Florida."[5] Jackson biographer Robert Remini acknowledges that the president probably never discussed the Florida situation with Rhea—and speculates that the obstinate General simply believed what he wished and dared others to say different:

In his own mind Jackson always believed he had permission to seize Florida and that the permission came straight from Monroe. For years he vehemently argued his defense and found or invented excuses to close loopholes in that defense wherever they appeared. He even claimed he had burned Rhea's letter at the writer's insistence in order to prevent it from falling into the hands of those who might make improper use of it. This was pure invention.[6]

It is worth asking the extent to which Jackson's success in the recent Division Order controversy emboldened or even occasioned his challenge to the War Department's order that he steer clear of Spanish forts in Florida. Certainly in neither instance did Monroe hold his Southern Division commander accountable. Jackson was allowed to follow his own dictates without repercussions, perhaps because, at least in the latter case, they dovetailed so vitally with the administration's. The two episodes differed, of course, in one vital respect. Jackson had demanded during the order dispute that the War Department follow a strict chain of command, yet he now sought with Rhea a secret back channel to the president. He seems to have understood that a majority of Americans would warmly welcome success against the Seminoles and their Spanish allies, and thus justify his actions in the eyes of the political class.

Using Fort Scott as a launching point, Jackson led twenty-eight hundred regular, militia, and volunteer soldiers, supplemented with fourteen hundred (mainly Lower Creek) Indians, into Florida on March 10 and headed for the former site of the Negro Fort. From there his army moved east, destroying Seminole villages and killing or seizing their occupants, many of whom bolted to St. Marks, a Spanish citadel on the Apalachee Bay. The invading force followed them, arriving at the stronghold on April 6. On that day Jackson forwarded a letter to Francisco Caso y Luengo, commander of Spanish forces at St. Marks. "I have penetrated to the Mekasukian Towns & reduced them to ashes," he wrote to introduce his army, justifying its presence both by the numerous white scalps it had discovered in the council houses along the way and by damaging information presumably relayed to him from Pensacola's governor. "The Governor stated," so he maintained, "that the Indians & Negroes had demanded of you large supplies of munitions of war, with a threat in the event of a refusal, of taking possession of your fortress."

Noting "your defenceless state," Jackson presented himself as a defender, eager to protect the Spanish fort. Concerned with Spain's "gross . . . violation of neutrality," and the need to "exclude our savage Enemies from so strong a hold as St. Marks," he offered Caso y Luengo the only, as he saw it, possible option: "I deem it expedient to garrison [your] fortress with American Troops untill the close of the present war." Such an operation he thought admissible "on that universal principal of self defense" and, less abstractly, because "under existing treaties . . . the King of Spain is bound to preserve . . . peace" in Florida, but has not.[7]

Caso y Luengo paused. Writing to Jackson on the 7th, he commenced ironically, congratulating the General on "your expedition against [the] Mickasuckey," agreeing to lodge ill American soldiers "in the royal hospital," and making assurances of his desire "to keep a strict & perfect neutrality." He acknowledged, however, the impossible premise of Jackson's request: "I beg of your Excellency leave to state to you what difficulties I should involve myself in with my Government if I were to conform with what your Excellency proposes [and] garrison this post with United States troops without first receiving orders to that effect." But his protest failed to persuade. Jackson's forces occupied the fort that same day, furnishing the exiled commandant "with," so Jackson informed Calhoun on the 8th, "transportation to Pensacola."[8]

From St. Marks, the American force continued some one hundred miles east toward the village of Chief Billy Bowlegs, an eighty-acre settlement on the Suwannee River; its Tennessee volunteers and Indian auxiliaries engaged in deadly skirmishes with Seminoles along the way. Reputed to be a haven for runaway slaves and a stronghold of Seminole power, Bowlegs's town largely emptied upon Jackson's approach, though more than two-dozen blacks and Indians were killed or captured in its taking. Shortly thereafter Robert Ambrister, a young, charismatic white Bahamian oblivious to Jackson's rapid march through Florida, walked into the town only to be arrested. Stationed in Spanish Florida during the latter stages of the War of 1812 and discharged in 1815 at the rank of lieutenant in the British Corps of Colonial Marines, he had returned to trade in the region, encouraging the Seminoles in their struggle against American settlers.

Ambrister proved to be the second "foreign integrator" who had fallen captive to Jackson's forces. Two weeks earlier Alexander Arbuthnot, a seventy-year-old Scotsman, had been arrested in St. Marks. Operating in the colony as a translator and merchant, Arbuthnot sympathized with the Gulf tribes to the extent that the Creeks had entrusted him with representing their interests. "These men are children of nature," he wrote in a journal, "leave them in their Forests to till their fields, and hunt the stag, and graze the cattle, their ideas will extend no farther and the *honest* trader in supplying their moderate wants may make a handsome profit on them. They have been ill treated by the English and robbed by the Americans, cheated by those who have dealt with them, receiving goods and other articles at the most exorbitant prices, with their peltry which has been much undervalued." Ambrister, by contrast, entertained less altruistic plans. Along with a handful of other former British officers/soldiers of fortune, he hoped to organize a filibuster expedition using Indian allies to extricate Spain from Florida. As one student of these two unfortunate British subjects has noted, "If Jackson was justified in the execution of anyone, it was certainly Ambrister."[9]

Jackson decided, however, that both men must die. After having torched hundreds of Indian homes, his army returned to St. Marks, where, in a stone fort, over three days, Ambrister and Arbuthnot faced trial. A discovered note in the former's handwriting, attesting to having organized a raid against the invading Americans, convinced a court of twelve officers to decree a death sentence. Apparently impressed with the dashing veteran's frankness and comportment, however, they quickly reduced the punishment to fifty lashes and a year's confinement to hard labor. The charges against Arbuthnot—accused of spying and inciting the Indians—appeared less conclusive. Yes, he warned those at Bowlegs's town of the oncoming Americans, but did this constitute spying? "I close my reply to the charges and specifications preferred against me," he said and bowed before the court, "being fully persuaded that, should there be cause of censor, my judges will, in the language of the law, lean to the side of mercy." Instead, "my judges" sentenced Arbuthnot to swing. Given both verdicts on April 28, Jackson, that very evening, rendered his own decision: "The Commanding General approves the finding and sentence of the court in the case of A. Arbuthnot, and approves the finding and first sentence of the court in the case of Robert C. Ambrister, and disapproves the re-consideration of the sentence of the honorable court in this case." Rather, Jackson ordered "Ambrister to be shot to *death*."[10] The following day both men were executed.

Why such hasty justice? Perhaps because Jackson, a former attorney and Tennessee state Supreme Court justice, understood the unusual conduct of the trials. Neither of the men were allowed to have counsel or present witnesses on their behalf; hearsay evidence was used against Arbuthnot, including the testimony of a man he had recently fired for stealing. A rough frontier justice administered during the pressures of an invasion might satisfy certain constituencies, but would it stand up to appellate inspection? Quashing any chance of an appeal, Jackson took no chances. "These individuals," he wrote Calhoun a few days after the executions, "were tried under my orders by a Special Court of Select officers—legally convicted as exciters of this Savage and Negro War, legally condemned, and most justly punished for their iniquities." Jackson wanted more than the blood of these men, however; he wished as well to intimidate all—British or banditti, Indian or Spanish—who challenged American power in the Gulf. Legal distinctions, he believed, could not be permitted to impede this progress; rather, he aimed with the executions to set, so he wrote, "an awfull example to the world."[11]

Leaving a contingent of soldiers behind to man St. Marks, Jackson returned to the former Negro Fort—now Fort Gadsden—on May 2. There, he wrote Calhoun of his intention to march on Pensacola, 180 miles to the west. That city, Jackson argued, offered "free access," supplies, and ammunition to the "Indians at war with the U States," while allowing hundreds of warriors to collect in its precincts. On the road to Pensacola, Jackson received two communications (one addressed "Protest") from Colonel José Masot, interim governor of Spanish West Florida. The American general's illicit presence, Masot insisted, constituted "an infringement and insult" to the King of Spain, and the American general could expect in reply "an effusion of blood"—"I will," he promised, "repulse you force to force." Jackson kept coming, of course. In a note to Masot written "on the line of March," he justified his actions in Florida on "the immutable laws of self defense," chastised Spain's failure "to enforce existing treaties," and even claimed to have fought "her battles" against hostile Indians. He asked for a "peaceable surrender" of Pensacola and promised to "enter . . . by violence" otherwise. "My resolution is fixed," he assured the governor, "& I have strength enough to enforce it."[12]

The following day, on the 24th, Jackson took the town, facing only token resistance; Masot and his garrison had already vacated to Fort Barrancas overlooking Pensacola Bay, eight miles to the east. This decampment, however, only delayed the inevitable. Trading one tenuous position for another (and facing a handful of American howitzers), Masot, after a slight and perhaps obligatory show of force, surrendered the fort on the 28th. Jackson's Florida campaign—improbable, illegal, and utterly effective—had come to an end; on June 1 he passed through Fort Montgomery in the Alabama Territory, on his way back to Tennessee.

Jackson's cavalier conducting of foreign policy in the field put the administration in a difficult position. His seizure of Spanish forts and execution of two British subjects fairly cried out for an international response, perhaps even declarations of war from the injured nations. Calhoun and treasury secretary William Crawford were quite willing to sacrifice Jackson should, say, Spain, make demands. Calhoun, so secretary of state John Quincy Adams observed, was "extremely dissatisfied" with the General, believing that he hoped "to produce a war for the sake of commanding an expedition against Mexico." Even Adams, Jackson's only defender in the cabinet, had his doubts. Upon learning of the army's execution of Indian prisoners and the General's "half inclined" decision "to give [Arbuthnot] no quarter," he hesitated for a moment, confessing, "I was not prepared for such a mode of warfare."[13]

In a July 21 diary entry, Adams succinctly outlined the difficulty facing the cabinet:

> The Administration were placed in a dilemma from which it is impossible for them to escape censure by some, and factious crimination by many. If they avow and approve Jackson's conduct; they incur the double responsibility of having commenced a War against Spain, and of warring in violation of the Constitution, without the authority of Congress. If they disavowed him, they must give offence to all his friends, encounter the shock of his popularity and have the appearance of truckling to Spain.[14]

What was it to be? Were the men advising Monroe willing to entertain a "violation of the Constitution" or might they risk "the shock of [Jackson's] popularity"? There appeared some early momentum for the latter path. Reading over Jackson's Florida campaign communications, Monroe complained to former president Madison that the General "has not made his case as strong as I am satisfied he might have done." Ten days later, on July 20, he wrote Madison again, noting that the Spanish wished to know if Jackson followed government orders when taking the forts. "We have yet given no answer," he explained about the situation, "but as the fact is . . . General Jackson was not authorised to take them, & did it on his own responsibility." Calhoun carried this point to its logical conclusion when writing to Georgia senator Charles Tait, "As you know, the act was unauthorized; and done by Jackson on his own responsibility. . . . It belongs to Congress, and not to the Executive, to make war on Spain. However improper the conduct of Spain has been, and however desirable to us to possess the Floridas, I am decidedly of the opinion, that the peace of the country ought to be preserved."[15] So Calhoun, so Monroe, and so most of the cabinet believed; still, Jackson received no comeuppance, served no penance. The most vital voice in the July deliberations proved to be Adams's, and he sided with the General.

"The President and all the members of the Cabinet except myself," Adams said, summarizing the situation, "are of opinion that Jackson . . . has committed War upon Spain." Dissenting, the secretary of state opted for only "an apparent violation." The general's "proceedings," he argued, "were justified by the necessity of the case, and by the misconduct of the Spanish commanding Officers in Florida." And though he recognized that "the question" of the invasion "is embarrassing and complicated" in that hostilities were carried out without a declaration of war, he contended that as Jackson had received permission from the president to enter Florida in pursuit of the Seminoles, anything that transpired on that sojourn, even the taking of a Spanish fort or three, "was," as he casually put it, merely "incidental." And in any event he thought it "better to err on the side of . . . our own Officer who had rendered the most eminent services to the Nation, than on the side of our bitterest enemies." Should the government punish Jackson, he concluded, "it would be said that . . . after having the benefit of his services, he was abandoned and sacrificed to the enemies of the country."[16] Adams's rationale won out— the president, the cabinet, and no doubt popular opinion sustained the decision.

An ambitious continentalist, Adams grasped immediately the implications of Jackson's actions. For years the United States had nibbled away at West Florida, extending its border claims, since 1810, from

Baton Rouge to Pensacola. Now the 1818 raid demonstrated conclusively Spain's inability to maintain its empire in East Florida.[17] As a
result, in February 1819, the United States and Spain signed the Adams-
Onís Treaty, which, among its several provisions, ceded Florida to the
U.S. Combined, Jackson, Monroe, and Adams were the major players
in a compact considered for its time a triumph of American diplomacy.

Jackson's Florida offensive stressed certain possibilities and problems
in the young republic. It confirmed the growing appetite for expansion
in the Gulf region, it demonstrated the difficulty of a distended nation
maintaining civilian control over its military officers, and it bolstered
Jackson's already impressive popularity. From the comparative quiet
of winter, the old Virginia dynasty lingered in letters over the Florida
crisis. Collectively, they gave the controversial general every benefit of
every doubt. Monroe, in a February 1819 communication to Madison,
suggested that his support for the assault on Spanish forts hinged, at
least in part, on Jackson's elevated standing among westerners—"Had
General Jackson been brought to trial for transgressing his orders, I
have no doubt that the interior of the country, would have been much
agitated, if not convulsed." The following month, on March 3, a hawkish
Jefferson wrote Madison, "I certainly never doubted that the military
entrance into Florida, the temporary occupation of their posts, and the
execution of Arbuthnot & Ambrister were all justifiable." Although he
acknowledged feeling some initial concern over the two deaths, "mature
reflection" convinced him that "the example will save much blood."
And three days later Madison weighed in, replying to Jefferson, "I have
always expressed the fullest confidence in the patriotism of [Jackson's]
views," adding that "if he should have erred on any point" this "ought
not to be separated from [the campaign's] merit."[18] Three of the nation's
greatest symbols of republican government, in other words, sanctioned
Jackson's unsanctioned conquest of Florida. Some in Congress, however, wished to take a closer look.

22

Congressional Qualms

By mid-June rumors and reports of Jackson's illegal seizure of Pensacola had begun to ripple through Washington. The invasion's potentially dire consequences on the diplomatic front kept Adams particularly busy that summer. First, he faced the British. His diary entry for the 25th notes that Ambassador Charles Bagot somewhat dryly stated during their recent interview a need to "say something" to his London superiors "about the Execution of the two British subjects Arbuthnot and Ambrister, and the occupation of Pensacola by General Jackson." Could Adams provide "copies of the proceedings of the Court-Martials?" He could not. Adams did assure Bagot, however, that the General's confiscation of the Florida forts "was not authorized" but rather quite "unexpected." Bagot replied that he had guessed as much and confessed a complete ignorance on what circumstances might possibly have led to the strange deaths of his countrymen. "He could," Adams recorded, "not indeed imagine any." At this point in the meeting, the secretary sighed and said, "I was willing to change the subject of Conversation."[1]

Two weeks later, the Spanish wanted their own answers—and their forts back. Spain's minister to the United States, Luis de Onís, additionally demanded Jackson's punishment. Adams replied aggressively and without a hint of apology or contrition. He described the invasion as "necessitated and justified" by Spain's unwillingness or inability to live up to the 1795 treaty, which stipulated that both contracting parties "shall . . . maintain peace and harmony" on their shared frontier. Spain had failed, he contended, to effectively police its pale. Rather, he continued, American citizens "had been exposed to the depredations, murders and massacres of a tribe of Savages . . . the greater number of them dwelling within the borders of Florida." Adams then smoothly placed the blame for the invasion on the Spanish officers who refused to abide by the treaty "and to the duties of good neighborhood." This had forced Jackson, he argued, with no recourse, to fall back "upon the immutable principles of self defence." Playing this bold hand to its logical conclusion, he cantingly called upon "his Catholic Majesty for the punishment of those officers, who, the President is persuaded, have therein acted contrary to the express orders of their Sovereign."[2] Pensacola and St. Marks would of course be returned—as soon, in the latter's case, as a force strong enough to hold it from Indian incursion arrived. The secretary's swaggering performance proved compelling. Jackson's belligerent argument for occupying Spanish forts had coaxed from Adams an equally petulant defense. And in this way did he aid in Jackson's legitimization as a national figure, defended in the highest councils of government and vouched for by a distinguished New Englander with an indelible name.

Monroe meanwhile, having returned to Washington on July 14 after a Virginia holiday, wrote to Jackson for the first time since the invasion. As with the Division Order controversy, the president seemed eager to assert the chief executive's constitutional prerogatives without alienating a popular subordinate. No doubt he knew from experience that said subordinate would massage, elide, or flat-out deny any accusation or allegation of misconduct. Monroe's communication to Jackson both absolved the administration of wrongdoing—"In transcending the limit prescribed by [your] orders, you acted on your own responsibility"—and allowed that the General may have had good reason for his actions—"you acted . . . on facts and circumstances, which were unknown to the government when the orders were given." The note further justified sending troops into Florida—"It is not an act of hostility to Spain"—while acknowledging "an order, by the government, to attack a Spanish post, would assume another character"—that of war. And only Congress, Monroe pointed out, could by "our constitution" make such a declaration. Accordingly, the forts were to be returned to Spain. "Should we hold the posts . . . it is not improbable that war would immediately follow," perhaps involving "Britain & other countries." This seemed entirely unnecessary, he told Jackson. "The events which have occur'd in both the Floridas, shew the incompetency of Spain to maintain her authority in either." If relations between the two countries soon soured, he concluded, and "if we engage in . . . war, it is of the highest importance . . . that Spain commence it, and above all, that the govt. be free from the charge of committing a breach of the constitution."[3]

Exactly one month later a note from Nashville arrived in Washington. After begging Monroe to "allow me fairly to state that the assumption of responsibility will never by shrunk from . . . ," Jackson did a bit of shrinking. Whole sentences—"It is . . . a grammatical truth that the limits of . . . an order cannot be *transcended* without an entire desertion of the objects it contemplated"—give the air of practiced muddle. Monroe and the War Department are scolded both for ambiguity—"an order generally, to perform a certain service . . . without any specification of the means to be adopted . . . leaves an *entire discretion* with the officer as to the choice and application of means"—and for failing to inform Jackson that he could not do as he pleased in Florida—"In no part of [my instructions], is there a referrence to . . . the limits of my power." Jackson sent Monroe a copy of his December 26 order, a directive to move against "the Seminole Towns," as though it somehow justified his occupation of Spanish forts; he never referred to the alleged Rhea letter, whose existence would have been his strongest defense.[4]

Jackson's criticism of Monroe is shaky at best. In his pre-campaign communication to the president suggesting Rhea as a relay, the General understood all too well the limitations placed on him. Which is precisely why he recommended a back channel that Monroe might use to convey the orders Jackson wanted (pushing, as he had put it in this note, for "possession of the Floridas"), rather than the orders that he received and now claimed were unclear.[5]

Though the administration agreed to support Jackson in the official record, perhaps for his own private account Monroe wished to restate that he never ordered the capture of Spanish forts. In an October 20 letter to the General, he once more maintained "that you understood your instructions relative to operations in Florida differently from what we intended." Shortly thereafter, however, he offered a somewhat altered interpretation to the nation. His second annual message to Congress, delivered in November, firmly defended the campaign. Lawlessness on the frontier required the American military's intervention ("the Indian tribes have constituted the effective force in Florida"); Ambrister and Arbuthnot were justly punished ("men who thus connect themselves with savage communities and stimulate them to war . . . deserve to be viewed in a worse light than the savages"); and the forts were taken for purposes of protection ("the right of self-defense never ceases"). Adopting Jackson's version, Monroe insisted "there was reason to believe that the commanders of these posts had violated their instructions." This consideration contained twin conveniences, justifying Jackson's actions and telling the American people that a cohesive cabinet had backed the decision to occupy the stations.[6]

Congress, however, wished to take a closer look. House speaker Henry Clay, rumored to be in some quiet partnership with Treasury Secretary Crawford, moved forward with an investigation of Jackson's conduct in Florida. Both men harbored presidential ambitions and perhaps recognized the Hero of New Orleans as a possible impediment. Others in Congress, with no such dreams or designs, were quick to line up behind the speaker. Some of these men feared the erosion of their constitutional right as representatives to declare war; others regarded Jackson as a military chieftain whose Florida raid endangered the nation's republican character. On January 12 a majority of the House Committee on Military Affairs denounced the executions of Ambrister and Arbuthnot, perhaps the least defensible of Jackson's actions. Having received word of Congress's investigation, Jackson, at home in Nashville, rushed to Washington, eager to defend his name. As the inquiry excluded his participation, however, it seems more likely that he came to glower, fume, and generally intimidate.

Arriving on the 23rd, Jackson missed by three days what turned out to be the investigation's climax—Clay's "Speech on the Seminole War," a twenty-four-page evisceration of both the administration and the General. "There was," the speaker bluntly insisted, having looked over Jackson's orders, "no justification for the occupation of Pensacola, and the attack on the Barrancas." Rejecting the General's assertion that hostile Indians commanded the forts, he countered that the "posts were not in the possession of the enemy. One old Indian only was found in the Barrancas, none in Pensacola, none in St. Marks." Clay further dismissed Monroe's circuitous claim, made in the president's November address to Congress, that Jackson had not made war in Florida. Rather, the speaker argued, "The President had acted in conformity to the constitution when he forbade [in his orders] the attack of a Spanish fort, and when, in the same spirit, he surrendered the posts themselves."[7]

The invasion, Clay continued, imperiled the American experiment in democratic government—the ideological hope, he grandly argued, of the entire world. "Obscure that, by the downfall of liberty here," he said, "and all mankind are enshrouded in one universal darkness." This sacred trust, he noted, faltered by "suffering to be trampled . . . the rights of other people" or by "exhibiting examples of inhumanity, and cruelty, and ambition." The very health of the republic, in other words, lay in muting men such as Jackson. In a particularly wounding comparison, Clay earned the General's lifelong enmity by suggesting that he belonged in a rogue's gallery of history's despots, dictators, and tyrants. "Beware how you give a fatal sanction, in this infant period of our republic, scarcely yet two score years old, to military insubordination," he cautioned. "Remember that Greece had her Alexander, Rome her Cæsar, England her Cromwell, France her Bonaparte, and, that if we could escape the rock on which they split, we must avoid their errors."[8] The threat of warfare on the Gulf frontier paled, Clay said, appealing to the gallery, before the greater danger of Jackson.

Most of the nation, however, as well as Congress, thought otherwise. It is difficult to overemphasize Jackson's staggering popularity and the belief that he, perhaps more so than any other living American, embodied the nation's fate, will, and resiliency, as its borders extended westward. Asked in a series of early February votes to stand by or to censure the celebrated general, a majority of congressmen, meeting as a committee of the whole, sustained Jackson. A number of resolutions—denouncing the seizure of Pensacola and condemning the executions of Ambrister and Arbuthnot among them—were soundly beaten back by an average of 98 nays to 54 yeas. On a subsequent formal House ballot, the body refused, by a 100–70 vote, to define Jackson's capture of the Florida forts as unconstitutional.[9]

Sufficiently vindicated, Jackson left Washington on February 11, traveling to Baltimore as part of a brief East Coast tour, which included stops in Philadelphia and New York. While on the road, however, he received word that a small Senate committee investigating the Seminole War and chaired by Crawford ally Abner Lacock of Pennsylvania had turned in a report sharply critical of his actions. "It went dead against Jackson on every point," one nineteenth-century biographer accurately put it. The general appeared, the brief stated, to have taken deliberate measure "to involve the nation in a war without her consent"; the committee further considered the executions of Ambrister and Arbuth-not "an unnecessary act of severity on the part of the commanding general, and a departure from that mild and humane system towards prisoners, which, in all our conflicts . . . has heretofore been consid-ered . . . honorable to the national character," and it further made sport of Jackson's insistence that the Spanish forts represented a clear and immediate danger: "This war was waged when the United States were at peace with all the world, except this miserable undisciplined banditti of 'deluded Indians' and fugitive slaves, their whole strength when com-bined not exceeding one thousand men. . . .What, then, in this state of the case, becomes of the plea of necessity?"[10]

More broadly, and echoing the tenor of Clay's January address, which had attacked Jackson as a nascent Caesar, Lacock's committee warned of a potential turn toward a perpetual American war state eager to plunder and appropriate:

> But the weakness of the Spanish authorities is urged in justifica-tion of this outrage upon our Constitution. And is the weakness of an independent Power to disparage their neutral rights, or furnish pretences for a powerful neighbor to weaken them further by hos-tile aggressions? And is it thus we are to be furnished, by an Ameri-can officer, with a justification of the dismemberment of Poland, the capture of the Danish fleet by Great Britain, and the subjugation of Europe by Bonaparte? And [if] the United States be called upon to imitate the example, or silently acquiesce and thereby subscribe to doctrines and approve measures that are in direct opposition to the repeated and invariable declarations of the Government . . . will it not be said that we have changed our national policy?[11]

In sum, the committee condemned Jackson's Florida invasion as completely as (rhetorically) possible. He had, so it insisted, operated incautiously and violently, and had endangered the nation's republican heritage. "A departure from these forms," it concluded, "is calculated to inflict a wound on the national character and tarnish the laurels so justly acquired by the commanding general by his former victories."[12]

Learning of the damning report, Jackson, now in Baltimore to sit for the artist Rembrandt Peale, rode through the night, making for the capital, eager to show Washington that he assumed no shame or stigma.

On March 2 the *National Intelligencer,* the District's major paper of the antebellum period, published the Lacock committee's findings, though nothing seemed to injure or even threaten the General's popularity. The February Adams-Onís Treaty put to rest the border dispute between the United States and Spain, while the British government seemed at this late date certain to silently pass on pursuing vindication for Ambrister and Arbuthnot. Such salutary repercussions only burnished Jackson's growing reputation, making him something more than a regional phenomenon, a mere thing of the backwater West. Louisa Catherine Adams, the London-born wife of John Quincy Adams, recorded in her diary of seeing the General for the first time at a February fête.

> Went to the Drawing Room but the crowd was so great that I nearly fainted. Gen Jackson made his first appearance there which occasioned this great assemblage of company—He is tall and very thin and when he smiles his countenance is very agreeable his manners are those of a Gentleman neither confident or timid and on the whole he produced the most favourable impression—I heard much astonishment expressed by some persons not friendly to him at his being so polite as they expected to have seen him at least half *Savage.*[13]

So Jackson weathered yet another storm, collecting critics along the way but to little effect. The Lacock committee's exacting attention to the Florida campaign seemed to cap an extended period of conflict in America that corresponded with Jackson's emergence as a national figure. But what was his place in a new era of peace? Would his honor allow for a quiet retirement or might the accusations of his enemies prolong the fight, keeping him in contention, unwilling to leave the ring?

23

Florida's Revenge

Following the War of 1812 and the acquisition of Florida, an economy-minded Monroe called for a contraction of the country's military budget. In March 1821 Congress clipped away at the army, halving troop strength from twelve thousand to six thousand, eliminating regiments, and pruning its officer corps.[1] This last item affected Jackson directly. As a commander he often clashed with other commanders and, as noted, secretaries of war and even the president. It remains an open question as to whether any of these particular constituencies regarded Jackson as a Gulf-waters-warlord-in-waiting, though Secretary Calhoun's efforts to adopt a more centralized hierarchy among his diminishing field of officers is suggestive. As part of the Reduction Act of 1821 the army high command narrowed to a single major general and two brigadier generals. That meant that either Jackson or Jacob Brown, the only major generals in the army, would have to accept a demotion.

Though Brown's résumé lacked a spectacular battle vita à la New Orleans, he nevertheless could claim a distinguished military record. Appointed brigadier general to a New York militia in 1811, he soon attained the rank of major general in the regular army, where he engaged in several important northern theater campaigns. Brown's troops defeated the British at the Battle of Chippewa; he took two wounds at the Battle of Lundy's Lane and subsequently participated in a successful defense against a British siege at Fort Erie. A national hero, he earned a Congressional Gold Medal (a year prior to Jackson's receipt of the same) and received honorary membership in 1818 in the Society of the Cincinnati, a hereditary organization that promoted the ideals of the Continental Army officers who had served in the American Revolution. Canadian military historian Donald E. Graves has written, "By the end of the War of 1812, Jacob Brown was one of the most successful generals in the U.S. Army. Other leaders, notably Andrew Jackson and William Henry Harrison, had won major victories but not, like Brown, against large numbers of British regulars in open battle."[2] Finally, in regard to the rank question, Brown possessed a most precious asset—seniority. Accordingly, Monroe appointed him commanding general of the army in June.

But what to do with Jackson? Two years earlier, while taking a western presidential tour, Monroe had offered the General the governorship of Florida, only to be rebuffed. What did Jackson want? According to his communications with Monroe, nothing more than a quiet withdrawal from public life. "You know my earnest wishes for a retirement," he wrote the president in late 1819, "and I am convinced will permit it as early as it would be honourable to myself, and the interests of our common Country, will permit." Just weeks later, pleading health concerns and growing financial commitments, he wished Monroe might at the earliest possible convenience, "signify . . . to me, that I may tender to you my resignation." But days, months, and years passed, and Jackson, by choice, remained at his post, kept there perhaps out of a sense of duty, or self-importance, or possibly because he feared his critics might dare to rewrite history lest he cast a long shadow in saddle. Now, however, the looming 1821 reorganization of the military promised to retire him on terms beyond his control. And so months before Brown's inevitable appointment, he slowly came around to seeing Florida as a face-saving sinecure. Monroe appears to have felt much the same. "The President has determined to appoint General Jackson Governor of the whole Territory," Adams informed his diary. "This office of Governor of Florida presented itself as a fortunate occasion to save the nation from the disgrace of even appearing to discard without compunction a man to whom they are so deeply indebted." Monroe made the official offer to Jackson in January 1821, promising, "The climate will suit you, and it will give me pleasure to place you in that trust."[3]

Jackson's answer eighteen days later reeked of reservation. "I first determined not to accept it," he admitted, citing "not competent . . . expenses" and concerned that "the present appointment" might appear to be a payoff for the Seminole campaign. But he took it and within weeks knew that he had made a mistake. "I assure you," he wrote to his friend John Coffee, "it will be with great reluctance I will go to that country"; and to his nephew and namesake Jack Donelson he expressed "regret that I did not adhere to my first determination not to accept the Government of Floridas." He promised to quickly organize that entity "and retire to private life."[4] On April 14, Jackson and Rachel left Nashville with a small group for New Orleans. By June they were all in Florida, the General's retirement from the army having taken effect the first of the month. A small train of civil officials accompanied Jackson—judges and district attorneys, secretaries and a single marshal—to administer a territory of some ten thousand citizens. On July 10 Commander Robert Butler accepted at St. Augustine the transfer of Spanish East Florida to the United States, and one week later, after some slight skirmishing over "the subject of the rations" and "the Inventory of the Ordnance," Jackson entered Pensacola to receive West Florida from outgoing governor José Maria Callava.[5]

From that day on, until the second week of October when he and Rachel returned to Tennessee, the governor grew increasingly annoyed with his post. The president's appointees soon trickled in, bearing evidence of the limited patronage power enjoyed by Jackson, who discovered, as he possibly had expected all along, that administering a small colony blanched beside the autonomy he assumed while campaigning in the field. Rachel fared no better. Grown pious since her flirtatious younger days, she found Pensacola sinful and Sabbath-breaking, a minor entrepôt aspiring to be the next New Orleans. "I have been in this place four weeks," she wrote to one correspondent on July 23. "In all that time I was not an idle spectator. The Sabbath profanely kept; a great deal of noise and swearing in the streets; shops kept open; trade going on, I think, more than on any other day." The governor's wife, primly eager to dampen the festal air, and exhibiting a certain adamancy often associated with her husband, turned the law loose on Pensacola: "They were so boisterous on that day I sent Major Stanton to say to them that the approaching Sunday would be differently kept. . . . Great order was observed; the doors kept shut; the gambling houses demolished; fiddling and dancing not heard any more on the Lord's day."[6]

Refusing to reconcile with Pensacola, Rachel, in a fit of white Protestant pride, looked suspiciously on the sea of Catholics and blacks before her: "the worst people here are the cast-out Americans and negroes"; "The inhabitants all speak Spanish and French"; "There are fewer white people [by] far than any other, mixed with all nations under the canopy of heaven . . . in this dark region." The following month she wrote to her brother John Donelson, "I have not injoyed myself no ways Contented," and told him to "tell our friends and all I hope to see them againe in our own Country and to know it is the best I Ever seen." She spoke as well for her husband; "ther never was a man more Disappointed then he," she complained, citing among a list of grievances Jackson's inability "to apoint one of his friends which I thought was in part the reason of his Comeing."[7]

If denied the opportunity to aid "his friends," Jackson nevertheless oversaw the organization of civil government in Florida's two counties. Under his eye, judges, *alcaldes*, and aldermen received appointments, though this kind of bureaucracy-building could hardly have appealed to the defender of New Orleans. An unexpected, but one suspects not unwelcome, confrontation with Callava offered some relief. Briefly, Mercedes Vidal Palao, the illegitimate daughter and one of several half-caste heirs to a long-deceased former West Florida civil official, approached Pensacola mayor Henry M. Brackenridge. Cheated for years out of her inheritance—said to consist of "sixteen thousand acres at Baton Rouge" with additional "valuable property" in Florida—she now wanted justice. A powerful commercial house, Forbes and Company, oversaw the estate, and its Pensacola representative, John Innerarity, proved adept at putting off her appeals. Having collected enough material to place the company's actions regarding her late father's estate into question, she enjoined Brackenridge to act. Papers demonstrating the veracity of her claim, she maintained, were soon to be carried off to Havana. A convinced Brackenridge prevailed upon Jackson, who then ordered Callava to hand over the materials in question. Claiming both jurisdiction over Spanish officers and diplomatic immunity, Callava resisted the command; that very evening American soldiers entered his home and, finding him in bed, brought him before Jackson. The former governor knew no English, the present governor knew no Spanish, and when an emotional Callava attempted through a translator to protest, an annoyed Jackson cut in, "I will not permit him to protest." Instead, he ordered Callava jailed and issued a writ to have the disputed documents seized. Callava's friends went to Eligius Fromentin, the federal district judge, who granted a writ of habeas corpus to release Callava from custody. Jackson, insisting that Fromentin's purview extended only to federal slave trade and revenue laws in Florida, ignored the writ.[8]

Considering Jackson's peculiar history of arresting personal enemies and ignoring writs of habeas corpus, Monroe could hardly have been surprised at his governor's high-handedness. In an October 7 communication between the president and Attorney General William Wirt, Monroe recognized that Jackson "may have displayed some degree of zeal & warmth, & have executed the Spanish powers, too much in the Spanish way, makeing no nice distinction, according to the principles of our system." Wirt replied four days later that he too recognized the excitable governor's need to constantly control situations: "Our friend the General certainly takes to this same Spanish power as kindly as if it was natural to him: but you may rely upon it, it will require all his popularity to gild this pill."[9] Of course Jackson enjoyed popularity to burn.

And on this point Secretary of State Adams entertained no doubts. Stopping at the president's house on the 29th, he counseled Monroe to take a soft line with Jackson. The governor, he pointed out, might resign in a fit "and then . . . make it a matter of controversy with the Administration." One must consider, he needlessly reminded Monroe, that Jackson "had a strong hold on the affection of this people."[10] Reminiscent of the Spanish forts controversy, the cabinet, with Adams's prodding, backed Jackson.

While Monroe and his advisors discussed the governor's actions, the governor and his wife vacated Florida, leaving Pensacola on October 8 and arriving at the Hermitage on November 4. In all, they had spent fewer than 120 days in the territory. As with his earlier turn in the Senate, the job had defeated Jackson, requiring both skills and an emotional makeup beyond his ken. His letter of resignation to Monroe, dated November 14, sounded much like his previous pleas for a quiet retirement. "I can only observe for the present," he wrote, "that I am truly wearied of public life, I want rest and my private concerns imperiously demand my attention. It is true my duties have been laborious and my situation exposed me to heavy expense which makes it more necessary that I should retire to resusitate my declining fortune to inable it to support me in my declining years."[11]

And, true enough, Jackson was coming to resemble a physical wreck. He suffered from inflammation of the lungs, writhed with what he called an "old bowell complaint," and occasionally coughed up "slime."

His teeth had all but rotted away.[12] Having lived a hard fifty-four years he may have supposed his career complete, but hindsight offers an altogether different answer. Though in a self-imposed exile, he remained in retirement improbably significant, strangely relevant, and inexplicably ascendant.

24

Ebbing Old Republic

Both Jackson and the United States reached respective crossroads in 1821. The pensioned general no longer commanded an army, while his country struggled to reconcile with the recent and still reverberating Panic of 1819 and the controversial Missouri Compromise (1820). The former, an injurious and far-reaching financial crisis, emphasized the nation's economic interconnectedness and with it the growing influence of major bankers, merchants, and manufacturers; the Compromise, admitting Maine and Missouri into the Union as, respectively, free and slave states, gave sanction to black servitude's westward expansion. It became evident with these episodes that serious sectional and ideological divisions threatened to split the country. To meet this challenge, a new partisan pattern slowly began to surface.[1]

The Panic of 1819 constituted the nation's first serious economic depression. Really part of a general readjustment of global markets in the wake of the Napoleonic Wars, its American version fed on excessive speculation in public lands and the largely unchecked circulation of paper money to pay for these properties. Just three years earlier the country's financial prospects had appeared to be altogether healthy. In 1816 both Congress and the president endorsed two vital engines of economic development, the second Bank of the United States (Alexander Hamilton's now extinct 1791 depository was the first) and a protectionist tariff to aid the country's budding industrial base. Along with earlier support for a promising transportation artery, the National Road (begun in 1811), the central government appeared to be actively promoting prosperity. Some years later Henry Clay called this amalgam of high tariffs, centralized banking, and internal improvements the American System and saw in its potential to link food-producing western farmers to eastern factory workers who processed southern cotton a solution to sectional tensions.[2] The Panic of 1819 called all of this into question.

Jackson joined many in blaming the banks for the economic collapse, and he opposed absolutely efforts to establish a National Bank branch in Nashville. "You know my opi[in]on as to the Banks," he wrote a friend in 1820, "that is, that the Constitution of our State, as well as the Constitution of the United States prohibited the Establishment of Banks in any state." More than a legal question, the lending and spending crisis raised serious concerns about government's role in encouraging a speculative economy. State banks starved of their specie (metallic currency such as gold and silver as opposed to checks and credit) were under intense pressure by the country's parent bank to call in loans on heavily mortgaged properties. This set off a wave of foreclosures—and these assets were often assumed by the National Bank. As William Gouge, a young Philadelphia political economist, all too pointedly put it, "The Bank was saved and the people were ruined." Some of this ruin rubbed off on Jackson, who also struggled with debt and credit issues. "From the great pressure of the times & our banks having suspended Specie payments it is difficult to procure Eastern paper," he wrote a nephew in July 1819, "in fact I have been trying to obtain some to remit you & as yet have entirely failed." The following month he observed to James Gadsden, a commissioned officer then part of Jackson's military family, "Times are dreadfull here confidence entirely destroyed, specie payments suspended, and no foreign notes to be got." And still another month later he complained to a correspondent, "The distressed state of the mercantile world has introduced its effects every where—money has disappeared & brought the great mass of mankind into distress."[3]

The second great issue of 1819—Missouri statehood with slavery—proved, even more than the Panic, to be a portent of discontent. Congressional debate began in December and lasted until February; much of the nation held its collective breath, and this included too a few old Founders. During the discussions, Jefferson wrote to John Adams, "The Missouri question is a breaker on which we lose the Missouri country by revolt, and what more, God only knows. From the battle of Bunker's hill to the treaty of Paris we never had so ominous a question." Adams replied in kind, going so far as "to express . . . doubt of the perpetual

duration of our vast American Empire."[4] The carefully tendered historical balance between free and slave states appeared suddenly in danger.
Missouri's bid to become the first state taken entirely from the Louisiana Purchase suggested to some that the vast territory in toto might be
opened to enslavers. Over the winter a compromise brokered largely
by Henry Clay took shape: Missouri's admission was to be balanced by
that of free labor Maine's, with slavery excluded from the remaining
Purchase lands north of the 36 degrees, 30 minutes latitude line (the
southern border of Missouri). Though called a compromise, the narrow
sectional nature of the vote indicated that the peculiar institution's place
in the territories beyond the Mississippi remained unsettled.

The westerly advancing slave economy was one Jackson knew well.
Owner of several properties, he maintained a sharp eye on captive labor,
looking to replenish his stock in regional sales. One April 1822 communication to his nephew Jack Donelson indicates the close continuity between a fluctuating paper money currency and the trafficking of
enslaved people. "On the subject of the purchases of the negroes," he
wrote Donelson:

> I have to observe, that I still intend to make the purchase contem-
> plated at or in the neighborhood of Lexington, but . . . I have not
> as yet been able to get to Nasvhill to enquire of the exchange. I see
> from the Louisvill paper that the paper [money] of Kentuckey is still
> depreciating and if I can get forty percent advance on your paper
> will purchase the fellow you name at $700, or I will give the man
> $500 in Nashville paper for him. perhaps he would rather take our
> paper at 40 percent advance than the Kentucky paper say $700 in as
> much as we can get specie here at 17 pr ct advance and in Kentucky
> the paper is at 70 for sp[ecie] however you can advise me on this
> subject, and if the fellow is not more than 22 years old, if he is not
> subject to runaway and is healthy and stout I will remit to you seven
> hundred dollars in Kentucky paper or $500 in our Nashville paper
> for him any time after the 23rd day of next month.[5]

Jackson further indicated to Donelson yet another purchase pref-
erence: "I want two or three girls about fifteen or Eighteen years old."
These he apparently hoped to "make a contract for . . . at $450 each, our
[Nashville] paper."[6]

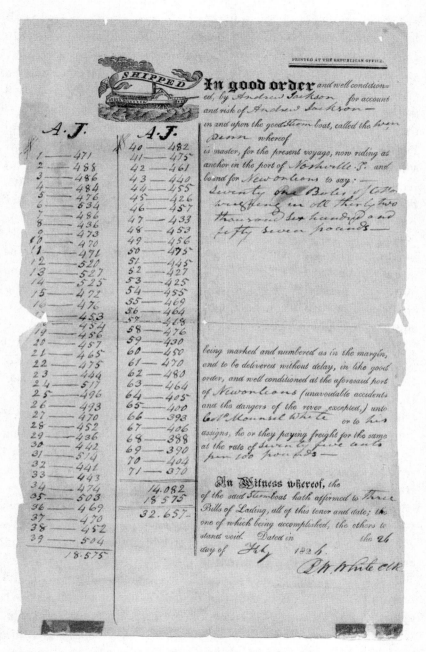

An 1826 shipping order charging Jackson $240 to haul 32,657 pounds of cotton from the Hermitage to New Orleans. This thriving cotton trade defined the economic contours of the Deep South, while giving it the character of a "slave country."

The institution of slavery, as the Master of the Hermitage knew, paralleled the nation's development in the period of the early republic. In 1810 the country counted a census of 7.2 million, of whom 1.2 million were enslaved. By 1830 these figures had swollen to 12.8 million and 2 million, respectively. The number of states making up the Union also increased during this period, from seventeen to twenty-four, most of these admitting slaves, while the center of U.S. population continued its westward pull, moving 120 miles from Loudon County, Virginia (just east of Washington, D.C.), to Grant County in present-day West Virginia.

Sensitive to Congress's fraught deliberations on slavery's extension, Jackson harbored the concerns typical of his section and station. Like Jefferson and Adams he despaired for the republic's future: "The Missouri question so called," he wrote one colleague, "has agitated the public mind—and what I sincerely regret & never expected—but what now I see, will be the entering wedge to separate the union." Dismissing entirely the possibility that moral concerns motivated men eager to limit chattel slavery's expansion, he supposed that a cynical regional partisanship explained their votes: "It is a question of political asscendency, and power, and the Eastern interest are determined to succeed regardless of the consequences." Instead, he predicted, "they will find the southern & western states equally resolved to support their constitutional rights." He took an extra and angry swipe at abolitionists, "Demagogues, who talk about humanity," so he complained, "but whose sole object is self agrandisement regardless of the happiness of the nation."[7] In standing by slavery—and a credit-suspicious specie currency—Jackson remained wedded to an old republic, although it was slowly giving way to a more complex, integrated, and industrial future.

In December 1820 the Missouri question, assumed solved by Clay's compromise, resurfaced after a clause in that territory's proposed state constitution permitted the exclusion of free blacks and mulattoes. This article contradicted the U.S. Constitution's "privileges and immunities" clause—"The citizens of each state shall be entitled to all privileges and immunities of citizens in the several states"—and renewed northern opposition to Missouri statehood. On the 13th, the House of Representatives refused to admit the territory into the Union. Nearly three weeks later Jackson denounced the lower chamber's decision in a letter to Monroe. "I sincerely regret the unpleasant situation in which the House . . . have placed the nation by the vote respecting the State of Missouri," he wrote. "Should the House not reconsider the subject I shudder for the consequences. The feelings of the South & West are aroused. The Eastern & Northern people have fully unmasked themselves, & if I can judge correctly Missouri will not retrograde or humble herself. What then will be the consequences? Missouri may seize the public property & funds within her limits. What course will Congress then adopt? I hope the majority will see the evil of this rash despotic act & admit the State and prevent the evil."[8] Following a so-called second compromise in which it was inexplicably agreed that the Missouri constitution's exclusionary clause—still very much in place—should never be interpreted in such a way as to violate the federal Constitution, Missouri entered the Union in August 1821.

Together, the Missouri debates and the Panic of 1819 helped to upend a tottering political order. As Monroe's second term wound down, so too did the antique Virginia dynasty and its pretensions to a kind of quasi-aristocratic hold on national office. Other players, representing various sections, interests, and opinions, correctly discerned a system in flux, pressured by an increasing number of voters increasingly distanced by both space and living circumstances from older Atlantic constituencies. Since the end of the War of 1812 six new states had been admitted to the Union. Their presence underlined both the nation's western bent as well as its continued drift from a deferential republic to a selective, imperfect, but growing democracy.

25

Call of the People

Befitting his political times, Jackson scorned any suggestion of one day claiming the presidency. A republican, after all, sought to emulate Cincinnatus, wanting nothing more after a spell of civic service than a quiet retirement on a green grace of land. "Those who labour in the earth," Jefferson had written in *Notes on the State of Virginia*, his treatise on the agrarian good life, "are the chosen people of God."[1] Consequently, the farmer theme proved decisive in the republic's formative decades. It aligned with cultural expectations to have chief executives serenely living off the land (or Highland, as Monroe called one of his two estates) and cultivating a field (the Adamses lived at Peacefield). A trio of Virginia presidents garnished their rustic plantations with an alliterative ring—Mount Vernon (Washington), Monticello (Jefferson), and Montpelier (Madison)—suggesting a pastoral rather than political emphasis. As a military hero, a national figure, and the occupant of yet another m-inflected plantation (the Hermitage), Jackson stood among a rather select assemblage of men who, despite a de rigueur lack of interest in the presidency, nevertheless were the de rigueur candidates for the same.

Interest in a Jackson candidacy began to slowly percolate following the Battle of New Orleans. In November 1815 Anthony Wayne Butler, a recently retired colonel in the regular army, informed the General, "On my way through Pennsylvania and Virginia I had numerous conversations with persons of the first consideration . . . and I found a strong disposition manifested to run your Name for the Presidency." That same year Aaron Burr, no fan of the congressional caucus that all too reliably returned Virginians to the executive office, could sense from his New York exile a persistent momentum already beginning to build behind the "Naturally dull & stupid . . . [and] indecisive" James Monroe. "The Moment is extremely Auspicious for breaking down this degrading system," he insisted to one correspondent, "if then there is a man in the U. S. of firmness and decision & having standing enough to afford even a hope of success it is Your duty to hold him up to public view." Burr left little doubt of his own beau ideal: "That man is Andrew Jackson— Nothing is wanting but a respectable Nomination."[2] But that would take several more years and one final Virginia presidency to arrive.

In the winter of 1821–1822 a political struggle in Tennessee resulted in Jackson's first candidacy. The out-of-power Overton faction (a legatee of the Blount machine) believed that by nominating the General it might galvanize the state's electorate in 1824 and capture the gubernatorial and senatorial races from the Erwin party (something of a successor to the old Sevier faction). Many Overtonians actually wished to see the ubiquitous Henry Clay, the western candidate, president and were willing to use a Jackson boom as a stalking horse to forward their local interests. In doing so, they completely underestimated the General's appeal beyond the state's borders.[3] Months before the Tennessee house and senate caucuses nominated Jackson in the summer of 1822, the *Philadelphia Columbian Observer* had already endorsed his candidacy.

Naturally Jackson affected a lack of interest. In late July, as the caucuses met, he complained to Monroe of a broken body: "My health is not good, nor have I much hope of regaining it, retirement & ease may prolong my life, but I fear never can restore health." Five days later, he said to a former aide, "I never have been an applicant for office I never will. . . . I mean to be silent. I have no desire, nor do I expect ever to be called to fill the Presidential chair." And yet, he calmly continued, "should this [endorsement from the legislature] be the case, contrary to my wishes & expectations, I am determined it shall be without any exertion on my part—and on this unexpected event, all that can be expected of me, is to obay the call of the people."[4] Jackson may have determined by this time that he had earned the office. Among conceivable candidates, Quincy Adams and he were the same age while Crawford, Clay, and Calhoun were respectively five, ten, and fifteen years younger. Sensitive to snubs, both real and imagined, Jackson possibly saw in the presidency a kind of ultimate vindication, one that placed him, in effect, above all his critics. Before these men, some who thought him a danger to the Constitution, he might yet play the coveted role of tribune.

The prospect of a Jackson candidacy altered the calculus of the impending presidential campaign, though not everyone could see it. Clay, Harry of the West, the only other trans-Appalachian candidate with a national profile, initially refused to take the Tennessee assemblies' nominations seriously. He thought them, so he confided to one correspondent, intended "as a mere compliment to the Genl. from his own State," or possibly done in order "to produce division in the West" and thus assist a non-western aspirant. In any case, Clay continued, "I think it may be asserted very confidently that no other Western State will lend its support to him," and he looked to "My friends in Tennessee" to offer their "undivided support" should "the General be out of the way."[5] No doubt most of Monroe's cabinet shared Clay's hope that Jackson would simply disappear. The secretaries of state (Adams), treasury (Crawford), and war (Calhoun) were all candidates in a single-party system quickly balkanizing into a politics of regions. More contestants simply produced greater uncertainty.

Perhaps in the interest of thinning down the field, Adams, with Monroe's less than robust assent, offered Jackson the post of American minister to Mexico, the country just having won its independence from Spain. The president, so Adams reported, "received favourably the name of Jackson, but doubted whether he would accept, and made some question whether his quickness and violence of temper might not in the opinion of

An 1824 print portraying the year's presidential race: Jackson (long and lean with a sword), Quincy Adams (momentarily in the lead), and William Crawford are all striding toward the finish line.

a great part of the Nation make the expediency of his appointment questionable." Adams replied by characterizing the General's erratic emotional
responses as simply surface: "I said that although the language of General
Jackson was sometimes too impassioned and violent, his conduct had
always appeared to me calm and deliberate. Acting under responsibility,
I did not apprehend he would do any thing to the injury of his Country;
and even if he should commit any indiscretion, he would bear the penalty
of it himself, for the Nation would not support him in it." This last line
is particularly eye-catching considering that Jackson's seizure of Spanish
forts and execution of British subjects were improprieties of the highest
order, for which, and due in great part to Adams's unflinching support, he
managed to quite cleanly evade "the penalty." The secretary did acknowledge to Monroe one apparent sticking point—"To send him on a Mission
abroad, would be attributed by some perhaps to a wish, to get him out
of the way." The president agreed, saying "there [is] something in that."[6]

It is difficult to imagine Jackson in any diplomatic post, let alone,
bearing in mind his distaste for Spain, serving as an envoy to Mexico, a
nation peopled by Hispanic Americans who shared with the U.S. a frontier that Jackson wished to see extended farther to the south and west.
Writing to Adams on March 15, 1823, the General, citing "the present unhappy revoluntionary [sic] state of Mexico," and his belief "that
no minister from the U States could at this period effect any beneficial
treaty for his country," agilely extracted himself from the snare.[7]

Jackson, in fact, had already publicly indicated his willingness to
run for the presidency. In the early weeks of 1823 several Pennsylvania newspapers backed his nomination, while a January 21 Dauphin
County meeting produced a statement proposing the General as Monroe's successor; some ten thousand copies were printed and the appeal
appeared in the *Harrisburg Commonwealth*. One of the authors, H. W.
Peterson, then wrote Jackson on February 3 asking if he approved of his
name "being used at this time as a candidate for the Presidency of the
U States." The general's response on the 23rd ended any doubts. After
offering the correct cautionary line on power-grasping—"My undeviat-
ing rule of conduct through life . . . has been neither to seek, or decline
public invitations to office"—he said yes. "The office of Chief Magistrate
of the Union is one of great responsibility . . . so it cannot with propriety be declined when offered by those who have the power of selection."
He closed by pretending that this coming out letter was anything but—

"My political creed prompts me to leave the affair uninfluenced by any expression on my part."[8] The signal now given, supporters, Jacksonians, could fully take up the General's candidacy.

A senatorial contest in Tennessee that year, however, threatened to undermine Jackson's momentum. The incumbent, John Williams, a soldier, statesman, and critic of the General's actions in Florida, appeared to be a shoo-in to keep his seat. It soon dawned on Jackson's backers that his presidential ambitions might falter if a political enemy in his own state held such high office. Efforts were made to reconcile Jackson and Williams, but to no avail. On June 9 the General replied to one presumptive peacemaker, "The war was made upon me without cause, & secretely when I had a right to expect the warmest friendship from Colo Williams." Attempts to secure Williams's support for Jackson in the upcoming presidential campaign proved equally futile, the senator having already committed to Crawford. Amid this labored backdrop, the legislature convened in Murfreesboro on September 15, and despite the politicking of Jackson men, Williams's support appeared firm. This prompted two House members, William Brady and Thomas Williamson, to write the General on the 20th, requesting he come to Murfreesboro "to thwart them." They stated that "Public opinion" in Tennessee backed Jackson's presidential bid, but a Williams victory in the legislature would doubtlessly qualify such support. "Believing as we do that attempts have been made by certain individuals high in trust from Tennessee, to have it whispered at Washington City, that you were not seriously talked of as our next president," they wrote, "requires that we should well weigh the character and conduct of the aspirants now before us, before we surrender out of our hands this great constitutional trust." Jackson's presence in Murfreesboro, they concluded, "would disperse some of the small atoms now floating in our atmostphere to the obstruction of the formation of correct opinions."[9]

Jackson refused, however, to make the thirty-five-mile journey south to circulate among the legislators. "My Political view," he carefully replied to Brady and Williamson on the 27th, "does not under present circumstances sanction the pleasure which a visit to my friends at Murfreesborough would afford me." His friends thought otherwise. John Eaton and William Lewis, part of the General's military family and now his de facto political managers, realized that only he could defeat Williams and, without asking his permission, adroitly engineered his nomination.

"Great uneasiness and alarm" ensued, Lewis later acknowledged, "among the more timid members." But Jackson, his name and reputation now suddenly before the public, paused not at all; the would-be senator suited up, saddled up, and immediately rode to Murfreesboro. On October 1 the legislature elected Jackson by a thirty-five to twenty-five vote. Of the dissenters, only three were reelected to the next assembly, no doubt solidifying Jackson's opinion that the people backed him completely.[10]

That December, the initial session of the 18th Congress convened; the new junior senator from Tennessee proudly reported to Overton that a series of warm receptions attended his journey to Washington:

> I . . . was greeted by the people on the whole rout—indeed I had set out with the determination not to participate in their hospitality any where—I could not get by Kingston & Knoxville without dining by candle light with them—at Rogersville Blountsville, Staunton & Fredericksburgh I was invited to tarry & dine with them, this I declined, & altho I reached Fredericksburgh in the stage at three in the evening and proceeded on at half after 4, I was escorted out of Town by the aged & the young accompanied with two companies of their independent corps of Infantry.[11]

Writing to Rachel, Jackson suggested that the public's praise served as a kind of absolution. His controversial activities over the years—the duel with Dickinson, the brawl with the Benton brothers, the capture of the Spanish forts, the arrest of a federal judge in New Orleans, and so on—elicited considerable criticism from, as he might have put it, elites, partisans, and patricians. He delighted now in the notion that numbers made right: "It is gratifying to find that I have triumphed over the machinations of my enemies, & still possess the confidence of the people."[12]

In the winter of 1823–1824, the impending presidential contest consumed the capital. Ever since Washington announced his retirement in 1796, the Democratic-Republican Party (Jeffersonian) had decided its presidential candidates by caucusing; Federalists had caucused only in 1796 and 1800 and subsequently held small convention-like gatherings in 1808 and 1812. Federalism's extinction and Monroe's unopposed candidacy in 1820 had suggested the beginning of a partisan-free era in American politics, though with several aspirants vying for the crown

in 1824, the caucus once again loomed large. Crawford, a serious chal-
lenger to Monroe in 1816, seemed to have the nomination's inside track.
A Virginian by birth, he fit a certain presidential pedigree. Decamping in youth with his family first for South Carolina and then Georgia,
he'd enjoyed an impressive public career, sitting in the Senate, serving
as minister to France, and heading the war and treasury departments in
two presidential cabinets.

Of all the possible candidates, Crawford, master of Woodlawn, a
thirteen-hundred-acre plantation upon which more than three-dozen
enslaved people labored, appeared to be the most agrarian, favoring a
states' rights stance that looked with some skepticism upon the power of
the central government. He faced, however, great and, as it turned out,
insurmountable opposition. With the Virginia dynasty fading and the
seemingly automatic linkage between Democratic-Republican nominees
Jefferson, Madison, and Monroe now interrupted, the other candidates—
at this point Jackson, Adams, Clay, and Calhoun—saw no reason to defer
to Crawford. The caucus system itself, rather, struck them as anachro-
nistic, a relic of past politics. In something of a representative statement,
Charles Fisher, a former North Carolina congressman, complained during the campaign that Virginia assumed an arrogant proprietorship of
the presidency, and he called on citizens of the Tar Heel state to "break
the charm of Virginia influence—and think and act for ourselves."[13]

If a fresh and comparatively wide open political dynamic complicated Crawford's candidacy, so did health concerns. The Georgian
suffered a stroke in September 1823 shortly after leaving muggy Washington for the cooler Piedmont climes of Orange County. He took ill on
the journey and early nineteenth-century medicine may have exasperated the situation. Believing Crawford had experienced a heart attack,
a well-meaning doctor, two historians have written, "administered dig-
italis, an extract of the poisonous foxglove plant and toxic if incorrectly
dosed. In fact, it was an extremely dangerous drug. The measure separating a fruitless from a fatal dose could be less than a drop. The doctor
gave Crawford too much. With his heart beating wildly out of control,
Crawford suffered a massive stroke."[14] Though he returned to some cabinet activities early the next year, he never fully recovered.

Jackson took his Senate seat on December 4 and quickly made
amends with some of his old enemies; he had come to the capital, after
all, to adopt a presidential posture. The proffering of olive branches

extended to Missouri senator Thomas Hart Benton, whose brother's lead ball Jackson still carried inside him. Both men belonged to the Committee on Military Affairs, and as its chair, Jackson approached Benton about meeting times and shortly after inquired of his wife's health. The General later left his card at Benton's boardinghouse, and the two, over a Washington winter of suppers and social gatherings, grew into cordial acquaintances. No one could have achieved Jackson's level of political success without learning how to play politics.[15]

Critics of the caucus, which is to say anyone who backed anyone other than Crawford, denounced it as a gathering of oligarchs. For in effect a small number of congressmen convened and foisted a candidate upon the people. In protest the state legislatures of Tennessee, Maryland, and Alabama passed resolutions condemning the practice as undemocratic; the process moved inexorably on, however, pushed in part by New York's shrewd junior senator Martin Van Buren. Architect of the Empire State's Albany Regency, a well-disciplined political machine, Van Buren, short and sturdily built, with rapidly receding sandy curls and strong blue eyes, had gravitated to the agrarian politics practiced by the Democratic-Republicans as a hedge against a narrowing New England Federalism. He hoped, as he once put it, to unite under the pressures brought about by the Panic of 1819 and the Missouri Compromise, "the plain republicans of the North and the planters of the South." "My earliest political recollections," he wrote,

> were those of the day when I exulted at the election of Mr. Jefferson, as the triumph of a good cause over [a Federalist] Administration and Party, who were as I thought subverting the principles upon which the Revolution was founded and fastening upon the Country a system which tho' different in form was nevertheless animated by a policy in the acquisition and use of political power akin to that which our ancestors had overthrown. I had ever since regarded the continued success of Mr. Jefferson's policy as the result of the superiority of the principles he introduced into the administration of the Government over those of his predecessor, and was sincerely desirous that they should continue to prevail in the Federal Councils.

As a Jeffersonian, he continued, "I announced [in 1824] my intention to support Mr. Crawford." New York thus joined Georgia and Virginia in supporting the treasury secretary, undoubtedly hoping to give his candidacy an air of inevitability. These friends of Crawford moved to call for the quadrennial caucus. A notice appeared in the February 7, 1824, *National Intelligencer* signed by several congressmen asking their colleagues to convene with them the following week "in the Representatives Chamber, at the Capital," to "recommend" a presidential candidate. The same *Intelligencer* edition, however, carried a competing article by two dozen congressmen declaring it "inexpedient, under existing circumstances, to meet in caucus"—and promising that scores of their associates would boycott.[16]

As things turned out, a great many did. Following some discussion of putting the meeting off, sixty-six congressmen, barely a third of all Republicans in Congress, attended; two appeared by proxy. Combined they predictably nominated Crawford with sixty-four votes—Adams received two, Jackson and North Carolina senator Nathaniel Macon each collected one. Only three attendees represented western states, while well over half (thirty-eight) came from Georgia, Virginia, and New York. Rather than elevate a candidate, the disappointing results merely magnified the rejection of both King Caucus and its irrelevant nominee. On February 22, Massachusetts representative Daniel Webster observed with a striking clairvoyance, "The caucus has hurt nobody but its friends. . . . Mr. Adams and General Jackson are likely to be the real competitors at last.[17]

Jackson's second Senate term proved to be altogether more successful than his first. Now in his late fifties, he bestrode the upper chamber, a national hero praised widely for his military exploits and past much of the gnawing insecurity that had haunted him in 1797. As importantly, he advanced toward a definite goal, the rapidly approaching election of 1824. Thus, he served for a mere eighteen months, with Congress meeting only a third of that time. He proved to be an engaged if undistinguished senator, balloting on bills he might have ducked, though never proposing legislation. As chairman of the Military Affairs Committee he spoke on four occasions, for a total of perhaps twenty minutes. Twice he advocated military-related road construction, and he pled separately for armament fortification funds and a pension for a veteran of the Battle of New Orleans.[18]

Two related and long contested issues, the national tariff and federal expenditures on internal improvements, continued to be discussed and debated. Many southerners regarded these objects of central state power as antithetical to both states' rights and an agrarian economy. But not Jackson. As a senator he consistently voted against tariff reduction and for public works bills that he considered national (rather than merely local) in scope. On both accounts, he cited state security. "The experience of the late war convinced me," he wrote an Alabama judge during this period, "that our Liberty was too precious, to be left for the means of its defence upon the precarious supply to be derived from commerce in a state of war." The federal government, that is, needed to provide those precious roads, canals, and turnpikes that an army might, in an emergency, require. Thus, in order to "prepare our country for defence," he supported certain internal improvements, and rather than see American manufacturing suffer before European competition, he advocated an equitable protective tariff "that will place the american labour in a fair competition with that of [E]urope."[19]

These are certainly practical and defensible views, though it might also be noted that they were considerably to candidate Jackson's advantage. Revered throughout much of the South, the Senator could afford to take unpopular positions on the twin questions of the tariff and internal improvements without alienating the region's voters. Conversely, his acclaim expanded in nascent industrial states like Pennsylvania, which supported protective federal excises on iron products and textiles. In this, as in other respects, Jackson shrewdly leveraged his scant time in the Senate to full advantage. He cultivated friendships in the capital that proved both enduring and important, relishing the opportunity to play the gentleman before a host of politicos who expected to encounter a ruffian. "I am told the opinion of those whose minds were prepared to see me with a Tomahawk in one hand, & a scalping knife in the other has greatly changed," he smiled to one correspondent, "and I am getting on very smoothly."[20]

Early in 1824 Jackson's presidential ambitions were advanced considerably when a Pennsylvania convention meeting at Harrisburg nominated the General. Hitherto many assumed that Calhoun, at this point in his career a southern nationalist like Jackson, could count on the Keystone State's support. Instead, the electoral landscape began to shift, confounding conventional opinion. "The movement at Philadelphia," Calhoun wrote, "was as unexpected to me as . . . to any of my friends. . . . Had Pen[a] decided favorably the prospects would have been most fair. Taking the U. S. together I never had a fairer prospect than on the day we lost the State."[21] Now considered a serious candidate, Jackson attracted a raft of detractors who questioned his temperament, judgment, and past conduct. The Dickinson duel, executions of militiamen, and imprisonment of Callava were all revisited, among a host of other questionable actions.

This print criticism infuriated Jackson, who seemed to regard it as yet another contest of wills. Enemies were everywhere, the papers lied, and the truth would destroy the malicious. Only two days after the Pennsylvania nomination, he appeared already to be in fighting form. "I have allways wished that my name had not been brought before the nation as President," he posed for Donelson. "But as it has been," he continued, "and the Radicals now heap upon me every scurrilous slanderous abuse that falshood can suggest, I am glad."[22] Captive to his combative personality, Jackson marched eagerly into the cockpit, in search of exoneration and restless for an ill-defined revenge.

26

To Make a Myth:
The Election of 1824

Prior to 1824 several of America's presidential elections were largely uncontested affairs. Washington's victories in 1788 and 1792 were de facto coronations giving the distinct impression of the office being out-fitted for the man; in 1804 Jefferson captured 92 percent of the electoral vote, while in 1820 Monroe carried every state in the Union, as well as 80 percent of the popular vote. Turnout during this era never exceeded 40 percent (1812) and averaged only 22 percent, easily the lowest voter participation in the nation's history. And then came a great change. The emergence of professional political organizations, the kind advanced by men like Van Buren, catalyzed a tremendous uptick in the popular vote—to 57 percent of those eligible in the 1828 contest, an astound-ing 80 percent in 1840, and from that point on averaging 72 percent until the Civil War. Equally striking is the steep increase in western and southern Gulf Coast electoral strength. In 1812 these regions counted collectively thirty-eight electoral college votes or 35 percent of the total needed for victory, though by 1824 the numbers had jumped to sixty-four and 49 percent respectively.[1] Clearly such a dramatic shift in sec-tional politics prefaced a new political age.

But first the aristocratic strain of provincial potentates, the old Vir-ginia and Massachusetts regimes, needed to evaporate. Jackson was only too happy for this to happen. Evidence for his displeasure may be gleaned in *The Letters of Wyoming*, a series of missives written anony-mously by John Eaton for the friendly *Philadelphia Columbian Observer*

in the early summer of 1823 and more widely republished the following year. Considering the candidate's assistance with the project, *Letters*
stands as Jackson's strongest pre-presidential ideological statement, one
thick with contempt for the presumed decay in republican verity. The
"author" Wyoming rhetorically asks "Can it be that there is less virtue
with the people than formerly?" before denouncing the capital's culture
of privilege and patronage: "Yes, my countrymen, there is less: not with
the honest yeomanry of the country do I mean; but with the few—those
who with the confidence of the people on their side appear at Washington, and who, in quest of their own interest and promotion, are disposed to favour the man, who in return can best promote their views."
No doubt a healthy dose of regional and class resentment informed this
pointed analysis of what ailed America, as did an anxious assumption
of cultural decay. "We are not as once we were," Wyoming complains,
"the people are slumbering at their posts; virtue is on the wane; and the
republican principles with which we set out, are fast declining."[2]

It is further possible that Jackson's notion of a deteriorating nation
gained traction in the print whipping he took from his critics. Editors
assailed his presumably crude western manners, questioned his commitment to constitutional rule, and worried over his rising cult of personality. All of these concerns informed former treasury secretary
Albert Gallatin's dismay over the General's candidacy. "Whatever gratitude we owe him for his eminent military services," he wrote in a May
1824 communication, "he is not fitted for the office of first magistrate of
a free people and to administer a government of laws." Perhaps unsurprisingly, Gallatin, a member of the old guard that Jackson rejected,
embraced the caucus politics of the past. Accordingly, he condemned
Jackson as a maverick barging in on a game traditionally played by gentlemen: "His doctrine of paying no regard to party in the selection of
the great officers of government is not only in direct opposition to the
principles of the Republican party . . . but it is tantamount to a declaration that political principles and opinions are of no importance in the
administration of government."[3]

Certainly the kinds of legacy "principles" prized by Gallatin were in
flux, and a striking number of politicians proved amenable to standing
near the shine of Jackson's luminous star. Adams, for one, decided to
hold a reception for the Hero, on January 8, 1824, the ninth anniversary of the Battle of New Orleans. Despite the protests of Adams's wife,

Louisa Catherine—"I objected much to the plan but was overpowered by John's arguments"—the event came off and, with attendance exceeding by hundreds the already ample five hundred invitees, proved an immense success. "The party at [M]rs. Adams was the largest I ever witnessed at a private house," Jackson later wrote with evident pride to one correspondent, "every room was crowded." Dolley Madison's friend Phoebe Morris reported to the former first lady shortly after the fête, "Mrs. Adams' reception . . . was really a very brilliant party and admirably arranged. The ladies climbed on chairs and benches to see General Jackson and Mrs. A[dams] very gracefully took his arm, & walked through the apartments with him, which gratified the general curiosity." The following month Daniel Webster informed his brother that the General's elegant bearing gave him a decided advantage in the upcoming election—"Jackson's manners are more presidential than those of any of the candidates. He is grave, mild and reserved. My wife is decidedly for him."[4]

Throughout 1824 Jackson played the interwoven roles of candidate and sage. He posed for a portrait by the American neoclassicist John Vanderlyn, received a Congressional Gold Medal for war service, and attended any number of public dinners. These also passed, no doubt, as suitable activities for an executive-in-waiting (both Madison and Monroe having already sat for Vanderlyn). That late autumn, while voters and six state legislatures cast presidential ballots, the Jacksons, having taken rooms in Washington's Gadsby's Tavern, were swarmed by a crush of supporters and exploiters certain of victory.[5] Within a couple of weeks the electoral results began to collect, and a coherent if awkward picture emerged. Jackson captured a higher percentage of the popular vote (41 percent) than either Adams (31 percent), Clay (13 percent), or Crawford (11 percent), and he won more electoral votes as well—his 99 exceeding Adams's 84 and surpassing Clay and Crawford's combined total of 78. The Constitution requires, however, that a candidate attain a majority of electoral votes, and this Jackson failed to accomplish, falling well shy of the necessary 131. Only Calhoun, with the support of both Adams and Jackson backers, could claim a victory—as vice president.

Of all the aspirants, Jackson proved to have the greatest national standing. He won several southern states (Tennessee, North Carolina, South Carolina, Alabama, Mississippi, and a majority of Louisiana's electors), took most of the electoral votes in two western states (Indiana and

Illinois), and performed well in the mid-Atlantic (claiming Pennsylvania, New Jersey, and a majority of Maryland's electors). The other candidates, by contrast, were largely creatures of regions. Adams secured New England and 26 of New York's 36 electors, but earned only 3 in Maryland, 2 in Louisiana, and 1 each in Delaware and Illinois. Crawford predictably claimed Virginia and Georgia, with New York furnishing 5 electors, Delaware 2, and Maryland 1. Clay, finishing fourth, competed well in the West, winning Ohio, Kentucky, and Missouri, but elsewhere could secure only 4 electors in New York. There are other indices of Jackson's attractiveness to voters; he finished second in three western states, while four of the states he lost allowed their legislatures—not the people—to conduct elections; too, he lagged considerably in blue-blooded Virginia, trailing both Crawford and Adams.

As per the Constitution, the election now belonged to the House of Representatives, where each state cast a single ballot. According to the Twelfth Amendment only the top three candidates were included, thus excluding Clay, relegated as house speaker to the role of kingmaker. In a January 9, 1825, letter to a Kentucky friend, the speaker revealed his "painful" verdict:

> We are beginning to think seriously of the choice which we must finally make. I will tell you then, that I believe the contest will be limited to Mr. Adams & Genl. Jackson; Mr. Crawford's personal condition [having suffered a stroke] precludes the choice of him; if there were no other objection to his election. As to the only alternative which is presented to us, it is sufficiently painful, & I consider whatever choice we may make will be only a choice of evils—To both those Gentlemen there are strong personal objections—The principal differences between them is that in the election of Mr Adams we shall not by the example inflict any wound upon the character of our institutions; but I should much fear hereafter, if not during the present generation, that the election of the General would give to the Military Spirit a Stimulus and a confidence that might lead to the most pernicious results—I shall therefore . . . support Mr Adams.[6]

Later that day Clay and Adams met in the latter's library to discuss the election. "Mr. Clay came at 6," Adams recorded in his diary:

He said that the time was drawing near, when the choice must be made in the House of Representatives, of a President, from the three Candidates presented by the electoral Colleges. . . . He wished me as far as I might think proper to satisfy him with regard to some principles of great pubic importance, but without any personal considerations for himself—In the question to come before the House, between General Jackson, Mr. Crawford and myself, he had no hesitation in saying that his preference would be for me.[7]

This decision made sense. Clay's views on nationalism, federal power, and internal improvements—the American System—aligned much more closely with Adams's than with the other candidates. Clay, moreover, ruminated anxiously and somewhat doubtfully over Jackson's commitment to republican government; he would always be, to the Kentuckian, a military chieftain. "I cannot believe," he wrote to a colleague in late January, "that killing 2500 Englishmen at N. Orleans qualifies for the various, difficult and complicated duties of the Chief Magistracy."[8]

Beyond a common nationalism, Clay and Adams had never really gotten on. Sparring colleagues in 1814 while negotiating the peace at Ghent, their temperamental differences—a case of the prim Puritan and the carousing card-player—grated. In one disapproving diary entry recorded in Flanders, Adams wrote, "Just before rising, I heard Mr. Clay's company retiring from his chamber."[9] It seems both unlikely and unnecessary that in their January conversation the topic of presidential appointments came up. Certainly Clay, a diplomat, senator, and now house speaker, could make his way. As a coming western man, he had received (and declined) invitations from Madison and Monroe to serve as secretary of war in two presidential cabinets. He now looked forward to demonstrating the potency of his political skills by engineering an Adams majority in the House. That he should have a place in that administration—as he might in a Jackson administration—he no doubt assumed.

On February 9, one month after the Clay-Adams tête-à-tête, the House met to conduct the contingent election. To the surprise of many Adams received the required majority (thirteen)—and did so on the first ballot; Jackson came in second with seven and Crawford trailed further behind with four. Clay's support proved crucial as his own strongholds—Ohio, Kentucky, and Missouri—all went for Adams. The fact that the Kentucky House had earlier passed a resolution insisting that its congressmen support Jackson in the contingent campaign made no difference. Jackson also saw the delegations of Illinois, Maryland, Louisiana, and North Carolina vote against him, despite the fact that he had claimed twenty-seven of their thirty-four electoral votes in the general election. Thus emerged the founding myth of the Jacksonian party: the people had spoken, had chosen Jackson, but a cabal of politicians and businessmen stole the election. The ever agitable General himself anticipated the worst, writing to Eaton and Overton just prior to the House decision, "Excitement here is considerable, & is fast spreading every where[.] The bare suspicion of any existing combination to deprive the people of their choice, commenced the excitement." The day after the election he complained further to Overton, "The people of the west have been disregarded, and demagogues barter them as sheep in the shambles, for their own views, and personal agrandisement." Adams, of course, exulted. "May the blessing of God," he happily scribbled in his diary, "rest upon the event of this day."[10]

Jackson's partisans were outraged, and the cry quickly surfaced that, as Jack Donelson carped to John Coffee on the 19th, a series of "corrupt bargains" snatched the presidency from the people.[11] Actual evidence for this is thin. Nearly 59 percent of the electorate, after all, had voted for one of the General's opponents; put another way, though Jackson captured some 151,000 ballots, the field collected about 214,000. Further, while a plurality of the popular vote in both Maryland and Illinois went for Adams, a majority of their electoral votes had gone to the General, and thus their support for Adams in the contingent contest might be regarded as a democratic outcome. Additionally, because of the number of strong regional candidates in 1824, a victory by any one of them required a coalition—and Jackson's provocative past may at last have caught up with him. Finally, the Twelfth Amendment simply asserts that when the House selects the president "a majority of all the states shall be necessary to a choice"—it does not stipulate that the candidate with the most popular votes should receive any advantage.

Much of the public, however, deplored the decision. One southern newspaper editor recalled that "on the afternoon of the day of election in the house . . . not a doubt was entertained in Baltimore, but that [Jackson] would be elected, and the office of the *Chronicle*, in that city, was crowded with men waiting the arrival of the express, to bring the pleasing intelligence. He came, and the reader may imagine, I cannot describe, the indignation that was both felt, and expressed on the occasion, when they found that Jackson was defeated." Shortly before the March swearing-in ceremony the *Allegheny Democrat* damned Henry Clay as "morally and politically a gambler, a blackleg and a traitor." Invoking her own version of the corrupt bargain theme, Rachel Jackson condemned Washington's wicked ways—"The pious here are not like those at home," she wrote a sister-in-law, "they are too much Divided with the world."[12]

Following the Senate's adjournment, the Jacksons departed for home on March 10. Crowds met them in several cities, perhaps helping to harden in the vanquished candidate's mind the impression that the politicians had defied the will of the people. Clay figured as the preeminent demon in this narrative, though Adams, as the beneficiary of the speaker's machinations, needed to be demonized as well. Just four years earlier Jackson had written to a correspondent, "You know my private opinion of Mr Adams Talents, virtue, and integrity—and I am free to declare that I have never changed this opinion of Mr Adams since it was first formed, I think him a man of the first rate mind of any in america as a civilian and scholar—and I have never doubted of his attachment to our republican Government."[13] Now, to nourish his anger, Jackson could do nothing but doubt Adams.

Part IV

KING OF THE COMMONS

His strength lay with the masses and he knew it.
Martin Van Buren, 1854

A drawn-from-life portrait of Jackson in 1829, marking the early years of a presidency that dramatically extended the powers of the executive branch.

27

In Slavery's Shadow

In October 1825, a mere seven months into the Adams administration, the Tennessee General Assembly, meeting in Murfreesboro, defiantly nominated Jackson to be the next president. One week later the General, citing this resolution "to present my name to the American people," resigned his Senate seat, doubtlessly relieved to relinquish a post that, like the governorship of Florida, he'd never wanted.[1] Thus commenced for Jackson a three-year period passed in public dinners, ceremonial civic offices, and the inevitable defense of his reputation. It additionally offered the often-itinerant planter the opportunity to maintain a careful eye on his farms. One December 1825 note to Coffee details Jackson's involved reflections on the rhythms of pig tending and the vicissitudes of weather:

> I suppose there will be some corn to spare from little Hutchings farm—you will be the best Judge how much—and when to offer it for sale—the quantity that can be spared, can be bested Judged of, after the crop is housed, & the Hoggs killed—as soon as the pork is fatted, direct that it be killed—This will save corn, as well as ensure the safety of the pork—for I anticipate an open winter after this month, with a great deal of rain; If in this I should be correct—some danger may be expected in saving pork after this month—I have killed half of mine—and on the change of this moon will slaughter the ballance.

He further instructed Coffee on matters of woodland clearing, fence repair, and a possible plow schedule predicated on "a dry winter."[2]

Combined, Jackson's several financial interests—farming, land speculation, and slaveholding, along with operating a tavern, general store,
and tracks for racing horses—turned a tidy profit. As a consequence
Rachel and Andrew, living since 1804 in a log cabin at the Hermitage, had erected on its grounds between 1819 and 1821 a two-story,
Federal-style brick mansion with four rooms on each floor divided by
broad center halls. The Jacksons' bedroom, along with a dining room
and two parlors, were located below, with additional bedrooms above.
French wallpaper, several fireplaces, and a separate summer kitchen distinguished the home. Preferring company, Jackson enjoyed both brief
and extended stays from any number of wards, nieces, and nephews.
Just why the Jacksons raised no family of their own remains a mystery. It could be that the General's youthful contraction of smallpox left
him sterile, though it is interesting to note that Rachel's first husband,
Lewis Robards, fathered four boys in a second marriage. Conspicuously
devout since her divorce, Rachel ensured that the Hermitage ménage
included any number of local or sojourning clergy, while Jackson's hero
status more generally attracted a cult of the curious. A young artist of
modest talents, Ralph E. W. Earl, also enlivened the scene, first visiting
Nashville in 1817 to arrange a depiction of the Battle of New Orleans.
Instead, he painted portraits of the Jackson family and married one of
Rachel's nieces, Jane Caffery, who died in childbirth in 1820. A particular favorite of Rachel's, Earl remained at the Hermitage, excepting
several years spent in the Jackson White House, until his own death in
1838. Earning his keep, he produced, as a kind of artist-in-residence,
a number of competent if undistinguished depictions of the General.[3]

Though the Jacksons fashioned a long and devoted marriage, the
public's intrusion into their privacy clearly affected Rachel—as did her
husband's frequent absences. Often when the General departed the Hermitage for military or civil service, Rachel would exhibit symptoms of
neuroses including hypertension, palpitations, and hysterics. Following
doctor's orders she medicated herself with tobacco, which piqued the
interest of others. "She was the first woman I ever saw smoke a cigar,"
noted one northern caller to Nashville many years after her death. "She
was correct," he warmly added, "and easy in her manners, playful in
conversation and fond of a joke."[4] A depiction from the daughter of an
officer who served under the appearance-conscious General empha-
sizes the evident contrasts that marked the couple:

Picture to yourself a military-looking man, above the ordinary height, dressed plainly, but with great neatness; dignified and grave—I had almost said stern—but always courteous and affable, with keen, searching eyes . . . expressive of deep thought and active intellect. . . . Side by side with him stands a course-looking, stout, little old woman, whom you might easily mistake for his washer-woman. . . . Her figure is rather full, but loosely and carelessly dressed, so that when she is seated she seems to settle into herself in a manner that is neither graceful nor elegant.[5]

Still another report on the marriage comes from Juliana Margaret Conner, a young Charleston bride who visited the Hermitage with her husband in 1827. Upon entering the house, she wrote, "the General and the Lady," as if performing on cue, "were in the act of descending the stairs." After taking refreshments, Conner received a tour of Rachel's garden, "which is very large and quite her hobby." Following a supper festooned with "French china, rich cut glass, [and] damask Napkins," conversation ensued "until we retired." Conner thought the Hermit-age "furnished in fashionable and genteel style"; a tasteful space, "there was no splendour to dazzle the eye but everything elegant and neat." Charmed by the Jacksons, she thought the General "perfectly easy and polished," while finding his wife "replete with kindness and benevo-lence."[6]

Rachel spent her final years entirely a captive of her husband's ambi-tions. Critical of Pensacola, she liked Washington little better and per-haps felt the condescension of the General's enemies and admirers alike, who found her "motherly," "stout," "plain," and even "uncommonly ugly." The unseemly circumstances of her long ago divorce increasingly drew the attention of Jackson's opponents. Perhaps her chest pains and hypertension were part of the price she paid for being the wife of a hero. "I could have spent at the Hermitage the remnant of my days in peace," she assured one correspondent shortly after Jackson captured the pres-idency in 1828, "& were it not that I should be unhappy by being so far from the General no consideration could induce me again to abandon this delightful spot."[7]

The "spot" referred to by Rachel undoubtedly meant something quite different to the Hermitage's many enslaved. Over the years these bondsmen and -women increased in number, making Jackson one of the larger plantation owners in Tennessee. He held 15 captives in 1798, 44 in 1820, about 100 in 1830, and some 150 at the time of his death in 1845. Typical of many planters, Jackson adopted a paternal pose, referring to his slaves as "the family" and the grounds they worked on as "the farm." More to the point, these people were first and foremost financial assets, from which he expected to accrue profits. Historian Mark R. Cheathem notes that between 1818 and 1822 alone "Jackson invested at least $5,599 [approximately $130,000 in current dollars] in slave property." The general also sold chattel, which meant that he engaged in the breaking up of families. Such a cruel practice served as a powerful counter to the master class's preferred self-image, making even the masters occasionally waver. In the spring of 1810 Wade Hampton, a South Carolina planter and one of the country's largest slaveholders, wrote to Jackson asking to have a recent sale rescinded as "the Boy" he had purchased

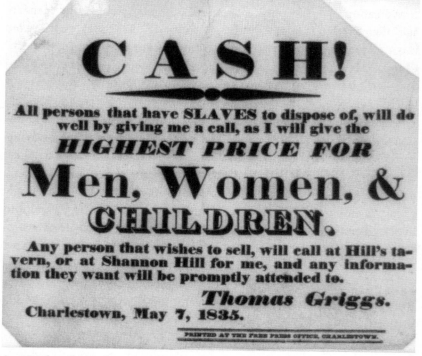

An 1835 broadside advertising the sale of enslaved "Men, Women, & Children." As a master to some 300 slaves on multiple plantations, Jackson periodically engaged in such sales, breaking up families in the process.

from the General was "a family Negroe." He expressed concern that "the *distance* would create great affliction amongst [his] relations." We don't know the outcome of his request. About this time Jackson, a partner in a mercantile concern, led an armed band transporting more than two dozen slaves from Natchez to Nashville, a hotbed for human trade. Critics of the General's presidential ambitions later condemned him for peddling flesh.[8]

Jackson enjoyed the cultural ritual of performing as a gentleman, though on a plantation this could involve frank instances of physical brutality. When an enslaved male mulatto ran away in 1804, Jackson put an advertisement in the *Nashville Tennessee Gazette* offering a reward of $50 for "any person that will take him, and deliver him to me, or secure him to jail, so that I can get him." He indicated further a willingness to pay "ten dollars extra, for every hundred lashes any person will give him, to the amount of three hundred." One wonders if Jackson considered the possible death of this particular runaway as a fitting sentence for something perhaps approximating in his mind mutinous behavior. As Cheathem writes, "Benevolent expressions toward his slaves were rare; much more frequent was the episodic violence that he authorized or endorsed. It was a risk, of course, but like other southern slave owners, Jackson strove to find a balance that demonstrated his power while not inciting active, organized slave resistance."[9]

Such probing calculations factored always into Jackson's thinking. He seemed—as master, general, and public official—to understand just how far he could go, how much he could take, assume, or assert without inviting calamitous repercussions. An emotive man teased by his passions, he nevertheless possessed the self-awareness to successfully negotiate frontier feuds, state patronage fights, and Washington politics. Driven by an intense sense of superiority, he wished above all to avoid public humiliation. Thus, in allowing others to advance his candidacy in the 1828 presidential race, Jackson gave every indication that he expected to win.

28

Jacksonians

Adams's unconventional election served as a provocation to a number of constituencies. Some embraced the corrupt bargain argument, more than a few worried over the new president's active nationalism, while still others considered him a kind of crowned head reclaiming his banished father's throne. All such constructions called for resistance. Correspondingly, Tennessee's nomination of Jackson in 1825 rang the death knell for the brief period of partisan-free politics that presumably distinguished the Monroe era. For even in the fractious contest just passed, each of the several candidates had assumed himself to be a generic Jeffersonian. On the surface their differences appeared merely regional. Now ideological distinctions, grounded most immediately in questions of federal versus state sovereignty, came increasingly to the fore. This in turn inspired a broader, more robust, and concentrated kind of polling culture, exchanging both the politics of caucus (the coronation of a single candidate) and regions (allowing, inevitably, the House to choose the president) for a politics of parties in which two sharply defined voting blocs competed for power. Even before Adams took the oath of office, close observers sensed a shift in aspect. A "party is forming itself here to oppose Mr. Adams' administration," the old Federalist and New York senator Rufus King observed to a colleague in February 1825 upon hearing of a rumored Jackson-Calhoun dinner summit. "This first step," he supposed, "may serve to combine the malcontents."[1]

That December, in his first annual message to Congress, Adams all but egged on his emerging opposition. Appealing to "the spirit of improvement . . . upon the earth," he emphasized the need for the central state to play a vital role in building "roads and canals" as a means of "multiplying and facilitating the communications and intercourse between distant regions and multitudes of men"; he advocated further government provision for the establishment of a national university as well as "the erection of an astronomical observatory" (he called them, much to the hooting derision of critics, "light-houses of the skies"); and more generally Adams accentuated the need for Congress to use every ounce of its constitutional powers in the act of "promoting the improvement of agriculture, commerce, and manufactures, the cultivation and encouragement of the mechanic and of the elegant arts, the advancement of literature, and the progress of the sciences, ornamental and profound." To do otherwise, he insisted, "would be treachery to the most sacred of trusts." He closed by advising his colleagues to embrace the future, steer the ship of state boldly, and resist any constituent-raised reservations to this brave vision: "Were we to slumber in indolence or fold up our arms and proclaim to the world that we are palsied by the will of our constituents, would it not be to cast away the bounties of Providence and doom ourselves to perpetual inferiority?"[2]

Such an ambitious call to congressional action advertised equally the president's grand plans as well as his notoriously tin political ear. Considering the controversial nature of the late election, he might have trod, in this first address, more lightly and chosen less polemical language. The "palsied" comment in particular raised eyebrows, suggesting to some that Adams aimed to push his notions of national internal improvements on an ambivalent country. North Carolina senator John Branch declared in reaction, "I never will be *palsied* by any power save the Constitution, and '*the will of my constituents.*'"[3] This ill-received epistle, along with the earlier elevation of Clay into the cabinet, launched the new administration into rather choppy waters. Considering that Adams, Monroe, Madison, and Jefferson had all headed the State Department prior to their presidencies, the choice smacked of a double investiture—Clay gave Adams the scepter and Adams returned the favor. This only fueled the "corrupt bargain" charge, while giving Jackson, in one of his final acts as a senator, a soupçon of satisfaction—he voted no to confirm Clay, who nevertheless claimed the office by a contested 27–15 vote.

Retired in name only, Jackson maintained a broad correspondence designed to deflect, as he observed to his friend Tennessee congressman (and future Texas president) Sam Houston, "the slanders or falshoods propagated against me by the hired minions of the Govt." This proved to be a rather large job. He filled friendly hands with copies of letters to the War Department "exonerating" his actions in Pensacola; he passed along testimonials of Rachel's "Most prudent & virtuous" behavior when the old utterances of adultery and bigamy once again broke; and he more generally made himself available to furnish "with great pleasure," so he informed a Virginia supporter, "any official public documents necessary" to set the historical record straight—by which he meant, of course, to justify every one of his every actions the opposition dared to condemn.[4] He refused to go quietly; in fact he refused to go away at all.

Looking beyond its Virginia dynasty roots, the Democratic Party's formative decades are equally embedded in the cult of Jackson. Nashville loyalists and the Tennessee legislature may have initiated the movement, though it inescapably began to attract, following the 1824 election, the interest of Crawford and Calhoun supporters. Collectively, these constituencies formed over time into a strong and relatively cohesive national organization of networks and committees. In June 1826 Vice President Calhoun—then in the process of abandoning his War of 1812–era nationalism to embrace a more southern vision of limited government and states' rights—wrote to Jackson, offering, in a communication marked "private," his aid in the coming campaign. "In my opinion," he observed, "liberty was never in greater danger." He believed "the next three years" would determine "whether the real governing principle in our political system be the power and patronage of the Executive, or the voice of the people." One might almost confuse Calhoun for a democrat in such affirmations and forget that South Carolina featured the most planter-dominated state chamber in all of Dixie, with high property requirements for office holding. Taking a swipe at the Adams-Clay concord, Calhoun maintained that "a corrupt patronage from hand to hand" threatened to make elections "a mere farce" that might soon lead to "power by hereditary principle, in some imperial family." No doubt he feared, or at least affected to dread, a third or even fourth Adams presidency. Pledging loyalty to the cause of "liberty," he expressed "my sincere wish" to Jackson, "that you may be the instrument, under Providence, of confounding political machinations and of . . . perpetuating our freedom."[5]

The following month Jackson answered in a communication filled with the appropriate candidate encomiums—he praised "the people," petted "the virtuous yeomanry of the country," and condemned "the enemies of freedom." He declared further a willingness to "march hand in hand" with Calhoun, in the common cause to turn Adams out of office. "An artful management of patronage," after all, could never be abided in a people's republic.[6]

On the charge of offering offices to supporters, however, Adams could justly plead clean—disastrously so. With a high-minded if rather sniffy "Such a system [of political rewards] would be repugnant to every feeling of my soul," he seemed perversely willing to allow men championing Jackson to remain in their posts, which, particularly in the case of postmasters overseeing the public mails, they might easily use for partisan ends. Clay, a strictly practical pol, once complained to the president, "The friends of the Administration have to contend not only against their enemies . . . but against the Administration itself, which leaves its power in the hands of its own enemies."[7] Adams, in effect, pursued Monroe's nonpartisan policy, though its brief and not altogether bright day, along with the caucus and the Virginia dynasty, had clearly passed. Echoing Jefferson's famous plea for ideological unity—"We are all Republicans, we are all Federalists"—Adams too stressed the need to avoid faction. "There still remains one effort of magnanimity, one sacrifice of prejudice and passion, to be made by the individuals throughout the nation who have heretofore followed the standards of political party," he maintained. "It is that of discarding every remnant of rancor against each other, of embracing as countrymen and friends, and of yielding to talents and virtue alone that confidence which in times of contention for principle was bestowed only upon those who bore the badge of party communion."[8] Determined to place his presidency on a high plane, Adams spent the next four years paddling vigorously, vainly, upstream.

Van Buren, a former Crawfordite, patiently opposed the anti-faction creed. Startled by the recent crisis over the extension of slavery in Missouri, he sought instead to substitute party spirit for sectionalism. Back in the 1790s the Jeffersonians had worked toward this end by establishing the famous Virginia–New York axis, a partnership leading to nearly continuous Old Dominion presidents and Empire State vice presidents. Van Buren believed the breakdown of this system threatened the country's cohesion, as regional issues, particularly slavery, were certain to take center stage if partisanship became regional as well. In other words, while a number of Founders had deplored the popularity of parties as a grave danger, Van Buren presumed just the opposite, touting their unique ability to unite disparate interests around the country. He sought now to usher in party discipline as a replacement to the old patrician system. Monroe he thought a naïf. The former president's failed fusion policy, so he argued, had led to the fractious Missouri debates, the caucus disaster, and the House's controversial elevation of Adams in the contingent election. None of this would have happened, he presumed, had a two-party structure been in place to promote discipline in the ranks.[9]

A sampling of Van Buren's assorted nicknames—"The Red Fox," "The Little Magician," "The Great Manager," and "The Careful Dutchman"— gives some sense of his reputation as a master political wire-puller. Such skills he now put in motion, moving himself by 1826 out of what remained of the Crawford camp and into Jackson's. He did so in part, so he later professed, because both Adams and Clay "embraced with avidity and supported with zeal" Monroe's position on the partisanship question. "They understood too well my feelings on the subject of Mr. Monroe's fusion policy," he observed, "to expect me to sustain it." A Jeffersonian favorable to the agrarian, states' rights perspective and anxious over the ascendant influence of finance and industry, Van Buren hoped to link the old republicanism to a rising Jacksonianism.[10]

Looking back on the recent past, the Little Magician believed the vintage issues defining the Jeffersonian era—including concerns over economic development, central government power, and slavery's place in the republic—continued to inform the electorate. "The politics of this state [New York] like those of Pennsylvania & most of the northern states," he wrote Jackson from Albany in 1827, "are yet governed by old Party feelings." Nothing that Monroe or Adams might do could apparently suppress the timeless struggle in America between power and liberty, aristocrats and agrarians. New York, Van Buren reminded Jackson, had played a critical role in the Jeffersonians' success—"For four fifths of the time since 1800 the old Republican Party has possessed the power of this state"—suggesting strongly that it would now like to do the same for him.[11]

29

First from the West

In 1828 American politics became, for the first time in the country's history, a popular pastime. Parades and picnics, rallies and barbecues pandered to an expanding electorate. Jackson, though reticent to engage in such public activities, proved nevertheless an ideal candidate for the new campaigning culture. The sobriquet Old Hickory lent itself to any number of tree planting ceremonies, while the Battle of New Orleans continued to resonate among a large share of voters, many of whom regarded Jackson as the greatest American since Washington—or perhaps a Washington of the new West. In the wake of Federalism's collapse, the election constituted the first since 1816 to offer voters a choice between parties. The Adams-Clay side of the old Jeffersonian combination now took the name National Republican to emphasize its backing for a central banking system and federally funded internal improvements; Jackson's supporters simply called their coalition the Democratic Party.

As the 1828 campaign gained speed, a remarkably malicious partisanship, targeting both candidates, took hold. Adams was denounced as a secret monarchist enamored of European manners and appended to a foreign wife (London-born Louisa Catherine Adams admitted to having an English mother). One crazy story alleged that as U.S. ambassador to Russia during the Madison administration, Adams, improbably doubling as a pimp, had procured a young chambermaid on his staff to sexually service the czar.

Of course Jackson, owner of a far more violent, colorful, and controversial past, attracted even greater attention. Portrayed by his supporters as a curative to the corrupt politics cankering Washington, he now found himself attacked for complicity to adultery and marrying an already married woman. *Cincinnati Gazette* editor Charles Hammond, in arrangement with Clay, began spreading these charges in the later winter of 1827, spuriously adding, for good measure, that the General descended from a mixed-race father and a prostitute. The Jackson camp, headed by John Eaton, responded alertly to the bigamy charge by putting together a labored narrative filled with documents and testimonials purporting to exonerate, sort of, the candidate and his wife. There is no doubt that Lewis Robards obtained a divorce in 1793 (approximately two years after Rachel began living with Jackson), so the General's friends were forced to argue for the couple's well-meaning ignorance in assuming that Robards had received the dissolution prior to their marriage. This explanation reduced, among friendly ears, Rachel's embarrassing infidelity to being merely technical and unintended.

Jackson's dubious repute as a violent chieftain—evident, National Republicans argued, in his duel with Dickinson, execution of mutinous soldiers, brawl with the Bentons, and recurrent quarrels over the years with civilian officials—also drew generous attention. One engraving by the Boston printmaker David Claypoole Johnston made Jackson out to be a modern King Richard III (1452–1485), commemorated by Shakespeare as cruel in deed, ruthless at heart, and monstrously ambitious. Jackson's face is tattooed with the bodies of his victims, he wears a military tent for a hat, and an inscription at the bottom of the illustration quotes from the Bard, "Methought the souls of all that I had murder'd came to my tent."[1]

A still more direct accusation of Jackson's actions surfaced when the Dublin-born journalist John Binns, editor of the *Philadelphia Democratic Press*, published an attack on the General under the heading: "Some Account of some of the Bloody Deeds of GENERAL JACKSON." Known as the coffin handbill, it featured six caskets bearing the names of the six Tennessee militiamen executed *after* the victory at New Orleans and *after* reports of peace had reached Jackson. More than two-dozen versions of the handbill appeared during the election cycle. Binns's pamphlet further noted that while campaigning in Florida, Jackson "indiscriminately exterminated" Indian towns containing "WOMEN and CHILDREN" (illustrated with four caskets), and refused to pardon the "generous hearted" John Woods (commemorated with one). On the charge of putting to death mutineers, at least, Jackson made no apolo-

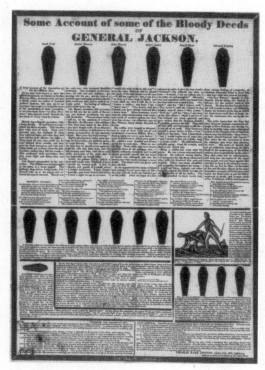

The famous coffin handbill ("Some Account of some of the Bloody Deeds of GENERAL JACKSON") used by his political opponents during the 1828 presidential election. The coffins represent soldiers and Indians condemned by Jackson for execution during the Creek War.

gies. "It will be recollected in the Revolutionary war, at a time of great trial," he wrote one correspondent in an 1827 letter that subsequently appeared in the *Lexington Kentucky Gazette*, "General Washington ordered deserters to be shot without trial."[2]

In a memoir, newspaper publisher Thurlow Weed offered a glimpse into how National Republicans further sought to exploit Jackson's many misdeeds. Only thirty at the time, the tall, lanky upstate New Yorker would go on to become a powerbroker in the Whig and Republican parties. In 1828 he stumped for Adams. "In August preceding the November election," he later recalled:

I received from the National General Committee two large dry-goods boxes containing campaign documents, upon opening which I found two pamphlets, one containing an account of the trial and execution of six militia men by General Jackson. This document was generally known, and will be better remembered, as the "Coffin Hand Bill." The other document was entitled "General Jackson's Domestic Relations," and gave an account of the General's duel with Mr. Dickinson, and his . . . marriage. A letter from the committee advised me that these boxes contained valuable campaign documents, the distribution of which throughout the western counties of this State was instrusted to me, adding that if more should be required, they would cheerfully furnish them.

Offering some insight into Jackson's victory, Weed contended that "the enlightened and able statesmen, editors, etc., etc., who supported Mr. Adams," were oblivious to a good portion of the country's attachment to the General. "The impression of the masses was that the 'six militia men' deserved hanging." And any attempt to embarrass Jackson "by ruthlessly invading the sanctuary of his home" via the bigamy charge could only "damage the cause" of their own candidate.[3]

If the executions of the militiamen failed to generate enmity toward Jackson, neither did the killing of one of his slaves—Gilbert—by an overseer. A Virginian by birth, purchased by the General and taken to labor on his northern Alabama plantation, Gilbert ran away in 1822, only to be apprehended. Later brought to the Hermitage, he again fled in 1824, was captured, and escaped yet again in August 1827, only to be returned. Following this last attempt Jackson ordered his overseer, Ira Walton, to whip Gilbert in front of his other slaves. According to Walton, he and Gilbert were walking to a field to enact the punishment when Gilbert managed to unfree his bound hands and attacked him with a piece of wood. Fearing for his life, so Walton claimed, he stabbed Gilbert several times; the man died a few hours later. Jackson called the death an "unfortunate occurrence" and seemed to back Walton—"I believe the fatal stab," he wrote the Davidson County coroner, "was given in self defense." A local nine-man jury predictably agreed.[4]

Jackson, however, perhaps sensing or alerted to the potential political damage of the situation, suddenly decided to pursue the matter. On August 30 he wrote Andrew Hays, state prosecutor for the Fourth Circuit Court, requesting that he investigate Gilbert's death. "I have discharged Mr Walton from my service," he provocatively added. The following day, after examining Gilbert's body, Hays offered the following opinion: "There exists a considerable doubt as to the absolute necessity of killing the slave Gilbert. . . . The wound in Gilbert's back, afforded a strong presumption that he was stabbed in the back whilst running, and not in the first scuffle; and among other circumstances, which induce me to think that it is not a case of justifiable homicide, is, that his hands were tied." Hays advised Jackson to "have Mr Walton before the circuit court to answer a bill of indictment for the death of Gilbert." In November a grand jury discharged Walton from prosecution.[5]

The following year, as the election neared, the *National Banner and Nashville Whig* published "Gen. Jackson's Negro Speculations, and His Traffic in Human Flesh," which included a few sharp words on Gilbert's death. This commentary soon circulated more generally as a pamphlet. Andrew Erwin, its author and a longtime Jackson critic, wrote in part, "I never had a slave brought before me for offending against whom I gave an unmerciful sentence, such as you are said to have done at or near your own fire side at the Hermitage of late, in the attempt to execute which, it is said your own slave was killed." Days later the *Nashville Republican*, returning fire, exonerated Jackson—"whatever might have been the conduct of the overseer, the General was entirely free from blame."[6] Gilbert, like John Woods, Florida's Seminoles, and the six militiamen, would simply become a footnote of the campaign.

The personal attacks on both Jackson and Adams in 1828 underlined the growing influence of newspapers in America. Successful candidates were soon to grasp that editors could make strong allies in campaigns, shaping public opinion while offering ideas on which issues to accentuate. Amos Kendall, a Kentucky transplant and editor of the *Frankfurt Argus of Western America*, proved to be a tremendous asset to Jackson. Originally a Clay supporter (and tutor of Clay's children), Kendall, an unprepossessing asthmatic with myopic vision and a slight stoop, drifted into the opposition during the Panic of 1819, supporting the interests of debtors in what became known as the Kentucky Relief War. Many in the Bluegrass State blamed the country's National Bank, the cash and credit engine behind Clay's grand American System vision, for the financial collapse. Kendall and his *Argus* associate, Francis P. Blair, both Relief War veterans and western defenders of hard money, would play important roles in fashioning Democratic Party economic policy under Jackson.

In 1828 the tariff question, the major economic issue facing the nation, became a political plaything. Congress, composed mainly of Jackson supporters, passed a bill in May designed to encourage support for the General's candidacy. Presumed swing states—Pennsylvania, New York, Kentucky, Ohio, and Missouri—stood to benefit from the new protective rates, even as the resultant tax on foreign goods threatened to increase the cost of living in the South, though that section was assumed safe for Jackson. When pressed for his views, the General, retired at the Hermitage, referred to a cautious 1824 letter in which he blandly spoke in favor of tariffs, but only so long as they produced the result of "fostering, protecting and preserving within ourselves, the means of national defence and independence, particularly in a state of war."[7] At this point, no firm Jacksonian position on the impost had gelled; some favored higher rates, while others, particularly below the Mason-Dixon Line, demurred.

Jackson's own view on the tariff remained conveniently open to interpretation. His connection to Tennessee's Blount faction suggested an active economic outlook on such issues as banking and land speculation, on par with Clay's American System; his support in the Senate for the protectionist tariff of 1824 only reinforced this notion. But the General's economic nationalism had limits. He supported hard money over paper in the Tennessee and Kentucky relief wars, and, as noted, defended the 1824 tariff for reasons of national defense rather than as a broad economic principle. Moreover, he had congratulated then President Monroe in 1822 for vetoing a bill designed to allocate federal funds for the maintenance of the Cumberland (also known as the National) Road. "My opinion has allways been," he wrote Monroe at the time, "that the Federal government did not possess that constitutional power [to oversee improvements]—That it was retained to the States respectively, and with great wisdom."[8]

Perhaps it is fair to say that Jackson's position on protection remained fluid in 1828. Like many Jeffersonians he seemed to casually accept, following Federalism's disintegration and the near disastrous war with Britain, a national bank, a protective tariff, and the Cumberland Road—all Republican initiatives. But then the Panic of 1819, the relief wars, and the revitalization of a partisan system in which supporters of Clay and Adams so conspicuously touted internal improvements, challenged him to question these initiatives. He never abandoned his belief, however, in the tariff's constitutionality; he regarded the principle of protectionism as both legal and necessary to secure the republic against its European rivals.

The tariff's actual impact on the election is debatable, as Jackson hardly needed it to claim victory. His appeal ranged widely, a factor that disappointed some adherents of a more deferential political order. "In this state [Virginia] as in Kentucky the people in mass are favorable to General Jackson," Supreme Court chief justice John Marshall complained to a nephew. "A great portion of the intelligent and unambitious are in [fa]vour of the reelection of Mr. Adams," he continued, but "th[ey] constitute a decided minority."[9] Elections in the states occurred over a two-week period between October 31 and November 14 and these admitted to wide discrepancies of participation. Virginia's restrictive franchise laws resulted in only 39,000 white men going to the polls; in Ohio, by contrast, the number was nearly 131,000, and yet due in part to the Constitution's three-fifths clause, the Old Dominion wielded twenty-four electoral votes to Ohio's sixteen.[10]

Jackson carried the contest handily, winning 55.5 percent of the popular vote and 68 percent of the electoral college (178–83). Even so, a (to be sure improbable) shifting of only 11,517 ballots in five states—Ohio, Kentucky, Louisiana, Indiana, and New York—would have produced a slender 132–129 Adams victory, along with impassioned calls from his supporters to reform the process of presidential selection.[11] Voter participation, spurred on by vicious campaigning and uncommonly effective party organization, increased dramatically from some 350,000 in 1824 to well over 1,000,000—about 57 percent of those eligible. Jackson ran strong, if unevenly so, throughout the Union, taking 50.3 percent of free state votes and 81.4 percent in the South; in all he captured a majority of electoral ballots in fifteen of the twenty-four states. Perhaps sensing defeat, Adams had ceased, since early August, attending his diary. He picked it up again in early December, including a theatrical entry on the 3rd: "The Sun of my political life sets in the deepest gloom."[12]

On the evening of December 22, a few weeks after the election, Rachel Jackson, complaining of severe chest pains and suffering from an irregular heartbeat, died.[13] Two days later, on Christmas Eve morning, a steady flow of carts and carriages, wagons and horses, choked the roads leading to the Hermitage. "Thousands from the city and from all the country around flocked to her funeral," reported Henry Wise, a young Tennessee lawyer from Virginia:

The poor white people, the slaves of the Hermitage and adjoining plantations, and the neighbors crowded off the gentry of town and country, and filled the large garden in which the interment took place.... Following the pall-bearers came General Jackson, with his left hand in the arm of General Carroll, holding his cane in his right hand, not grasping it with the hand over the head, nor with the thumb up, but with the back of the hand up and holding the point of the cane forward as he would have held a sword, and where he stopped at the pile of clay its point rested on the clods.[14]

Rachel's last months were likely a trial. Humiliated by the campaign's focus on her first marriage and depressed at the notion of living in the capital—"I would rather be a doorkeeper in the house of God," she is reported to have said, "than live in that palace at Washington"—she seems a collateral casualty of her husband's career.[15] The inscription Jackson had placed over Rachel's grave, describing her as "a being so gentle and so virtuous, slander might wound but could not dishonor," can be read as a defense of himself as well as of her. In this conspicuous mood of mourning he prepared to go to Washington, perhaps in search of yet another variation of vindication.

30

The People's Pell-Mell

As the first president-elect since Washington to have to travel to the capital city for his inauguration, Jackson looked every bit that winter like a political outsider. Those former executives-in-waiting—Adams, Jefferson, Madison, Monroe, and Quincy Adams—had been serving as either vice president or secretary of state at the time of their selections. None, in any case, lived so far from the seat of government. Jackson and a small party left the Hermitage on January 19 and shortly thereafter took the steamboat *Pennsylvania* west on the Cumberland River, where, near Paducah, Kentucky, it merged into the serpentining Ohio River; from there the General and company turned east and continued for some 600 miles to Pittsburgh. Having disembarked, the group moved 30 miles south to the small town of Washington, where it picked up the Cumberland Road and proceeded yet another 250 miles to the capital. The trip took three weeks. In mourning and perhaps exhausted from both the long journey and its attendant demands from well-wishers (the English novelist Frances Trollope espied the General in Cincinnati and noted "his harsh gaunt features"), Jackson parted from most of his entourage in Rockville, Maryland, and took a separate carriage, led by nearly a dozen men on horseback, to Washington.[1]

Until the inauguration Jackson stayed at the National Hotel, located on the corner of Pennsylvania Avenue and Sixth Street, just north of the space now occupied by the National Gallery of Art. His comfortable accommodations—a parlor, bedroom, and drawing rooms— offered Jackson the capacity to both entertain and conduct business. When leaving the hotel, indeed, whenever appearing in public during this period, he conformed to, if not exceeded, the sartorial expectations of his bereavement, dressing in a black suit and tie, accompanied by a jetty armband and a mourning veil encircling his tall hat and sliding down his slim back. About this time Daniel Webster brooded a little uneasily on the country's future. "Nobody knows what he will do," he wrote his brother Ezekiel of Jackson. "Many letters are sent to him; he answers none of them. . . . My opinion is That when he comes, he will bring a breeze with him. Which way it will blow, I cannot tell. He will either *go with the party,* . . . or else, he will . . . *be President upon his own strength.* . . . My *fear* is stronger than my *hope.*"[2]

On February 14, three days after arriving in Washington, Jackson invited Martin Van Buren to head the state department. This proved to be his strongest and most astute cabinet selection. The other appointees—including Pennsylvania congressman Samuel Ingham and Jackson's Tennessee friend John Eaton for, respectively, the Treasury and War departments—were widely considered undistinguished. Jackson might have simply made conspicuously innocent or even poor choices, though it is possible that he wished to dominate his cabinet and sought not strong men to serve under him. Van Buren, easily the most adept of the lot, quickly ingratiated himself to Jackson, aware that his personal political ambitions were now tied to the General's. This cabinet's collapse within two years and Jackson's resort to a kind of shadow—called Kitchen—ministry allowed the president to seek advice from hard-core loyalists, some of whom were quite capable. It came, however, at the cost of stability within the executive branch. A constant churn of advisors would mark Jackson's presidency; the State and Treasury departments alone saw a combined nine separate secretaries come and go.

The evening prior to the inauguration the John Quincy Adamses absented the White House, occupying a residence on nearby Meridian Hill. Taking advantage of, as his diary records, the "warm and Spring-like" weather, Adams rode into the city with a companion the following morning but conspicuously avoided the swearing-in ceremony. He thus became only the second outgoing president (his father being the other in 1801), to miss the inauguration of his successor. In defense of the senior Adams's decision, one historian has written, "There was no such tradition"—but this condition had changed with the Virginia presidents, who seemed eager to emphasize continuity, legitimacy, and perhaps even a bit of amity. Monroe's main biographer has written, "In accordance with established tradition Monroe played a subsidiary role in the inauguration of his successor, honoring custom by accompanying [Quincy] Adams from his home to the Capitol for the ceremony."[3]

As the Adamses exited, others arrived, as if to signal a great changing of the guard. Margaret Bayard Smith, the influential Washington political commentator and close friend of Dolley Madison, wrote of the days leading up to the inauguration: "Immense crowds were coming into the city from all parts, lodgings could not be obtained, and the newcomers had to go to George Town, which soon overflowed and others had to go to Alexandria." On Inauguration Day Jackson, moving slowly with an escort through a large crowd, arrived at the Capitol Building. After attending Calhoun's Senate chamber swearing-in at 11:30 a.m., he walked to the East Portico, which hosted the inauguration for the first time—a ritual that held, with few exceptions, until such ceremonies were moved (beginning in 1981 with Ronald Reagan's) to the Capitol's west front, facing the National Mall. A staggering fifteen to twenty thousand were in attendance. Watching a ship's cable stretched across the portico's steps to contain the swelling crowd, an enthusiastic Francis Scott Key thought the surge of well-wishers "beautiful" and called the spectacle "sublime!"[4]

Prior to taking the oath of office, Jackson delivered a brief address. Running to little more than two printed pages, it touched only obliquely upon the various issues confronting the country. On the question of internal improvements, the new president offered a single nebulous platitude: "So far as they can be promoted by the constitutional acts of the Federal Government, [they] are of high importance"; on the tariff debate he waxed equally esoteric: "With regard to a proper selection of the subjects of impost with a view to revenue, it would seem to me that the spirit of equity, caution, and compromise in which the Constitution was formed requires that the great interests of agriculture, commerce, and manufacturers should be equally favored"; and he offered a similar imprecision regarding relations with the Native Americans: "It will be my sincere and constant desire to observe toward the Indian tribes within our limits a just and liberal policy, and to give that humane and considerate attention to their rights and their wants which is consistent with the habits of our Government and the feelings of our people." More substantively, Jackson insisted that the election mandated change.

Accordingly, he called for a sizable turnover of government personnel, in effect an end to the sinecure system, which he blamed for his—nay, the people's—defeat in 1824. "The recent demonstration of public sentiment inscribes on the list of Executive duties," he read, "in characters too legible to be overlooked, the task of *reform*, which will require particularly the correction of those abuses that have brought the patronage of the Federal Government into conflict with the freedom of elections, and . . . have placed or continued power in unfaithful or incompetent hands." On an altogether different note Jackson, sensitive to charges that he domineered like a chieftain, promised to respect the nation's checks and balances tradition: "In administering the laws of Congress I shall keep steadily in view the limitations as well as the extent of the Executive power, trusting thereby to discharge the functions of my office without transcending its authority."[5]

The old Federalist John Marshall administered the oath to Jackson and, having attended a number of inaugurations, marveled to his wife Mary at the new president's popularity. "We had . . . a most busy and crowded day," he wrote, "a great number of them ladies." Webster too wondered at the large numbers who came out for Jackson—and at their peculiar belief in having discovered a redeemer. "I never saw any thing like it before," he told his sister-in-law Achsah Pollard. "Persons have come 500 miles to see Genl Jackson; & they really seem to think that the Country is rescued from some dreadful danger."[6]

Many among the throng followed Jackson back to the White House for what was supposed to be a simple public reception but, due to the terrific numbers, quickly turned into a chaotic scene laced with unintended menace. The crowd, having spied freezers of ice cream, barrels of lemonade, and pails of whiskey-spiked orange punch—among a powdery mountain of pies and cakes—rushed inside, smashing glasses, destroying furniture, and otherwise trying to get near the president. Sensing danger, a group of men formed a circle around Jackson, locking arms and slowly escorting him out of the building's south front, from which he escaped to his hotel. "But what a scene did we witness!" an exasperated Bayard Smith observed. "*The Majesty of the People* had disappeared, and a rabble, a mob, of boys, negros, women, children, scrambling, fighting, romping. What a pity what a pity! No arrangements had been made no police officers placed on duty and the whole house had been inundated by the rabble mob." As a commentary on democracy, the frenzied reception, Bayard Smith believed, set an ominous tone. She wondered a little desperately at a republic whose hero was "nearly pressed to death and almost suffocated and torn to pieces by the people."[7]

Looking to hold the line against such raw equality, the scolding *Washington City Chronicle* thought that Jackson's "hospitality . . . was in some measure misapplied." Eager to condemn the joyous pie and punch revelers, the paper insisted that "many were admitted . . . [that] certainly ought not to have been there."[8] Such words captured still more broadly the views embraced by those members of an elite governing class unable to make sense of the Jackson movement.

In many respects a bold new political arrangement beckoned. Party building, rotation of office, and reform were each to take commanding positions in the early days of Jackson's presidency. Some commentators, accustomed to the deferential principles of the past, looked with no little trepidation at the impending purge of the old political order. "What a change will take place in our society," Bayard Smith speculated upon Jackson's ascendency, "how many excellent families shall we lose."[9] Such concerns neglected, however, to touch upon an equally critical truth. For if Jacksonianism reflected a more populistic strain of democracy, it also perpetuated southern planters' rule in the republic. The Virginia school may have given way to a Tennessee creed, though the protection and even expansion of slavery remained a sine qua non for many Democrats. On this perilous note, Jackson represented more consensus than clash.

Jackson's remarkable first inaugural (1829), when a vast crowd descended upon—and inside—the Executive Mansion and forced the new president to make a hasty escape. Critics of the General said the actions of the ebullient "mob" showed the dangers of popular rule.

31

New Politics, New Men

Though absent at the inauguration, John Quincy Adams received a copy of Jackson's address from Washington mayor Joseph Gales, Jr. The skeptical New Englander described the speech as "short, written with some elegance; and remarkable chiefly for a significant threat of Reform." Clearly Adams scorned the new president's notion that America's governing institutions needed a thorough overhaul, a removal of the country's familiar custodians of which, of course, he might himself be regarded as the first casualty. More generally, Monroe's idealistic aim to create a no-party political culture gave way to Van Buren's belief that "political combinations . . . are unavoidable." Although respecting in principle the idea of a loyal opposition, Jackson now wished to institutionalize this division between Democrats and National Republicans by favoring the former in public appointments. He engaged, that is, in party building, a still suspect activity at the time. His predecessor had announced in 1825 as "my great object" an intent "to break up the remnant of old party distinctions and bring the whole people together in sentiment as much as possible."[1] Obviously the times had changed.

A program based on rotation of office, rather, became the principal feature of Jackson's first year in power. As a tool to institutionalize partisanship, it attracted equally a sea of supporters and dissenters. There is much to be said in favor of Jackson's view. Too many civil service jobs were in fact frozen, clasped on to year after year, in some cases decade after decade, in a kind of bureaucratic boondoggle. A certain degree of garden-variety greed and malfeasance, moreover, had no doubt sunk into the system, as had the inevitable superannuation of numerous clerks, accountants, and secretaries. Jacksonians were easily able to identify examples of corruption, as occasional cases like Tobias Watkins, a Treasury auditor, Adams acolyte, and modestly proficient swindler of government funds (to the tune of some $3,000—about $80,000 in current dollars), demonstrated.[2] More broadly, Jackson believed that the recent election, one in which the executive branch and both chambers of Congress had gone solidly Democrat, clearly indicated the people's desire for change. A newly inaugurated Jefferson had made a similar supposition in 1801 when Republicans, victorious in the previous year's elections, watched Federalism retain power in numerous appointed posts. "If a due participation of office is a matter of right," Jefferson lectured a group of concerned New England merchants early in his presidency, "how are vacancies to be obtained? those by death are few. by resignation, none. can any other mode then, but of removal, be proposed?" This is precisely the clear if convenient logic Jackson followed as well, and as with Jefferson it allowed him to cloak patronage as a form of reform.[3]

In defense of his removal agenda, Jackson attacked the value of expertise, insisting that any man could theoretically serve in any public office. Eschewing experience, he sought, at least rhetorically, to promote the notion of rotation as an egalitarian alternative to an entrenched Washington aristocracy. He articulated this position most fully in his first message to Congress in December 1829:

> Office is considered as a species of property, and government rather as a means of promoting individual interests than as an instrument created solely for the service of the people. Corruption in some and in others a perversion of correct feelings and principles divert government from its legitimate ends and make it an engine for the support of the few at the expense of the many. The duties of all public officers are, or at least admit of being made, so plain and simple that men of intelligence may readily qualify themselves for their performance; and I can not but believe that more is lost by the long continuance of men in office than is generally to be gained by their experience.[4]

Jackson came in time to favor popular elections—of presidents, senators, and federal judges—as a means of protecting the will of the people from electors and state legislatures alike. No doubt a strong personal antipathy to such institutions, cultivated during the contested 1824 election, informed his animus, though others have on occasion since pushed for similar measures. Perhaps most recently the presidential contests of 2000 and 2016, in which the winners of the popular vote lost in the electoral college, have raised concerns not entirely unlike Jackson's.

Despite fears from the General's opponents of a rotation reign of terror, only about 10 percent of government placeholders actually lost their positions, a sum roughly equal to that of Jefferson's removals. The percentage climbed higher, however, in regard to presidential appointments, which Jackson himself could affect quickly and easily. Consequently, turnover in the nation's customhouses, land offices, and postal system reached a rate of perhaps one half. In retrospect, and within an antebellum context, it appears that Jackson tried to prevent the rise of what might today be termed the deep state—a concern that a cadre of relatively permanent government bureaucrats, along with top-tier financiers, effectively govern the country, and do so beyond the reach of the people. In place of this unelected oligarchy, evident, some Democrats then argued, in the shadowy machinery that made Quincy Adams president and in the vast monetary power of the National Bank, Jackson offered a program of swap, switch, and exchange. Presumably if incoming presidents practiced the rotation principle, evicting "dangerous centinels over the public purse," as Jackson called them, the republic would remain strong.[5]

Much to his distaste, Jackson quickly discovered that a good many of the "centinels" fully expected to retain their posts. "Now every man who has been in office a few years," he wrote in a "Memorandum Book" shortly after taking office, "believes he has a life estate in it, a vested right, & if it has been held 20 years or upwards, not only a vested right, but that it ought to descend to his children, & if no children then the next of kin—This is not the principles of our government. It is rotation in office that will perpetuate our liberty." The following month he complained to John Coffee of being inundated with pleas from the current occupants of government assignments: "The most disagreable duty I have to perform is the removals, & appointments to office—There is great distress here, & it appears, that all who posses office, depend upon the emoluments for support, & thousands who are pressing for office do it upon the ground, that they are starving, & their families, & must perish without they can be relieved by the emolument of some office."[6]

1.

THE BRAVE BOY OF THE WAXHAWS.

Jackson, in his early teens, was assaulted by a British officer during the American Revolution. Commemorated in this 1876 Currier & Ives print, the attack laid a foundation for the notion of Jackson's invincibility.

2.

Rachel Donelson Jackson, apparently the General's only romantic interest. The couple married while she was still wed to another man; during Jackson's political career the opposition press attacked her as a "convicted adulteress."

3.

1893 photo of the log buildings at the Hermitage. This is the home Jackson built in 1804 and lived in when he led the U.S. defeat of the British at New Orleans.

4.

Engraving of an interview between General Jackson and William Weatherford, a Red Stick Creek chief. Jackson had just successfully prosecuted the Creek War (part of the War of 1812 in the American interior), and Weatherford surrendered to the General at Fort Jackson (Alabama).

5.

The American victory over the British at the Battle of New Orleans, coming on the heels of the successful Creek War, turned Jackson into a national hero.

6.

Thomas Hart Benton nearly killed Jackson in a gunfight in a Nashville hotel. He later became a loyal Jacksonian and promoted the president's policies in the Senate.

7.

Martin Van Buren played a key role in supporting Jackson for the presidency, in serving as his first secretary of state, and then succeeding him in the executive office. He was Jackson's most resourceful political ally.

8.

John Quincy Adams, a great defender as secretary of state of Jackson's (illegal) war against the Seminole Indians (1817–1818). Quincy Adams defeated Jackson for the presidency in 1824—though the General had the most popular and electoral votes of all four candidates. The Jacksonians cried corruption and defeated Quincy Adams's bid for reelection. For another generation, as the two men aged, Jackson and Quincy Adams cordially loathed each other.

9.

The Eaton Affair consumed much of Jackson's early presidency; this is Margaret (Peggy) Eaton in the 1870s. Her husband committed suicide and she quickly thereafter married a powerful Tennessee senator (and good friend of Jackson's). Polite Washington society snubbed her, and the fallout shook Jackson's cabinet, causing several of its members to resign. The Eaton Affair further substantiated the argument that the old eastern aristocracy refused to accept western ways.

10.

Emily Donelson, Jackson's niece and his first White House hostess (his wife Rachel having died just weeks before he assumed office in 1829). Siding with anti-Eaton sentiment, Emily refused to return social calls with the controversial couple and soon returned to Tennessee.

11.

A 1939 photo of the Philadelphia-based national bank—the "monster" bank that Jackson destroyed a century earlier.

As a National Republican and then a Whig, Henry Clay was Jackson's chief political opponent, running against him for the presidency in 1832, fighting him during the Bank War, and attacking his Indian Removal policy. For Jackson it was personal, as Speaker of the House Clay swung House votes to Quincy Adams in the contingent election of 1825 to give Adams the presidency.

13.

John C. Calhoun, Jackson's first vice president and an early supporter of the General, who he thought would prove to be a firm advocate of states' rights. Instead, Jackson and Calhoun broke, bitterly, during the nullification crisis, and the presidency went next to Van Buren.

14.

Jackson's Hermitage (1856), twelve miles east of Nashville.

15.

Jackson's Hermitage bedroom. Here, in his last years, the old General maintained an active correspondence, perused stacks of newspapers, and greeted well-wishers.

16.

Alfred Jackson, the General's manservant (as he called him), an enslaved man at the Hermitage. Alfred, thought to have been born by 1812, died in 1901. He is buried in the Jackson family plot.

17.

Texas president Sam Houston. He and Jackson were both eager to see the Lone Star Republic, yet another piece in a growing coastal cotton empire, brought into the Union.

18.

Andrew Jackson
Just before death June 8, 1845

Jackson in his final days. "Death has no terrors for me," he insisted at the end. "When I have suffered sufficiently the Lord will take me to himself."

Many of these longtime retainers correctly recognized the push for
party building in their removals, though it is no less true that the country's increasingly westward tilt made it incumbent at some very near
date that trans-Appalachian peoples also receive representation—their
share—in the administration of their government. Jackson, himself a
part of that migration, understood this as well as anyone.

There is no doubt that in the rotation rush and scrum certain mis-
takes, some quite significant, were made. The case of Samuel Swartwout,
a Poughkeepsie-born soldier, speculator, and embezzler extraordinaire,
is famous for its picaresque quality and the sizable sum of its protago-
nist's sin. An early Jackson supporter (and a former ally of Aaron Burr),
Swartwout received from the new president appointment as collector
of customs for the Port of New York—among the federal government's
largest sources of revenue, with some $15 million (about $440 million
in current dollars) coming in each year. Van Buren, intimately privy to
New York politics and personalities, fruitlessly warned Jackson away
from the man. Swartwout nimbly kept his appointment through Jackson's presidency, after which he dashed off to England, having skimmed
staggering sums in public funds. An investigation called for by Van
Buren put the figure at $1.2 million. Remarking in his diary on the
breathless "reports of a defalcation" in Swartwout's accounts, former
Federalist and New York City mayor Philip Hone condemned by association the entire rotation policy:

> President Jackson, on his accession to office, made a great fuss
> about public defaulters, prosecuted several petty offenders, whom
> he got imprisoned, and swore in his usual amiable manner that they
> should never be released, and at the same time appointed his per-
> sonal friends, who were notoriously irresponsible, to offices of the
> highest trust, whose claims consisted only in their unscrupulous
> devotion to him and his party.[7]

The astute Van Buren knew Jackson too well ever to touch upon
the topic again. "The subject was never afterwards referred to between
us," he later noted. "Even during my visit to the Hermitage in 1842
when most of the transactions of that and still earlier periods interesting to himself were brought into review . . . this matter was studiously
avoided. He did not refer to it and I was too sensible of the extent of

his disappointment and mortification to do so myself."[8] The resourceful Swartwout returned to the United States in 1841 and, having forfeited property in this country in an agreement with the government, managed to stay out of prison. He died in 1856 and is interred in Manhattan's Trinity Church Cemetery, resting, in that upscale potter's field, near former treasury secretaries Alexander Hamilton and Albert Gallatin.

Despite inevitable lapses and blunders, of which Swartwout is the most prominent example, the rotation policy boldly challenged certain existing class norms. Its role in the American social mobility story has attracted perhaps too little attention. By securing government positions for, as we might say today, underrepresented populations, Jackson challenged the notion of who could assume civic service. And this is precisely what bothered the comparatively privileged Henry Clay, son of a Virginia slaveholder and tutored at William and Mary College by George Wythe, a noted legal scholar and signer of the Declaration of Independence. Writing to a colleague in July 1829, Clay blamed the country's "present misrule" on the too humble origins of those in the highest ranks of government: "I hope both you and I shall live to see the . . . Jacksons and . . . the Eatons and the host of kindred spirits driven back to their original stations and insignificance." Clay could see only chaos "if such men . . . are to be sanctioned" and allowed to hold the golden keys of government.[9]

The quiet class war that informed the rotation debate continued well beyond the 1830s. In time the aggrieved patricians took the lead, demanding an end to a spoils system that cared little about their college degrees and ancient pedigrees. In 1869 Henry Adams, grandson of John Quincy Adams, published an angry essay in the important *North American Review* that frankly encouraged a return to elite rule. "It is one of the unfortunate but inevitable results of the situation," he wrote, "that the better class of politicians on whom a President ought to rely, men of dignity and self-respect, will not lower themselves to this struggle for patronage. Their suggestions or wishes once expressed and met by refusal or neglect, they retire, offended and mortified but too proud to beg for favors. Not so with the baser type of professional politicians. These are never wearied and never absent."[10] Adams's view is a variation of Clay's—the collective sigh of men equally fearful, suspicious, and cynical about seeing power in the hands of those hitherto powerless. This is the struggle that rocked American politics in the 1830s.

32

Peggy vs. the Moral Party

Though the rotation commotion consumed much of Jackson's energy in 1829, still another issue, the by turns combative, farcical, and wholly self-inflicted Eaton Affair proved markedly more contentious. Briefly, the circumstances surrounding the recent marriage of Jackson's friend John Eaton to Margaret "Peggy" Timberlake, coming so soon after the mysterious death of her first husband, aroused a stormy reaction in respectable Washington society. Critics and gossips alike doubted if she met the moral standards of a cabinet wife. The ensuing ostracizing of the Eatons only aroused Jackson's determination to stand by the beleaguered couple. For a little over two years, before the president reorganized his divided cabinet in the late spring of 1831, the Eaton Malaria, as some dubbed it, dominated the administration. It "exerted perhaps a more injurious influence upon the management of public affairs," Van Buren later insisted, "than could be ascribed to any of the disturbing questions of the excited period of which I write."[1] These difficulties included, incredibly, Indian removal and the Bank War. Perhaps the Eaton controversy cleaved so indelibly to Van Buren as one of its unexpected outcomes proved to be his presidency. In maintaining cordial relations with the Eatons, he did so as well with Jackson—and the General typically took care of his friends.

In a memoir published more than a half century after her 1879 death, Margaret recalled with pride an impressionable youth: "While I was still in pantalets and rolling hoops with other girls I had the attentions of men, young and old, enough to turn a girl's head." These few words suggest a great deal. They detail Margaret's physical attractiveness, ascribe a condensed adolescence, and perhaps imply a sense of superiority; she could be forward, liked to feel important, and thought a great deal of herself. She almost certainly learned early to take her value from men. One of six siblings, Margaret was born in Washington in 1799 to William and Rhoda O'Neale, proprietors of a multistory brick boarding residence just a few blocks northwest of the Executive Mansion. A collecting place of senators, congressmen, and government officials, the inn, after considerable expansion, became the Franklin House in 1813 and soon after opened a bar to complement its seventy rooms.[2] The Treasury Department, its own building destroyed by the British in the War of 1812, did business in the bustling tavern until 1816.

Confident in their daughter's capabilities, the O'Neales afforded Margaret an education. She studied conventionally female subjects including drawing and dance, music, and needlework, though English and French grammar, history, and mathematics also drew her attention. She enjoyed some proficiency on piano. Handsome, articulate, and unself-conscious, she joked and flirted with the Franklin House's itinerant clientele; inevitably, in the summer of 1816, she married one of them—John Timberlake, a thirty-nine-year-old purser in the navy, plagued by persistent debts and said to like his liquor a little too much. Margaret later recalled that her wedding guests included both first lady Dolley Madison and a cabinet member, though no evidence sustains this assertion. In December of the following year she gave birth to a boy, William, who died within a few months; she subsequently delivered two girls—Mary Virginia (Ginger) and Margaret Rose.[3] The latter was born in March 1825, precisely nine months after Timberlake shipped to sea. He never returned home. In April 1828, said to be anxious and depressed, he slit his throat while in the Mediterranean. He received burial at a cemetery on the Balearic Islands off the coast of Spain; the navy politely identified "pulmonary disease" as the official cause of death.

Years earlier, while in Washington, the Timberlakes had struck up an acquaintance with Tennessee senator John Eaton. A former Jackson military aide and biographer, Eaton had entered the upper chamber in 1818 and regularly roomed at the Franklin House, sometimes with the General. Writing to Rachel in December 1823, an obviously enamored Jackson expressed his avuncular interest in Margaret: "I can with truth say I never was in a more agreable & worthy family—When we have a leisure hour in the evening we spend it with the family—Mrs. Timber-lake the maryed daughter whose husband belongs to our navy, plays on the piano delightfully, & every Sunday evening entertains her pious mother with sacred music." Nuptials having done little to dampen her coltish behavior around men, Margaret invited innuendo, acting, as some took it, like a single woman. She once complained to Jackson of being "grossly insulted" by a certain lodger who presumed her amenable to carnal relations with the tavern's clientele.[4] In this environment the widower John Eaton seems, once Timberlake shipped off to sea, to have anointed himself Margaret's protector.

Of course some leeringly presumed that he had simply moved into her bed. Such hearsay gained currency with Timberlake's suicide and Eaton's ensuing resolve to marry the recently widowed Margaret. But first he sought Jackson's advice, perhaps certain that, due to the unusual circumstances surrounding his own marriage, the General would bless the union as a way to stay the "detraction & slander" Margaret suffered. Accordingly, Eaton stated in a December 1828 communication to Jackson that he hoped to make Margaret something of a proper lady—"by interposing myself" in a legal union and "snatch[ing] her from that injustice . . . [of] a gossipping world." He did voice some small concern regarding the "deep rooted prejudice" against marrying Margaret less than a year after Timberlake's death, though in his reply Jackson, now president-elect, entirely encouraged Eaton's plan—"Why, yes, Major, if you love the woman, and she will have you, marry her by all means." Understanding that some questioned Margaret's reputation, Jackson naively thought matrimony the perfect solution. "Well," he said, "your marrying her will disprove these charges, and restore Peg's good name."[5] Having received this presidential imprimatur, John and Margaret were wed the following month.

But far from absolving Margaret, the marriage only roused rumor-mongers, carpers, and critics. "Her reputation," Adams indelicately informed his diary at this time, "was not in good odour," while Delaware senator Louis McLane meanly opined, "Eaton has just married his mis-tress, and the mistress of eleven doz. others!" Word invariably circulated that the unfortunate purser Timberlake took his life because a more powerful man determined, in a kind of *droit du seigneur*, to have his wife.[6] Considering the storm surrounding the Eatons, Jackson would have done well to steer clear of the controversy. Instead, he fairly begged it by making Eaton his secretary of war, thus bringing Margaret into the cabinet family. In these difficult winter weeks, coinciding with Rachel's sudden death, he might have attached some attenuated vindication to standing by the Eatons. John, in any case, had proven a good friend to Rachel, often defending her honor during Jackson's two presidential campaigns when the circumstances of her bigamy were brought up. Jackson, moreover, clearly wished to place a loyalist, a man of the Cumberland Settlements, in the cabinet. He narrowed the decision down to Tennessee's two senators, Eaton ("a man," so Van Buren not unfairly thought, "of moderate intellectual capacities") and Hugh Lawson White, a more astute and respected figure. Longtime rapport and affection won out as Eaton, once referred to by Jackson as "more like a son to me than anything else," received the position.[7]

Following Jackson's swearing-in ceremony a grand ball held at Carusi's Assembly Rooms ministered to Washington's new elite; there, several women, including Vice President Calhoun's petite, raven-haired wife Floride, Jackson's occasionally sharp-tongued niece Emily Donelson, and a few cabinet wives, openly snubbed Margaret Eaton. These "old tabbies," "petticoats," and "broken down dowagers," as some depicted them, assumed the station of ethical arbiters of polite capital society. Digging in, Deborah Ingham, the second wife of Treasury Secretary Samuel, insisted to Donelson, "I . . . will not yield one inch of ground." Undoubtedly many in Washington shared her opinion, including Bayard Smith, who waspishly called Margaret "one of the most ambitious, violent, malignant, yet silly women you ever heard of."[8] Such heated responses suggest that the Eaton Affair presented yet another side of Jackson's insurgent presidency. If the General's critics regarded Eaton's appointment as a break from traditional values, his champions could just as easily say that Margaret's martyrdom reflected the conceit of established elites to keep an outsider out. The common man may have swept John Quincy Adams from office, but a group of well-bred ladies refused to admit a common tavern keeper's daughter into their clean company.

Jackson claimed in correspondence to care little what the petticoats thought. "I was making a Cabinet for my self," he wrote one Tennessee colleague just a few weeks after the inaugural. "I did not come here to make a Cabinet for the Ladies of this place, but for the nation, and that

I believed, & so I do, that Mrs. Eaton is as chaste as those who attempt to slander her."[9] In this note and elsewhere, however, he concentrated less on the ladies than on Henry Clay who, he argued, was trying to get at him by getting at the Eatons. Under assault, so he thought, from a number of sides, he soon took the offensive. Rather than devote his undivided energies to the presidency, he lavished precious time in the pursuit of letters, affidavits, and admissions seeking to exonerate John, Margaret, and no doubt himself.

Jackson quickly, perhaps predictably, came to see Washington's anti-Eaton prejudice as a plot to undermine his barely launched administration. Giving a formal dinner party for his cabinet, he noticed the icy demeanor of several cabinet wives, and the evening, plagued by stilted exchanges around a rushed meal, proved a perfect disaster. Such humiliating encounters threatened to make Margaret, expected to participate in any number of suppers, parties, and receptions, an object of public derision. Each event would expose not merely Washington's low estimation of her, but implicitly rebuke Jackson for bringing such a woman into its society. Privy to the capital's grapevine, Adams thought Jackson his own worst enemy: "The President makes her [Margaret] doubly conspicuous by an overdisplay of notice—At the last drawing-room the Night before last she had a crowd gathered around her, and was made the public gaze—but Mrs. Donelson, wife to the President's private Secretary, and who lives at the President's House . . . held not conversation with her." Learning that his cabinet officers excluded the Eatons from their own parties, Jackson demanded they do otherwise. Summoning Secretaries Ingham and John Branch (Navy), and Attorney General John Berrien for individual interviews in late January 1830, he hoped to quiet, as he wrote in a memorandum, "the personal dificulties between some of the members of my cabinet."[10]

These three men had recently and separately held large receptions that conspicuously omitted the Eatons. "When we met," Jackson related, "I said to them . . . That the course pursued by them towards Major Eaton & his family as reported to me was in my opinion under the circumstances not only unjust in itself but disrespectful to myself." He further accused these men—and their wives—of having "taken measures to induce others to avoid intercourse with Mrs Eaton and thereby sought to exclude her from society." Aside from attacking the Eatons, Jackson continued, such a course demonstrated "a wanton disregard of my feelings & a reproach of my official conduct." He now insisted on absolute loyalty from each member of his administration—or else. "I will not part with Major Eaton from my cabinet," he warned the three, "& those of my cabinet who cannot harmonise . . . had better withdraw, for harmony I must and will have." In conclusion, he extended to Ingham, Branch, and Berrien a vague threat should they conspire to use the scandal against him politically: "Therefore have I sought this interview, to assure you if there are any truth in the report that you have entered into the combination charged, to drive Major Eaton from my cabinet that I feel it an indignity & insult offered to myself, and is of a character that will remain hereafter to be considered."[11]

The Eaton Affair had clearly turned into the Jackson Affair. It bore all the earmarks of the president's outlook, suspicions, and tactics— blaming, declaiming, and demanding vindication all the while eliding his own responsibility for the situation. It seemed uncertain who, if anyone, could possibly benefit from this society scandal, excepting the cunning Van Buren. A widower, the secretary of state paid courtesy calls on the Eatons, heedless of what others (other than Jackson) might think. Some observers, aware of Van Buren's reputation for shrewd maneuvers, believed the Little Magician proposed to use the Eaton Affair to feather his own nest. As the opposing sides began to form, retired Pennsylvania congressman Thomas Patterson wrote to Clay that the opportunistic Van Buren "has no wife & will not fail to advantage even by this case or matter."[12]

Despite efforts to bully his cabinet into bullying their wives to socialize with the Eatons, Jackson met with little success. In one astonishingly desperate effort to exonerate Margaret, he even interrogated two intrusive clergymen who presumed to save the administration and perhaps the country from such a woman. Having heard whispers that Margaret's last pregnancy occurred with her husband away at sea, the Reverend J. M. Campbell, pastor of the Second Presbyterian Church (Jackson's occasional Washington congregation), passed this gossip on to the Reverend Ezra Stiles Ely, pastor of Philadelphia's Pine Street Church, for several years Jackson's acquaintance, and described by Quincy Adams as "a busybody" and a "mischief-maker." Shortly after the inauguration, Ely had sent a long "Private & Confidential" communication to the president on the subject of Margaret's many iniquities. Opening on a reluctant note— "With deep regret I now approach you"—Ely then quite unreluctantly unpacked an itemized list of innuendo carefully collected in both Washington and Baltimore. Some said "that she was a woman of ill fame before Major Eaton knew her; and had lived with him in illicit intercourse," others accused her of "having been a lewd woman, excluded from society, before her *first* and *second* marriage," and still another ("I shall not call a gentleman") at a public table at Gadsby's, the very hotel sometimes used by Jackson, told a small circle of "the time when I slept with her." Displaying a dangerous lack of delicacy, Ely warned that many Americans would connect the Eatons' secure Washington berth to Jackson's own sexual past. "The public who generally believe Mrs. E____ to have been a licentious woman for years," he wrote, "will consider her elevation to society through the influence of the President as a reflection upon the memory of Mrs. J____. It is uttered by a thousand malicious tongues, '*He* could not make an objection to Genl. E on account of his wife.'" Ely closed wishing Jackson "the happiest presidency, and heaven at last."[13]

Jackson replied to the parson less than a week later, naming "Clay and his partisans" as the cause of the uproar against the Eatons. He brushed the hearsay repeated by Ely aside as meaningless "unless accompanied with indubitable evidence," and refused to desert a friend: "Mr. Eaton has been known to me for twenty years—his character, heretofore for honesty and morality, has been unblemished, and am I now for the first time, to change my opinion of him, because of the slanders of this City? We know, *here* none are spared." Having questioned, doubted, and dismissed all the accusations raised by Ely, Jackson, the presumed tribune of the common man, now played the role of protector to a lady under attack from an eastern aristocracy: "If you feel yourself at liberty to give the names of those secret traducers of female reputation, I entertain no doubt, but they will be exposed."[14] Over the next few months Jackson and Ely exchanged several notes, their positions each unmoved by the evidence and arguments of the other.

Finally, in early September Jackson called an evening meeting of his cabinet (excepting Eaton) along with the Reverends Ely and Campbell, the latter having confessed to the president of approaching Ely with information on Margaret. Acting like a lawyer before a jury, Jackson offered evidence of Margaret's good character, including, in regard to the pregnancy rumor, dates of Timberlake's time at sea. The president claimed that in conversation with him, Campbell, having spoken with Margaret's physician, stated that she had miscarried in 1821. But

Campbell interjected, insisting he had said 1826—at which time Timberlake had been some two years at sea. Jackson ignored the clergyman and pressed on. Focusing now on a story that Margaret and Major Eaton had, prior to their marriage, spent a night together in a New York hotel, he asked Ely, who had made inquiries, to inform the group of his findings. Jackson knew that the accusation had become cloudy, moving from a night in a hotel room together to an accusation that the couple had merely engaged in conversation while sitting on a bed. Ely related this information, observing that no evidence indicated that *Mr. Eaton* had engaged in improper conduct. Jackson then chimed in, "Nor Mrs. Eaton either," only to have Ely contradict him: "On that point, I would rather not give an opinion." Incensed, Jackson declared, "She is as chaste as a virgin!"[15] After that rare presidential decree, the disastrous meeting soon broke up, having served only to accentuate the division in the president's cabinet.

An equally uncomfortable rift now dominated Jackson's domestic circumstances. Eager for company, he had brought Andrew and Emily Donelson to live in the Executive Mansion. The couple (each claimed Rachel as an aunt) served respectively as the president's private secretary and as hostess—in effect, acting first lady. But Emily took a quick and distinct disliking to the Eatons; she wrote her sister early in Jackson's presidency, "I think if Eaton had felt any disinterested friendship he never would have accepted the appointment," and she disparaged Margaret's attempt to affect a closeness where none existed: "She ... talked of her intimacy with our family and I have been so much disgusted with what I have seen of her that I shall not visit her again." Emily proposed, as part of her duties as his hostess, to receive Margaret as her uncle's guest but not to return calls.[16] A young woman only in her early twenties, she demonstrated a strong resolve to stand by her principles—even against Jackson's orders.

Then again, the General's influence in this affair ran distantly behind the wishes of several cabinet wives. A stern note from Deborah Ingham to Emily—"I am prepared to defend our course"—reflected their rigid opposition and left no doubt that intimacy with Margaret might leave the presumptive first lady vulnerable to social isolation.[17] Emily's initial dislike of Margaret could only have hardened in light of her more experienced Washington friends' unbending attitudes, women she needed to pave her way in the capital.

Jackson, who seemed to grasp few of the situation's subtleties, loathed the predicament in his home. How could he expect the cabinet wives to socialize with Margaret if his own niece refused? Relations between the president and both Emily and her husband, if always cordial, soon soured. Emily's biographer notes that in one six-day period during the Eaton Affair, "nine letters passed between uncle and nephew—four in one day—while they were living under the same roof, eating at the same table, and Donelson performing the duties of secretary." Upset at her treatment from Emily, Margaret complained to Jackson: "Circumstances my dear Genl are such as that under your kind and hospitable roof I cannot be happy. . . . I ask to say to you that whatever may be the cause of the unkind treatment I have recd from those under your roof, whose course could not but be a serious injury in the opinion of others one consolation is had, that I have done all in my power to avoid it."[18]

Trying too hard to please Margaret, Jackson appointed her father inspector of the District of Columbia prisons. This only drew attention to the growing cancer in the president's cabinet. One Jacksonian wrote to Van Buren, "For God knows we did not make him president . . . to work the miracle of making Mrs. E. an honest woman, by making her husband *Secy of War*, or by conferring some crumbs of comfort on every creature that bears the name O'Neale."[19] Finally, the political calendar brought some relief. During the summer of 1830 Jackson, his household, and the Eatons all variously retreated to Tennessee. That fall both Emily and Margaret remained there—Andrew Donelson, who proposed to stay with his wife, relented to his uncle's pleas and returned to Washington in September, though only for another congressional session. Feeling like a guest in Jackson's house, he too then retired back to Tennessee.

Unrelenting, Jackson wrote in October to Mary Ann Eastin, Emily's orphaned niece and companion, "I have . . . only to add, that it would give me much pleasure to see you both here, provided you will persue my advice, and assume that dignified course that ought to have been at first adopted, of treating every one with attention, & extending the same comity and attention to all the heads of Departments, & their families which is the only course that my situation can permit."[20] Certainly Jackson's situation as president did call for amity among his colleagues, but he never seemed to question his own ragged role in the Eaton Affair— his reasons for bringing John into the cabinet or for devoting so much of his time to gathering evidence of Margaret's innocence, or the dubious justice in demanding that others accept his account of circumstances and follow his will.

Wanting an adversary upon whom to aim his frustration, Jackson, casting a wide net, inevitably began to concentrate on Calhoun. Ironically, the vice president and his wife were in South Carolina during most of Jackson's first year in office, though it is true that before returning home, Floride, describing Margaret as "a woman of reputation," refused to return a social call made by the secretary of war and his wife. Expecting loyalty, Jackson appreciated Van Buren's solicitation of the Eatons, a piece of conspicuous domestic diplomacy widely whispered about the capital. In early 1830 Adams wrote in his diary, "The Administration party is split up into a blue and a green faction upon this point of morals. . . . Calhoun heads the moral party, Van Buren that of the frail sisterhood." In this instance the fortunes of the frail were decidedly on the rise. As the Eaton Affair raged, Jackson praised his secretary of state's capabilities to Overton: "Permit me . . . to say of Mr. Van Buren that I have found him every thing that I could desire him to be, and believe him not only deserving *my* confidence, but the *confidence* of the *nation*." He appeared to be making arrangements for a successor. Jackson pointedly referred in the note to "the most cordial good feeling" between Van Buren and Major Eaton—"It gives me," he assured Overton, "pleasure."[21]

Calhoun's failure to best Van Buren for Jackson's favor hinged, of course, on more than Margaret's wavering reputation. Beholden in South Carolina to uncompromising critics of the federal tariff and indifferent to Jackson's brewing opposition to the National Bank, soon to exceed even the Eaton Affair in its repercussions, he invariably lost the General's confidence. Van Buren then swooped in and claimed the prize. In a deft maneuver that deepened Jackson's respect for him, the secretary of state tendered his resignation in the spring of 1831. He recognized the cabinet's paralysis and the president's corresponding difficulty in removing those officials snubbing the Eatons without drawing attention to the reason why. But if Van Buren—and Eaton—resigned on the more general justification of disharmony, then Jackson had an excuse to conduct a purge and begin anew.

The president, so Van Buren maintained in an autobiography, initially resisted his retirement—"Never, Sir!"—though during a four-hour ride around the capital, the secretary crafted a compelling argument.[22] Two days later, after consulting with Eaton, William Lewis, and Postmaster William T. Barry, Jackson accepted Van Buren's proposal. Accordingly, over several tense days in May the secretaries of state, treasury, war, and navy, and the attorney general, all resigned.

The Eatons, perhaps nursing pride, remained in Washington until September. By this time a definite break between Jackson and Calhoun had occurred, and John Eaton used it to explain the friction in the president's previous cabinet. Four days before departing, he presented the capital with "MR. EATON'S REPLY," a massive conspiracy theory filling the pages of the *Washington Globe*. "Their plan," he wrote of the vice president's supporters, "was that General Jackson should be president but for four years, and that Mr. Calhoun should succeed him." Van Buren's unexpected ascension presumably upended this scheme, and in need of reinforcements, the Calhounites worked to remove Eaton from the cabinet, that a Calhoun man might take his place. "All the visiting cards that were ever printed and circulated in this city," he insisted, referring to the kerfuffle among cabinet wives, "were as nothing, compared to this grand—this important design." Margaret took the same line in a memoir, writing, "The fact is, John C. Calhoun and his friends were at the bottom of this whole business."[23]

The Eatons' eventual removal from the capital proved a little humiliating for its principals, and according to Van Buren, Margaret never forgave Jackson for this unwanted exile. After the cabinet resignations were announced and she was now "sensible of the change in her position," Van Buren and Jackson paid a social call at the Eaton home and were treated with evident reserve:

> Our reception was to the last degree formal and cold, and what greatly surprised me was that the larger share of the chilling ingredient in her manner and conversation fell to the General. Since my first acquaintance with her there had been no time when such a change towards myself would have very much astonished me. We staid only long enough to enable us to judge whether this exhibition was that of a passing freak or a matured sentiment, and after we had fairly quitted the house, I said to my companion—"There has been some mistake here." His only reply was "It is strange" with a shrug. As the topic was obviously not attractive it was dropped, but I was satisfied that our brief interview had been sufficient to convince him

that in his past anxiety on her account he had at least overrated her own sensibilities.[24]

John Eaton briefly held the presidency of the Ohio and Chesapeake Canal Company before Jackson made him governor of the Florida Territory (1834) and then minister to Spain (1836), where he and Margaret remained until recalled by Van Buren in 1840. A number of small strains and transgressions, including keeping only token contact with Washington, did the ambassador in—with Jackson's blessing. "I regret to hear the unaccountable silence of Major Eaton," the old General wrote Van Buren. "My rule was where my friend failed to his duty faithfully I removed him sooner than an enemy." Apparently in reply, Margaret spread rumors of Van Buren's unsuccessful "attempt" to court her young daughter Virginia. The Spanish government, in any case, thought Eaton a "most stupid man . . . entirely destitute of talent."[25]

Back in America, John Eaton became a Whig and, perhaps in some attitude of cold revenge, supported William Henry Harrison against Van Buren in the 1840 election. According to the latter, Jackson showed his disgust by cutting off communication with his former friend—"Gen. Jackson . . . silently closed the troublesome relations that had existed between them by turning to the wall the face of his portrait, which hung in the drawing room at the Hermitage."[26] Four years later, however, the two men reconciled when Eaton brought to Jackson a cache of old correspondence. Jackson died the following year and Eaton in 1856. In 1859, the year she turned sixty, Margaret married Antonio Buchignani, a nineteen-year-old Italian immigrant, dance instructor, and self-described descendent of royalty. A few years into their marriage, he stole her money and returned to Italy with one of his stepgranddaughters. Margaret received a divorce in 1869 and died a decade later; then first lady Lucy Webb Hayes sent flowers to the funeral.

33

Economy and Expansion

In 1806 Congress authorized construction of the Cumberland Road to replace the old foot and wagon traces connecting the Potomac and Ohio rivers. Built between 1811 and 1837, it commenced in western Maryland and stopped at Vandalia, Illinois, some seventy miles east of St. Louis. Jefferson thought the artery an excellent way to unify an increasingly extended country. Despite such evident progress, however, the employment of federal funds to advance internal improvements in America remained controversial. The more states' rights–minded pointed out that Congress lacked the Constitution's explicit authority to make such allocations. In his last official act as president, Madison, concerned with the rapid pace of post–War of 1812 nationalism, had vetoed the Bonus Bill, designed to earmark for internal improvements the presumed revenue bonus generated from the newly established National Bank. In 1822 Monroe exercised his only presidential veto on a bill authorizing the introduction of tolls to pay for repairs along a government-financed thoroughfare—he thought such projects were the province of state governments. Neither man, however, was particularly consistent on the issue. Madison had signed bills extending the Cumberland Road, and Monroe believed that the Constitution's general welfare clause might be massaged so as to permit federal money to be funneled toward such improvements. Two generations into the life of the republic, in other words, the government's relationship to public works remained uncertain and inconsistent.

Western states like Kentucky, short of funds and eager to promote development, leaned toward a nationalist approach to improvements. In

that spirit, Kentucky congressman Robert P. Letcher, a Clay ally, introduced a bill in April 1830 to extend the Cumberland Road from the
Ohio River town of Maysville to Lexington, sixty miles to the southwest.
After three days' debate, the bill passed the House 102–85. Jackson then
asked Van Buren his opinion of the legislation, and the secretary of state
responded with a long denunciation. The president thought the paper
exceedingly strong. He replied to Van Buren on May 4:

> I have been engaged to day as long as my head and eyes would per-
> mit, poring over the manuscript you handed me; as far as I have
> been able to decipher it I think it one of the most lucid expositions
> of the Constitution and historical accounts of the departure by Con-
> gress from its true principles that I have ever met with. It furnishes
> clear views upon the constitutional powers of Congress. The ina-
> bility of Congress under the Constitution to apply the funds of the
> Government to private, not national purposes I never had a doubt
> of. The Kentucky road bill involves this very power and I think it
> right boldly to meet it at the threshold.[1]

Understanding Jackson well, Van Buren, after thanking him for
his "favorable opinion," ventured that the bill constituted a conspiracy designed to angle the president into either accepting improvement
projects that lacked a national scope or risk offending the friends of
public works. The strategy, he argued, involved "draw[ing] you into the
approval of a Bill most emphatically *local* [the entirety of the proposed
Maysville Road being in Kentucky] . . . or to compel you to take a stand
against internal improvements generally, and thus draw to their aid all
those who are interested in the ten thousand schemes which events and
the course of the Government for a few past years have engendered."
He assured Jackson that an appropriately worded veto would send to all
parties the proper message—"I think I see land."[2]

Less than two weeks later, on the 15th, the Maysville Bill passed the
Senate (24–18). Over the next few days the president, Van Buren, and
Tennessee congressman James Polk worked on a reply—a veto. Anticipating this, several western Democrats, eager for improvements in
their own states, tried to dissuade Jackson from killing the bill, a few of
whom showed up at the Executive Mansion one morning to make their
case directly. Later that same day Van Buren, in a separate meeting with

the president, inquired of their progress. "Don't mind that!" Jackson responded, pointing to the veto message resting in his breast pocket, "the thing is here."[3]

That thing opened with Jackson's pledge of support for public works and "the improvement of our country by means of roads and canals." He further acknowledged, however, that a "difference of opinion in the mode of contributing to it" existed between himself and Congress. In regard to this particular bill the president disparaged its local nature, identifying "an interior town" in Kentucky—Lexington—as its chief beneficiary. "Such grants have always been professedly under the control of the general principle," he offered, providing a hasty lecture on the history of internal improvements, "that the works which might be thus aided should be 'of a general, not local, national, not State,' character." To ignore this rule, he argued, "would of necessity lead to the subversion of the federal system." He emphasized further the need for economy. "The appropriations for internal improvements are increasing beyond the available means of the Treasury," he argued, and "without a well-regulated system . . . the plain consequence must be either a continuance of the national debt or a resort to additional taxes." The bill's questionable legality also troubled Jackson, who called it "indispensably necessary" that an amendment to the Constitution delegating and defining the parameters of federal spending on public works be put in place "if it be the wish of the people" to seek additional funding for roads and canals. He concluded by repeating his qualified praise for improvements, "as long as the encouragement of domestic manufactures is directed to national ends."[4]

Though Jackson's message recognized Congress's right to employ federal funds for nationwide projects, it more deeply emphasized the president's concern that the promise of internal improvements could, when abused by office seekers, debase American politics. This unease he articulated perhaps most clearly when arguing two years later in another address that such appropriations promote "a mischievous and corrupting influence upon elections by holding out to the people the fallacious hope that the success of a certain candidate will make navigable their neighboring creek or river, bring commerce to their doors, and increase the value of their property. It thus favors combinations to squander the treasure of the country upon a multitude of local objects, as fatal to just legislation as to the purity of public men." The states' rights wing within the Democratic Party took heart in such neo-Jeffersonian sentiments. The old republican John Randolph said that Jackson's veto message "falls upon the ears like the music of other days."[5]

Defeated on the Maysville Road, Congress quickly passed three additional appropriation bills that same month—to authorize the sale of stock in both the Washington Turnpike Company (connecting Frederick, Maryland, to the capital) and the Louisville and Portland Canal Company (a waterway around the falls of the Ohio River at Louisville), and to improve various harbors by making subsidies for light-boats, lighthouses, and buoys. An irritated Jackson, no doubt regarding these fresh requests as a rebuke to his Maysville message and unwilling to allocate public funds to private corporations, vetoed the bills on the basis, so he said, of economy. "Congress has this day adjourned," he wrote to Coffee on the 31st, "after a very stormy session, and on Saturday night and Sunday morning, after they knew the Treasury was exhausted by former appropriations, passed many laws appropriating nearly one million of dollars—two of which, containing upwards of half a million, I have retained under consideration until next session of congress, having before put my veto upon one & today upon another."[6]

Jackson's four vetoes in May 1830 are significant on several accounts. Most immediately they slowed momentum toward the kind of extensive outlays for public works proposed by men like Adams and Clay, thus indicating the president's hesitancy to advance economic development through the central government—essentially anticipating his veto two years later of the second Bank of the United States. Jackson believed that such federal aid to financiers and industrialists resulted in an unfair advantage to these special interests at the expense of other Americans. The vetoes further buttressed the president's popularity in many parts of the South, while also prefacing the enlargement of presidential power that came to define his tenure in office. Over two terms he used the veto a dozen times, more than all of his predecessors combined, half of whom had never employed it. "The Presidential veto has hitherto been exercised with great reserve," Adams wrote that June, but Jackson "has rejected four in three days. The overseer ascendancy is complete."[7]

By invoking the specter of "overseer ascendancy," Adams identified the southern hold on public power that shaped the early American republic. Questions of national expansion along the country's Gulf Coast began to be raised early in Jackson's first term, building toward a crisis that would eventually lead, in the 1840s, to the controversial admission of Texas into the Union. The Adams-Onís Treaty (1819) had defined the boundary between the United States and New Spain, though Mexico's independence from (Old) Spain in 1821 opened the door for Jackson to seek a new settlement. Resolved to take Texas off the Mexicans' hands, he ached to negotiate a purchase; though concerned with expenditures on internal improvements, he was willing to commit $5 million (some $147 million in current dollars) toward this enterprise. He enumerated several reasons for proceeding in an August 1829 communication with Van Buren: the safety of New Orleans demanded it; fresh western lands could be used "for the purpose of concentrating the Indians" to be removed from the East; and a distant "natural boundary" (the Rio Grande) promised to prevent border disputes.[8]

Just one year earlier, American minister to Mexico Joel Poinsett, working under the previous administration, had negotiated an

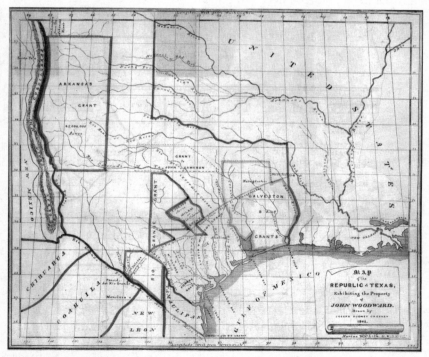

A longtime advocate of American expansion, Jackson coveted Texas—seen here as a republic in a map from 1842, along with various rivers and grants—which he unsuccessfully sought to purchase during his presidency.

agreement recognizing the Sabine River—the present-day line separating Texas and Louisiana—as the U.S.-Mexican border. Now, when Poinsett, upon Jackson's orders, pushed for the more southerly Rio Grande
boundary, the affronted Mexican government requested his recall. Jackson responded by replacing him with an old military acquaintance, Colonel Anthony Butler, in the post of chargé d'affaires to Mexico. Described
by one historian as a "free-wheeling, fast-talking land speculator," Butler formerly served in the South Carolina and Kentucky legislatures. He
knew no Spanish, liked to lecture, and seemed "thoroughly ignorant of
diplomatic protocol"; the president expected him to move quickly.[9] For
several years the Mexican government, looking to augment its sparsely
populated northern border, had pursued a policy of Anglo immigration
into Texas. This infusion of whites impelled Jackson's interest in acquir-
ing a new frontier line; he believed, accurately as things turned out, that
these *Texians* would soon take power for themselves, and he wished for
the area to be incorporated into the United States before that uncertain
day. "I feel great anxiety with regard to the boundary between us and
Mexico," he wrote to Butler in the summer of 1831:

> It is very important that it should be permanently fixed, before the
> meeting of our next Congress. I cannot, therefore, refrain from
> again bringing it to your view, and urging that no pains be spared
> to accomplish this desirable object. . . . I am just informed that daily
> preparations, by a wealthy company, are making in Boston, New
> York, and New Orleans to transport, this Summer, ten thousand
> emigrants to that Country. When these get possession and become
> permanently fixed, they will soon avail themselves of some pre-
> text to throw off the Mexican authority and form an independent
> Government of their own. This would beget great disquietude, and
> might eventually endanger the peace and tranquility of both coun-
> tries that now so happily exist.[10]

Thus did Jackson insist upon the plural virtues of Texas statehood. It
promised both Mexico and America border security while ensuring, as
he put it, that "adventure[r]s from the United States, acting in concert
with disaffected citizens of Mexico" were prevented from declaring an
independent republic.[11] The government of Mexico thought otherwise,
however, and kept Butler at bay.

The Texas question resurfaced repeatedly over the next several years, frustrating Jackson, who failed during his presidency to acquire the territory. "She is the Key," he wrote in retirement, "to our safety in the south and West."[12] More broadly, the pursuit of Texas was emblematic of the contradictions in Jackson's attempts to both economize and expand. He criticized the country's (mainly northern) economic nationalists for promoting an American System of internal development that looked to the central state for guidance, energy, and funds; his Maysville Road veto, among others, condemned this effort. In the dubious name of national security, however, he seemed altogether eager to allocate the public's monies for the acquisition of territory that would primarily benefit a southern cotton kingdom looking to control the Gulf Coast. In such preferences, choices, and initiatives did Jackson pursue an agenda that subsidized the expansion of slavery deeper into the continent, deeper into the century.

Part V

A WORLD OF ENEMIES

My course have been always to put my enemies at defiance.
Andrew Jackson, 1839

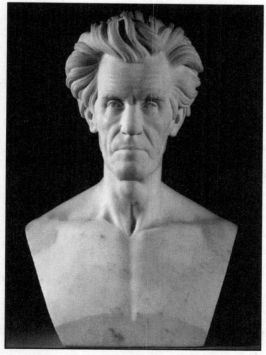

Jackson's tenacious resolve—evident in his Indian removal policy and his "war" on the second Bank of the United States—is captured in this marble bust by the German sculptor Ferdinand Pettrich.

34

The Graves of Their Fathers

Following the War of 1812, the long-standing Indian question assumed a paramount importance. Between the censuses of 1810 and 1830 the combined populations of Alabama, Mississippi, Georgia, and Tennessee trebled from roughly 550,000 to more than 1,640,000; this latter figure included some 50,000 Indians.[1] Jackson referred to these southern tribes in his first message to Congress in December 1829, arguing that the federal government pursued self-defeating policies by trying to both introduce "the arts of civilization" to the native peoples while simultaneously taking every "opportunity to purchase their lands and thrust them farther into the wilderness." Those Indians seeking progress, he continued, now presumed "to erect an independent government within the limits of Georgia and Alabama." Appealing to the Constitutional clause declaring, "no new State shall be formed or erected within the jurisdiction of any other State," he found the Indians' assertion of autonomy untenable. Perhaps looking to defend the southern right to removal, Jackson identified several northern states as justly jealous of their own authority. "Would the people of Maine," he asked of one, "permit the Penobscot tribe to erect an independent government" in Bar Harbor? Claiming that continued contact with whites only doomed the Indians to destruction, he argued for their relocation. "This emigration should be voluntary," he stressed in a now famously shameful statement, "for it would be as cruel as unjust to compel the aboriginies to abandon the graves of their fathers and seek a home in a distant land."[2]

Jackson's Indian policy largely followed the aggressive course of earlier presidents. The great difference is that Jackson possessed the military power in the 1830s to make removal a reality. A half century earlier George Washington, like Jackson an old Indian fighter and land speculator, believed that "the gradual extension of our Settlements will as certainly cause the Savage, as the Wolf to retire." Officially the Washington administration embraced a program of civilization—coaxing Indians into becoming Christian farmers living in nuclear families—and recognized tribal rights. In practice, however, it continually pressed upon Indian sovereignty and in the Treaty of Holston (1791) prompted the Cherokees to sell off a large section of their territory in eastern Tennessee in return for an annual payment and the promise of "perpetual peace" with the United States. According to historian Colin G. Calloway, Washington, both in and out of government service, had "spent a lifetime turning Indian homelands into real estate for himself and his nation."[3]

Jefferson also believed that the republic's future depended on the acquisition of native lands. Though interested intellectually in Indian history, language, and forms of government—the latter subject receiving respectful attention in his 1781 book *Notes on the State of Virginia*—he invariably worked as president to undermine Indian autonomy. In 1803, the year of the Louisiana Purchase, Jefferson counseled General William Henry Harrison on how to use indebtedness as a tool to extract territory belonging to native peoples:

> The decrease of game rendering their subsistence by hunting insufficient, we wish to draw them to agriculture, to spinning & weaving. . . . When they withdraw themselves to the culture of a small piece of land, they will percieve how useless to them are their extensive forests, and will be willing to pare them off from time to time in exchange for necessaries for their farms & families. to promote this disposition to exchange lands which they have to spare & we want, for necessaries, which we have to spare & they want, we shall push our trading houses, and be glad to see the good & influential individuals among them run in debt, because we observe that when these debts get beyond what the individuals can pay, they become willing to lop th[em off] by a cession of lands.[4]

In correspondence Jefferson sometimes seemed open to the idea of whites and Indians living side by side, though his words on this subject sound wooden and unconvincing. Perhaps more telling is his suspicion, communicated to John Adams in 1812, that there will always be a "backward" contingent of natives and "we shall be obliged to drive them, with the beasts of the forest into the Stony mountains."[5]

Following the Treaty of Ghent, the United States negotiated increasingly from a position of strength as those Indian peoples formerly tied to the British were now without allies. "They have, in great measure, ceased to be an object of terror," Secretary of War John C. Calhoun informed the House of Representatives in a December 1818 report on Indian trade, "and have become that of commiseration. The time seems to have arrived when our policy towards them should undergo an important change." Anticipating Jackson's position, Calhoun said of the natives, "They neither are, in fact, nor ought to be, considered as independent nations. Our views of their interests, and not their own, ought to govern them." Calhoun's superior, President Monroe, seemingly caught between the poles of removal and what he called "the great purpose of their civilization," recommended on multiple occasions to Congress legislation to pursue both a policy of voluntary emigration and one that aimed to elevate, educate, and domesticate the Indians. Presumably having undergone "a complete change in their manners," they might retain their land rights.[6]

But this view proved untenable. Monroe's successor, John Quincy Adams, faced fierce pressure from the state of Georgia, which removed most of its Creek population during his presidency. Adams complained about this but chose not to interfere. In a January 1828 diary entry he exhibited, apropos Georgia's still extant Cherokee population, a wide register of opinions, ranging from disapproval of Indian sovereignty, to anger over white efforts at removal, to support for the citizenship of native peoples. The germane passage reads in part:

The Cherokees in Georgia have now been making a written Constitution; but this imperium in imperio [a state within a state] is impracticable; and in the instances of the New-York Indians removed to Green Bay, and of the Cherokees removed to the Territory of Arkansas, we have scarcely given them time to build their wigwams before we [in government] are called upon by our own people to drive them out again. My own opinion is that the most benevolent course towards them, would be to give them the rights and subject them to the duties of citizens as a part of our own people.[7]

Historians have generally regarded Adams as equivocal on the Indian question. Michael D. Green writes in regard to removal, "Adams's sensitivities required that it be done legally, but there was not disagreement between [him and the Georgians] on the goal"; Robert Remini observes that "Adams felt . . . removal was probably the only policy to follow but he could not bring himself to implement it"; and David S. Reynolds argues that "although Adams later criticized Jackson's Indian policy as ruthless, Adams's irresolution had the same result as Jackson's firmness: the removal of natives from their ancestral lands."[8] One might add that two of Adams's most decisive actions on this subject were decidedly unsympathetic. He refused, while negotiating the Treaty of Ghent, to consider an independent Indian state in the Old Northwest, and as noted, he subsequently abetted Jackson's destruction of Seminole villages in Spanish Florida. Placing both Adams and Jackson in context, the logic of United States Indian policy up to 1830 pointed to the westward expulsion of the native peoples. It was a project well underway politically, culturally, and economically by the time Old Hickory assumed office.

That many if any of the men mentioned in the previous paragraphs sincerely wished the civilization project to succeed is doubtful.[9] The remaking of native communities along white lines is, rather, precisely what most whites resisted. As "savages" the Indians were ripe for removal, but as "civilized" their expulsion would expose decades of deceit and Anglo cant. Some natives, no doubt, recognized this hypocrisy even as they attempted to use it to their advantage when dealing with the federal government. Such is the case of Cherokee chiefs John Ross and William Hicks. Both were mixed-race, educated, and had welcomed Christian missionaries into Cherokee territory. Ross resembled Jackson in several respects—he engaged in land speculation, bought and sold enslaved people, and affected the mien of a southern gentleman. In 1825 he and Hicks addressed a long communication to President Adams asking for federal assistance to prevent the state of Georgia from confiscating lands belonging "to the Cherokee people whom we represent." They insisted that unlike "certain tribes" in the South who went through a process of "degradation and extinction," the Cherokees had successfully adopted white standards. It was now incumbent upon those whites, they maintained, to make good on their promises to respect this achievement. "If Indian civilization and preservation is sincerely desired, and is considered worthy [of] the serious attention of the United States," they wrote, it must become the government's policy to "never urge the removal of those tribes who are now successfully embracing the habits of civilized man within their limits."[10]

Such carefully argued appeals meant little to Jackson. As president he reduced the complexities of removal to a simple certainty: neither Alabama nor Georgia would allow a separate Cherokee nation to exist within their respective borders. Accordingly, he counseled the Deep South's Indians in his first annual message to Congress "to emigrate beyond the Mississippi or submit to the laws of those States." Of course he knew that "those states" showed little interest in permitting their native peoples to remain. Though still braying about civilization, Jackson deemed removal the only conceivable outcome other than outright annihilation. The question of justice, he shrugged, was now beside the point. "It is too late to inquire," he stated, "whether it was just in the United States to include [the Indians] and their territory within the bounds of the new States, whose limits they could control. That step can not be retraced." Identifying the Narragansett, Delaware, and Mohegan among the "dead tribes" in the North, he maintained that the same fate presently faced the Creek, Cherokee, and Choctaw. He did not mention those thousands of decidedly undead Iroquois in New York then living peacefully in the midst of white settlements.[11]

Jackson explicitly called in this annual message for Congress to pass legislation putting in motion a removal process that empowered government officials to negotiate for native lands. "I suggest for your consideration the propriety of setting apart an ample district west of the Mississippi," he offered as direction, "and without the limits of any State or Territory now formed, to be guaranteed to the Indian tribes as long as they shall occupy it, each tribe having a distinct control over the portion designated for its use." Georgia knew now that it could count on Jackson's support.[12]

There were roughly twenty-five thousand Georgia Creeks in the 1820s. The state claimed that as one of the original thirteen colonies, it preserved a charter right to deal peremptorily with its domain. It noted further that in exchange for ceding its western territory to the federal government in 1802 (much of which became Alabama and Mississippi), that government had promised to extinguish Indian titles in the state. During the Monroe presidency, Secretary of War Calhoun had suggested such a removal plan be put in place, though it gained little support in Congress. Instead, a small group of Creek chiefs agreed in the Treaty of Indian Springs (1825) to sell their lands east of the Chattahoochee River to Georgia and Alabama for an equal amount in the West, along with an allocation of $400,000 (approximately $11 million in current dollars). Representing only eight of the forty-six Creek towns, the chiefs, some of whom accepted bribes, had no right to conclude the compact. Having alienated tribal lands by operating in league with their white allies, several of the Creek signatories were subsequently executed by warriors commanded by other Creek chiefs.[13]

Though he had signed the Indian Springs accord, Adams, informed of its fraudulent nature, called for renewed negotiations. These resulted several months later in the Treaty of Washington. Voiding the previous agreement, it authorized the cession of some Indian lands to the state of Georgia while recognizing others, primarily a thin strip along the Alabama-Georgia border, as belonging to the Creeks. Unwilling to accept native sovereignty in his state, Governor George Troup ignored the new accord and ordered a survey of the treaty lands, including those reserved for the Indians. Troup further threatened to employ the state's militia if Adams sent federal soldiers to Georgia—and the governor got his way. "By 1826," two scholars have written, "Georgia's efforts had largely achieved the expulsion of the Creek Nation."[14]

Having decimated the Creeks, the Georgia assembly then turned its attention to the state's Cherokees. In July 1827 the Cherokee Nation, eager to counter stereotypes of savagery, drafted a U.S.-style constitution complete with executive, legislative, and judicial branches. A symbol of tribal sovereignty (and civilization), it only antagonized Troup and the legislature. In December of the following year the assembly responded by passing laws extending the state's police, judicial, and legal power over Georgia's remaining Indians. Three months later Jackson assumed the presidency. Perhaps emboldened by this, the legislature subsequently approved the Cherokee Code, which, among other articles, annexed Indian lands, forbade Cherokees from testifying against whites in court, and prohibited Indians from meeting in groups.[15] By this time, Jackson had determined to settle the removal question forever.

Working with Democratic leaders, the president pushed through a removal bill in the spring of 1830. It cleared the Senate (28–19) in late April and far more narrowly negotiated the House (102–97) the following month; Jackson signed the bill on May 28. It endorsed the establishment of lands west of the Mississippi to be carved into several districts and given to the Indians in exchange for their eastern settlements. It further promised assistance, protection, and money for those forced into the removal process. The bill's sectional nature surfaced for all to see. Sixty-one of seventy-seven southern congressmen voted for the act while more than eighty northern legislators voted against it. Jackson understood the bill's controversial nature and never asked for an explicit removal of the Indians. There is no language in the act permitting the government to take land unless it be ceded by treaty. Jackson could thus claim continuance of the policies pursued by his predecessors, trading land in the West for land in the East. Future president James Buchanan, a Pennsylvania Democrat and chairman of the House Judiciary Committee, dubiously guaranteed his colleagues during the removal debate that Jackson never intended "using the power of the government to drive that unfortunate race of men across the Mississippi."[16]

Political assurances aside, critics of the act attacked both Jackson and U.S. Indian policy. The Christian missionary Jeremiah Evarts, writing under the nom de plume William Penn (the Quaker founder of Pennsylvania whose 1683 peace treaty with the Lenape held for more than seventy years), noted the government's historical recognition of Cherokee sovereignty through numerous treaties, and argued that these covenants took precedent over Georgia state law. They further, he persisted, obligated the United States to protect Cherokee territory from illegal incursions by whites.[17] In reviewing this history, Evarts touched on one of the bill's great underlying contradictions. For though Jackson insisted on the errancy of treating tribes as sovereign entities, he had himself done so many times as a military officer. In such parleys, Evarts pointed out, he represented a government that recognized Cherokee autonomy.

In the Senate, New Jersey's Theodore Frelinghuysen held the floor for parts of three days, correctly identifying the true intent of the bill as a forced removal of the Cherokees rather than a voluntary program. Like Evarts, he argued that the rights of Indians in Georgia were clearly protected by their treaties with the U.S. government. He further raised the obvious issue of racism embedded in the legislation. "Do the obligations of justice change with the color of the skin?" he asked. "Is it one of the prerogatives of the white man, that he may disregard the dictates of moral principles, when an Indian shall be concerned?"[18] In reply, Georgia senator John Forsyth insisted that nothing in the act authorized a forced deportation and that to suggest otherwise revealed among some of his colleagues an ugly anti-southern prejudice. Northerners, he contended, were hypocritical on the relocation riddle considering their own convenient expulsions of the Pequods, Hurons, Senecas, and Eries, among other tribes.

Resisting removal, the Cherokee Nation sued in 1830 for a federal injunction against laws passed by Georgia designed to deprive them of their rights. The Nation's lawyer, former attorney general William Wirt, maintained that the Cherokees enjoyed the sanction of self-government as a separate entity, a status long recognized by the United States in its many treaties with the native peoples. The court heard the case but refused to rule on its merits. Chief Justice Marshall, rather, speaking for the majority in March 1831, noted that as the Indian tribes resided within the borders of the United States and accepted its protection, they were not foreign nations; he described them as "domestic dependent nations" and thus lacking the right to initiate an action in the U.S. courts. Two justices, Smith Thompson of New York and Joseph Story of Massachusetts, dissented, arguing that the Cherokees did constitute a foreign state. Dissatisfied with his own ruling, Marshall, seeking, as he put it, "a proper case, with proper parties," contacted Wirt over the summer and suggested that he "identify an individual with . . . standing whose rights were denied before a Georgia state court." Marshall and his colleagues could then, through the appeal process, rule on the state bench's decision.[19]

The following year such a case did come before the court—*Worcester v. Georgia*. Briefly, two Christian missionaries, Samuel Worcester and Elihu Butler, had been arrested for living in the Cherokee Nation, thus violating a Georgia law preventing the presence of whites (unless licensed by the state) on native lands. The men were sentenced to four years of hard labor. Their appeal went to the Supreme Court, which voided the convictions on the grounds that states had no criminal jurisdiction in Indian country. As the inheritor of British rights on former British lands, the United States, Marshall noted, enjoyed the sole right to negotiate with Indian nations. The order for the detainees' release (they were being held in a prison in Milledgeville, then the state capital) came down on March 5, 1832; twelve days later the court went into recess, not to reconvene again for several months. During this break Story, accurately reading the situation, wrote to a colleague of his concern that the court's decision might go unheeded:

> Georgia is full of anger and violence. What she will do, it is difficult to say. Probably she will resist the execution of our judgment, and if she does, I do not believe the President will interfere unless public opinion among the religious of the Eastern and Western and Middle States should be brought to bear strong upon him. The rumor is, that he has told the Georgians he will do nothing. I, for one, feel quite easy on this subject, be the event what it may. The Court has done its duty. Let the Nation now do theirs.[20]

The following month Jackson justified Story's suspicion, writing to John Coffee, "The decision of the supreme court has fell still born, and they find that it cannot coerce Georgia to yield to its mandate." True enough, the Georgia superior court refused to reverse its ruling and free Worcester and Butler. An obdurate Governor Wilson Lumpkin insisted on seeing the missionaries hang before going so far as to "submit to this decision made by a few superannuated *life estate* judges." For his part, Jackson backed Georgia, denouncing the court's "wicked" decision and thus signaling that states might enact within their borders legislation hostile to tribal sovereignty. Having carried his point and wishing to avoid making martyrs, the president prevailed upon Lumpkin to pardon Worcester and Butler, who were released in January 1833.[21]

By that time, the unrelenting machinery of removal had commenced in earnest. While on his American travels, Alexis de Tocqueville watched from the left bank of an ice-occluded Mississippi as a number of Choctaws, driven from their lands during an uncommonly cold winter, briefly congregated in Memphis. They came in families, some ill, some old, some near death. They took what they could and renounced the rest. "All the Indians had already got into the boat that was to carry them across," Tocqueville reported, "as soon as [their dogs] finally realized that they were being left behind forever, they all together raised a terrible howl and plunged into the . . . waters of the Mississippi to swim after their masters."[22]

In supporting Georgia, Jackson facilitated a new phase in Indian removal, though it unexpectedly left the president vulnerable in his dealings with another southern state. Long emphatic on the federal tariff's unconstitutionality, South Carolina observed carefully Georgia's refusal to comply with Marshall's decision. This successful assault by a state on a Supreme Court ruling fairly begged notice. Some believed that with Jackson's blessing a self-willed southern legislature had effectively nullified federal law, possibly establishing a precedent for other aggrieved parties. Thus in watching Georgia's fight against Indian rights, some defenders of states' rights felt emboldened to challenge the central government on yet other issues.

35

Cornering Calhoun

As the oldest president yet to be sworn in (61 years and 354 days), Jackson, so a host of parlor room politicians presumed, needed to identify a successor quickly. Early on Van Buren looked a bad bet. Once the estimable ally of Crawford and the caucus, both abhorrent to the General, Van Buren came a little late to the Jackson campaign. Calhoun, by contrast, bore all the earmarks of an apprentice president. His relations with Jackson were correct and cordial, his crowded résumé impressed, and he fit a certain if unstated regional requirement. A former cabinet official, vice president under two men, and a southerner, he seemed destined, so many assumed, to become the nation's eighth president. Contrarily, New Yorkers like Van Buren were customarily expected to rise no higher than the second slot; already three—Aaron Burr, George Clinton, and Daniel Tompkins—had served a combined five vice presidential terms. Crucially, Jackson considered Calhoun personally loyal, a faithful political friend in a city filled with critics and careerists. Back in the difficult winter of 1825, just days after Adams captured the presidency in the House's contingent election, a seething Jackson wrote to a Tennessee colleague, "I have, *now*, no doubt, but I have had opposed to me all the influence of the Cabinet, except Calhoune."[1]

Early in Jackson's White House residency, however, relations between the two men began to sour. Believing that the vice president and his wife had joined the general cabinet snubbing of the Eatons played a part, though a far more consequential issue—the constitutionality of the federal tariff—seriously divided them. Behind the tariff debate lay the subject of states' rights and behind that the footing and future of slavery.

247

All were aired in a riveting impromptu Senate debate between Robert Hayne of South Carolina and Massachusetts's Daniel Webster over several late January days in 1830. What began as a discussion of public land policy quickly grew into an unexpected and spirited deliberation on the nature of power in the republic. Summarizing a position staked out (anonymously) by Calhoun in the *South Carolina Exposition and Protest*, an 1828 tariff-bashing treatise made (in)famous for arguing that states might veto—nullify—federal laws within their borders, Hayne declared the Constitution merely a treaty among sovereign states rather than an ironclad compact creating a single nation. Webster replied by describing the American federal system as one entrusted to a central government "made for the people, made by the people, and answerable to the people," words later to be paraphrased by Lincoln in the Gettysburg Address. He further endorsed the idea of national supremacy, refused to accept the argument that sovereignty ultimately resided in the states, and famously concluded his oration with a tribute to "Liberty *and* Union, now and forever, one and inseparable!" On the subject of states' rights Jackson, the Tennessee slaveholder, could find considerable common ground with men like Calhoun and Hayne, but as an old patriot and a retired major general in the U.S. Army, he refused to entertain the legitimacy of nullification, which he believed synonymous with secession and treason.

That April, the Democratic Party's annual Jefferson Day Dinner provided its states' rights wing with an opportunity to press Jackson on the tariff. In office for more than a year, he seemed content with the 1828 impost, which many southerners believed both unconstitutional and injurious to their agrarian economy. A day before the event a colleague, having read the proceeding's program in the *United States Telegraph*, established in 1826 as a Jackson newspaper but truer to Calhoun's point of view, advised Jackson to look at the notice. After perusing the piece, the General concluded that "the celebration was to be a *nullification affair altogether*."[2] Infuriated, he determined to boost nationalism instead.

At the dinner Jackson gamely sat through two-dozen toasts to states' rights, several extolling Georgia's recent efforts to remove its Indians. When his own turn came, he cut these men down in six quick words— "Our Union: It must be preserved"—which caused a flummoxed Hayne to request that "Our *federal* Union" be substituted instead. Having delivered his message, Jackson easily agreed. "There was no misunderstanding the effect it produced upon the company," Van Buren later wrote, "neither could any sentiment from another have occasioned a tithe of the sensation that was witnessed throughout the large assemblage." But Calhoun did try. Tendering the next toast, he publicly crossed swords with Jackson: "The Union—next to our liberty the most dear; may we all remember that it can only be preserved by respecting the rights of the States and distributing equally the benefit and burden of the Union." Amid such high dinner theater Van Buren offered a perfectly nonpartisan pledge, one compatible with his reputation for smiling on all sides in self-interest: "Mutual forbearance and reciprocal concessions; thro' their agency the Union was established—the patriotic spirit from which they emanated will forever sustain it."[3]

Some months after the dinner Joel Poinsett, the former South Carolina congressman and ambassador to Mexico, and a critic of nullification, wrote Jackson of affairs in Charleston. The tariff's critics, he stated, were now claiming the popular president as one of their own: "The Nullifiers try to make us believe that the union party are acting against your wishes." In return, Jackson reaffirmed his negative view on nullification:

> I had supposed that every one acquainted with me knew, that I was opposed to the nulifying doctrine, and my toast at the Jefferson dinner was sufficient evidence of the fact. I am convinced there is not one member of Congress who are not convinced of this fact, for on all occasions I have been open & free upon this subject. The South Carolinians, as a whole, are too patriotic to adopt such *mad projects* as the nulifyers of that state propose.[4]

Revisiting a favorite formula, Jackson framed nullification as a doctrine advanced by freaks and elites, the purveyors of "mad projects" out of tune with the people "as a whole."

As Calhoun's prospects for succeeding Jackson dimmed, Van Buren's steadily increased. The Jefferson Day Dinner demonstrated serious cracks in the Democratic coalition, and the secretary of state insisted to Jackson that he, the General, must secure a second term for the good of the party. Not everyone agreed. Calling such sentiments "ill timed" and "unadvised," *Telegraph* editor Duff Green, an extravagantly bewhiskered Missourian favorable to the *Exposition and Protest* position, wanted to hear a solid defense of states' rights from Jackson before begging him to run again. He soon learned how little his paper mattered. After William Lewis encouraged Pennsylvania Democrats to pass a resolution in Harrisburg renominating Jackson, Van Buren coaxed a caucus of New York Democrats in Albany to do the same. Party organizations in other states, including Ohio and New Hampshire, followed suit. Watching from afar, Adams called this clever choreography "a trick of Van Buren's against Calhoun."[5]

The aforementioned Kentucky journalist Amos Kendall, serving as a Treasury auditor and less officially in Jackson's Kitchen Cabinet (an informal circle of advisors), observed with some amusement as the Little Magician maneuvered frictionlessly into the president's favor. "Van Buren glides along as smoothly as oil and as silently as a cat," he wrote a colleague. "If he is managing at all, it is so adroitly that nobody perceives it. . . . He has the entire confidence of the President and all his personal friends, while Calhoun is fast losing it."[6]

A rigid logician, the vice president, gaunt, brooding, and highbrow, with an intensity suggested by penetrating, deep-set eyes, lacked Van Buren's ability to "glide." One Senate colleague, Dixon Lewis of Alabama, found him "too intelligent, too industrious, too intent on the struggle of politics to suit me except as an occasional companion."[7] He was also, some thought, too tied to his section. Jackson demanded personal loyalty, but for Calhoun South Carolina came first. This produced a definite and deep tension between the occupants of the nation's two highest political offices. Calhoun sometimes refused to publicly support the president's policies, while Jackson quietly chafed over the vice president's failure to temper Charleston's nullification party. The Eaton Affair and dueling Jefferson Day Dinner toasts had further distanced the two, when suddenly, destructively, the old Florida controversy flared up again.

Somehow Sam Houston had procured a pilfered copy of a September 1818 communication in which Monroe criticized Jackson's seizure of Spanish forts to then Secretary of War Calhoun: "Our view, of his powers, is decidedly different, from his." In the late winter of 1828 the contents of this letter had reached Jackson, who subsequently wrote to a colleague, "I cannot disguise . . . when the letter . . . reached me, it smelled so much of deception that my hair stood on end for an hour."[8] His irritation focused mainly on Monroe, though Calhoun was clearly if somewhat less directly implicated as well. Jackson did not pursue the matter with the South Carolinian at this time.

Others, however, were clearly interested in alienating Calhoun. At Van Buren's behest, James Hamilton, the third son of Alexander Hamilton, wrote to Georgia's Governor Forsyth requesting that he inquire of the now retired William Crawford if "the propriety or necessity for arresting and trying General Jackson was ever presented as a question for the deliberation of Mr. Monroe's Cabinet." Committing his version to paper in April 1830 and leaving aside his own determination in those meetings to see Jackson disciplined, Crawford apprised Forsyth, "Mr. Calhoun's proposition in the Cabinet was that Genl. Jackson should be punished in some form, or reprehended in some form, I am not positively certain which." On May 12 a transcript of this letter (endorsed by Forsyth as "A true copy from the original in my possession") was given to Jackson, providing the evidence he needed for an open rupture.[9] The president and the vice president, for many months at odds, could now go to war.

The day after receiving Crawford's testimony, Jackson wrote Calhoun: "That frankness which I trust has always characterised me thro' life, toward those with whom I have been in habits of friendship induces me to lay before you the enclosed copy of a letter from Wm. H. Crawford Esqr. . . . The statements and facts it presents, being so different from what I had heretofore understood to be correct, requires that it should be brought to your consideration." That same day—both men were in Washington—Calhoun told Jackson that he would soon send a communication addressing Crawford's accusations. For now, he wrote, "I must express my gratification, that the secret and mysterious attempts, which have been making by false insinuations for political purpose for years to injure my character, are at length brought to light."[10]

Later that month Calhoun formally replied to Jackson, in several crisp pages of political suicide. Denying Jackson any right to "question my conduct," the vice president defended his decision in 1818 to see Jackson disciplined—"I acted on that occasion in the discharge of a high official duty, and under responsibility to my conscience and my country only." Thus, he continued, "I do not place myself in the attitude of apologyzing." Underscoring Jackson's dubious conduct in Florida—and skirting the question of whether for several years he had given the General a false impression of his loyalty—Calhoun proceeded to insist upon the invasion's illegality and Jackson's abuse of his orders. He quoted for good measure a March 1818 message from Monroe to the House in which the president declared, "orders had been given to the General in command not to enter Florida, unless it be in pursuit of the enemy, and, in that case, to respect the Spanish Authority." Calhoun now claimed to have long presumed Jackson's awareness that, in this contentious matter, "I concurred in the opposite construction, which you gave to your orders."[11]

The following day, after attending a church service, Jackson read Calhoun's letter. He responded immediately with an icy if controlled anger: "I had a right to believe that you were my sincere friend, and until now, never expected to have occasion to say of you, in the languauge of Cesar—*et tu Brute*. The evidence which has brought me to this conclusion is abundantly Contained in your letter now before me. . . . Understanding you now, no further communication with you on this subject is necessary." That same month, as mentioned previously, Jackson had begun to collect the resignations of most of his cabinet officers. Clearly he sought to disencumber himself from the tangle of issues—the Eaton Affair, the tariff controversy, and the perils of presidential succession— sapping his administration's strength.[12]

Several months later, Calhoun hit back with a pamphlet printed for public consumption, "Correspondence Between Gen. Andrew Jackson and John C. Calhoun," a long and tiresome indictment containing mainly the germane letters between the president and the vice president pertaining to the Florida invasion. Calhoun no doubt considered the piece vindicatory but this airing of Democratic Party disharmony did him no good. Who, after all, other than the political opposition rallying around Clay, would benefit from such an unseemly display? Calhoun's desire to acquaint the nation with the "artful operations" of those seeking "my political destruction" underlined both his questionable judgment and deep sense of persecution. He sounded a bit like the ever-suspicious president he now opposed.[13]

In a perfectly uneven contest, Jackson got the better of Calhoun by far. Effective when identifying an enemy, he maneuvered the badly outflanked vice president into a rash and self-destructive explication of his actions. Pleased, he wrote confidently to Overton that Calhoun "has been cutting his own throat as fast as he can politically."[14] Though nominally a dispute over Jackson's ancient Florida transgressions, the president's break with Calhoun in the spring of 1830 actually involved more immediate questions regarding the perils of presidential succession and South Carolina's unresolved relationship to the federal tariff. Those delicate subjects remained as yet unresolved.

36

Kitchen Politics

Bereft of consensus, Jackson's presidency ran ragged its first year. Calhoun and Van Buren skirmished for advantage, the Eaton Affair scandalized polite Washington society, and the unwieldy Democratic coalition lacked control. Eager to form a new cabinet and build momentum for a second term, Jackson took decisive action to create a party responsive to his will. Most immediately, he moved to replace Duff Green's unreliable *Telegraph* as the administration's mouthpiece. As Kendall put it, "The disposition which . . . Green has exhibited to identify Gen. Jackson and his friends with the nullifiers of South Carolina has excited anew [the Jackson camp's] desire for another paper here."[1] Loyal to Calhoun, the *Telegraph* emphasized tariff reform while taking a moderate line on an issue increasingly critical to Jackson—the constitutionality of the National Bank.

Consequently, Jackson found a new print agent in the *Washington Globe*, edited by the Kentucky Democrat Francis Blair, a Kendall protégé and soon to become part of the president's Kitchen Cabinet. "He looks like a skeleton," one Virginia Jacksonian said of Blair, "lacks but little of being one, and weighed last spring, when dressed in thick winter clothing, one hundred and seven pounds, all told; about eighty-five of which, we suppose, was bone, and the other twenty-two pounds, made up of gristle, nerve, and brain . . . flesh he has none. His face is narrow, and of the hatchet kind. . . . His complexion is fair, his hair sandy, and his eyes blue—his countenance remarkably mild."[2]

A hard-money man, Blair had formerly edited the *Frankfurt Argus of Western America*, which, following the disastrous Panic of 1819, helped elect Debt Relief Party candidates to office. Capturing majorities in both houses of the state's General Assembly, they passed a stay law preventing creditors (say, bankers) from taking debtors (say, farmers) to court for one year. Considering that Blair, Kendall, and postmaster general William Berry were all Kentuckians of the Relief Party persuasion, Jackson could be said to have moved to the left on economic issues and sought the contact of western men who shared his views.

Blair arrived in Washington in the fall of 1830; his duties, as specified by Kendall, were clear: "The course a paper should pursue here is obvious. It must be for a thorough reform in the govt." On the subject of states' rights Kendall wrote, the *Globe* will be "mildly opposed to the South Carolina nullifiers," while otherwise "in favor of a judicious Tariff[,] . . . against the [National Bank], and in favor of leaving the states to manage their own affairs without other interference than the safety of the whole imperiously requires."[3] Jackson's allies in the Treasury and War departments subsidized the paper with government printing contracts, while its connection to the administration aided circulation. The first edition appeared in early December. As a party-building instrument, coming on the heels of the old caucus system's collapse, its importance can hardly be overstressed. Still in a developmental stage, the Democratic Party had struggled to organize, delegate, and discipline. The *Globe* helped to do this by articulating the issues that Jackson wished to emphasize. No doubt certain constituencies within his early coalition, including both states' rights irreconcilables and National Bank defenders, would become alienated and leave, though their absences more generally strengthened the party by providing it a sharper focus.

In the spring of 1831, not long after the *Globe* began operation, Jackson accepted the resignations of nearly his entire cabinet. To some around the country the administration appeared to be in a state of disintegration. "These were the men," grumbled Charles Francis Adams, son of Jackson's predecessor, "who claimed to know how to administer this government, and to bring it back to its original purity." Putting a positive connotation on the resignations, Jackson wanly reported to one correspondent, "We all separate with good feelings." In more candid moments, however, he regarded the purge as necessary to blunt the "schemes" of his political enemies. "The plot was to take up Calhoun for President," he wrote to a colleague. "Whether an attempt may not now be made to unite with Clay & Webster, I cannot say. The late movement & reorganization of my Cabinet has frustrated all their organised plans."[4]

This near sweep of executive departments produced a somewhat more competent administrative group. New York's Edward Livingston took over the state department while Louis McLane (Delaware), Lewis Cass (Michigan), Roger B. Taney (Maryland), and Levi Woodbury (New Hampshire), headed, respectively, the offices of Treasury, War, attorney general, and navy. Interestingly, considering Jackson's difficulties with South Carolina's nullifiers, his new cabinet lacked a delegate from the Deep South. Two hailed from border states, while the other three represented New England, the mid-Atlantic, and the West.

Throughout the spring and summer the *Telegraph* regularly badgered Jackson, reporting, accurately enough, of the embarrassing connection between the "petticoat affair" and the cabinet crisis. This raised serious questions about the president's judgment. That an administration should fall into paralysis because of a social scandal involving public officials and their wives seemed a little ridiculous. Jackson's decision to make the Eatons part of his official family, moreover, looked like a clumsy mistake—as did his gratuitous efforts to exonerate Margaret. This difficult period probably constituted the nadir of the General's presidency. The prominent shape and substance given to it by the Bank War and the nullification crisis were yet to come, and it was by no means a certain thing in the summer of 1831 that Jackson, his first two years in office dogged by infighting among Democrats, could capture a second term. In a vital sense, the cabinet cleansing offered him the opportunity to start anew with loyalists like Taney, Cass, Kendall, and Blair.

The last two, western wordsmiths, proved particularly important to Jackson in helping to sharpen his criticism of the Bank, expound his narrow view of internal improvements, and defend his rejection of radical states' rights. These two Kentuckians were the leading figures of Jackson's Kitchen Cabinet, a shifting cadre including Jack Donelson, New Hampshire senator Isaac Hill, John Overton, William Lewis, and, when out of the formal cabinet, Roger Taney. Depending on the issue, Jackson approached certain men over others. Taney proved to be a tenacious opponent of the Bank, while Eaton and Lewis angled for its recharter; Kendall contributed a draft of the president's Proclamation on Nullification. As a Washington outsider Jackson had a particular need to tap into a wide range of opinions, competencies, and connections beyond his ken—and of course the personal loyalty that he demanded could best be found independent of a system that filled cabinet vacancies by considering party rank or sectional design. The descriptive "Kitchen Cabinet" gained currency in 1831 when used by National Bank president Nicholas Biddle as a pejorative contrast to the proper parlor cabinet. The expression soon seasoned political conversation. In 1834 the old Federalist Philip Hone, criticizing Jackson's Bank policy, wrote, "The language of the message in relation to the Bank of the United States is disgraceful to the President and humiliating to every American. It smells of the kitchen."[5] When used by Hone, a prominent figure in New York society, the epitheting of "Kitchen" adds context to Jackson's appeal. More Americans, after all, were conversant with kitchens than parlors, and more of them were voting than ever before.

As vital as Kendall and company proved to be, only Van Buren, recently resigned from the State Department, could, so to speak, extend the General's presidency beyond the two-term norm—as Madison and Monroe had formerly attempted to govern along Jeffersonian lines. Eager to signal a connection of succession, Jackson, in August 1831, with Congress out of session, granted a recess appointment to Van Buren as U.S. minister to Great Britain. Considering that three previous occupants of that office later served as president, no one could mistake the appointment's importance. The following month the dapper minister-to-be sailed to the Isle of Wight on his way to Southampton and thence to London, where he headed the legation at the Court of St. James's. That December, however, the Senate reconvened and within weeks Jackson's opposition had contrived a tie vote—23–23—on Van Buren's nomination, leaving Calhoun, presiding as the upper chamber's president, the presumed pleasure of casting the deciding negative ballot. The maneuver appears in retrospect lamentably in line with Calhoun's recent series of self-inflicted wounds, for Van Buren's humiliating rejection could only bind the New Yorker closer to Jackson, certain to take the negation of his nominee personally. As Missouri senator Thomas Hart Benton later noted, "it was Mr. Gabriel Moore, of Alabama, who sat near me, and to whom I said, when the vote was declared, 'You have broken a minister, and elected a Vice-President.'"[6]

Credit, if that is the proper word, for strategizing the negative vote belonged principally to the newly seated Kentucky senator, Henry Clay. Anxious to attack Jackson in the months leading up to the general

election, he determined to hand the president defeat after defeat in confirmation votes. "The character of an eminent public man resembles a
fortification," he wrote Webster. "If every attack is repelled, if no breach
on any point be made, he becomes impregnable. But if you once make a
breach, no matter how small, the work may be carried."[7]

Far from weakening the General, however, Clay and Calhoun effectively gave Jackson the things that motivated him most—adversaries, a
cause, a crusade. These designing men, he stated in one communication, were industriously "at work to destroy me."[8] Though burdened by
the Eaton Affair and the necessary but humbling cabinet overhaul, Jackson's two greatest assets, an immense public popularity and tenacious
resolve, remained in place. Most active when threatened, he faced a host
of obstacles in 1832, including critics of his reelection, radical nullifiers,
and backers of the National Bank. He personalized each of these challenges, making of public policy a bid for private vindication, and doing
so in the sacred name of the people.

37

Breaking the Bank

Ever since the adoption of the Constitution, the country's depository system had stirred controversy. The First Bank of the United States, proposed by Hamilton, promoted by Federalists, and approved by Washington, received a twenty-year charter in 1791. In opposition, Jeffersonians denounced the Philadelphia-based bank as a corruptive force in the republic, tending to spur on speculation while favoring eastern creditors over southern and western farmers. Writing to John Adams, Jefferson condemned "the tribe of bank-mongers, [for] seeking to filch from the public," that they might embellish "their swindling, and barren gains."[1] Predictably the Republicans, having come to power, retired Hamilton's bank in 1811, though to unexpectedly difficult results. During the War of 1812 inflation skyrocketed, credit and tax revenue plummeted, while the Treasury provided poor leadership. Once the war ended, Madison, swallowing his constitutional scruples, signed an act establishing the second Bank of the United States in April 1816—it too enjoyed a twenty-year charter.

Capitalized at $35,000,000 (about $680,000,000 in current dollars) and overseeing twenty-five branch offices, this tax-exempt bank functioned as a kind of exchequer extraordinaire. By manipulating the money supply, it could slow down an overheating economy, or when offering easy access to credit, it could stimulate a stagnant market. At least in theory. For in 1819, the year of the Panic, it failed its first big test. Many in the country, including Jackson, Kendall, and Blair, took note. The Bank further provoked debate by making capital available to select investors in internal improvements. Some Jacksonians saw in this practice an effort to advance a small aristocracy, while men like Quincy Adams and Clay believed it vital for promoting the American System. Why, they asked, should the nation hamper its material development by relying on modestly funded state banks when the capital and credit existed to create a teeming network of factories, canals, and turnpikes?

Nicholas Biddle, a Philadelphia financier and since 1823 the Bank's president, wondered as much as well. More energetic, efficient, and capable than his predecessors, he won the confidence of most men in Congress. In November 1829 Biddle, interested in securing an early recharter, initiated a meeting with the budget-minded president in which he unveiled a Bank-driven plan to retire the national debt. Jackson, both courteous and candid, refused the bait. "I think it right to be perfectly frank with you," he said. "I do not think that the power of Congress extends to charter a Bank out of the ten mile square [of the District of Columbia]. I do not dislike your Bank any more than all banks. But ever since I read the history of the South Sea bubble I have been afraid of banks. I have read the opinion of John Marshall who I believe was a great & pure mind—and could not agree with him."[2] Jackson, in other words, believed the Bank to be both unconstitutional and a corrupting force in American life. The infamous South Sea Bubble, the rapid 1720 rise and collapse of a British joint-stock company operating in South America, stood as something of an object lesson on the perils of speculation, insider trading, and the paying off of politicians. Some saw further in the disaster a still deeper danger in Parliament's incautious promotion of a credit-and-debt economy largely beyond its purview.

The question of the Bank's legality further troubled Jackson. His contrary reference to "the opinion" of Marshall alluded to the Supreme Court's important ruling in *McCulloch v. Maryland*. In 1818 the Maryland General Assembly passed an act to tax all banks in the state not chartered by the legislature—in effect the Baltimore branch of the Bank of the United States. The Bank refused, however, to pay the $15,000 tax (about $320,000 in current dollars) and faced a lawsuit. The Supreme Court sided with the Bank, declaring that Congress enjoyed the right to create depositories. The justices observed as well that the power to tax implied the power to destroy and denied that a state could abolish what Congress had created. Placed in context, the Marshall Court's ruling affirmed the constitutionality of both Hamilton's (1791) and Madison's (1811) banks and by inference any that might follow. But Jackson disagreed.

On December 8, shortly after meeting with Biddle, the president sent his first annual message to Congress, making public his criticism of the Bank. Noting that its charter expired in 1836 and that "its stockholders will most probably apply for a renewal of their privileges," Jackson, in effect, told them not to. Setting *McCulloch v. Maryland* aside and appealing instead to public opinion, he observed that "both the constitutionality and the expediency of the law creating this bank are well questioned by a large portion of our fellow-citizens." Possibly looking for a less contested reason to criticize the Bank than constitutionality, the president also and somewhat disingenuously blamed it for "fail[ing] in the great end of establishing a uniform and sound currency." He concluded that some future depository might be "deemed essential to the fiscal operations of the Government," and left it open to "the wisdom of the Legislature" to decide whether such an institution might be devised in such a way as to "avoid all the constitutional difficulties and at the same time secure all the advantages to the Government and country that were expected to result from the present bank."[3] Now the entire nation knew Jackson's position.

Naturally the president's message disappointed Biddle, though he considered the situation salvageable. "The consolations on the present occasion are," he wrote to a director of the Baltimore and Ohio Railroad, "that it is a measure emanating exclusively from the President in person, being the remains of old notions of constitutionality, that it is not a Cabinet measure nor a party measure."[4] But Biddle radically underestimated both Jackson and the fluid political landscape. The president's appetite for a fight and his ability to incite popular opinion created a new governing dynamic. True, cabinet sentiment on the Bank, as Biddle noted, dissented from Jackson's, and Democrats did seem disinclined to make an issue of recharter. That all of these obstacles might be wiped away in a flurry of aggressive, unprecedented executive action, however, eluded the banker. It appears that he too trafficked in "the remains of old notions of constitutionality."

The following year Jackson declared in his December 1830 annual message a desire to see an entirely government-operated depository, one bereft of the private investors who currently dominated Biddle's Bank. Critical of the president's position, Charles J. Ingersoll of the

Pennsylvania House of Representatives put together a resolution supporting the existing system and wrote to former Presidents Madison and Monroe asking for their opinions of Jackson's preference for a new financial entity attached to the Treasury Department. Both men expressed doubts. In March, Monroe, citing a desire to extend "candour" to a "friendly relation," wrote directly to Jackson, explaining his evolving position on the Bank. "Being a member of the Senate of the U States when the first bank was instituted, under the administration of Genl. Washington," he noted, "I voted against it, and . . . when the second was instituted under Mr Madison being then a member of his admn. I concurr'd with him, and voted for it. This change in my opinion, was produced, by my experience of the embarrassments and losses of the govt., during the last war. . . . It has been a cause of serious regret, that we should entertain sentiments so different, on so very interesting a subject."[5]

That fall Jackson's new treasury secretary, the pro-Bank Louis McLane, knowing the General's aversion to deficit financing, proposed to employ the Bank in such a way as to erase the country's considerable national debt—some $48 million (slightly more than $1.5 billion in current dollars)—by the end of the president's term in March 1833. The plan involved liquidating some Bank stock and using the revenue to pay off the government's obligations. McLane further dangled before the martial-minded Jackson the prospect of using these fresh funds for provisioning the military, improving state militias, and erecting armories. Might such enticements be enough to produce a favorable presidential opinion on recharter? Jackson refused, however, to show his hand; his 1831 message to Congress offered only a single ambiguous paragraph on the Bank that promised "to leave it for the present" to the thoughts of "an enlightened people."[6] McLane's annual Treasury Department report, by contrast, called for an early recharter. That Blair's *Globe* pushed right back on the report is indicative of the sharp divisions in Jackson's administration.

Eyeing the coming 1832 presidential contest, Clay began to formulate his own plans to extend the Bank's life. In the fall of 1830 he wrote to Biddle, "But suppose . . . instead of postponing, Congress was to pass a [recharter] bill . . . and it should be presented to the President, what would he do with it? If, as I suppose, he would reject it, the question would be immediately, in consequence, referred to the people, and . . .

[become] the controlling question in American politics."[7] The following year, in a small Baltimore convention containing some 150 delegates, Clay captured the National Republican Party's nomination and, in the midst of such momentum, counseled (as did others) Biddle to move for recharter. These men very questionably believed that if Jackson vetoed such a bill he would lose Pennsylvania—the Bank's home—and thus the election, and if he did not he risked alienating parts of the agrarian South and West, to the same end.

Biddle hesitated, uncertain how much congressional support he could count on. Moving methodically, he sent a Bank official, Thomas Cadwalader, to the capital on a fact-finding mission. The results, however, were inconclusive. Positively, Cadwalader believed that small majorities existed in both the House and Senate for recharter; less positively, a cautious McLane suggested to him that pro-Bank Democrats were unlikely to overturn a presidential veto in an election year, but might subsequently assert their independence. An early application for recharter would further, McLane suggested, infuriate Jackson, pushing him into a corner and all but ensuring a veto. Presented with conflicting advice, Cadwalader nevertheless advised Biddle to initiate a Bank renewal bill in 1832, which he did on January 6. This risky decision counted on a number of conjectures—that the Bank was too popular, too necessary, to disappear, that Jackson would seek to avoid a potentially nasty struggle with congressional Democrats in the commotion of a reelection campaign, and that should a contest between Jackson and the Bank arise, voters were likely to side with the latter. Biddle counted, that is to say, on reading public opinion better than the president.

Having idled over the Bank question for three years with no need to take action, Jackson now moved openly in opposition. The coming struggle reacquainted him with an old enemy (Clay), offered him a new adversary (Biddle), and stoked the impression of persecution never far from Jackson's thoughts. His own cabinet leaned toward the Bank. One ally, the Virginia agrarian John Randolph, warned the president to proceed carefully. "You . . . have no suspicion," he wrote, "of the influences which operate on all around you."[8]

Importantly, the Bank War offered the Democratic Party an identity beyond the cult of Jackson. Federalism discovered its personality in the Hamiltonian system of finance that took root in 1790–91, while Jeffersonianism found its abiding issue in the Louisiana Purchase (1803), which exemplified the agrarian ideology of the Virginia squirearchy. A large, unwieldy coalition in 1832, Jacksonianism needed to shed some of its softer support in order to develop an agenda beyond the generic reform platform applied four years earlier.

A second party-galvanizing opportunity occurred in late May when Democrats, in the wake of the old caucus system's collapse, collected in their first national nominating convention. More than three hundred delegates from twenty-three states gathered in Baltimore, too many to be packed, as planned, into the city's athenaeum and so the St. Paul Street Universalist Church hosted the event. With Jackson's nomination a foregone conclusion, the assembly was primarily concerned with identifying a running mate. The president's support for Van Buren, however, made that perfunctory as well. The Little Magician won on the first ballot with 208 votes; former Virginia senator James Barbour could muster only 49. From this point on, the campaign and the Bank's fate were inexorably linked.

Anti-Bank sentiment in both the House and Senate slowly built throughout the election year. If not a majority, it constituted a powerful interest eager to undermine the recharter effort. In late April a House committee investigating the depository released a sharply critical report of its practices, which included providing "loans" to favorite politicians, subsidizing certain influential newspapers, and even funneling money to sway political campaigns, perhaps most notably to aid Adams in New Hampshire in 1828. Besides Jackson, four individuals in particular— Polk in the House, Benton in the Senate, Taney in the cabinet, and Blair at the *Globe*—carried on the public fight against the Bank. In response, Biddle came to Washington to speak with congressmen, line up support for recharter, and calmly predict financial doom if the depository lost its special role in the economy. He seemed unaware that such vigorous lobbying only confirmed to Jackson the danger of allowing a powerful and lavishly funded semiprivate corporation to encroach upon the legislative process.

The extent to which Biddle's campaigning impacted the recharter bill is an open question, as sentiment in Congress appeared for years generally favorable to the Bank. What we know is that the bill passed the Senate 28–20 in early June and by an equally comfortable 107–85 margin in the House a few weeks later. Considering the president's opposition and the fact that the Jacksonians enjoyed majorities in both legislative chambers, the votes demonstrate the Party's awkward lack of cohesion. The National Republicans, by contrast, were unanimous in supporting the bill and so, although smaller than its opposition, the party could claim to have more clearly defined itself. Regionalism may go some way in explaining why. National Republicans were more geographically concentrated, being strongest in New England; Jacksonians, by contrast, held majorities just about everywhere else and thus represented an unwieldy coalition of contrasts, including southern planters, western farmers, and New York merchants. These groups began to diverge rather openly—and sectionally—on the Bank bill. In the Senate, northern votes accounted for 85 percent of the yeas while southerners cast 70 percent of the nays.[9]

One week after the recharter bill passed the House, Jackson submitted his veto message to Congress. Substantially influenced by Kendall, the communication is one of the iconic documents in American history, articulating the idea of republican equality against the perils of corporate monopoly and special privilege. More than merely denouncing the bill as unconstitutional, Jackson insisted that it threatened to upend the nation's democratic principles by giving a select few—a number of

An 1833 illustration of "The Downfall of Mother Bank." Jackson, like a god, smites the depository's defenders.

well-placed foreign speculators and what he called "our own opulent citizens"—exclusive rights. The veto further stressed the president's provocative claim that the Supreme Court's ruling on the depository's constitutionality in the *McCulloch v. Maryland* case did not bind him. "The Congress, the Executive, and the Court," he countered, "must each for itself be guided by its own opinion of the Constitution." Might this not lead to rule by potentially unstable forms of power, populism, or prejudice? Apparently. The "supreme judges" could claim, Jackson swore in a disquieting sentence, "only such influence as the force of their reasoning may deserve."[10]

Perhaps most striking is the message's strong whiff of class warfare. Jackson wrote: "The many millions which this act proposes to bestow on the stockholders of the existing bank must come directly or indirectly out of the earnings of the American people," as well as: "[The bill] seems to be predicated on the erroneous idea that the present stockholders have a prescriptive right not only to the favor but to the bounty of Government," and further: "Many of our rich men have not been content with equal protection and equal benefits, but have besought us to make them richer by act of Congress."[11] One paragraph in particular defended the economic rights of the nation's white working class in language as sharp and unambiguous as Jackson ever accomplished:

> It is to be regretted that the rich and powerful too often bend the acts of government to their selfish purposes. . . . In the full enjoyment of the gifts of Heaven and the fruits of superior industry, economy, and virtue, every man is equally entitled to protection by law; but when the laws undertake to add to these natural and just advantages artificial distinctions, to grant titles, gratuities, and exclusive privileges, to make the rich richer and the potent more powerful, the humble members of society—the farmers, mechanics, and laborers—who have neither the time nor the means of securing like favors to themselves, have a right to complain of the injustice of their Government.[12]

The president having taken a public stand, several previously pro-Bank Jacksonians fell in line. The Senate failed on July 13 to overturn the veto; needing thirty-two votes, it could muster only twenty-two. Three days later, both houses adjourned.

Biddle quickly countered, distributing—via Bank funds—some thirty thousand copies of Jackson's veto message, with which he mistakenly sought to sway public opinion. "When the Bank was denounced by the President," he said in defense of this mass circulation, "it was an obvious duty not to suffer the institution to be crushed by the weight of power—but to appeal directly to the country." Believing Jackson to have put "his will" over "large majorities of both houses of Congress," Biddle considered taking more drastic action: "The question now is whether the Bank ought to exert itself to defeat the reelection of that person who is now the only obstacle to its success." He admitted the "very great" incentives to play politics with the people's money, but reverently declared "it to be the duty of the Bank to resist them." Of course he resisted very little. In widely distributing Jackson's message—"It has all the fury of a chained panther biting the bars of his cage," he told Clay—in continuing to advance pro-Bank politicians credit, and in spending some $100,000 to defeat the president in November, Biddle gave in to temptation.[13]

Jackson, it might be said, did much the same. His veto message challenged the nation's checks-and-balances system by placing the executive office firmly in the legislative process. Noting that past Congresses both supported (1791, 1816) and opposed (1811) the nation's previous banks, he argued that his own personal opinions—"Each public officer who takes an oath to support the Constitution swears that he will support it *as he understands it*"—took precedence.[14] Congress, in other words, would presumably have to take into account Jackson's private views on legislation or face future vetoes. To many observers, this put too much power into the president's hands and smacked of an internal menace to liberty unseen in America since the Revolution.

And there is no doubt that scores of pro-Bank men considered Jackson, not Biddle's institution, the real threat facing the republic. Daniel Webster (on retainer to the Bank) swore to his Senate colleagues, "We have arrived at a new epoch. We are entering on experiments, with the government and the Constitution of the country, hitherto untried, and of fearful and appalling aspect." An equally exasperated Biddle evoked the French Revolution in a rather frantic insistence that the veto message "is really a manifesto of anarchy—such as Marat or Robespierre might have issued to the mob of the faubourg St. Antoine." Massachusetts politician Alexander Everett, by contrast, thought Jackson's actions wholly unprecedented: "For the first time, perhaps, in the history of civilized communities, the Chief Magistrate of a great nation . . . is found appealing to the worst passions of the uninformed part of the people, and endeavoring to stir up the poor against the rich."[15]

When applied to Jackson, however, the class war argument has clear limits. In no sense did the president wish to see the propertyless attack the propertied. He was, rather, comfortable with gradations in wealth—"Distinctions in society will always exist under every just government," the message stated—so long as the government played no role in elevating some over others. He called for equality of opportunity, not outcome. And though the message emphasized the need to even the playing field for "the farmers, mechanics, and laborers," the Bank's better connected critics included competing depositories, substantial merchants, and rising professionals. These interests resented the Bank's ability to regulate economic development by policing credit.

The struggle over the Bank helped to frame the fall election as a contest of contrasts. Clay stood as the candidate of federally subsidized internal improvements while Jackson ran as a protector of equality and limited government. Both of these portraits lacked precision, though they do suggest certain truths. Suspicious of elites, eager to restrain the Constitution's power to promote change, and culturally agrarian, Jackson's vision represented in many respects a nostalgic longing for the old pre–War of 1812 republic. To these localist-oriented constituencies drawn reluctantly into a national economy beyond their control, Jackson offered up the Bank as the devil incarnate of their concerns. With this firm hold on the popular imagination, he demonstrated a remarkable capacity to make voters believe they could retain what was already lost.[16]

38

More Popular than a Party

A dismissive Henry Clay once described the Democratic Party to a small group of Louisville notables as "the Jackson party . . . a mere *personal* party."[1] And certainly as the 1832 presidential election approached, the coalition, entering only its second national contest, lacked Jackson's prestige and popularity. What is more, the president seemed to will even his unfolding opposition into existence. The National Republicans attacked the Indian Removal Act and Bank veto while stressing the emanating danger of executive usurpation, thus making Jackson himself the main campaign issue. Certainly no single individual did more to provide a rallying cry for enemies and allies alike during this pregnant period of partisan formation.

Another party, the Anti-Masonics, also fielded a candidate, former attorney general (and defender of Cherokee rights before the Supreme Court) William Wirt. The nation's first third party, it opposed Freemasonry as a dangerous secret society, an elitist order in an egalitarian republic. It looked upon the Freemasons, that is, much as Jackson looked upon the Bank. Though regarded as a single-issue coalition, the Anti-Masonics, favoring internal improvements and a protective tariff, shared with National Republicans a similar economic vision. Despite organizing Wirt's candidacy, the Anti-Masonic Party proved to be, like Freemasonry, in decline by 1832, largely a victim of its success. It never sponsored another national ticket, and by 1840 its remnants had found a place in the Whig Party, heritor to the National Republicans.

The election of 1832, held over several weeks in late autumn, resulted in a strong Jackson victory. The president, taking 54.2 percent of the popular and 76 percent of the electoral vote, carried sixteen states to Clay's six, and one each for Wirt (Vermont) and the states' rights candidate and Virginia governor John Floyd (South Carolina). Clay proved to be a disastrous candidate, running three states and six percentage points behind Adams's numbers four years earlier. Jackson, by contrast, claimed a robust national following in winning reelection. In 1828 New York and the New England states combined to give the General only 24 percent of their electoral votes, but in 1832 he captured 62 percent, while his party added one Senate and three House seats in the Northeast.[2] Jackson predictably won most of the South, swept the Northwest, and did well in the mid-Atlantic; Maryland, one of the eight states he lost, went for Clay by a razor-thin four votes out of more than thirty-eight thousand cast.

There were, to be sure, limits to Jackson's popularity. Several presidents running for reelection have equaled or bested his 54 percent of the vote. These are: Jefferson (72 percent in 1804), Lincoln (55 percent in 1864), Grant (55 percent in 1872), Theodore Roosevelt (56 percent in 1904), Franklin Roosevelt (60 percent and 54 percent in 1936 and 1940), Eisenhower (57 percent in 1956), Nixon (60 percent in 1972), and Reagan (58 percent in 1984).[3] Jackson is also one of four presidents to win reelection with a smaller percentage of the vote than that which had brought him into office; down 1 percent, he joins Madison (14 percent in 1812), Franklin Roosevelt (6 percent and 1 percent in 1940 and 1944), and Obama (nearly 2 percent in 2012). Of course Jackson faced third-party opponents (siphoning off almost 8 percent of the vote), and it is likely that in a more conventional two-candidate contest he would have captured perhaps as much as 58 percent of the popular ballots, and thus exceeded his 1828 percentage.

Also worth noting is the relative struggle of the president's party. Democrats lost control of the Senate in the 1832 elections while their percentage in the House, hovering four years earlier in the low sixties, dropped in the last two electoral cycles to the high fifties. Neither of these outcomes is particularly unusual in American politics, though they do indicate an electorate willing to separate a popular candidate from his party.

Reactions to the election were somewhat predictable. From the once formidable House of Adams, John Quincy's son Charles Francis offered a studied lament—"The disastrous result of the Presidential Election throws a gloom over the political affairs of the Country which is deeper and darker than it ever has been before. The fate of our currency is sealed, and the Judiciary is in imminent danger. Office ceases to be honorable and vicious principle is every where triumphant." Clay, the beaten candidate, invoked in his misery a meteorological metaphor—"The dark cloud which had been so long suspended over our devoted Country, instead of being dispelled, as we had fondly hoped it would be, has become more dense, more menacing, more alarming." Tennessee congressman James Polk, by contrast, chirped to Coffee from the capital, "The President is in excellent health and in good spirits. How could he be otherwise after his late triumphant victory? Did you ever know such a complete route? The enemy is literally driven from the field."[4]

Considering the Senate's new anti-Jackson majority, Polk's definition of a "complete route" obviously applied only to the president. And that might be fitting. For in 1832 the election appears to have been more about Jackson than the Bank. Clay and Biddle were wrong. Jackson could kill the depository and keep his crown. The extensive assets he brought to the presidency four years earlier—his popularity, indelible connection to the Battle of New Orleans, and ability to capture the national imagination as the orphan who became the apprentice who became the hero—remained firmly in place.

Jackson relics were the subject of a brisk business during—and of course after—his life. A lock of the General's hair, as seen here, was commonly requested.

Sectionalism's impact on the election is perhaps less clear, considering that the main candidates were both southerners. Jackson showed strong in Dixie, winning seven states, losing four, and collecting eighty electoral votes; in the five-state northern tier connecting New York to Illinois he also performed well, tallying 105 electoral votes. The southern balloting was rarely competitive. Jackson won 61 percent in Louisiana, 75 percent in Virginia, 84 percent in North Carolina, and 95–100 percent in Mississippi, Alabama, Georgia, and Tennessee. The northern states that went for Jackson, by contrast, were much closer, if still, excepting tight races in Ohio and New Jersey, comfortably in the president's column.

Looking at the election through a longer lens, one notes that Jackson became in 1832 the first of only three Democrats to win multiple terms and claim a majority of the popular vote—a feat equaled more than a century later by Franklin Roosevelt (three times) and later still by Obama.[5] Jackson also became the first presidential candidate to win a plurality of the popular vote in three elections, Grover Cleveland and FDR being the only others. In at least one respect, however, 1832 proved to be the end of an era. Five of the nation's first seven presidents were reelected, but after Jackson seven contests passed before another president, Lincoln in 1864, was returned to office. That generational interregnum, one leading straight to civil war, brought to a violent culmination the welter of issues, framed preeminently around sectionalism and slavery, that did so much to define Jackson's presidency.

Part VI

CENTER OF THE STORM

He never had any half confidence. He did not like or dislike people: he loved them or hated them.

Margaret Eaton, 1873

This print of a placid Jackson belies the energy with which he imposed his will upon American politics, earning an unprecedented censure from a Senate whose Whig contingent sometimes compared him to Caesar.

39

The Nullification Crisis

Managing the precarious nullification struggle to a bloodless conclusion proved to be Jackson's most popular presidential achievement. Unlike the contested Bank War and the controversial Indian Removal Act, it largely cut against partisan lines. More than a few critics, however, accused his administration of unwittingly egging the crisis on. John Quincy Adams, for one, believed South Carolina's attempt to nullify federal law a logical extension of Georgia's ignoring—with Jackson's blessing—the Marshall Court's ruling in the Worcester case. "This example of the State of Georgia," Adams guessed all too correctly in 1831, "will be imitated by other States, and with regard to other National Interests. Perhaps the Tariff." On account of the executive branch failing to "sustain the Judiciary," he argued, "The Union is in the most imminent danger of dissolution from the old inherent vice of Confederacies."[1]

The first protective tariff became law in 1816, passing the House 88–54. A reaction to the recent and near disastrous war with Britain, it recognized the need for a self-sufficient industrial base and received fairly wide support, even in the planter South. This changed with subsequent imposts, particularly the so-called 1828 Tariff of Abominations, in which certain import custom duties rose dramatically. At that point many southern free-traders, including Calhoun (a friend of the 1816 act), argued that protectionism too completely aided northern manufacturing without offering an equal advantage to the slave states' agricultural commodities. In effect, some of them contended, the South sacrificed economically to subsidize a factory system based on free labor and thus antithetical to the plantocracy's long-term self-interest.

Jackson thought the tariff both constitutional and essential for developing the nation's economic strength, though he took a moderate line when considering rates, understanding the issue's divisiveness. "I regretted to see the subject of a Tariff question discussed under the strong feelings of political excitement that pervaded the whole nation, & congress," he wrote to a colleague in June 1828, shortly after the tariff bill passed:

> To regulate a Judicious tariff, is a subject of great dificulty at all times, & ought to be discussed, with great calmness & due deliberation, with an eye to the prosperity of the whole Union, & not of any particular part. . . . There is nothing that I shudder at more than the idea of a seperation of the Union. Should such an event ever happen, which I fervently pray god to avert, from that date, I view our liberty gone—It is the durability of the confederation upon which the general government is built, that must prolong our liberty, the moment it seperates, it is gone.[2]

This brief statement anticipated Jackson's subsequent reaction to the nullification crisis—he believed in the perpetual nature of the Union and refused, albeit with Georgia's Cherokee policy constituting a rather large caveat, to entertain the idea of a state rejecting federal law.

That same summer of 1828 Calhoun had explained the southern position to Jackson, whom he considered amenable to tariff reduction. "The impression, as far as I have observed, is nearly universal," he wrote, "that the system acts with great severity against the staple [crop] states, and that it is the real cause of their impoverishment." Anticipating Jackson's election that fall, he predicted "a better order of things . . . in which, an equal distribution of the burden and benefit of government, economy, the payment of the publick debt, and finally the removal of oppressive duties," will take precedence. Such optimism, he assured the General, "is what mainly consoles this quarter of the Union under existing embarrassment."[3] Five months later Calhoun anonymously drafted—though his authorship was widely suspected—the *South Carolina Exposition and Protest*, which argued that as the states (rather than the people) had ratified the Constitution, sovereignty ultimately resided in them. The *Protest*'s defense of nullification is skillfully constructed, if ultimately impractical. How could the nation survive if any state wished to nullify any law within its borders that it deemed unconstitutional—or merely inconvenient?

A nationalist in 1816, Calhoun took note in the postwar period of South Carolina's recent decline. Soil depletion and the rapid opening of new cotton lands to the west, in what would come to be known as the Black Belt, appeared to threaten the Palmetto State's future. Though growth continued in the 1820s, the rate slowed signally compared to previous decades. Casting about for blame, many state officials identified the tariff. Filled with planters and lacking a robust middle class, South Carolina tilted toward an extreme on the impost question. Outside opinions were rare as few migrants or immigrants took root in this society of enslavers and enslaved; an astonishing 96 percent of its population, both black and white, were natives.[4]

The *Exposition and Protest*'s sectarian tone—"the encouragement of the industry of the manufacturing states, is in fact discouragement to ours"—found varying degrees of sympathy throughout the South. Tennessee congressman Davy Crockett remembered that from a young age, "we have always been taught to look upon the people of New England as a selfish, cunning set of fellows, that . . . cut their wisdom-teeth as soon as they were born; that made money by their wits, and held on to it by natur; that called cheatery mother-wit; that hung on to political power because they had numbers; that raised up manufacturers to keep down the South and West; and, in fact, had so much of the devil in all their machinery, that they would neither lead nor drive, unless the load was going into their own cribs."[5] No doubt the economic pain prompted by the Panic of 1819—combined with Yankee resistance to slavery in Missouri and John Quincy Adams's elevation to the presidency in preference to a Tennessean with more popular and electoral votes—conditioned many southerners' response to the tariff. Some discerned a deliberate pattern of northern ascendency at their own section's expense.

When considering the tariff's impact on South Carolina in particular, the role of black bondage must be raised. With more than 320,000 slaves in 1830, the Palmetto State registered the highest percentage of chattel of any state in the Union (55 percent), making whites a racial minority. "In the district of Charleston," one historian reports, blacks "outnumbered whites three to one; in Colleton the ratio was four to one; in Beaufort, five to one; in Georgetown eight to one." No other region in the South "contained such a massive, concentrated" black population.[6] A recent series of direct and tangential attacks on South Carolina's vast system of enslavement had rendered the institution unusually brittle. In 1822 the Charleston carpenter and former slave Denmark Vesey was accused, convicted, and executed (along with more than thirty co-conspirators) of organizing a large-scale rebellion; a few years later officials at the port of Charleston seized copies of *Appeal to the Coloured Citizens of the World* authored by David Walker, a free black living in Boston who encouraged active and if necessary violent resistance to enslavers; in January 1831 the radical New England abolitionist William Lloyd Garrison began publishing the *Liberator*, while in August of that year the bloody Nat Turner rebellion in Southampton County, Virginia, resulted in dozens of white deaths and many more black casualties and executions. Under such intense pressure, white South Carolinians began to see in the tariff an effort to undermine their society. The promotion of industry implied the preferment of free labor, and the protective tariff's mere existence advertised its supposed constitutionality, though Calhoun and others argued that an impost could only be raised for necessary government expenditures, not to shield private industry from competition. A Congress with the power to pass such legislation, they knew, could presumably outlaw slavery someday.

Jackson attempted to undercut South Carolina's nullifiers by advocating a general contraction of the impost, a position he publicly advanced when calling, in his December 1831 annual message, for "a modification of the tariff" in order to "relieve the people from unnecessary taxation." The following July Congress, with respectable southern support, complied, agreeing to a new tariff bill that produced a moderate reduction in rates. The principle of protection remained intact, and yet the impost seemed no longer a provocation. Later that month Jackson bragged, prematurely as things turned out, of having defused the nullifiers—"The modified Tariff that has passed," he crowed to Coffee, "has . . . killed the ultras."[7]

But the new tariff only inflamed those South Carolinians who believed that the country's industrial sector remained inappropriately protected. Throughout the summer and fall, as the nation prepared to hold its presidential election, the impost controversy stubbornly refused to recede. Writing to his aide William Lewis on the subject, Jackson indicated a willingness to employ force to make South Carolina comply with federal law:

> I am prepared to act with promptness & energy—and should the laws be resisted, to enforce them with energy & promptness—our Government is sufficiently strong for self preservation, and under my administration, the laws will be duly executed and the union preserved—regardless of the reckless course of the great nullifier of the South [Calhoun] and all his satilites.[8]

In early October the South Carolina state elections favored the nullifiers who, capturing majorities of more than two-thirds in both legislative houses and claiming approximately 60 percent of the popular vote, defeated the unionists.[9] Public campaigning in places like Charleston occasionally resulted in mob violence, which only heightened tensions.

The nullifiers, now in control of the legislature, called for a state convention, which met in Columbia on November 19. This gathering demanded a dramatic drop in the tariff—to a uniform rate of 12 percent—but more remarkably passed an ordinance by a wide margin (136–26) declaring the tariffs of 1828 and 1832 to be null and void in the state of South Carolina. Payment of import duties, the ordinance indicated, would cease on February 1, 1833. The following month a concentrated reshuffling in South Carolina's leadership ensued. Hayne, considered less able than Calhoun to articulate the nullifier's position, surrendered his Senate seat and, following a quickly called legislative election, assumed the governorship; fifteen days later Calhoun resigned the vice presidency to fill Hayne's vacant upper chamber post. The new governor, at the general assembly's request, promptly began to raise a state army of volunteers. At the same time unionists, under the leadership of Joel Poinsett, a former congressman, minister to Mexico, and Jackson's de facto agent in South Carolina, struggled to establish a voluntary force in opposition. If violence broke out, Jackson preferred that it come internally, thus smoothing the way for U.S. soldiery to assist South Carolina's nationalists. "Congress will aid me to put down this outrageous rebellion," he wrote Poinsett in early December, "& I mean to put it down by the exertions of the Patriots of South Carolina, who at my call will rally under the banners of the constitution & the law to enforce it."[10]

For several months Jackson, though hoping to avoid armed confrontation, had quietly been making military preparations to neutralize Charleston. In September he arranged to have the military leadership in and around the city replaced to ensure its allegiance to the president. "I am confidentialy advised," he wrote to an assistant, "that the nullifyers of the south, have corrupted both the Naval officers, and those of the army in charleston—that they nullies are determined to push matters to extremities, and expect to get possession of the forts &c. . . . Therefore let the officers & men be relieved by a faithful detachment, and this carried into effect as early as possible." He further transferred troops to Fort Moultrie, sent "five thousand stand of muskets with corresponding equipments" to Castle Pinckney, and ordered Major General Winfield Scott (with whom he had skirmished several years earlier in the Division Order controversy) to prepare for military operations. Jackson also sent his private secretary, George Breathitt, to circulate through South Carolina in November, strategizing with the state's unionists, noting the strength of the city's federal military instillations, and more generally keeping his ear to the ground. "You will collect all the information touching the subject instrusted to your inquiries that you can obtain, which may be serviceable to the government," Jackson enjoined. And then he paused. "It is the most earnest wish of the President," Secretary of War Lewis Cass advised Scott, "that the present unhappy difficulties in South Carolina should be terminated without any forcible collision; and it is his determination that if such collision does occur it shall not be justly imputable to the United States."[11]

Seeking to further marginalize the nullifiers, Jackson struck a note of conciliation in his annual message, dated December 4. Citing the continued contraction of the country's debt, he recommended that Congress, excepting "what may be necessary to counteract the regulations of foreign nations and to secure a supply of those articles of manufacture essential to the national independence and safety in time of war," virtually abolish the tariff. "In effecting this adjustment," he candidly observed, "it is due, in justice to the interests of the different States, and even to the preservation of the Union itself." Gesturing to southern complaints on protectionism, he noted further, "If upon investigation it shall be found, as it is believed it will be, that the legislative protection granted to any particular interest is greater than is indispensably requisite for these objects, I recommend that it be gradually diminished, and that as far as may be consistent with these objects the whole scheme of duties be reduced to the revenue standard as soon as a just regard to the faith of the Government and to the preservation of the large capital invested in establishments of domestic industry will permit." Though refusing to abandon entirely the principle of protectionism, Jackson argued that it must be something considered "temporary" and "incidental" rather than "perpetual," lest it breed "a spirit of discontent and jealousy." Just as the National Bank, so Jackson believed, profited a privileged few, so the tariff gave undue advantage to industrialists. No longer, the president maintained, could these factory, shop, and mill owners "expect that the people will continue permanently to pay high taxes for their benefit."[12]

Just a week later, in response to receiving South Carolina's ordinance to block tariff collection within its borders, Jackson, aided by Kendall and Secretary of State Livingston, issued a second and more assertive statement, *Proclamation on Nullification*. It reviewed the president's opinions on states' rights and the Constitution, while scolding the "strange position that any one State may not only declare an act of Congress void, but prohibit its execution." What stands out, however, is Jackson's personalization of South Carolina's action. In a string of "I," "me," and "my" assertions, the old General again played the gallant, the great hero called in troubled times to save his ailing nation. A single long sentence early in the document strikes this sublime note of indispensability:

> To preserve this bond of our political existence from destruction, to maintain inviolate this state of national honor and prosperity, and to justify the confidence my fellow-citizens have reposed in me, I, Andrew Jackson, President of the United States, have thought proper to issue this my proclamation, stating my views of the Constitution and laws applicable to the measures adopted by the convention of South Carolina and to the reasons they have put forth to sustain them, declaring the course which duty will require me to pursue, and, appealing to the understanding and patriotism of the people.[13]

From there, Jackson denied completely the right of nullification. If one state deemed the impost unconstitutional, he asked, how could it then be enforced in others? And what might then become of the federal government's revenues? And who, after all, gets to decide the legality of a federal law? The Constitution prescribes the federal court system—so noted the man who ignored the Marshall Court's ruling in favor of Georgia's Cherokees—but the nullifiers of South Carolina presumed that this power resided with themselves. Jackson thought this absurd. "Every law operating injuriously upon any local interest will be perhaps thought, and certainly represented," he pointed out, "as unconstitutional, and, as has been shown, there is no appeal."[14]

If the principle of nullification was recognized, Jackson continued, the Union would surely collapse. And so, in the *Proclamation*'s most ringing sentence, he wrote, "I consider . . . the power to annul a law of the United States, assumed by one State, *incompatible with the existence of the Union, contradicted expressly by the letter of the Constitution, unauthorized by its spirit, inconsistent with every principle on which it was founded, and destructive of the great object for which it was formed.*" He then proceeded to pick apart South Carolina's ordinance, denying its pointed claim that the tariffs were chiefly in place to aid industry or that the state's cotton economy suffered as a result. In sum, he ridiculed the nullifiers' reasons for seeking "an open opposition to the laws of the country" in a liberal, legal system of governance their fathers had helped to create.[15]

Jackson further adopted in the *Proclamation* a position on sovereignty embraced by many nationalists, particularly in the North. "The people of the United States formed the Constitution," he contended, "in which the people of all the States, collectively are represented" under a single government. He likened his election and reelection to the presidency as an embodiment of that principle, one in which a state or even an entire section might give its support for one candidate but abide by another if elected. "The people, then, and not the States," he argued, "are represented in the executive branch."[16] That line did more than make a point on democratic governance in America, it also stressed Jackson's belief that the president, more so than the courts or even the legislatures in Columbia, Albany, Boston, and elsewhere, served as the people's protector.

The *Proclamation*, communicated to Congress on January 16, 1833, accomplished Jackson's goal to effectively isolate the nullifiers. Speaking directly to the "Fellow-Citizens of my native State," he reminded them of their advantages—"You are free members of a flourishing and happy

Union"—while agreeing that the tariff possibly tilted too high—"You have indeed felt the unequal operation of laws which may have been unwisely, not unconstitutionally, passed"—and promised that "that inequality must necessarily be removed." Above all, he said in closing, they might take pride that more than merely South Carolinians, they "too are citizens of America."[17]

It is unclear how many Charlestonians embraced Jackson's message— or even if they constituted his primary audience. Possibly above all he sought to quarantine secessionist sentiment and keep proximal states such as Georgia and Virginia from making common cause with South Carolina. The *Proclamation*, logical, lawyerly, and pitched in a patriotic key, did just that.

Northern opinion in particular rallied around Jackson's manifesto. A reliably dry Charles Francis Adams called the paper "ably written . . . In several of its passages reminding me of my father's style." He thought it just good enough to wonder "who could have been the Author." A delighted Philip Hone described "the language of the President [as] that of a father addressing his wayward children, but determined to punish with the utmost severity the first open act of insubordination."[18] Clay, by contrast, saw in the *Proclamation* a chieftain-president's determination to dominate equally states, congresses, and courts:

> After 44 years of existance under the present Constitution what single principle is fixed? The Bank? No. I[n]ternal Improvement! No. The Tariff? No. Who is to interpret the Constitution? No. We are as much afloat at sea as the day when the Constitution went into operation. There is nothing certain but that the *will* of Andw. Jackson is to govern; and that will fluctuates with the change of every pen which gives expression to it. As to the Tariff now pending, before the House, whether it will pass nor not in that body depends upon his commands."[19]

The tariff bill alluded to by Clay in fact fulfilled Jackson's call for a general reduction of duties. Auspiciously introduced in the House on yet another Battle of New Orleans anniversary (January 8, 1833), the measure proposed to halve the present duties over a two-year period— really an altogether extensive revision. It might be said to have graciously addressed the nullifiers' concerns or, conversely, to have signaled a sizable concession on the part of the central government. To accompany this carrot, however, the president quickly produced a rather thick stick—the Force Bill. Time was running out, South Carolina's February 1 deadline to resist the collection of revenue loomed, and Jackson now sought authorization to use, if necessary, federal troops to enforce the law. Privately, he thought such a possibility likely. "If I can judge from the signs of the times," he wrote to Secretary Cass in late December, "Nullification, & secession, or in the language of truth, *disunion* is gaining strength, we must be prepared to act with promptness, and crush the monster in its cradle before it matures to manhood."[20]

Accordingly, eight days after the proposed tariff revisions went before Congress, so did Jackson's Force Bill. Tensions eased considerably when, on the 21st, the nullifiers gathered in a public assembly in Charleston and—both uncertain of their support from neighboring states and impressed with the reform tariff bill's proposed reductions—suspended the nullification ordinance while Congress debated the impost. For the time being, they announced, "all occasions of conflict . . . should be sedulously avoided."[21] The House and Senate took up the Force (called by its detractors the Bloody or War) Bill in late January, and nearly a month later, after a vigorous if somewhat anticlimactic debate, it passed 32–1 in the upper chamber. The appearance of near unanimity is deceptive. Most of the nullifiers and their allies, certain to be on the short end of the count, refused to vote; this passive resistance came primarily from the slaveholding states and cut across party lines. Some days later the bill eased through the House, 149–48.

During the Force Bill debate, Clay, with Calhoun's support, proposed a competing bill to lower the tariff. It sought a reduction of duties to 20 percent ad valorem over a period of nine years, a slower reduction than the act supported by Jackson, though neither Clay nor Calhoun wished to see the General claim such a resounding series of recent victories—the Bank veto, reelection, the Force Bill—on so many fronts without a challenge. Defeated by Jackson only three months earlier in the general election, Clay still eyed the presidency and may have hoped by the bill to attract future southern votes. Known as the Compromise Tariff, the act passed the House on February 26, 119–85, and three days later the Senate obliged 29–16. The crisis had come to an end.

On March 2, Jackson signed both the Force Bill (first, as though to prioritize) and then the revised tariff legislation. A convention in South

Carolina subsequently repealed the nullification ordinance and then contemptuously nullified the Force Act. Though nationalists throughout the country claimed victory—Yankee farmers took to calling their scarecrows Calhouns—a longer lens suggests a more mixed outcome.[22] South Carolina sought a strong tariff reduction and received, after much blustering, beseeching, and threatening, precisely that. Its cause might more broadly be coupled with that of Georgia, which had also faced down federal power and benefitted. The accumulated outcomes of these challenges to centralized authority—the removal of mostly free laboring Native Americans in the South and the sharp contraction of an impost designed to benefit industrial manufactures and thus wage-earning factory workers—aided a southern economy predicated upon enslavement. In a period of less than three years Jackson, by vetoing the Maysville Road and Bank recharter bills and reducing the tariff, advanced in certain vital respects a states' rights vision for America.

Still, some southerners refused to see Jackson as an ally. They distrusted his nationalism and loathed his rhetorical insistence on rule by the people. A meeting of Milledgeville, Georgia, men denounced the Force Bill as an effort to "insidiously restore to the Federal party, the power which they lost under the elder Adams," while one disaffected North Carolina Democrat warned James Polk, "General Jackson's proclamation will not satisfy the South. It is thought to be an abandonment of the rights of the states." Even Jackson's friend Thomas Hart Benton said he "could not concur in some of the doctrines of the Proclamation."[23]

A generation later these sectional concerns echoed powerfully among the plantocracy. In the secession winter of 1860–61, as South Carolina separated from the Union and then wondered what to do with the federally held Fort Sumter in Charleston Harbor, the *New York Times* proclaimed Jackson "the favorite hero" of a rising Republican Party. That early March, in his much anticipated inaugural address, Lincoln, sporting a new black suit and adjusting his glasses, declared before an anxious crowd, "The Union . . . [is] perpetual," and eagerly drew upon Jackson's argument that the people rather than the states had made the nation—and made it enduring. No nullification, no secession.[24]

40

New England Swing

A few months after the nullification crisis, Jackson commenced an extended early summer tour of the Mid-Atlantic and New England states. Only the third president to journey widely about the country—Washington and Monroe having set precedent—he submitted to an exhausting season of banquets and barbecues, parties and parades. Such festive occasions were invariably freighted with meaning. Assuming the obligation of a nation-builder, Washington had gamely barnstormed the North (as far up as Kittery, Maine) and South successively between 1789 and 1791, careful to visit each of the original thirteen states. By appearing as both a symbol of the central government and a hero of the Revolution, he hoped to shake his fellow citizens' residual suspicion of federal power. Monroe, making two trips, also negotiated the nation's several regions; the latter trip, a southern swing, included a stopover in Nashville and a quick tête-à-tête with Jackson. His first excursion, amid a wave of post–War of 1812 nationalism, seemed calculated to put an end to partisanship in the United States. Following a brief stopover in Boston, one Federalist newspaper, the *Columbian Centinel*, cooperatively employed the phrase "Era of Good Feelings" to describe the visit.

The origins of Jackson's elaborate circuit ride are a little hazy. That he received in early February 1833 an invitation by a committee of Hartford, Connecticut, citizens to visit their state and region is clear. This summons and his acceptance probably hinged, however, on the enormous goodwill aroused in various Yankee enclaves following the showdown with South Carolina. Certainly local Democrats, noting that Jackson had earned more than 46 percent of the section's popular votes in the previous November's election and followed that up by smiting the detested nullifiers, desired his association. Even the region's irreconcilables were otherwise amenable to showing this particular Tennessee slaveholder an amicable face. "Jackson had come to us at a period," a former Massachusetts congressman recalled, "when his bitterest opponents, if not quite ready to forget their grievances ... were prepared to remain in the background and make no protest to mar the popular cordiality." Eager to display the fruits of their civilization, Hartfordians expressed a wish that Jackson might view the section's "commercial cities and manufacturing towns; her temples of worship, colleges, and seminaries; and to visit and mingle with her active and virtuous population."[1] Entreaties from other quarters of New England quickly followed.

The president's touring party left the capital on June 6, making the forty-mile journey north to a raucous Baltimore. Following a three-day stay in which Jackson became the first president to ride in a train— boarding the Baltimore and Ohio Railroad in Ellicott's Mills for a short trip into the city—his cortege, after a brief sortie to New Castle, Delaware, to meet the governor, traveled to the Philadelphia Navy Yard aboard a steamship greeted by a crowd of thirty thousand. Having negotiated the obligatory pilgrimage to Independence Hall, followed by a military parade in a fierce sun that blistered his weathered face, Jackson next stepped onto the steamer *North America* at Perth Amboy, New Jersey, for the short sally to Manhattan. "The landing took place on the wharf at Castle Garden [now known as Castle Clinton]," Philip Hone recorded. "It was impossible to preserve order. The wharves and housetops and vessels were covered with people; the troops were drawn up on the Battery." From Castle Garden the president slowly rode up Broadway on horseback, to a reception at City Hall. The raspy crowds, immense and excited, formed "a solid mass of men, women, and children," Hone noted, and in their earnest affections wore against the old man's stamina. Days earlier the president had confided to his son Andrew Jackson, Jr., of discomfort—"I have seen Doctor Phisic, who encourages me, and says my heart is not effected in any way, and the pain in the side can be removed by cupping. I sincerely wish my trip was over. except to my Hermitage, or to the watering places, I think it is the last journey, I shall ever undertake."[2]

Perhaps the infectious enthusiasm of the people summoned the old soldier up each morning. After visiting three towns in New Jersey "and passing," as he put it, "over in procession three fourths of the city of Newyork," Jackson wondered at the astounding reach of his popular appeal. "I have witnessed enthusiasms before," he wrote one relative, "but never before have I witnessed such a scene of personal regard as I have to day, and ever since I left Washington. I have bowed to upwards of two hundred thousand people to day—never has there been such affection of the people before I am sure been evinced." Eager to drop, if just for a few weeks, the strain of partisanship, he insisted, "Party has not been seen here."[3]

Beyond the daily bobbing and bowing, Jackson managed here and there to conduct more practical affairs. In Baltimore he had met with Black Hawk, the ancient Sauk warrior who had the previous year led some one thousand Indians, compelled under a disputed treaty to cede their property and relocate to what is now Iowa, back across the Mississippi in an attempt to resettle on tribal lands in Illinois. Quickly confronted by frontier militia, a desperate Black Hawk instead conveyed a band into present-day southern Wisconsin where, greatly outnumbered and trying to withdraw, it fell to U.S. forces at the Battle of Bad Axe. Soon after, Black Hawk surrendered. In custody he met two future presidents, Colonel Zachary Taylor and Lieutenant Jefferson Davis, the latter accompanying him by steamboat to confinement in St. Louis. In early 1833 he was brought, as something of celebrity prisoner, east and held for several weeks in Virginia's Fort Monroe. Upon release Black Hawk, hazel-eyed and broad-shouldered, with a fine-edged nose, was required by U.S. officials to visit a number of cities along the East Coast. That is how he happened to find himself in a Baltimore hotel with Jackson, who he referred to as "Our Great Father." In effect the president, touring the nation to observe its vigor, population, and capacity, demanded that Black Hawk do the same: "You will see the strength of the white people. You will see, that our young men are as numerous as the leaves in the woods. What can you do against us?"[4]

The question of the Bank also came up during Jackson's trip. Though having failed to secure a recharter, it operated under an existing franchise that ran for three more years; Jackson wished to see it expire quietly. In New York the president discussed with Van Buren the feasibility of directing future revenues away from the Bank and placing them in state depositories—his cabinet having already criticized the idea. Shortly after the meeting Jackson informed his son that plans were now under way to "make the arrangement with the different Banks."[5] Managing the ongoing battle with Biddle from afar, Jackson now left New York and headed to New England, the only section of the country to provide anti-Jackson majorities in the last two presidential elections.

In Connecticut the General visited Bridgeport, New Haven, and Hartford before crossing over to Rhode Island and from there, via the Pawtucket Bridge, to Massachusetts. Josiah Quincy, Jr., the sandy-haired thirty-one-year-old son of Harvard's president, met him at the border, assigned by Governor Levi Lincoln to serve as the president's personal chaperone through the state. The party enjoyed a convivial breakfast in Attleboro before moving on to Quincy (ancestral home of the Adams family), then Roxbury, and finally, on the 21st, Boston. There, Benjamin Brown French, a young New Hampshire Democrat, recorded the erstwhile Puritan city's robust reaction to Jackson:

> Soon after four a flag was run up upon the flagstaff at the top of the dome of the State House, which was the signal that the President was within the city, a salute was fired and all the city bells commenced ringing. Tremont Street was crowded with the populace all pushing toward the Common. I . . . passed up to the Common with the multitude, where I found all the Engine Companies paraded in two lines & the Scholars of the schools of the city within them, also in two ranks, leaving a passageway between for the President & his suite to pass through. . . . The crowd, like a vast river, came rolling back through Tremont Street.[6]

Jackson was exhausted. On the road for over two hard weeks and "finding myself," so he noted in one communication, "a good deal fatigued after the labors of the day," he canceled several scheduled activities.[7] A large public reception at the State House, however, went off as planned.

After being soberly addressed in a packed House chamber by the governor, Jackson greeted, as one observer put it, "a continual stream of citizens passing through for two or three hours, to everyone of whom the President bowed. He became so much fatigued that it was thought advisable to close the doors, or Heaven only knows how long they would have kept him bowing." While in Boston Jackson's lungs, never strong, began to hemorrhage, causing an attending physician to twice bleed the president. This act of heroic early American medicine coaxed from John Quincy Adams, doubtlessly annoyed at New England's strong turnout for the president, a waspish retort—"He is so ravenous of notoriety that he craves the sympathy for sickness as a portion of his glory. He is now alternately giving out his chronic diarrhœa and making Warren bleed him for a pleurisy. . . . Four-fifths of his sickness is trickery, and the other fifth mere fatigue."[8] Jackson's ailments were authentic, though after two days of bed confinement he felt well enough on the 26th to write a long letter to his treasury secretary, William Duane, on the deposits question and to make the short trip to Cambridge to receive the honorary degree of Doctor of Laws.

No doubt much of Harvard blanched at the notion of making the General even a nominal doctor, partly because of his politics and partly because the distinction between ceremonial and academic degrees was less clear than it is today. Insisting that he lacked the requisite literary or scientific achievements for such an award, Millard Fillmore discreetly refused Oxford's offer in 1855 to make the touring former president an honorary Doctor of Civil Law.[9] But it would have been both impolite and impolitic for Harvard, having conferred degrees on Washington and Monroe as they visited Cambridge on earlier presidential tours, to now ignore Jackson. Even so, wags and critics alike sniggered at the apparent incongruity of Jackson sharing a stage with scholars, struggling to comprehend a Latin-solemn ceremony. Josiah Quincy, Jr., held a higher opinion of the man he had observed over the previous few days, calling him "in essence, a knightly personage,—prejudiced, narrow, mistaken upon many points . . . but vigorously a gentleman in his high sense of honor and in the natural straightforward courtesies which are easily to be distinguished from the veneer of policy; and I was not prepared to be favorably impressed with a man who was simply intolerable to the Brahmin caste of my native State."[10]

Adams, among the cream of that caste, retained his reservations. Having turned down an invitation to attend the Harvard ceremony, he apprised his diary, a little indignantly, of the painful reason why:

As myself an affectionate child of our alma Mater, I would not be present to witness her disgrace in conferring her highest Literary honors upon a barbarian, who could not write a sentence of gram-

mar and hardly could spell his own name. [Harvard president]
Mr. Quincy said he was sensible how utterly unworthy of Literary
honors Jackson was, but the Corporation [one of the university's
two governing boards] thought it was necessary to follow the precedent, and treat him precisely as Mr. Monroe his predecessor, had
been treated. As the People of the United States had seen fit to make
him their President, the Corporation thought the honors which
they conferred upon him were compliments due to the station, by
whomsoever it was occupied. Mr. Quincy said it was thought also
that the omission to show the same respect to President Jackson
which had been shown to Mr. Monroe would be imputed to party
spirit, which they were anxious to avoid.[11]

"I was not," the former president bristled, "satisfied with these reasons." His youngest son, Charles, also a chronic diarist, confirmed the
official family attitude—"father is somewhat indignant," while Louisa
Catherine chose to commemorate the occasion in a nervy verse:

> Discerning old Harvard presents the degree
> Old Hickory asks pray *what means* LLD?
> The Corporate Sages afraid of excess
> Reserve for themselves that of A.S.S.[12]

It is perfectly reasonable to consider, however, that Jackson, a former justice on the Tennessee Supreme Court and a recent (if certainly
controversial) interpreter of constitutional law in the Worcester, Bank,
and nullification controversies, believed that he had earned Harvard's
respect. In an undated paper written late in life, the General wrote, "I
never could accept of an honorary title, where I had not a claim to the
honor, conferred, by some personal acts of my own."[13] It might be that
both Harvard and Jackson found themselves in similarly unwanted situations. Jackson could hardly have toured New England without stopping
in Boston, while Harvard could scarcely have let him pass by without
offering the same honor it had bestowed upon other presidents. All
played their parts, and following the ceremony the president genially
received students in the parlor of the old gambrel-roofed Wadsworth
House, which, in its circa 1720 splendor, had previously sheltered nine

Harvard presidents and briefly served as Washington's headquarters during the Revolutionary War.

Dr. Jackson continued his tour in nearby Charlestown, inspecting the still incomplete Bunker Hill memorial. After giving a concise address at the site, he sat for two hours as Congressman Edward Everett unlimbered a lengthy speech. (A celebrated orator, Everett delivered a similarly extended address thirty years later at Gettysburg, Pennsylvania, this time with another president offering a brief remark.) Heading north, Jackson passed through Lynn, Salem, and Andover on his way to Lowell; several scheduled engagements were canceled due to the president's persistently flagging health. Surprisingly, Lowell appealed to him immensely. Jackson the agrarian, the owner of enslaved labor, and the recent signatory of a reduced tariff bill, was absolutely intrigued by Lowell's famous mills, epicenter of America's nascent industrial revolution. A factory town, the City of Spindles housed the ubiquitous mill girls, who worked, worshiped, and boarded there. Perhaps some five thousand of these women, "all under thirty and all dressed in snow-white dresses with sashes of different colors to designate their different manufacturing establishments," were brought out to smile and greet the president. Observing the mills in operation, he asked question after question. "Jackson was evidently much impressed with what he had seen," Josiah Quincy later wrote, "and, indeed, talked of little else till we reached the State line, about noon the next day."[14]

Now in New Hampshire, the president's party went to Portsmouth and from there to Concord. "I never saw people so happy as all appeared," one observer wrote, before adding, "There were some croakers who kept themselves hidden until all was over, & then commenced finding fault." At this point the tour, intended to bring Jackson yet farther to Maine, Vermont, and upstate New York, abruptly ended—the exhausted president simply could not go on. As John Quincy Adams gauged the situation, Jackson "must hasten back to Washington, or he will be glorified into his grave."[15] Returning to Lowell, he moved south, circumventing Boston, and caught a steamboat in Providence which took him to New York, at which point the party decided to push on to Washington. In all, this rapid three-day journey from Concord to the capital covered nearly five hundred miles.

More than simply a presidential tour, Jackson's New England swing brought tangible benefits to his party. In the 1836 election Van Buren held on to Vermont and Maine—won by the General in 1832—and captured Connecticut and Rhode Island as well. "President Jackson has been prodigiously successful in his excursion this Summer from Washington," Charles Francis Adams fairly lamented. "His Popularity has appeared unbounded even in the strong holds of opposition."[16] Drained from his arduous travels, Jackson expected little rest upon returning to Washington. He quickly reengaged, rather, in the battle to reduce Biddle's power and to finally put his bank out of business.

41

Shades of Caesar

Jackson's 1832 veto constituted the principal though by no means final act of what turned into a protracted Bank War. Concerned with Biddle's power to provoke a financial crisis, to impact elections, and to bestow upon politicians and newspaper editors various emoluments in the Sisyphean struggle to renew the depository's charter, Jackson sought to mute its influence. One particularly strong option drew his attention: putting future revenues into state banks while continuing each month to pay the government's bills out of Biddle's Bank. Though this policy was certain to meet the president's objective, many Democrats, much of his cabinet included, balked at what they regarded as a potentially disastrous decision. Unburdened by federal oversight, the unregulated state depositories might be tempted to over-lend and thus create, as one advisor told the president, a "great disturbance in commercial affairs."[1] While not without precedent—Congress's 1811 refusal to recharter the First National Bank forced Madison to park government dollars in state coffers—Jackson enjoyed other options, including maintaining the status quo. But fearing, with some reason, Biddle's reaction to the veto, he determined to do otherwise.

Seeking evidence of corruption that might aid his as yet private proposal, the president looked expectantly to a seven-member congressional Ways and Means Committee report investigating the Bank. But its findings, issued on March 1, 1833, declared the government's funds safe under the existing system; the House shortly thereafter approved of the study by a large margin, 109–46. Three members of the committee dissented, however, chief among them Jackson's fellow Tennessean

James Polk. This noncompliant cluster issued a separate minority report claiming ongoing corrupt practices with the people's money by Biddle. Ignoring the majority report exonerating the Bank, Jackson now took it upon himself to put the removal policy in play. In an anxious moment he linked his chief political opponents together in a grand, improbable conspiracy to now prop up the depository. "But before nullification had received its death blow," he wrote Hugh Lawson White, "a new combination between clay and calhoun is discovered. . . . I am very strongly impressed with the opinion . . . that one object, in [their] so arranging the Tariff Bill as that it should produce a large surplus, was to enable, *thereby*, the Bank to survive its present depressed condition."[2]

Jackson subsequently polled his cabinet on a number of questions relating to the management of Biddle's Bank, its right to continue receiving federal funds, and the feasibility of establishing a new banking system. In a long reply dated May 20, Treasury Secretary McLane strongly opposed removal. He had "no doubt" of the Bank's constitutionality; "of the usefulness of such an institution, surrounded with proper safeguards," he expressed but "little doubt." To now spend down the Bank's deposits, he argued, denied the nation of a valuable service. "As long as the Bank exists," he wrote, "the government and the People shall be deprived of none of the advantages they are entitled to derive from it," and he reminded Jackson that his recent veto, which refused to extend the institution beyond 1836, could not negate the fact that "the act chartering the bank is a part of the law of the land" and this charter tasked the Bank with handling the government's revenues *into* 1836. In regard to this important duty, McLane continued, "it has fulfilled its obligations." He then raised the question of whether the kind of corruption Jackson saw in Biddle's bank could not be repeated in state repositories. "The local banks might use the encreased means which the public deposites would give," he pointed out, for purposes "of gratifying private or political partialities or resentments."[3]

Jackson recognized the vigor of McLane's response, writing on his personal copy, "There are some strong points in this view—all ably discussed."[4] But this hardly stopped him. Because McLane maintained that only the treasury secretary could remove the deposits, and he declined, Jackson took the opportunity to shuffle his cabinet a second time. His secretary of state Edward Livingston pined to serve as U.S. minister to France, an office held during the first Jefferson administration by his older brother Robert. The post had opened months before, and Jackson now expediently sent Livingston to Paris and gave to McLane, a man he much respected and who had generally supported his policies, a nominal promotion to head the State Department. In his place Jackson tapped a relative unknown, William Duane, an Irish-born lawyer and loyal Democrat who had once sat in the Pennsylvania General Assembly. Jackson needed Duane to do only one thing, oversee the removal policy. It proved, maddeningly for the president, to be the one thing that Duane refused to do.

In a July 10 communication to Jackson, Duane laid bare his reasons for resisting removal: "It is very painful," he cautiously opened, "to be obliged to decline to adopt the course [prescribed by] . . . the President." But decline he did. Though affirming his support for Jackson's recharter bill veto ("The bank has forfeited all claims to favour. . . . It has put itself in the wrong"), he reminded Jackson that "the charter is the law of the land; it is a contract, that cannot be dissolved, or altered. . . . The public deposites are a benefit to the bank, for which it has paid a consideration, and their continuance is a part of the contract." If Jackson feared misconduct on the Bank's part, Duane continued, appealing to the nation's court system appeared to be the logical, legal alternative. "It is the right of the President to arraign," Duane argued, "and the right of the judiciary to try, the bank." But Jackson now proposed to assume all power, to arraign, try, and execute. Duane pointed out that by law only he, as treasury secretary, could remove deposits, only he was legally bound to file reports on Bank matters to Congress, and, though nominated by Jackson, his appointment was Senate confirmed. The House, he further pointed out, had recently voted by a significant majority that the government's money remained safe in the Bank—"Is there, then," he rhetorically asked Jackson, "any cause for sudden and extreme action?"[5]

More than questioning the president's removal plans, Duane raised the tricky question of executive power in the republic. Jackson lacked the authority, he contended, to divert public monies to state depositories as the sixteenth section of the Bank's charter, still good for three more years, clearly directed those funds to the Bank. And the president further enjoyed no jurisdiction, he maintained, to force the treasury secretary to do his bidding without first consulting Congress. But Jackson considered such concerns little more than legal hairsplitting. Without consulting Duane, he had sent Kendall to talk with the managers of several state banks in order to identify those institutions capable of receiving the government's monies. In selecting such depositories Kendall enumerated a single overriding condition—they must be loyal to Jackson. "With equal capital and character," he identified the criteria to one Connecticut correspondent, "those which are . . . politically friendly will be preferred." Thus, one of Jackson's more compelling charges against Biddle—he played politics—could now be leveled at him as well. In reply, the furious opposition to the president would refer contemptuously to these institutions as pet banks.[6]

It became increasingly evident to Jackson that Duane would have to be dismissed. The president feared the Bank's power to corrupt the political process, to pour money into congressional elections in a bid to yet finagle a new charter. The treasury secretary's unwillingness to contend with this possibility, his delay and disdain of overseeing a new system, placed him squarely in Jackson's sights. "It will be unpleasant for me to differ with these two gentleman [McLane and Duane] for whom I have such high regard," Jackson wrote Van Buren in August, "but when duty points the way, my private friendships must yield to public good, and if I should loose twenty more friends as highly prised as they, my feeling being now as it was on the Maysville Road bill, and the Bank veto; 'that it is a duty I owe to my country, my conscience and my god,' to put down this mamoth of corruption and to separate it from being the agent of the Government as early as possible for the safety of its fiscal concerns."[7]

Matters now moved quickly to a predictable end. On September 9 Jackson sent Duane the report and accompanying correspondence relating to Kendall's search for suitable state banks to assume the government's funds. Seven—three in New York, two in Boston, and one each in Philadelphia and Baltimore—had been deemed acceptable. But not to Duane. "The answers of some of the banks, willing to act, showed, that they ought not to be trusted," he later wrote. "Several of the most substantial institutions refused to act as fiscal agents, under any circumstances." The following day and again on the 17th Jackson convened his cabinet to discuss the impending removal. McLane and Secretary of War Lewis Cass objected while Secretary of the Navy Levi Woodbury equivocated; only Attorney General Taney supported the proposal. "Taney has been firm," Jackson wrote to Van Buren at this time, "others wavering." Frustrated, the president described himself as "determined to have the matter settled."[8] On the 20th, under his authorization, a notice appeared in the *Globe* declaring removal a reality.

Jackson assumed Duane would resign, indeed he hoped to part amicably and appoint him to lead the U.S. legation to the Russian Empire as a kind of consolation. Duane had other plans. He met with the president on the 21st and the two remained at odds. Having listened to the secretary reiterate his decision to neither remove the deposits nor step down, Jackson chose to see signs of personal discourtesy—"Then you do not mean," he said, flashing some evident frustration, "that we shall part as friends." The following day he dismissed Duane. Having now dispensed with two treasury secretaries in fewer than four months, the president appointed Taney, a safe, trusted, and effective loyalist; Benjamin Butler, a long-time New York ally of Van Buren, took over as attorney general. "Mr. Taney is commissioned, sworn into office, and the business of the Treasury is progressing as tho Mr. Duane had never been born," Jackson wrote a little testily to the Little Magician on the 23rd.[9] Actually he nearly faced another cabinet collapse. McLane and Cass briefly considered resigning before the *Globe*, nudged by the president, announced the cabinet's independence from the new policy. Aside from the unwanted but manageable tussle with Duane, Jackson had gotten what he wanted.

Reflecting some months later on the president's successful skirmish over the Bank's deposits, Supreme Court justice Joseph Story wrote to a fellow jurist in early 1834, "though we live under the form of a republic we are in fact under the absolute rule of a single man. . . . I seem almost, while I write, to be in a dream and to be called back to the last days of the Roman republic, when the people shouted for Cæsar, and liberty itself expired."[10] Many around the country, sharing Story's concerns of a polity in peril, determined to erect a stronger and better organized opposition than that which Jackson had toppled in 1832.

42

Censure

As Jackson's second term opened, a growing chorus of critics arraigned the president as a tyrant, a danger to the nation's delicate constitutional balance between the executive, legislative, and judicial branches. A host of angry nullifiers thought the Force Bill undermined states' rights, while the Bank veto offended advocates of state-aided modernization. Though disparate combinations—Calhounites embraced localism while Clayites fostered nationalism—they jointly arraigned Jackson for lodging an unprecedented and, to their minds, alarming degree of power in the presidency. Other potential allies were prone to agree. The Anti-Masonic Party, its candidate claiming nearly 8 percent of the popular vote in the 1832 election, could see in Jackson's partisan appointments the kind of corrupt insider politics that had fueled its crusade, while humanitarian objectors of Indian removal and slavery brought a moral tone to the table.

Combined, these various strands and sympathies formed something of an incongruous coalition. Conversant with past crusades against executive despotism, Jackson's opposition called itself the Whig Party, taking its name from those English advocates (circa the 1670s–1850s) of constitutional monarchism in place of absolute monarchism. One popular 1833 American political cartoon, playing to this theme, christened a crown-wearing, scepter-bearing Jackson, "King Andrew the First." Though the Party survived but a generation—rising in response to questions over banking, internal improvements, and Jackson himself, then collapsing in the 1850s when sectional discord proved paramount—its unease with the growth of centralized power endured, embedded in periodic complaints of imperial presidencies and codified in the Twenty-Second Amendment (1951) which, in the wake of Franklin Roosevelt's unrivaled four general election victories, placed term limits on executive office occupants.

As a growing opposition to Jacksonianism began to take shape, Jackson himself moved ahead with the contentious removal program. By the end of 1833 twenty-two pet banks held government funds—a number that grew to nearly one hundred by 1836. While the National Bank slowly contracted, Biddle remained busy, deciding, following a meeting in early October 1833 with the Bank's board of directors, to begin a general curtailment of loans. He believed that by causing economic pain, by slowing the spigot of available funds, he could threaten an economic crash and thus force Jackson to reverse course. "This worthy President thinks that because he has scalped Indians and imprisoned Judges," Biddle wrote to a colleague, "he is to have his way with the Bank. He is mistaken." Over the next several months a modest financial panic ensued as Biddle squeezed the nation's financial markets;

BORN TO COMMAND.

OF VETO MEMORY.

HAD I BEEN CONSULTED.

KING ANDREW THE FIRST.

An 1833 caricature of Jackson during the Bank War. This gets to the heart of the debate about Jackson: Was he a democrat, a representative of the "common man," or did he in fact rule as an aristocrat who made war on the Bank for his own reasons?

he called in loans from state banks, who were then forced to press their borrowers for repayment. As money became precious, loans dried up and some believed a panic on the order of 1819 in the offing. But Jackson held firm. "The curtailments by the U.S. Bank will oppress only their own friends," the president insisted to Van Buren, "and when done for mischiefs sake only, it will raise up the whole in hostility to it."[1] Having let Charles Dickinson put a bullet in him from eight paces, he refused to bow now before a mere banker.

A divided Congress, however, grew increasingly anxious as the economy gave signs of faltering. On December 26 Clay offered resolutions in the Senate designed to censure both Jackson and his removal policy. Presumably the Kentucky pol would have preferred impeachment proceedings, though only the House possesses that power. Instead, he pushed for an unprecedented senatorial condemnation of a sitting president, aware that the emerging anti-administration coalition enjoyed a majority in the upper chamber. The first resolution declared that in light of Jackson's dismissal of Duane "the president has assumed the exercise of a power over the treasury of the United States not granted to him by the constitution and laws, and dangerous to the liberties of the people." The second measure attacked Taney, Duane's replacement, for giving "unsatisfactory and insufficient" reasons for putting the public's money into state banks.[2] In support of these articles, Clay more generally warned of a coming despotism in America if the nation failed to rein in its too powerful president:

> We are in the midst of a revolution, hitherto bloodless, but rapidly tending toward a total change of the pure republican character of the government, and to the concentration of all power in the hands of one man. The powers of Congress are paralyzed, except when exerted in conformity with his will, by frequent and an extraordinary exercise of the executive veto, not anticipated by the founders of our constitution, and not practiced by any of the predecessors of the present chief magistrate.[3]

"You will have seen from my movements," Clay wrote at this time to Peter Porter, formerly secretary of war in the Quincy Adams administration, "that I do not mean to spare this wicked administration."[4] And certainly for several weeks in the winter of 1833–34, the debate over Jackson's actions consumed Congress. Clay, as well as Calhoun and Webster, repeatedly attacked the president's high-handedness; Senator Benton, who had nearly killed Jackson in a public brawl twenty years earlier, proved to be his old adversary's chief defender.

Finally, on March 28, Clay's now slightly altered December resolutions came to a vote before the Senate, where they were read on the floor:

> *Resolved,* That the reasons assigned by the Secretary of the Treasury for the removal of the money of the United States deposited in the Bank of the United States and its branches, communicated to Congress on the 4th of December, 1833, are unsatisfactory and insufficient.
>
> That the President, in the late executive proceedings in relation to the public revenue, has assumed upon himself authority and power not conferred by the Constitution and laws, but in derogation of both.[5]

The resolutions passed 26–20. An incensed Benton called the vote a "mere[ly] personal censure" and "having no relation to any business or

Jackson remains the only president censured by the U.S. Senate: for his constitutionally dubious role in denying federal deposits to the National Bank. Here Clay is shown stitching Jackson's mouth shut.

proceeding in the Senate."[6] This symbolic public scolding, the only such rebuke of a president ever conducted by the Senate, incited Jackson's indignation. Never one to walk away from a fight, he engaged his rivals, sending to the upper chamber a long message of protest dated April 15.

With the considerable aid of Taney, Kendall, and the newly installed attorney general Butler, Jackson vehemently denounced the Senate's censure. "I think my protest will shew," he wrote to Andrew Jackson, Jr., "that it is not I, but the Senate who have usurped power and violated the constitution." Making a strained historical analogy and discounting the dangers of a too powerful executive, he claimed the upper chamber the logical place for jobbery to lodge: "I am sure the people will recollect, that it was a corrupt and venal senate that overturned the liberty of Rome before ever Cezar reached her gates, and if ever our republic is overthrown, it will be by a venal Senate usurping all power and forming an alliance with a corrupt monied monopoly."[7] Jackson's complaint arraigned the Senate's upbraiding as "unauthorized by the Constitution," an extralegal effort to lessen the legal prerogatives of the executive office. Alluding to the recent Duane entanglement, the president defended his right to make cabinet appointments and to remove those appointments at will. Only "in the conclusion of treaties," he argued, is the executive obligated to seek "the advice and consent of the Senate." A president may be impeached, subject to private legal action, or held "accountable at the bar of public opinion," he continued, but a censure "is wholly unauthorized by the Constitution."[8]

After a long explication on the impeachment process, he then defended his actions throughout the Bank War, making in the process the kind of exaggerated plea for presidential power that worried critics. "Every species of property belonging to the United States," he astonishingly insisted, "whether it be lands, or buildings, or merchandise, or provisions, or clothing, or arms . . . is in [the] charge of officers appointed by the President . . . responsible to him, and removable at his will." If true, then the treasury secretary, along with any number of civil and military officials, was a mere clerk, ultimately under the direction of a single man. The president seemed to be reserving for himself the type of autonomy he accused Biddle of enjoying. This dangerous assertion needed to be walked back. On Van Buren's suggestion, Jackson subsequently sent an explanatory note to the Senate acknowledging "the power and right of the legislative department to provide by law for the

custody, safe-keeping, and disposition of the public money and property of the United States."[9]

Perhaps most remarkable is Jackson's startling assertion in the protest that the nation's constitutional system made him ultimately answerable to the public and thus, by implication, less so to Congress. "The
President is the direct representative of the American people," he contended, ignoring the even closer constituency-based relationships
institutionalized in both the Senate and particularly the House of Representatives. For Jackson, rather, "the Chief Magistrate elected by the people" assumed a greater "responsib[ility] to them."[10] This is precisely the
type of unfiltered appeal to popular democracy that caused the skeptical
Founders to erect a system of separate and counterbalancing branches
of government. Jackson's striking rhetoric raised for many the question
of whether rule of law or rule of man would rule in the republic.

Senate Whigs thought Jackson's message contemptuous and condemned his swollen assumptions of presidential powers, which
appeared to be limited only to the extent the people wished them to
be limited. Daniel Webster called the president's logic chimerical, a fic-
titious presumption resting on "remote analogies" and based on "an
undefined, undefinable, ideal responsibility to the public judgement!"
He could see only trouble ahead. "I ask, Sir, Is this republicanism? Is
this a government of laws? Is this legal responsibility?" No doubt he
saw an irresponsible populist commandeering the executive mansion,
an ignorant ruffian who produced with the aid of a few lieutenants a
self-aggrandizing protest "purely ideal, delusive, and vain."[11]

While Jackson and the Senate jousted in the early spring of 1834, the
Bank War inevitably wound down. Biddle's contraction of the money
supply, which resulted, as prescribed, in an economic downturn, only
offered ammunition to the Bank's growing list of critics. In the House,
where a Democratic majority resided, Polk pressed successfully for resolutions that both denounced the depository's bid to win a fresh charter
and, by a lesser margin, endorsed the new pet banks plan.

While this final phase of the Bank War played out, Jackson cannily
delayed sending Taney's treasury nomination to a Whig-controlled Senate for confirmation. Finally, on June 23, nine months into the acting
secretary's tenure, he forwarded the name. Some Whigs contended that
Taney's removal of the deposits as an unconfirmed official constituted
an illegal action—just another example, they believed, of Jackson's will-

ingness to circumvent the law. The Senate promptly, soundly, and perhaps a little vengefully rejected the nomination (28–18) on the 24th. Possibly out of spite it also rejected that same day, by a narrow 23–22 margin, the president's nominee to the Court of Saint James's, Virginia congressman Andrew Stevenson. A loyal Jacksonian, Stevenson was said, while serving in the House, to have organized committees and chairmanships along lines congenial to the president.[12]

The constant churn in Jackson's official family—nine new secretaries and two rotating attorneys general in little over a year—was unprecedented. While it is tempting to see the earlier Eaton Affair as sui generis, as an unusually disruptive feature in Jackson's administration, it might more accurately be said to have anticipated the greater chaos to come in the president's second term. The common denominator in both cabinet shuffles is neither John nor Margaret Eaton, Calhoun nor Van Buren, Biddle nor Taney, but Jackson, of course.

Those concerned over presidential power organized institutionally in Whiggery, a single-generation party mainly operating in the Democracy's electoral shadow. It embraced the American System and its Bank adjunct as instruments of economic development leading to moral progress. New roads, canals, and cleaner urban spaces populated by well-educated Americans implied a kind of cultural gentrification. Its connection to the Bank, however, proved problematic, and the coalition suffered for this association in the 1834 elections. "After staggering along from year to year with a doomed bank upon our shoulders," the New York Whig Thurlow Weed grieved shortly after the November contests, "both the bank and our party are finally overwhelmed."[13] Though wary of Jackson's aristocratic bearing, the Whigs were rarely able to overcome their own awkward reputation as the party of social conservatism in an increasingly egalitarian America. Competing in five national campaigns (1836–1852), the party elected only two presidents, both of whom, William Henry Harrison and Zachary Taylor, were pocket Jacksons—generals, southerners, and military heroes. These luckless Whig presidents, the first chief executives to die in office, combined to serve for only seventeen largely forgettable months.

The Bank War did more, however, than inspire an opposition party, it further slimmed down and solidified the Jacksonians. The unwieldy reform coalition of 1828, home to South Carolina nullifiers and

Pennsylvania high tariff proponents, western advocates of government-funded improvements and southern defenders of states' rights, gained focus and precision through the struggle against Biddle. "Our party is too large already," declared one Democratic newspaper in New Hampshire at the time.[14] Previously, major coalitions were relatively ephemeral affairs, tied to personalities and lacking institutional strength. After George Washington's passing, Federalism failed to sustain its progress and soon disappeared; once Monroe, the last of the Virginia dynasty, left office, the Democratic-Republicans quickly splintered. In 1834, by contrast, the Jacksonians gave every indication of gaining strength. Ironically, Jackson, the would-be Caesar, stands also as the leader of the first major American party to survive the retirement of its great hero. Inventing a new tradition, the coalition finally proved bigger than the man.

43

Facing Europe

Though internal issues dominated Jackson's presidency, he periodically engaged in foreign affairs with the major European powers. In contrast to the previous four executives—Jefferson, Madison, Monroe, and Quincy Adams, all of whom had served as secretary of state—he lacked formal experience in the art of international relations. No doubt his critics must have wondered, reflecting on the General's never forgotten invasion of Spanish Florida, if he retained the requisite temperament to keep the country at peace. He proved, however, to be a reasonably adept manager of American diplomacy, despite the fact that the State Department, headed by no fewer than five men during his two terms, lacked traction.[1] Jackson benefited enormously, of course, from the conclusion of the Napoleonic campaigns, a generation-long struggle that bedeviled Jeffersonian statecraft by invariably bringing European wars to American shores. In their wake the United States determined with the Monroe Doctrine (1823)—warning the Old World off future New World colonization—to master its geopolitical fate.

Jackson's first real diplomatic success involved a new trade agreement with Great Britain. This achievement, considering the president's deeply rooted loathing of British power, gives some suggestion of the more pragmatic qualities of leadership he sometimes employed. Following the War of 1812 a series of British navigation acts, followed by retaliatory American measures, combined to severely limit U.S. exports to the lucrative West Indies trade. The situation festered for several years, and finally, in 1825, American ships were barred entirely from these British colonial ports. Naturally Jackson supporters hammered away at then President Adams, presumably a master diplomat, for failing to find a way to open this commerce. The impasse—stemming in part from the poor relations between Adams and British secretary of foreign affairs George Canning—changed dramatically once Adams left office and Canning conveniently died. Charged to set aside older issues dividing the powers, Louis McLane, American minister to the United Kingdom, negotiated a treaty in October 1830 that reopened West Indies markets and in return granted British ships most favored nation status. "The trade will be placed upon a footing decidedly more favorable to this country than any on which it ever stood," the president subsequently informed the nation in his annual message, "and our commerce and navigation will enjoy in the colonial ports of Great Britain every privilege allowed to other nations." The New York Jacksonian James Hamilton boasted correctly enough that the compact satisfied "all ranks and parties, except the factious cavilers."[2]

The following year Jackson appeared to have scored another foreign policy success. Through the persistent negotiating of the American diplomat William Cabell Rives, France agreed on July 4, 1831, to award the United States nearly $5 million for damages incurred during the Napoleonic conflicts. The United States pledged in turn to pay France a significantly lesser sum to settle the Revolutionary War claims of the Beaumarchais family, whose polymath patriarch, Pierre Beaumarchais—inventor, spy, and author of *The Barber of Seville* and other Figaro plays—conducted covert aid (supplies, munitions, and money) from Spain and France to further the American Independence movement. Mutual adjustments, moreover, on American long-staple cotton and French bottled and casked wines were part of the compact. Two months later the Senate unanimously approved the treaty, and in early February both nations exchanged ratifications. Jackson thought the accord—and the one signed the previous year with Great Britain—marked a real turning point in America's international affairs. "Thus in two years," he wrote John Coffee shortly after receiving the French treaty, "we have been able to obtain justice from all Foreign Governments, which had been the subject of negotiation for many years." But the optimistic president presumed too much. For France's Chamber of Deputies took no positive action on the allotment until April 1834, at which time, having second thoughts regarding the cost of the claims, it refused to pass an appropriations bill. Two months later Jackson wrote with disappointment to Edward Livingston, U.S. minister to France, "I was not prepared to hear the result of our treaty with France."[3]

That December Jackson detailed in his annual message to Congress the rickety course of U.S.-French relations both before and after the 1831 treaty. In frustration, he denounced the current French government for "wanting in the performance of the stipulations it has so solemnly entered into with the United States." What to do? "We can not embarrass or cut off the trade of France without at the same time in some degree embarrassing or cutting off our own trade," he pointed out.[4] Still, he continued, a remedy other than a trade war stood at the ready—the confiscation of French property:

> It is my conviction that the United States ought to insist on a prompt execution of the treaty, and in case it be refused or longer delayed take redress into their own hands. After the delay on the part of France of a quarter of a century in acknowledging these claims by treaty, it is not to be tolerated that another quarter of a century is to be wasted in negotiating about the payment. The laws of nations provide a remedy for such occasions. It is a well-settled principle of the international code that where one nation owes another a liquidated debt which it refuses or neglects to pay the aggrieved party may seize on the property belonging to the other, its citizens or subjects, sufficient to pay the debt without giving just cause of war.[5]

France's rejection of the treaty, Jackson argued, its continued failure to indemnify Americans for legitimate claims, warranted such a drastic action. "This remedy has been repeatedly resorted to," he said, scrambling for the high ground, "by France herself toward Portugal, under circumstances less unquestionable." As some of Jackson's political enemies had recently rallied around the president during the nullification crisis, more than a few Whigs now wished him well. "I believe the only way to maintain the dignity of this country is not to allow itself to be trifled with," Charles Francis Adams maintained. "France has acted in a manner shamefully wrong and the sense of it ought to be expressed by this Country. General Jackson can do it."[6]

Predictably, Jackson's message to Congress played poorly in Paris. Did America's president presume to bully the deputies into accepting a treaty? The French replied twice—first, King Louis Philippe I ordered

Louis Barbe Charles Sérurier, his envoy to the United States, home, and second, a bill to indemnify the United States comfortably passed the Chambers in April 1835, 189–137. The legislation included, however, a proviso that made the payment conditional on Jackson explaining his hawkish December comments on France's tardy march to making good on the spoliation claims. Jackson's response, evident for the all world to see, appeared in the May 29 *Globe*—"France will get no apology."[7]

The idea of an American president, he argued, explaining to a foreign country an internal (and constitutionally prescribed) communication between separate branches of its government, would not do. Matters festered over the next several months as both sides dug in, the French perhaps planning to wait Jackson out and deal with his successor. This logjam eventually broke due to what the president did and did not say. In his December 1835 annual message he tactfully refused to flay or embarrass the French as many had predicted he might. He struck, rather, an even and somewhat conciliatory tone. Though Jackson did indicate that "the honor of my country shall never be stained by an apology from me," other statements in the address—that his earlier message was meant "to contain no charge of ill faith against the King of the French" and that "self-respect and regard to the dignity of other nations would always prevent us from using any language that ought to give offense"—were eagerly accepted by French officials as suitable indications of remorse.[8]

By this time the British had also entered the picture, promoting conciliation. Eager to avoid a costly maritime conflict that might disrupt American cotton imports to English factories, foreign secretary Lord Palmerston proposed, so he stated to Aaron Vail, chargé d'affaires of the United States to the United Kingdom, that the Franco-American quarrel not be "carried to extremities." He offered Britain's services, rather, to mediate the affair. Both France and the United States eventually accepted the help, though, in fact, the intervention never occurred. Acknowledging Jackson's "apology" in his most recent annual message, which followed the British overture, France allowed the indemnification treaty to go forward. Not long after, in May 1836, the first of four installment payments took place. Jackson described the action to Congress as a "satisfactory termination of our controversy with France."[9]

During Jackson's presidency, numerous Napoleonic era spoliation claims involving American merchants and several European governments were addressed. The total sought—some $14 million (about $430 million in current dollars), of which a bit more than half was collected—constituted a modest amount in what proved to be the final phase of antebellum America's Atlantic-oriented diplomacy.[10] From this point on, the country focused increasingly on its own hemisphere. The Latin American wars of independence (1808–1826), along with the push of white—and enslaved—settlement beyond the Mississippi, heralded a new dynamic in U.S. diplomacy. Much of Jackson's foreign policy thinking fixated in its final years on the unstable situation in Mexico and on his palpable desire to extend the nation's fluid borders farther south.

Part VII

SOUTHERN SYMPATHIES

The sacrifice of the rights of Northern freedom to Slavery and the South, and the Purchase of the West by the plunder of the public Lands, is the . . . system of Jackson.

John Quincy Adams, 1837

Jackson at the age of 64, nearing the end of a long public career committed to the removal of the southern Indians, whose former lands became the heart of a budding cotton belt reliant on enslaved labor.

44

Jackson and the Abolitionists

In the summer of 1835, amid the spoliation claims controversy, Jackson engaged in yet another unwanted entanglement, forced to respond to the willful destruction of U.S. mail by American citizens. In late July abolitionist literature directed toward Charleston, South Carolina, reached, via steamboat, the city's postmaster. Discovered in the sorting process, these several thousand pamphlets and tracts, addressed to specific Charlestonians, promptly excited the wrath of a furious mob led by a self-appointed vigilante society known as the Lynch Men. Within twenty-four hours the materials had disappeared into a great bonfire on the city's parade grounds before a cheering crowd of some two thousand. Soon thereafter a "committee of five," led by former governor Robert Hayne, proposed to inspect incoming mails and destroy materials deemed repugnant. Postmaster Kendall (elevated, just weeks earlier, into the president's cabinet) sympathized with the committee, yet knew the law did not. Though he hoped, so he wrote one Charleston official, to see the offensive items destroyed "with as little noise and difficulty as possible," he refused to give official sanction: "I am not prepared to direct you."[1] For the second time in three years, Jackson turned his attention to South Carolina and to the growing contradictions of slavery's existence in an increasingly liberal, industrial democracy.

The origins of the abolitionist petition campaign began in 1833 with the formation of the American Anti-Slavery Society (AASS). Situated in New York and presided over by ashen-whiskered Arthur Tappan, a devoutly religious operator of a successful silk-importing firm, the Society found itself by 1835 at a crossroads. Sparsely funded, it had begun to divide between its conservative wing and the more radical devotees of William Lloyd Garrison, the small, balding Boston-based editor of the *Liberator*, who was said by one contemporary to possess "the pert loquacity of a blue-jay." A spectacularly defiant gesture promised to energize the Society, publicize its mission, and generate financial support. Its leadership consequently decided to inundate the southern mails with abolitionist materials, a legal if enormously provocative action.[2]

The campaign caught the South at a particularly vulnerable moment. Just two years earlier Britain's Parliament, taking note of its nation's lessening reliance on West Indian trade and prodded by activists unrelentingly engaging in petitions, mailings, and speeches, passed the Slavery Abolition Act of 1833. It established a mix of immediate and gradual emancipation within most of the empire, while compensating owners. A defining strike against slavery, the act eventually freed more than eight hundred thousand people in the Caribbean, just off the Florida coast.

The materials sent south by the AASS were obviously intended to offend the eye. These easily hung broadsides, adorned with woodcut illustrations of enslaved men and women being beaten and brutalized, inflamed Charlestonians—many of whom insisted that the images were designed not primarily for white consumption but to agitate blacks into taking up arms. Though this particular fear misstated the Society's goal, one of its members, the Connecticut-born mathematician Elizur Wright, noted at the time, "We are beginning to see ahead of us a conflict which will outdo—far—all the skirmishes of the past."[3]

By August angry oratory, strident meetings, and torchlight parades characterized the responses of whites in southern port cities and elsewhere affected by the pamphlet petitions. One abolitionist was imprisoned in a Georgetown jail for circulating such materials; another supporter of the mail campaign barely escaped a mob in Lynchburg, Virginia.[4] The government now needed to protect both the law and U.S. citizens; instead, it did something a little different.

In a private August 9 communication to Postmaster General Kendall, Jackson candidly expressed his unvarnished views on the dispute. He described those involved in the campaign as "monsters" and seemed a bit bothered that the nation's laws protected such men from being summarily executed: "Could they be reached, they ought to be made to atone for this wicked attempt, with their lives." Jackson did acknowledge that their activities were perfectly legal—"we have no power to prohibit anything from being transported in the mail that is authorized by the law"—but, taking a cue from Kendall, he outlined a strategy for intimidating, harassing, and perhaps physically endangering those rare southerners who wished to peruse the AASS antislavery materials:

> Few men in society will be willing to acknowledge that they are encouraging by subscribing for such papers this horrid and most wicked procedure; and when they are known, every moral and good citizen will unite to put them in coventry, and avoid their society. This, if adopted, would put their circulation down everywhere, for there are few so hardened in villainy, as to withstand the frowns of all good men. . . . In every instance the Postmaster ought to take the names down, and have them exposed thro the publik journals as subscribers to this wicked plan of exciting the negroes to insurrection and to massacre.[5]

There is in this note an echo of Jackson's efforts, almost thirty years earlier, to gain the names of those who solicited the black mourning borders in a Tennessee newspaper tribute to the duelist Charles Dickinson. He hoped then to frighten his opposition into acquiescence. He now sought a kind of sequel, though in accommodating public pressure in the South to censor the mails, the stakes were considerably higher.

Predictably, the *Globe* used the abolitionist postal drive for political purposes. It blamed "Whig leadership" in an August 22 editorial for commencing the campaign and identified Tappan as "the archenemy of the present Administration."[6] Mere partisanship, in other words, lay behind the "assault" on the mails. This garbled argument aligned with Jackson's sense of persecution and long-standing unwillingness to respect the sincerity and moral seriousness of his opponents. He suspected the abolitionists of using slavery as a stalking horse, rather, to attack his administration. In Jackson's world of finely spun conspiracies, the rich and influential feared democracy and threw whatever they could—internal improvements, the Bank, and now abolitionism—to knock him down. He took seriously only his own ethical concerns, and the cares of others were variously dismissed as mere opportunism.

As the weeks passed, several southern communities tendered resolutions forbidding the circulation of abolitionist materials. In some of these towns extra-legal vigilante committees formed, as Jackson had hoped, to ensure that inflammatory materials placed in the federal mails went undelivered upon reaching the local level. Many postal officials in both the North and South complied with this unlawful practice. As one scholar has written, "anticipating Kendall's support, the postmaster of New York City had already made it his policy to stop abolitionist literature at its point of origin."[7]

That December, Jackson ruminated darkly on abolitionism in his seventh annual message. Insisting that "no respectable portion of our countrymen" could possibly empathize with enslaved people, he denounced the Society's efforts and claimed for good measure that an attack on slavery amounted to an assault on the Constitution. As that document recognized the property rights of the plantocracy, he argued, "the misguided persons who have engaged in these unconstitutional and wicked attempts" were on the wrong side of the law. An obvious solution, he continued, stood at the ready—the legal suppression of postal material: "I would . . . respectfully suggest the propriety of passing such a law as will prohibit, under severe penalties, the circulation in the Southern States, through the mail, of incendiary publications intended to instigate the slaves to insurrection."[8] By maintaining that prints and illustrations critical of slavery were essentially aimed at the enslaved, he hoped to couch his call for censorship by denying that any whites, aside from those obviously "misguided," were affected.

Jackson's old nemesis Senator John Calhoun perhaps predictably opposed the president's proposal. He argued that the states, not the central government, possessed the right to determine through local law what might and might not enter their borders. Neither got his way. Several months after Jackson's address a new postal law sustained the government's right to deliver the mails, thus endorsing rather than limiting freedom of speech. This statute—and several successors—Jackson refused to enforce. In practice, abolitionist materials were largely kept out of the South through the Civil War.

In the wake of the Society's mail campaign, some prominent Democrats joined the president and rallied to condemn abolitionism. Van Buren, requiring southern support in 1836 to succeed Jackson, needed Jacksonians in his native New York to lean in Dixie's direction on the slave question. Accordingly, Governor William Marcy declared the advocates of black freedom "visionary and pernicious" at an anti-abolitionist meeting in Albany; in October a violent crowd led by Congressman Samuel Beardsley interrupted an antislavery gathering in Utica before turning its attention to the neighboring headquarters of the abolitionist weekly *Oneida Standard and Democrat* and destroying its type. Speaking in an official capacity, Marcy praised the rioters' actions.[9] This spirit of violence in the North carried into the following year. In November 1837 Elijah Lovejoy, a Presbyterian minister, journalist, and abolitionist, was murdered by a crowd in Alton, Illinois, determined to cease his printing of antislavery materials.

On at least one occasion Jackson invoked the power of populism to reject abolitionism. In early 1835, a few months before the crisis in Charleston, the president enjoyed a convivial White House supper with a number of guests including Richard Robert Madden, an Irish abolitionist on his way home from the recently emancipated Caribbean. Madden later recalled their conversation:

> After we had discussed the subject of the emancipation of the slaves in the British West Indies, I said, *en résumé* of my views:—"The sooner, General, you adopt a similar measure in the United States the better. It would be a fitting finale of a great career like yours to connect it with such an act of emancipation." The President was standing with his back to the fire when I said this. He burst out laughing, and addressing his guest on either side said—"This gentleman has just come from the West Indies, where the British have been emancipating their slaves. He recommends me to make myself famous by following their example. Come here, Donaldson (turning round to his private secretary), put the poker in the fire, bring in a barrel of gunpowder, and when I am placed on it give the red poker to the Doctor, and he will make me famous in the twinkling of an eye."[10]

If Jackson embodied popular democracy, no less did he express the fading aspirations of the final generation of planter aristocrats to serve in the executive office. As some of his southern Democratic associates guessed, making the people's will a kind of extralegal sanction augured ill for minority opinion; and slavery, the peculiar institution, was becoming increasingly a minority opinion. Between the 1803 Louisiana Purchase and 1845, seven of the eleven states admitted into the Union came in with slavery; from 1845 to the April 1861 firing on Fort Sumter, however, six new states came in, all free. Planter apogee in an age of Jackson neared its end, giving way to a new age of abolition.

45

Removal Redux

In late December 1835, just a few months after northern abolitionists began to target southern mails, government officials and a minority Cherokee faction signed the Treaty of New Echota, which ceded the territory of the entire Cherokee Nation in the southeast. Approved by neither principal chief John Ross nor the Cherokee National Council, the accord, ratified the following March in the Senate, became the legal means by which thousands of Cherokees were forced to remove beyond the Mississippi. This process, part of the broader Trail of Tears trauma that included the Choctaw, Chickasaw, Chickamauga, Creek, and Seminole nations, constituted the logical conclusion of the Indian relocation policy initiated by Jackson five years earlier in the Removal Act. Though that agreement distinctly recognized existing treaty rights, it also empowered the government to negotiate land exchanges, while appropriating half a million dollars—be it in graft, gratuities, or bribes—for such purposes. The president and his legal negotiators, Eaton and Coffee, were thus able to manipulate divisions and factions within Indian nations in order to create the conditions by which removal inevitably ensued. That dire day had now come.[1]

The last desperate maneuvering began in early 1835 when Ross asked for a $20 million indemnity in exchange for the Cherokees' remaining eastern lands. The price, more than $600 million in current dollars, Jackson thought prohibitive (Jefferson had paid less for the Louisiana Purchase), and he supposed Ross was stalling. Days later, Secretary of War Cass responded with the government's counteroffer—$5 million—which Ross took as an insult and refused to entertain. The administration then opened negotiations with John Ridge, Elias Boudinot, Stand Watie, and several other Cherokee leaders; this Treaty Party concluded a draft agreement that exchanged seven million acres of Indian land in Georgia, Alabama, Tennessee, and North Carolina for territory in the West and the aforementioned $5 million.[2] Ross faction Cherokee subsequently assassinated some of the agreement's signatories in revenge.

The Cherokee national government rejected Cass's offer and created a committee to negotiate a more acceptable agreement, recognizing removal to be at this point unavoidable. Jackson's friend and envoy, John Schermerhorn, a Dutch Reformed minister and Indian commissioner, suggested that the two sides meet in December at New Echota, Georgia, the Cherokee capital. There, following a few days of discussion, a compact, much resembling the earlier draft treaty, was reached. Ross and other non–Treaty Party Cherokee leaders were discouraged at the results and hoped the Senate might scuttle the accord. But it passed through the upper chamber that spring 31–15, barely garnering the necessary two-thirds majority.[3] Over the petitions and protests of more than ten thousand Indians, Jackson signed the bill on May 23, making removal the law of the land.

The Treaty of New Echota called for a voluntary removal concluding in two years—May 1838. Though presumably protected until that time, many Indians were driven off their lands during the interregnum. Jackson, his term running until March 1837, did nothing to defend them. When the deadline arrived, some seventeen thousand Cherokees continued to occupy their homes, barns, and fields. About seven thousand U.S. Army and militia soldiers, under the command of the ubiquitous General Winfield Scott, charged five years earlier to move against Charleston's nullifiers if necessary, began to collect, intern, and otherwise extract the irreconcilables; removal commenced in the fall and extended through the early spring of the following year. Land and water routes cutting through several states over hundreds of miles were used by the Cherokees to reach their destination in present-day Oklahoma. Traveling in often harsh climatic conditions, they suffered incredible hardships. An estimated four thousand died during this forced exodus of hunger, exposure, and disease.[4]

Late in the removal process, the Transcendentalist Ralph Waldo Emerson, only thirty-four and not quite yet the Concord Sage, sent a furious manifesto to Massachusetts congressman John Reed, who eased its May 14, 1838, publication in the *National Intelligencer*. Emerson briefly reviewed the chicanery at New Echota that lent a dubious legitimacy to the seizure of Cherokee lands by producing an arrangement "pretended to be made by an agent on the part of the United States" and "persons appearing" to serve the Cherokee but "by no means represent[ing] the will of the nation." Emerson called this "a sham treaty," "a crime," and a "conspiracy" that mocked the American sense of fairness and rule of law. "Such a dereliction of all faith and virtue," he continued, "such a denial of justice, and such deafness to screams for mercy were never heard of in times of peace and in the dealing of a nation with its own allies and wards, since the earth was made." In cheating the Indians, he suggested, the country betrayed itself, ignoring the liberal enlightenment values that made it a New World republic rather than yet another abusive Old World imperial master. What path did it now propose to take? "Will the American government steal?" he asked. "Will it lie? Will it kill?"[5]

The removal policy continued for several years, during which a Second Seminole War, succeeding the earlier (1816–1819) conflict conducted by General Jackson, removed an additional four thousand Indians to the West. Resourceful fighters, the Native Americans inflicted hundreds of battle deaths on U.S. soldiers and perhaps as many as a thousand Seminoles managed to remain in Florida. This fighting proved to be the bloodiest, most protracted, and most expensive of the removal process.

In all, nearly sixty thousand Indians were dispossessed of their eastern lands as a result of the Indian Removal Act of 1830. Of the fewer than ten thousand that remained, most resided in upstate New York, the Middle West, and the Old Northwest. Jackson, while regarding his efforts as essentially humanitarian for rescuing the Indians from hostile white populations, had put into motion a large-scale relocation process that ultimately produced widespread suffering and death. Insufficient government funds were allocated, and this led to inadequate protection and limited supplies for exposed peoples traversing hundreds of miles, often during the winter months. These were the peoples Jackson said he wished to save.

By the early 1850s the California Gold Rush had combined with pressure from snaking interstate railroad systems to spur Congress into granting president Franklin Pierce the power to arrange treaties

permitting white set-
tlement on certain
Indian lands beyond the
Mississippi—territory,
so Jackson had prom-
ised the Choctaw peo-
ple in 1829, where "their
white brethren will not
trouble them ... [and]
it will be theirs forever."
During the Civil War,
Lincoln received author-
ity to negotiate a similar
arrangement in Kansas,
and still later, in 1887, the
Dawes Act sanctioned
the surveying and divi-
sion of Indian holdings
with the intent of extin-
guishing tribal owner-
ship in favor of individual
ownership.[6] As a result
the old southern tribes
were victimized yet
again, losing some one
hundred million acres to
settlers, speculators, and
railroads. All the while
U.S. forces waged a series
of violent Indian wars
throughout the century's
second half, involving
Apache, Comanche, and
Sioux, among numerous
other western peoples.
This violent, unedify-

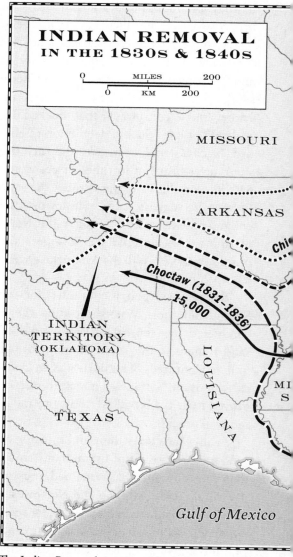

The Indian Removal Act signed by Jackson in 1830
resulted, by the end of the decade, in the forced dis-
placement of some 60,000 self-governing southern
Indians, at least 8,000 of whom died along the Trail
of Tears.

ing history accentuates Jackson's important role in the removal process
while also contextualizing it within a broader historical narrative that

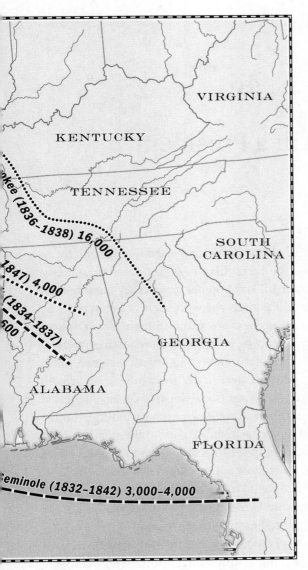

VIRGINIA

KENTUCKY

TENNESSEE

...kee (1836-1838) 16,000

...847) 4,000

(1834-1837)

...00

ALABAMA

SOUTH
CAROLINA

GEORGIA

FLORIDA

...eminole (1832-1842) 3,000-4,000

includes multiple layers, players, agendas, and tragedies.

For Jackson, the Treaty of New Echota capped a career-long effort to uproot Native communities from their southern lands. As a young man he had fought Indians in the Tennessee Territory, destroyed Red Stick power during the War of 1812, and not long after pursued the Seminoles into Florida. As Sharp Knife he forced the Creeks to cede a vast empire, more than twenty million acres, in Alabama and Georgia. Perhaps more than any other individual, Jackson fostered the expansion of a cotton belt kingdom connecting older southern Atlantic societies with newer Gulf states, an area encompassing, it might be noted, the core of the future southern Confederacy. His legacy must invariably be reckoned with the consequences these transactions entailed.

46

To Kill a President

The removal process attested to one particularly striking, though by no means solitary, example of the Jacksonian era's turbulent personality. Increasing mobility, materialism, and popular democracy combined to produce, among a people still conversant with their colonial past, an unprecedented flux. "Even in families," wrote the eminent New England theologian William Ellery Channing in 1835, "we see jarring interests and passions, invasions of rights, resistance of authority, violence, [and] force."[1] Older paternalistic patterns were in decline while urban growth and immigration, riots and poverty, sectionalism and slavery suggested to some a coming upheaval. Antebellum reformers—including promoters of temperance, abolitionism, women's rights, millennialism, and more—mixed hope with anxiety in seeking to remake the nation's fluid republican culture. It seems somehow apt that amid this unease Jackson should be the first president targeted for assassination. The arrival of an increasingly heated partisanship helped bring him to power and, in its moiling strength, nearly captured him in its confusion.

In yet another and more personal respect, the targeting of Jackson appears perhaps foreseeable if not grimly fitting. Occasionally belligerent, often bullying, and always self-righteous, he could invite malice in others. Many considered his duel with Dickinson a cold-blooded killing; he carried inside him the bullets fired by men in some combination of honor, odium, and fear.[2] As president he remained a remarkably contentious figure. In May 1833 Robert B. Randolph, a former naval purser discharged upon Jackson's discretion for stealing, coolly twisted the president's nose on the steamboat *Cygnet* while it docked in Alexandria, Virginia. Jackson and his party were on their way to nearby Fredericksburg, Randolph's home, to participate in a ceremony in honor of Martha Washington. Unexpected proximity to the president gave rise to a quick, convenient revenge. The episode is recorded in Parton's biography:

> "Excuse my rising, sir," said the General, who was not acquainted with Randolph. "I have a pain in my side which makes it distressing for me to rise." Randolph made no reply to this courteous apology, but appeared to be trying to take off his glove. "Never mind your glove, sir," said the General, holding out his hand. At this moment, Randolph thrust his hand violently into the President's face, intending, as it appeared, to pull his nose. The captain of the boat, who was standing by, instantly seized Randolph and drew him back. A violent scuffle ensued, during which the table was broken. The friends of Randolph clutched him, and hurried him ashore before many of the passengers knew what had occurred, and thus he effected his escape.[3]

Jackson's nose was reportedly bloodied and his pride predictably wounded. "I am not much hurt," he is remembered to have said on the *Cygnet*, while a few days later he complained to Van Buren of "the dastardly and cowardly insult offered me." John Quincy Adams thought the episode qualified for many of the General's victims as a case of vicarious cold revenge. "A President of the United States pulled by the nose, is a new incident in the History of this Country; and as he himself has countenanced personal violence against members of Congress, he will not meet with much sympathy."[4]

The attempt to assassinate Jackson occurred nearly two years later, in Washington in January 1835. The narrative of the young republic up to this time included internal rebellions in states, fierce partisanship, and widening sectionalism, but never before an effort to murder the occupant of the executive office. Following a memorial service for a South Carolina congressman in the cavernous House chamber, Jackson and a small group were walking through the Capitol Building toward the East Portico when Richard Lawrence, a thirty-year-old unemployed housepainter lingering by the entrance, suddenly confronted the president, only a few feet away. Lawrence drew and fired a pocket pistol which, according to Adams, also in the vicinity, sounded "like a squib," though

Benton upgraded the effect to "loud." The powder in the gun's barrel having failed to ignite, Lawrence quickly produced a second pistol with his left hand as Jackson, perhaps out of a combination of alarm, anger, and self-preservation, raised his walking stick as if to assail his assailant; Lawrence fired again, and again the cap refused to ignite the powder. A small pell-mell ensued as the would-be assassin was brought to the floor by a crush of men and taken into custody. "The attack," said an attending Harriet Martineau, describing Jackson, "threw the old soldier into a tremendous passion."[5]

The president's narrow escape, combined with his history of surviving duels, battles, and all manner of political opposition, offered true believers the faint yet discernible hint of divine intervention. The *Globe* endorsed the apotheosis of Saint Andrew, insisting, "Providence has ever guarded the life of the man who has been destined to preserve and raise his country's glory, and maintain the cause of the People." A dubious Daniel Webster acknowledged no such thing. He feared, rather, that "thousands" of ardent Jacksonians "will believe there was a plot in it" to remove this populist messiah from his masses. And that "many more thousands will see in it new proof, that he is especially favored and protected by Heaven."[6]

And indeed some artless partisans did detect a political plot behind the assassin's efforts—a sort of permanent censure. Though the British-born Lawrence gave evidence of mental illness, claiming that Jackson had both killed his father and hindered his right to be King of England, a few Democrats, including Jackson, wondered if a few Whigs were behind the effort to silence a president who seemed to best them at nearly every turn. Various responses that Lawrence gave in interrogation could be so wrenched to raise this suspicion. When asked by two physicians whom he wished to be president, he gave the names of Clay, Webster, and Calhoun; when asked why he wanted Jackson dead he stated that he "could not rise unless the President fell, and that . . . the mechanics would all be benefited . . . [and] have plenty of work; and that money would be more plenty." And why would there be additional money? Because, he explained, "it would be more easily obtained from the bank"; and when asked which bank, he replied, "the Bank of the United States." For good measure, Lawrence called the president "a tyrant." And how did he form this conclusion? "It was a common talk with the people," he observed, an opinion repeated "in all the papers."[7]

Brought to trial in April, Lawrence inspired more pity than fear. His defense produced several witnesses, including a few Washington physicians who attested to the accused's obvious instability. The one-day trial ended with the jury, after needing only a few minutes of deliberation, reaching a decision of not guilty by reason of insanity. Though acquitted, Lawrence was ordered remanded in custody until he no longer presented a danger to himself or to others. He never experienced freedom again, but lived, rather, in several hospitals and institutions until his death in 1861.[8]

Martineau, on a long visit to the United States gathering materials for books she subsequently published on American society, morals, and manners, called on Jackson the day after the assassination attempt. She later recorded his unwavering insistence on a conspiracy in terms strident enough to make her uncomfortable: "He protested, that there was a plot, and that the man was a tool, and at length quoted the attorney-general as his authority. It was painful to hear a chief ruler publicly trying to persuade a foreigner that any of his constituents hated him to the death; and I took the liberty of changing the subject as soon as I could." Jackson's suspicion of a cabal reflected the high tempers, on both sides of a political divide, that wished to make of Lawrence's failed effort something grander and more sinister. Several Democrats blamed the president's political enemies, while certain administration critics, noting the *Globe*'s recent publications of letters from cranks threatening Jackson, countered that the "plot" was nothing but a ploy to garner sympathy.[9]

Such corrosive posturing indicates the depths to which partisanship now embittered the nation. The actions of a single confused man set in motion a season of recriminations and responses among the country's elected leadership. A persistent tone of distrust, cankering government service ever since the old corrupt bargain charge, continued to conjure ill will in a restless age. Having had his home painted by Lawrence a few months before the assassination attempt, Mississippi senator George Poindexter, a Jackson critic, was accused by a scattering of Democrats of somehow being behind the assault—the kind of irresponsible denunciation that in other nations, in other times, gave way to reigns of terror. Amid this pernicious mood, the chronic problem of slavery's place in the republic—an even deeper source of dispute—began to attract greater attention and moral interest. This query Jackson invariably broached again when looking west, toward the future, toward Texas.

47

Texas Again

The Jacksonian appetite for expansion confirmed a certain continuity between the Tennessee republicans—Jackson, Sam Houston, and James Polk—and the earlier Virginia dynasty. Under Jefferson, Madison, and Monroe, the lands of the Louisiana Purchase, along with the annexation and acquisition respectively of East and West Florida, became part of an emerging American empire. Texas seemed next. Having gained independence from Spain in 1821, Mexico endured repeated efforts by the United States to "reclaim" the lands lying west of the Sabine River. This notion, as some including Jackson put it, of "reannexation," hinged on the hollow presumption (never shared by Jefferson himself) that the Louisiana Purchase included Texas—and was unaccountably bartered away in the 1819 Transcontinental (Adams-Onís) Treaty with Spain. Many years after the fact, John Quincy Adams, armed with decades of diary entries and eager to defend his reputation, vigorously attacked this attempt at revisionist history: "Jackson denies positively that he ever advised the acceptance of the Sabine for the western boundary. . . . [Perhaps he] has totally forgotten his interview with me of 2 and 3 February 1819. The memory of violent men, is always the slave of their passions."[1]

Anglo settlement in Texas emerged under the auspices of the Mexican government, eager to people a thinly occupied region. Enticed by the opportunity to claim hundreds or even thousands of acres, waves of Americans—about thirty-five thousand, mainly southerners—arrived between 1821 and 1835. Some of these émigrés, in violation of the law, brought with them enslaved people or purchased them after entering Texas. By 1830 the government in Mexico City, increasingly concerned that these colonists might one day demand independence or seek annexation into the United States, forbade future immigration. Their fears were well founded. In April 1833 the Americans in Texas, citing misrule, held a convention in San Felipe de Austin and drafted a constitution supporting self-governance. Mexican officials replied by passing a series of measures that briefly appeased the Anglos, but a certain inexorable momentum toward Texas's autonomy had taken hold.

As noted earlier, Jackson's appointment of Anthony Butler in 1829 as chargé d'affaires to Mexico only hindered American diplomacy on the continent. A shyster who readily interfered with Mexico's internal affairs and speculated in the lands he hoped to bring under U.S. control, he proved to be a disastrous choice. In October 1833, Jackson directed Butler to convince Mexico to grant Texas's independence in order to avoid "a bloody civil war." Should the latter occur, Jackson continued, "We cannot restrain our citizens from emigrating to any country they please, we can and will restrain all from arming and raising troops within our Territory. This is all the executive power can do—when beyond our limits our power ceases." In reply, Butler rashly advised the president to order "an immediate occupancy of the disputed Territory." Justifying this outrageous, illegal plan, he audaciously invoked Jackson's old assault on Spanish forts in Florida: "I recollect the advice you gave, and the opinion you expressed to Mr. Monroe in relation to East Florida, a case presenting features nothing like so strong as the present, and with not a tithe of the circumstances to justify the proceeding which we have in the T. affair, I cannot doubt but you will concur with me in the propriety of the movement."[2]

Jackson most definitely did not concur. "In your negotiation on the subject of the boundary," he warned the slippery diplomat, "you must keep within your instructions." This chiefly involved, as Jackson put it, "giv[ing] five millions of dollars for the cession of Texas as far west as the Grand Desert." Butler's follow-up query on how much of this amount to set aside for bribery—"There will be a large sum necessary, ½ a million or upwards"—only drew Jackson's official indignation. "I have read your confidential letter with care," he replied in late November, and noted with "astonishment that you would entrust such a letter, without being in cypher." He reiterated Butler's orders and noted for good measure, "we are deeply interested that this treaty of cession should be obtained without any just imputation of corruption on our part." Butler had reason, however, to construe his orders otherwise. First, he knew that Mexican officials would expect their individual shares of the "five millions," and second, he understood that Jackson himself had resorted to paying tribute when negotiating for Indian lands. Moreover, upon being appointed to his post, Butler had received a communication from the president clearly suggesting that he consider bribery a legitimate tool for conducting diplomacy with the Mexican government—"I scarcely ever knew a Spaniard who was not the slave of averice, and it *is not improbable* that this *weakness* may be *worth a great deal to us, in this case*."[3]

The truth is, Jackson badly wanted Texas. When justifying the old Florida invasion, he had repeatedly blamed Spanish weakness—its porous borders, he then argued, forced America's intervention. Now he claimed that the United States lacked the capacity to police its own perimeter. In effect, and apparently with no irony intended, Jackson told Butler to tell Mexican officials that they should acquiesce to U.S. expansion because the U.S. was unable—"We cannot restrain our citizens"—to control its frontier. The alternative, he argued, was Texan independence, a protracted guerilla conflict should Mexico City resist, and the inevitable augmenting of rebel forces by Americans. In place of this nightmarish scenario Jackson offered, so he said, an honorable peace. "We want," he told Butler, "a good and unincumbered cession," and he shied from actions that might leave his administration open to courting a war.[4] Butler's antagonistic negotiations did little to advance the president's agenda, though Jackson must take the blame for this debacle. He sustained the rapscallion for years, somehow entranced by his strange charisma and bolstered by the errant belief that he could at last deliver up Texas. In fact, the Texans delivered themselves.

In October 1835, the military phase of the Texas Revolution began at the Battle (perhaps more of a skirmish) of Gonzales between Mexican cavalry and Texas militia. Five months later, in early March, a convention of fifty-nine delegates met at Washington-on-the-Brazos and produced the Texas Declaration of Independence. Shortly thereafter a Mexican force under President General Antonio López de Santa Anna wiped out Texas defenders—including Davy Crockett and co-commander James Bowie—at the Alamo Mission near San Antonio de Béxar. But the following month some nine hundred rebels led by Sam Houston smashed a Mexican army at San Jacinto near present-day Houston. A captured Santa Anna ordered his army out of the region and subsequently signed treaties at Velasco both ending the war and acknowledging Texas's independence. A new government in Mexico City, however, repudiated the agreement, even as it lacked the power to bring the revolutionaries in line.

At this point the Texans sought annexation into the United States. Jackson wanted this too, but thought it might irreparably sectionalize the Democratic Party and threaten his more immediate goal of seeing Van Buren elected president that fall. All along he had hoped to purchase the territory and thus follow the pattern established by his Virginia predecessors. Despite pressure from droves of Texas commissioners in Washington, Jackson now took an uncharacteristic backseat to others. Nearing seventy, eager to avoid an open break with Mexico, and perhaps desiring to close his controversial tenure in office on a quiet note, he let Democrats in the national legislature do the heavy lifting. And sure enough Congress came through for the old man—though shy of annexation. On the last day of February 1837 the House passed resolutions in support of recognition, and the following day the Senate narrowly concurred (23–19). Two days after that, in one of his final acts as president, Jackson appointed former Louisiana state representative Alcée La Branche American chargé d'affaires to the Republic of Texas. Its inclusion in the Union, however, would have to wait.[5]

48

The Jackson Court

While Jackson dreamt of Texas, his second term turned on domestic as well as foreign policy, and never more so than when appointing Supreme Court justices. His six picks are exceeded only by Washington's ten and Franklin Roosevelt's eight. The General's total is all the more notable considering that Washington enjoyed the unique opportunity to select (with Senate approval) the original bench and Roosevelt served, by several years, longer than any other chief executive. Momentum toward creating a Jackson Court began to build in January 1835 when Gabriel Duvall, a Madison designate from Maryland, resigned. The president incautiously chose the loyal Taney, also from Maryland, to take his place. A Whig majority in the Senate thought otherwise. Beaten by Jackson on the Bank, anti-Jacksonians responded in part by holding up or refusing to confirm presidential appointments. "It is doubtful whether he will be approved," Clay wrote of Taney at the time. "He will not be by my vote." The Senate adjourned on March 3 without taking on the nominee—as good as a rejection. It did agree, however, to shrink the size of the court from seven justices to six and thus deprive Jackson of this latest appointment. The billed failed in the Democratic-controlled House.[1]

The situation grew both more complicated and yet more clear over the congressional recess. Chief Justice John Marshall's June death opened a second seat on the Court, while a new Democratic majority in the Senate assured Jackson of a timely vote. In choosing the Virginian Philip P. Barbour to succeed Duvall and tapping Taney to follow Marshall as chief justice, the president offered geographically correct nominations, proposing to replace judges from Maryland and Virginia with judges from Maryland and Virginia. Over Whig efforts to postpone acting on the selections, Taney and Barbour were both confirmed by comfortable margins on March 15, 1836. Two days later Taney thanked Jackson and, perhaps exhibiting a less than juridical temperament, condemned as well their mutual enemies: "I have been confirmed by the strength of my own friends, and go into the office not by the leave, but in spite of the opposition of the men who have so long and so perseveringly sought to destroy me, and I am glad to feel that I do not owe my confirmation to any forbearance on their part."[2] Like his patron, Taney too rejoiced in a public vindication against his political opponents.

Jackson's determination to see the trusted Taney on the court addressed a broader policy of rewarding loyalists. Having brought western hard-money men such as Blair and Kendall to Washington, welcomed fellow Tennessean Eaton into the cabinet, and established an informal kitchen ministry, Jackson clearly made devotion to party and patron a sine qua non for nomination. This pattern persisted when doling out judgeships. As one legal scholar has noted, while Jackson followed his predecessors in considering a range of criteria for Supreme Court appointments, including previous experience, geography, and partisanship, he "elevated the latter consideration to new heights, making certain that, despite all other aspects involved in the decision, political considerations, especially in terms of loyalty, mattered most."[3]

For John Quincy Adams, Marshall's death in particular signified a passing of the guard. "It was the last act of my father's Administration," he wrote privately of John Adams's January 1801 lame duck nomination of Marshall to lead the court, "and one of the most important services, rendered by him to his Country." Now, he continued, Jackson stood, with Taney's appointment, to put his certain stamp on the nation's highest tribunal: "The President . . . has not yet made one good appointment—His Chief Justice will be no better than the rest."[4]

The sharp enlargement of the federal judiciary at the end of Jackson's second term further flummoxed Adams as well as other critics. Thirty years had passed and nine new states added to the Union since the Seventh Circuit Act of 1807 increased the Supreme Court from six to seven seats. Justices were taxed at this time with "riding circuit"—traveling to designated towns to hear cases—and found it difficult to accommodate, over often primitive roads, the greater distances. Justice John McLean, an Ohioan nominated to the court by Jackson in 1829, complained to Tennessee senator Felix Grundy of an impossible itinerary sluicing about the Midwest during the spring rains: "Now it is this season of the year the roads through Indiana and Illinois are almost impassable. . . . Why are western judges required to perform five times as much labour as the eastern judges."[5] In response to such complaints Congress created two new jurisdictions in 1837, geographically reorganized some of the old circuits to ease the travel of justices, and enlarged the Supreme Court by two seats. The selection of two southerners—Tennessee's John Catron and John McKinley of Alabama—proposes an argument for sectional court packing, but it is ultimately lacking. Though it is true that Jackson's final four nominees (1835–1837) were all from Dixie and that Van Buren's two appointees, John McKinley and Peter Vivian Daniel, came from Alabama and Virginia respectively, the upshot is that in 1841, after Van Buren's final appointment, the court showed only a slight five to four planter advantage. In effect, southerners had been replacing southerners.

If the focus is less on section and more on partisanship, however, then a pattern becomes apparent. In 1857 Taney and his colleagues handed down what most commentators consider the Supreme Court's worst ruling—the Dred Scott decision. Along with denying U.S. citizenship to blacks (free or otherwise), the 7–2 majority proclaimed unconstitutional the Missouri Compromise, which had prohibited slavery in most of the Louisiana Territory. The decision dangerously stoked sectionalism and nudged the country closer to civil war. The Taney court's regional composition in 1857 contained, as it did in 1841, five southerners and four northerners. More importantly, six of the seven justices who ruled against Scott had been nominated by Democratic presidents— three by Jackson and one each by Van Buren, Polk, and Franklin Pierce. Virginia slaveholder John Tyler, a former Democrat who left the party to support South Carolina's nullifiers, proposed the seventh.

When assaying the legacy of Jackson's judicial appointments, the subject of slavery must take precedence. Though often regarded, in contrast to the nationalist Marshall Court, as distinctly states' rights, the Taney Court (1836–1864) frequently employed a powerful judiciary to defend the plantocracy against its growing opposition. It upheld in *Prigg v. Pennsylvania* (1842) a federal law guaranteeing slaveholders the right to recover—even in the North—their escaped human property; it struck down in *Ableman v. Booth* (1859) a Wisconsin law that denied the federal government's right to compel the states' citizens to cooperate in the rendition of runaway slaves; and, of course, it spoke most forcefully in the Dred Scott decision. One might gauge this court's impact by the furious reaction it aroused. Between 1858 and 1874, a period marked by the rise of Lincoln, the Civil War, and much of Reconstruction, ten new justices were appointed—nine by Republicans and all from northern states excepting one Californian.

For Jackson, judicial appointments, if important, seemed a somewhat secondary route to securing a governing legacy. He looked, rather, to Van Buren's election with great hope and anticipation. Having observed the smooth six-term presidency of Jefferson, Madison, and Monroe, he wished now to extend his own ideological influence. And Van Buren, more than any other man, seemed capable of granting Jackson a coveted third term.

49

The Politics of Succession

Aside from ideology, Jackson and Van Buren, the dominant Democrats of the 1830s, appeared to have little in common. The former, a military hero, tall and worn, seldom edited his opinions, impulsively courting controversy; the latter, diminutive and dapper, emotionally sober and lacking in personal popularity, relied on partisanship to pave his way in America's widening political world. Josiah Quincy, Jr., the president and vice president's escort through Massachusetts during Jackson's 1833 tour, observed both men over several days. Circulating through the same crowds, talking with many of the same people, they offered Quincy an opportunity to contrast their personalities and propensities. He found Jackson a natural, resting completely at ease from the superiority of his position and the vain certainty of his views; Van Buren, he considered, purred like a well-pet politician:

> As we rode through divers small towns, receiving salutes and cheers at their centres, the President talked constantly and expressed himself with great freedom about persons. His conversation was interesting from its sincerity, decision, and point. It was easy to see that he was not a man to accept a difference of opinion with equanimity; but that was clearly because, he being honest and earnest, Heaven would not suffer his opinions to be other than *right*. Mr. Van Buren, on the other hand, might have posed for a statue of Diplomacy. He had the softest way of uttering his cautious observations, and evidently considered the impression every word would make.[1]

In choosing Van Buren as his successor, Jackson no doubt believed the vice president capable of maintaining Jacksonianism's momentum. But this presumed a strong economy, the cooperation of a nation perhaps fatigued by the high drama of the last eight years, and Van Buren's ability to effectively navigate sectional tensions.

More than a few Democrats doubted the Little Magician's prospects, supposing him far more adept at jockeying than generalship. "Van Buren cannot be president," John Randolph once warned Jackson. "He is an adroit . . . little managing man, but he can't inspire respect, much less *veneration*."[2] The remark appears off, however, in at least two respects. First, while iconic early republic personalities—Washington, Jefferson, and Jackson—assumed the presidency, so did their less august legatees—Adams, Madison, and Van Buren—whose associations with more dominant figures aided their elevation. Further, fealty to political machines came to play a pivotal role in the antebellum electoral process. Dark horses (Polk and Pierce) and warhorses (Harrison and Zachary Taylor), men elevated at conventions or by dint of many years of service to their parties or armies, constituted the coming presidential profile. Accordingly, Van Buren is perhaps best seen as a transitional figure, reflecting both the old politics (as the outgoing president's preference) and the new (as a candidate less popular than his party).

Van Buren's candidacy also bears evidence of the nation's shifting sectional strength. The Little Magician proposed to become the first northerner to carry the electoral college since John Adams in 1796. His success correspondingly drew attention to the declining power of Virginia, whose native sons occupied the presidency nearly continuously from 1789 to 1825. Rising leviathans New York, Ohio, and Illinois emblemized the new politics, capturing between 1836 and 1944 more than half of all national elections. Thus, in backing Van Buren, Jackson sought to extend an agrarian, hard-money, and plantation-tolerant society whose peak had passed.

The Democratic convention, held over two days in Baltimore in May 1835, proved to be a mere coronation, with Van Buren nominated unanimously. His running mate, Richard Mentor Johnson, a Kentucky slaveholder and War of 1812 veteran said to have killed the great Shawnee warrior Tecumseh, approximated a poor man's Jackson. The ease of Van Buren's convention success, however, implicitly raised certain inconvenient questions. In 1824 Jackson had joined a coterie of men in

denouncing the caucus system then used to promote presidential candidates. But Van Buren's uncontested selection suggested a similar lock-
step strategy, a case of King Andrew replacing King Caucus.

The Whigs, by contrast, encouraged several candidates. These men—
William Henry Harrison (an Ohio transplant), Tennessee's Hugh Lawson White, North Carolina's Willie P. Mangum, and Daniel Webster of
Massachusetts—seemed collectively capable of causing a replay of the 1824
election, in which no candidate captured a majority in the electoral college. In practicing a politics of regions, in seeking to balkanize the vote,
Whigs obviously hoped to send the election to the House. No doubt such
a prospect only affirmed Jackson's low opinion of the opposition and its
"anti-democratic" impulse. Clay affirmed such a strategy when writing to
a colleague in July 1835, "Upon the supposition of there being three Candidates, it would of course be sound policy to cultivate the best relations of
amity between the two sections [North and South] of the Whig party; since
they might find it necessary to co-operate if the election were to devolve on
the House"; to another correspondent he blithely surmised, "If White can
get the South, and [another] Candidate can get Pennsa., should there be
no popular election [winner], as would be probable, V. Buren would enter
the House the lowest Candidate."[3] The fact that the Whigs refused to hold a
convention only emphasized their preference for multiple aspirants.

It soon became apparent that of all the Whig nominees, Harrison
attracted the greatest support. The scion of an old Virginia family (his
father, Benjamin, sat in the Continental Congress and signed the Declaration of Independence), he gravitated to political opportunities in the
rising West, represented Ohio in the House and Senate, and served as
governor of the Indiana Territory. Harrison achieved national fame in
the War of 1812 when his army defeated a combined British and Indian
force at the Battle of the Thames in Upper Canada near Chatham. That
Jackson's influence extended beyond even his party may be inferred in
Harrison's repute. For Jackson's life story—leaving the old South for the
new West, claiming civic offices on the frontier, and winning sudden
personal popularity fighting Indians and English—overlapped Harrison's. In several respects, even in earning a folksy by-name, did Old Tip-
pecanoe emulate Old Hickory.

In July 1836, just months before the election, Jackson again dominated
discussion by issuing an executive order requiring that specie—gold

and silver—be used as payment for purchasing public lands exceeding 320 acres after August 15. This Specie Circular responded to a sharp increase in speculation fueled in great part by both the Bank War and Indian removal. The former eliminated a useful regulatory break on soft currency (the issuance of notes susceptible to fluctuations in value), while the latter opened up vast new public lands for sale. A store of investors snatched up many of these parcels with rapidly depreciating paper money dispersed from state banks and typically unbacked by hard currency. Jackson, fearing a new Panic of 1819, now moved to contract credit.

For many Whigs the Specie Circular confirmed their faith in the president's fiscal idiocy. The idea of substituting a finite supply of precious metals for paper money in an expanding nation struck them as altogether absurd, primitive, and precarious. In a speech delivered before the Senate on December 21, Daniel Webster insisted that "an exclusive circulation of gold and silver is a thing absolutely impracticable; and if practicable, not at all to be desired; inasmuch as its effect would be to abolish credit, to repress the enterprise and diminish the earnings of the industrial classes, and to produce, faster and sooner than any thing else in this country can produce, a moneyed aristocracy." A caucus of concerned Democrats agreed and joined with Whigs in passing a bill several weeks later that effectively quashed the order. A furious Jackson denounced those Democrats who had jumped ship on the Circular: "I am free to declare that the course of some of our friends in the Senate are perfectly unaccountable to me on this paper system. Good, professed states right men, and professed hard money men . . . still they vote, and pass a bill to make bank bills part of our currency."[4] He more formally replied by vetoing the offending legislation on March 3, 1837, his last full day in the presidency.

Jackson's willingness to issue the controversial Specie Circular amid a presidential contest is telling of his confidence in Van Buren, and no doubt himself. Though some thought the slate of contenders altogether unimpressive—the dependably unsparing John Quincy Adams nagged that "all the candidates are at most third-rate men"—voter turnout, nearly 58 percent, exceeded all previous presidential elections. Van Buren captured 170 electoral votes, carried fifteen states, and collected slightly more than 50 percent of the popular vote. Combined, his four

Whig opponents took 124 electoral votes and eleven states. The contest in Pennsylvania proved critical. A shift of some 2,100 ballots would have given the commonwealth to Harrison and sent the election, as Whigs had hoped, to the House. Van Buren won states in every region of the country, though he lost Tennessee and Georgia, never before forfeited by a Jeffersonian or Jacksonian. In all, he claimed slightly less than half of the southern popular vote, a significant reduction from Jackson's 68 percent in 1832. His opponents, however, included two southern candidates, and no previous northern presidential aspirant had ever earned such a large percentage below the Mason-Dixon Line.[5]

The month following the election Congress reconvened, and Senator Benton, backed by a Democratic majority, moved to expunge the upper chamber's 1834 censure of Jackson. Benton's resolution claimed that this unusual manner of condemnation "was not warranted by the constitution, and was irregularly and illegally adopted by the Senate"; more, it had declared the president "guilty of an impeachable offence . . . without allowing to him the benefits of a trial, or the means of defence." Declaring Jackson's removal of Secretary Duane from the Treasury perfectly legal and in no sense a "violation or . . . derogation of the laws and constitution," Benton condemned the censure as wholly "unfounded," "erroneous," "unjust," and "irregular."[6] His own resolution called not merely for the annulment of the 1834 vote but for its physical deletion in the Senate Journal. It reads:

> Resolved, That the said resolve be expunged from the journal; and, for that purpose, that the Secretary of the Senate, at such time as the Senate may appoint, shall bring the manuscript journal of the session 1833 '34 into the Senate, and, in the presence of the Senate, draw black lines around the said resolve, and write across the face thereof, in strong letters, the following words: "Expunged by order of the Senate, this — day of —, in the year of our Lord 1837."[7]

Following three weeks of spirited debate, the resolution passed 24–19 and Benton moved for its immediate execution. The old journal was produced, the expunging commenced, and the Whigs walked out. Anxious as the audience grew unruly, a few Democratic senators "sent out," as one of their number noted, "and brought in arms" to clear the gallery. Amid "a storm of hisses, groans, and vociferations" a furious

Benton stood on the floor trying to identify, as he put it, "the bank ruffians" who mocked his resolution.[8] This unseemly episode of political theatrics perhaps appeared to some observers a fitting conclusion to a presidency filled with unprecedented drama and controversy. Jackson's opposition, though neither his personal popularity nor domineering presence, now became Van Buren's.

50

Administration's End

Shortly before his successor's early March inauguration, Jackson wrote to a colleague of the splendid vindication that day promised. Clearly the old pol warmly retained his catalog of complaints and took some private delight in leaving Washington with loyalists at the helm. "Tomorrow ends my official career forever," he noted with satisfaction, "on the 4th I hope to be able to go to the capitol to witness the glorious scene of Mr Van Buren, once rejected by the Senate, sworn into office, by chief justice Taney, also being rejected by the factious Senate." Inauguration Day, bright, calm, and pleasantly cool, proved uneventful. Jackson and Van Buren, sharing a carriage drawn by four gray-silvering horses, arrived in a House chamber thick with public officials to witness Johnson take the vice presidential oath. Directly thereafter Van Buren, before a crowd of some twenty thousand, delivered, in "a voice remarkably distinct," said one observer, a thirty-minute address from a wooden platform erected on the East Portico, after which followed a brief second swearing-in ceremony. The former and the new president then descended the capitol's steps and disappeared inside a phaeton which, attended by blue-coated dragoons, dropped its passengers off at the White House. "For once," Senator Benton observed, "the rising was eclipsed by the setting sun."[1]

Three days later Jackson, suffering, so he said, from "advanced age and a broken frame," left Washington for good, accompanied by a small party made up of immediate family, his friend the painter Ralph Earl, and an army physician. Taking a railroad to Ellicott's Mills, Jackson and his entourage then traveled by carriage and steamboat to Wheeling, Cincinnati, and Louisville. In Kentucky the former president paused to write Van Buren, "From the time I left you, I have been literally in a crowd. Such assemblages of my fellow citizens I have never before seen on my passage to or from Washington."[2] He arrived at the Hermitage on the 24th. As a final public act he left behind a "Farewell Address," becoming just the second president, following George Washington in 1796, to issue a formal valediction. Principally authored by Justice Taney, the document both reviewed what Jackson regarded as his administration's cardinal achievements and warned readers to remain vigilant against the nation's internal enemies, namely bankers and abolitionists.

As something of a summation on the currency and credit questions, the retired president offered a strong caution against the rising power of paper money to unjustly lift a privileged financial elite at the expense of others. "It is one of the serious evils of our present system of banking," he contended, "that it enables one class of society—and that by no means a numerous one—by its control over the currency, to act injuriously upon the interests of all the others and to exercise more than its just proportion of influence in political affairs."[3]

Jackson showed considerably less vision when ruminating on abolitionism. He might easily have let the subject pass, as it played no role in his presidency commensurate with Indian removal, the nullification crisis, or the Bank War. Instead, he endorsed the southern plantocracy in language that lightly evoked of all things Calhoun's old *Exposition and Protest*: "Every State must be the sole judge of the measures proper to secure the safety of its citizens and promote their happiness; and all efforts on the part of people of other States to cast odium upon their institutions, and all measures calculated to disturb their rights of property or to put in jeopardy their peace and internal tranquility, are in direct opposition to the spirit in which the Union was formed, and must endanger its safety." Jackson further refused to take critics of slavery seriously—"weak men," so he said, who only "persuade themselves for a moment that they are laboring in the cause of humanity"—despite the fact that in 1837 about half of the states in the Union had either outlawed enslavement or instituted gradual emancipation laws to end the practice. In these areas resided the preponderance of the nation's population, and Jackson most certainly considered himself a man of the majority. Instead, he took it upon himself to guide northern public opinion, both denouncing abolitionism and calling for its public condemnation in such a way that some might be encouraged to carry out acts of violence: "but everyone, upon sober reflection, will see that nothing but mischief can come from these improper assaults upon the feelings and rights of others. Rest assured that the men found busy in this work of discord are not worthy of your confidence, and deserve your strongest reprobation."[4]

The retired General inevitably attracted commentators and critics eager to assess the meaning of his presidency. In *The American Democrat* (1838) James Fenimore Cooper, author of *The Last of the Mohicans*, wondered at Jackson's imperious governing style, which he believed a product of "popular impulses" that "often work injustice." Philip Hone privately considered Jackson's "rule more absolute than that of any hereditary monarch of Europe," but considered the behavior of the nation's majority even more worthy of reflection—"that the people should not only have submitted to it, but upheld and supported him in his encroachments upon their rights, and his disregard of the Constitution and the laws, will equally occasion the surprise and indignation of future generations."[5] One New Yorker, by contrast, thought the people the true, evident, and unassailable spirit behind the era. This gentleman, one John Lawson, praised Jackson in verse for defying the weight of so much peasant past and bearing up, through the example of his own obscure origins, the condition of commoners. He ruled, Lawson supposed, in their good name:

> Raised by the voice of freemen to a height
> Sublimer far than kings by birth may claim[6]

Part VIII

WINTER'S WAGES

What do you think will be my fame with posterity? I mean, what will posterity blame me for most?
Andrew Jackson to Presbyterian minister John Edgar, 1845

A daguerreotype of Jackson in 1845, the year that Texas statehood precipitated the Mexican-American War, ushering in an intense era of sectionalism that led to the Civil War.

51

Unquiet Retirement

Less than two weeks after Jackson left office, the prominent New York exchange firm I. and L. Joseph, caught in the collapse of slipping southern cotton prices, tumbled into bankruptcy. Several equally vulnerable repositories and merchant houses quickly followed. Thus ensued the Panic of 1837, a product of excessive speculation in western lands brought about by reckless credit policies. The controversial Bank recharter veto, followed in the autumn of 1833 with the placement of government deposits into the president's pet banks, undermined Biddle's ability to manage the country's money supply.[1] In this new lending environment, state banks began to rather extravagantly flood paper into the economy, unmindfully conspiring, despite Jackson's Specie Circular, to create a land bubble that soon burst.

The Panic of 1837 ruined thousands of businesses and banks, invited inflation, and put a damper on economic development into the early 1840s, contributing perhaps decisively to Van Buren's failure to secure a second term. Jackson's enemies wasted no time in blaming the financial crisis on the Bank War's bitter fruit. In May 1837 Supreme Court Justice Joseph Story complained to a colleague, "The experiments of General Jackson, from his interference in removing the deposits and annihilating the Bank of the United States, down to the last infatuated act of the Treasury Circular, have produced their natural effects. They have swept over the country with the violence and desolation of a hurricane." Sensing opportunity, the Anglo-American economist Thomas Cooper encouraged Nicholas Biddle, now presiding over a Philadelphia bank, to pursue the ultimate vindication: "Why not look to the Presidency? Can your name be brought forward at a time more advantageous than the present? You are rising, your opponents are falling: strike the ball on the rebound, and I think this is the moment." That same frantic spring, Jackson privately and no doubt a little defensively justified the Bank War to Francis Blair, blaming the Panic on "Biddle and his corrupt mercenary merchants." "I have done my duty," he insisted, expressing only concern that the new administration thwart "Biddle and his satelites."[2]

He need not have worried. Van Buren responded to the crisis with a typically Jacksonian hard-money maneuver. He proposed in September to create an independent U.S. treasury to hold the public's monies in gold and silver, upon which the government might then draw to meet its financial obligations. This plan promised to separate once and for all federal banking from private banking—and thus presumably take politics out of the cash-and-credit industry. Jackson had contemplated such a division some years earlier and now assured Van Buren of his support: "I rejoice at the prospects of the divorce . . . passing congress." The bill, however, aggressively opposed by state banks, failed during consecutive congressional sessions. The Independent Treasury Act did eventually pass in 1840, though a Whig congressional majority repealed it the following year.[3]

As Jackson watched the nation's economy with varying degrees of dismay, frustration, and hope, his own personal finances were close to cratering. A few years earlier, in 1831, he had paid for a major remodeling of the Hermitage—adding new wings (accommodating a library, office, dining room, and pantry), a many-columned two-story front portico, and a rear portico. The structure's tendriling gutters were made of pricey copper. Three years later, in the fall of 1834, an afternoon fire, possibly caused by sparks in a chimney, quickly spread, devastating much of the house and destroying or damaging most of the upstairs furniture. The walls and structure were sound and Jackson determined to rebuild on the site. The new Hermitage (the house tourists visit today in Nashville) was completed in the summer of 1836; it included a graceful cantilevered staircase in the center hall and Greek-revival woodwork. Several Philadelphia suppliers and other merchants furnished the home, which featured pictorial wallpaper from Paris, crystal chandeliers, several mahogany chairs, three cherry bookcases, silk damask curtains, a Japanese bronze clock inlaid with enamel, pier tables, and any number of rugs, bedsteads, and bureaus. The expense of construction (roughly double the original estimate), when added to the cost of furniture, fittings, and fixtures, came to some $8,000 (about $235,000 in current dollars).[4]

Though the fire and its accompanying outlay to rebuild cut into Jackson's capital, much of his sad financial situation involved Andrew Jackson, Jr.'s mounting debts. Creditors were everywhere, seeking payment for unwise land purchases that forced the General, now in his early seventies, to liquidate his Alabama lots and other properties. Perhaps predictably, an anxious Jackson assumed that a few rogue Whigs had used the speculative paper system to embarrass him financially. Writing to a nephew in the autumn of 1840, he expressed both faith and fidelity, rather, to a slave and cotton economy entering its final phase:

> We have just received a letter from the overseer below—all well. . . . I hope our last years crop of cotton on its way to market . . . will relieve us from pecuniary pressure arising from Andrews imprudent debts. And I hope he will hereafter shun debt, as the greatest evil. I have paid for him in the last two months upwards of twelve thousand dollars in actual cash, and is not quite clear yet. I have been greatly distressed in mind and feeling. every Whigg that he was indebted to has either sued or warranted him.[5]

Jackson might have mentioned, for good measure, his own ill health. Afflicted with diminishing eyesight, severe headaches, a delicate stomach, and the accumulated impact of malarial fevers, ancient gunshot wounds, and mercury-laced calomel treatments, he suffered persistent and sometimes great physical discomfort in retirement. Such aches could only have exacerbated his often quick-tempered and occasionally compulsive responses to his assorted nemeses. One of them, Tennessee senator Hugh Lawson White, contended in an 1837 letter published in the *Knoxville Register*, that Jackson, a former ally, trafficked in megalomania, eager to assert and quick to condemn. The former president, he testily wrote:

> has come home determined to destroy every man who dared to differ with him in opinion as to his successor, and *that is the experiment* he is now making. . . . In the temper he now is, and with enfeebled faculties, he views everything as an *enemy* that stands in

the road of his ambition. He *personifies* truth, justice and . . . [is] determined he will die *having* the character of a *great* man.[6]

But *which* great man, White's skeptical colloquy implored, did he plan to emulate? Humble Cincinnatus relinquished power and returned to the plow; Caesar, the charismatic strongman, aroused the dread and alarm of assassins.

Jackson suffered a great blow when the Democrats lost the presidency and both houses of Congress in 1840. "The scenes of corruption at our late elections, are now so palbable, and so general," he wrote Van Buren in November, "that unless soon met by the Indignant frowns of the virtuous portion of the whole community . . . we will [be] ruled by the combined mony power of England and the Federalists of this Union." The lingering economic downturn combined with Whiggery's decision to unite upon a single candidate, General Harrison, made the difference. Voter turnout, on the rise since Monroe ran uncontested in 1820, climbed to an incredible 80 percent, though this time "the people" went against the Jacksonians—a first in the party's brief history now encompassing four national contests. The Whigs did well by emulating their opponents. Harrison played the rustic log cabin and hard cider candidate while Van Buren, who liked to entertain, was successfully accused, as one Pennsylvania congressman put it, of "*spending the money of the people with a lavish hand* [on] regal splendor." How could he represent the laboring class, critics insisted, while dining off fancy French china and reclining on fine mahogany sofas? An ever-sensitive Jackson, reading such casual accusations in the papers, reflexively took to his pen. In late October he groused to his old advisor William Lewis, "Much has been said and written on the expence and extravagance of my administration and that of Mr. Van Buren. . . . If ever due economy was observed by any public officer I trust I faithfully observed it, and as faithfully took care of the public mony and the public interest."[7] But Jackson no longer commanded the public stage.

Harrison, rather, captured a strong victory, winning nearly 53 percent of the popular vote and 234 of 294 electoral votes. He ran impressively in each section, taking eight southern and three western states, the mid-Atlantic, and nearly all of New England. No doubt the presence of former Virginia senator John Tyler on the ticket soothed some among the planter elite. Tyler had sympathized with South Carolina's opposition to the tariff and criticized both Jackson's Force Bill and removal of Bank deposits. A states' rights Democrat, he gravitated to Whig concerns regarding executive usurpation.

Sensing defeat in the offing, Jackson gave several speeches that autumn in western Tennessee. He bid his audience in one to indulge a "feeble" old soldier, eager to "exchange salutations with you . . . [for] probably the last time." He proceeded to condemn Whiggery as an echo of Hamiltonian nationalism, arguing that the forces rallying around Harrison sought "a revolution . . . of our institutions." Deigning to race-bait, he further condemned abolitionism as contrary to the Founders' wishes—though these same men had crafted in the Northwest Ordinance (1787) legislation that barred slavery from the nation's northern territories.

> Look, I pray you, at the efforts which are making to array one section of the union against the other. It is in this aspect that the movements of the abolitionists become fearful and portentous. . . . It is undeniable that the mass of the abolitionists acknowledge as political leaders those who have signalised their opposition to the measures which will keep the government in the path prescribed for it by its founders.[8]

Jackson doubted that even a single abolitionist could be found among Democrats, though he saw a link—accurately it must be said—between slavery's critics and supporters of a national bank, internal improvements, and a protective tariff. All pointed to a future more oriented toward free labor and industrial development than the fading agrarian establishment.

Despite Jackson's autumn efforts, and much to his mortification, Tennessee went solidly for Harrison. As evidence of his successor's imminent defeat began to filter in from around the country, elections taking place over several weeks, he kindly denied to Van Buren the reality of the situation. "Still, altho our friends here are all gloom," he wrote the president in early November from the Hermitage, "I do not believe one word of it, nor will I believe that you are not elected untill I see *all* the official returns." He did concede, however, that the forces of "bribery, and corruption" were no doubt at play.[9]

Though momentarily beaten, Jackson soon took heart when given indisputable evidence that a just God, like him, also hated Whiggery. In early April 1841, only thirty-one days into his presidency, Harrison died of pneumonia. Seeing in his restless retirement no need for false sympathy, the briny General rejoiced in having survived yet another enemy. "A kind and overuling providence has interfered to prolong our glorious Union and happy republican system," Jackson wrote to a former aide, "which Genl. Harrison and his cabinet was preparing to destroy under the dictation of that profligate demagogue, Henry Clay." Having survived a slew of duels and disputes, military campaigns, and an assassination attempt, perhaps Jackson really did believe his deity a hard-money Democrat. "I now view that providence by taking away Genl. Harrison has saved the Union," he wrote Van Buren, "and Federalism with its cooneries and modern Whigeries is down forever, and our republican system will long endure." In another communication he expressed "full confidence" in Tyler's "democratic and state right principles," though worried over the new president's inherited cabinet. He need not have. Tyler (His Accidency to the implacable) twice vetoed Clay-initiated bills for a national banking act and further vetoed legislation to raise tariffs. Frustrated House Whigs moved in the summer of 1842 toward building a case for impeachment—a therapeutic act, perhaps, for their earlier failure to tame Jackson—though the autumn elections returned a Democratic majority to the lower chamber.[10]

Tyler's clashes with congressional Whigs proved to be but one of many concerns that vied for Jackson's retirement attentions. His several and spirited letters to Van Buren, Lewis, and Blair indicate a restless and ongoing engagement with public opinion and partisan skirmishes. He reviewed too ageless animosities, idling sometimes in these communications on the New Orleans judge who had fined him in 1815, on his even older resentment of John Sevier, and of course on the corrupt bargain that briefly cheated the people of their champion. "I ask," he pettishly wrote to one correspondent, "what has John Q. Adams or Henry Clay ever done for their countries good—nothing, but much mischief."[11]

Possibly Jackson now saw these old foes as part of a rigged financial system that threatened to destroy him. In dire need of cash, he accepted a $10,000 loan (about $315,000 in current dollars) at 6 percent interest from Blair—secured by mortgaging "thirty odd negroes," as he put it, and a 1,200-acre northern Mississippi plantation for which he had paid $23,000 in November 1838. Though the General acknowledged the advance's urgency due to Andrew Jackson, Jr.'s "improvident debts," he also blamed unnamed "enemies" who had apparently "swindled" his son "out of thousands."[12] In appreciation for the loan, he sent a filly to Blair's daughter, Elizabeth. This miserable episode offers something of a sobering encapsulation of Jackson's southern sense of honor. For it included enslaved people, land, and a horse—the same symbols of power and prestige that teased him as a young Tennessee blade.

Though he was dogged by persistent debt, partisan issues continued to capture Jackson's attention. In the spring of 1842 Van Buren arrived at the Hermitage, and stayed for several weeks of discussion. Later that fall the General, pledged fully to his friend's candidacy in the next presidential election, promised victory. "I have no doubt but you will be the choice of the national convention," he wrote Van Buren in November. "There are many good reasons I could give for this, but one is anough, that is, that you are on the only one who the whole democracy can be brought now to unite on."[13] Time, however, had passed these relic public servants by. No more would the Bank War, Indian removal, or Jackson himself shape debate. The nettlesome subject of slavery on the unfolding frontier, rather, had replaced them all.

52

The Last Push

Jackson's fevered dreams of western expansion scarcely slackened in retirement. He demanded, rather, that Texas be brought into the Union lest the previous generation's signature military achievements—the reversal of British and Spanish power in the Gulf—now, somehow, be threatened. This pressure point on the American map teased Jackson mercilessly; it raised old issues, enemies, and anxieties. From a distant Nashville redoubt, he lived more than a little in the past. "Texas is viewed as absolutely necessary for the defence of Neworleans and keep foreign influence from tampering with our Indians, and slaves in war, and in peace," he wrote Blair in the spring of 1844. "We cannot bear that Great Britain should have a Canedy [Canada] on our west as she has on the north." To a Tennessee congressman he somewhat senselessly contended (in a communication subsequently published in Blair's *Globe*) that Great Britain might soon send "to Texas 20 or 30,000, organising her army near to the Sabine, when furnished with all supplies, and equipt for active service, she declares war against us, marches thro Louisiana and Arkansa, makes a lodgment on the mississippi, excite the negroes to insurrection, the lower country falls and with it Neworleans, and a servile war rages all over the southern and western country." To Jackson a perpetual state of national emergency, brought about by the unholy trinity of British treachery, vengeful Indians, and rebellious slaves, seemed to forever threaten white settlements below the Mason-Dixon Line.[1]

Invariably the Texas question got caught up in politics. Tyler saw annexation as a way to return to the Democracy, secure its nomination, and win the presidency in his own right; the party's Van Buren wing, strongest in the North and seeking a fresh term for its champion, wished to put Texas off. But Van Buren's old adversary, John C. Calhoun, now Tyler's secretary of state, enjoyed a cold and satisfying revenge. Under his guidance, the U.S. secured a treaty of annexation that went before the Senate in April 1844. Along with the accord Calhoun gratuitously included a letter he had written to Richard Pakenham, British ambassador to the United States, declaring that the treaty prevented Great Britain from interfering with slavery in Texas. In racializing annexation, Calhoun thus alienated a critical bloc of Yankee Democrats.

Van Buren, hitherto publicly silent on Texas, felt compelled to act. "His correspondence from northern and northwestern friends," writes one biographer, "his extensive reading of the northern press, convinced him immediate annexation was unpopular, even feared in some quarters as a conspiracy of slave owners to control the destiny of the Union." Consequently, on April 27 Van Buren published his ill-advised Hammett Letter in the *Globe*. The communication (a reply to Mississippi congressman William H. Hammett) counseled putting annexation off until it could be accomplished peacefully. Mexico, never having

An 1844 satire on the Democrats' divided approach to the annexation of Texas (depicted as a dagger- and whip-wielding hag of war). The party's southern wing wanted it, while its northern contingent demurred. Jackson, on the left, is pushing the New Yorker Van Buren to support the annexation. In the end, he did not, and lost the nomination.

recognized Texas's independence, might "regard the fact of annexation," so Van Buren put it, "as an act of war." He further reminded readers that "the United States are bound to Mexico by a treaty of amity and commerce," and he utterly rejected the panicky notion that European powers would swoop in to colonize Texas if the U.S. demurred. Van Buren had hoped the letter might persuade Jackson to join him and repudiate immediate annexation. It did quite the opposite. Ten days after its publication the General wrote to Blair, "I am . . . mortified at Mr. V.B. letter," and further declared himself "for the annexation regardless of all consequences."[2]

Van Buren's Hammett Letter compelled the General to actively promote the candidacy of Polk, who entered the year angling for the second slot on the Democratic ticket. Two weeks before the Party's Baltimore convention, held in the city's Odd Fellows Hall on Gay Street (the site, earlier that year, of an Edgar Allan Poe lecture on American poetry), Jackson requested Polk's presence at the Hermitage. Shortly thereafter the latter related to Tennessee congressman Cave Johnson the gist of what transpired:

> [Jackson] regards this step of *Mr. V.B.* (his opinion on Texas) as the only great and vital error he has committed since he has known him. He thinks this single error however must be fatal to him. He thinks the candidate for the Presidency should be an annexation man and reside in the Southwest, and he openly expresses (what I assure you I had never for a moment contemplated) the opinion that I would be the most available man.[3]

Jackson was right. Van Buren led a smattering of candidates on the first four ballots at the convention, though he failed to carry the necessary two-thirds majority. Polk, up to this point not included on the canvass, emerged as a compromise candidate. He captured the nomination on the ninth ballot. Less than two weeks later the Senate, led by a Whig majority aided by seven mainly northern Democratic defections, soundly rejected Calhoun's treaty 35–16.[4]

Clay, like Van Buren opposed to immediate annexation, managed to claim the Whig nomination as his party's southern wing remained committed to a program of internal improvements. Meeting in Baltimore's Universalist Church on Calvert Street, the convention proffered a single paragraph platform absent any word of Texas. From the Hermitage, a simmering Jackson dismissed Clay as "a dead political Duck."[5]

At this point, with the conventions over, the gravest danger to Polk's chances appeared to come from Tyler. Though bereft of major party backing, the president pondered staying in the race—a maneuver that, if carried out, promised to siphon Polk's southern support. That summer, Mississippi senator Robert J. Walker suggested to Jackson that he draft a letter for publication notifying Tyler's supporters that upon the president's "withdrawal from the canvass," they would be well treated by "all other democrats." This kind of direct intervention Jackson rejected. "Why my dear friend," he wrote Polk, "such a letter from me or any other of your conspicuous friends would be seized upon as a bargain and intrigue for the Presidency. Just as Adams and Clays bargain." Jackson then proceeded to do secretly what he refused to do in the open, suggesting to his old friend William Lewis, "that Mr. Tyler now withdrawing from the canvass would give great popularity, and as he can have no hope of being elected, that his own sagacity with his fondness for popularity will induce him to withdraw." Jackson knew that his words, in some construction, would get back to Tyler. On August 1 he applied yet more pressure, writing naval secretary John Mason, "With much frankness I give you my opinion of the course that Mr. Tyler ought to pursue with regard to the Presidency, if he expects to retire in the confidence of the democracy; and adding to his popularity. *He ought to withdraw from the canvass*, with such an address to his supporters for the Presidency as his good sense may suggest." On the 17th Tyler complied, writing directly to Jackson, "Your letter to Major Lewis was, as you requested, shown to me, and your views as to the proper course for me to pursue in the present emergency of public affairs has decided me to withdraw from the canvass."[6]

Throughout the summer Jackson remained active on multiple fronts. While vigorously promoting the Polk campaign—writing letters and drafting statements for publication—he appealed to his old Tennessee friend, now Texas president, Sam Houston, to rebuff European offers of an alliance. Discouraged by the Senate's unwillingness in June to annex the Lone Star republic, Houston cannily refused to narrow his options, though Jackson advised him to keep "Texas out of the *snares* of *England and France*." That fall Polk defeated Clay in a tight election, 170 electoral votes to 105; his securing of New York's 36 electoral votes by a popular

vote margin of 1 percent proved to be the difference. To Jackson's cha-
grin, Tennessee went Whig for the third consecutive national election. He
blamed "the vilest frauds that have ever been practised" for this apostasy.[7]

In September 1844, as the presidential campaign entered its final phase,
Tyler appointed Jackson's nephew Jack Donelson United States chargé
d'affaires to Texas. This move, so the president assured Jackson, rested
primarily upon the fact that Donelson was "a member of your family
and in your close confidence. This I doubt not will have a controul-
ing influence with Genl. Houston and incline him, if he entertains any
feelings antagonistical to the U. States and favorable to England." Perhaps more than any other former American president, Jackson retained
in retirement real influence in national affairs. In the late autumn of
1844, while advising Donelson on the situation in Texas and counseling
Houston to wait just a little longer for annexation, he engaged in lengthy
talks with president-elect Polk in Nashville. "If his health be sufficient,"
former Georgia senator Wilson Lumpkin wrote Polk that November,
"your *best adviser* will be the *Sage* of the *Hermitage*."[8]

Insisting in his December annual address that the election offered a
mandate for expansion, Tyler moved during the next legislative session
for annexation via a joint resolution (this required only a bare congressional majority in both chambers rather than a two-thirds Senate majority, which had previously failed). The House passed the act 120–98 on
January 25, 1845; two days later the Senate followed suit by a much tighter
27–25 tally. Tyler signed the bill on March 3, his final full day in office,
after which the Republic of Texas was offered immediate annexation. The
expansion of the American empire—and war with Mexico—awaited.

During the winter of 1844–45 Jackson wrote often to Polk, offering
the incoming executive uninvited guidance. "Keep from your cabinet all
aspirants to the Presidency" and "Keep Blairs *Globe* the administration
paper," he advised Polk. Playing patronage, he further suggested that
America's minister to Spain, the writer Washington Irving, author of
"The Legend of Sleepy Hollow," be removed in favor of Amos Kendall,
late of the old General's Kitchen Cabinet.[9] Few of these politely received
overtures were acted upon. Like Jackson, Polk determined to be his own
man, his own counsel, his own president. If too openly ignored, the
proud General, obviously unable to leave the arena, may have prompted
a confrontation with the new president—had he lived.

53

No Terrors

As Polk took office in the late winter of 1845 Jackson, now confined by physical infirmity to the Hermitage, felt death's imminent approach. Settled in his bedroom, he held court in a cushioned wooden chair on wheels, the inevitable tobacco box, newspapers, and enslaved boy by his side, as a steady stream of visitors and well-wishers were brought to praise and gaze. They wished to see the legendary General alive, the younger among them perhaps to enter the twentieth century with a remote memory of having shaken the hand of the man who had served in the Revolutionary War, knew Jefferson, and commanded the victorious American forces at the Battle of New Orleans. Jackson proudly played along, often donning his best dress for these impromptu interviews, complete with "a high stiff collar." He gamely accepted his fate. "This may be the last letter I may be able to write you," he addressed Blair in early March. "But live or die I am your friend."[1]

Jackson struggled through the spring, and on May 24, about, so he supposed, to expire, he took Holy Communion. "Death has no terrors for me," he is reported to have said at the time. "When I have suffered sufficiently, the Lord will take me to himself." But the old man endured. William Tyack, a family friend staying at the Hermitage during this period, kept a record of Jackson's ordeal: "May 30.—The General passed a distressed night; no sleep; extreme debility this morning, attended with increased swelling of the abdomen and all his limbs, and difficulty of breathing"; "June 2.—The General passed a bad night. No sleep. An evidence increase of water on the chest"; "June 3d.—Much distress through the night. Opiates were freely administered, but sleep appeared

361

to have passed from him," and so on. Lucid, if somnolent, Jackson's correspondence during these final days invariably expressed relief in Texas's impending annexation—"All is safe at last."[2]

The sinking General lingered on until Sunday, June 8. Hannah, an enslaved woman brought to the Hermitage about 1808 in payment of a legal debt, later remembered her master's last day: "I . . . brought in his egg and milk, he could not drink it—his eyes look so curious that I ran out and told Missus Sarah [the General's daughter-in-law, Sarah Yorke Jackson]. She was frightened and ran to the store room, got some brandy, loaf sugar and cinnamon, burned the brandy and carried it into . . . him. He took one or two tea spoons full of it and it seemed to revive him. He did not speak during the day. . . . About an hour before he died he come to—we had all thought he was dead before that. Dr. [John] Esselman was at his bedside constantly." Sam Houston, hoping for a final interview with Jackson, arrived too late. "At 6 o'clock this evening Gen. Jackson departed this life," he wrote Polk from the Hermitage. "He retained his faculties to the last hour. I lament that I was denied the satisfaction of seeing him in his last moments."[3]

For many years historians surmised that some combination of mercury and lead poisoning killed Jackson at the age of seventy-eight. His regular dosages of calomel and two leaching bullets embedded in his left lung and arm (the latter extracted in 1832) suggested as much, as did the General's diarrhea, heavy salivation, loss of teeth, and trembling hand. But a 1999 article in the *Journal of the American Medical Association* lead-authored by Ludwig M. Deppisch, M.D., a graduate of the Johns Hopkins

A stylized deathbed scene of Jackson by Currier (1888).

School of Medicine, ruled out both as critical factors. Granted access to two of Jackson's hair samples—from 1815 and 1839—the researchers discovered that while the General's mercury levels "were consistent with . . . a variety of populations consuming contaminated fish," they were hardly high enough to do him mortal harm. And as for lead poisoning, Deppisch et al. reported a decline in exposure by Jackson as he aged, likely due to the removal of one of the offending balls. Instead they concluded, "We suspect that Jackson probably died of chronic renal [kidney] failure." This would account for the swelling of his legs, feet, and ankles that Jackson first noticed in the late 1820s and which grew more pronounced. By the end of his life, they argued, Jackson likely had progressed from localized edema "to massive anasarca"—the widespread swelling of the skin. Evidence for this exists in the General's correspondence. He wrote Blair less than two weeks before his death, "I am I may say a perfect Jelly from the toes to the upper part of my abdomen, in any part of which a finger can be pressed half an Inch and the print will remain for minutes."[4]

Jackson's body was placed inside a black-draped coffin occupying the Hermitage's parlor; only the worn and sunken face remained exposed to a throng of well-wishers wanting their moment with history. By early Tuesday morning, thousands of mourners and curiosity seekers had invaded the plantation's grounds, eager to be near the 11:00 a.m. funeral. A minister read from Psalm 90—"Who knoweth the power of thine anger? even according to thy fear, so is thy wrath"— and Jackson's remains were taken from the parlor into the garden just east of the house, where, following a bit of jostling (the shallow grave unevenly accommodating the coffin), they were laid next to Rachel's in a limestone tomb resembling a Greek temple. The chimes of church bells vied with the volley of distant guns. "I have just returned from the Hermitage, where I attended the funeral of Gen. Jackson," reported Polk campaign biographer J. George Harris to the president. "It was estimated, fairly I think, that from 2500 to 3000 persons were present. There were . . . two hundred carriages in attendance to say nothing of horses, which as fastened to the boughs of the trees in front of the Hermitage yard literally filled the woods."[5]

Jackson enjoyed in death the amity that had eluded him in life. Philip Hone recorded in his diary that Manhattan mourned sincerely for the former president. A profusion of black crepe, liberty poles, and flags at half-staff issued a conspicuous attitude of grief, while newspaper boys less indecorously shouted out the only news of the day. "The

funeral procession and ceremonies [in New York City] took place yesterday," he wrote on June 25. "The military parade was exceedingly fine,
and the several societies and professions made a very respectable display. Everything was done in order and party seemed to have nothing
to do with it. The ex-President, Mr. Van Buren, Mr. Secretary [of War]
Marcy, and Gov. Silas Wright were in the procession, with a host of the
personal and political friends of the deceased chieftain. . . . [Even] . . .
many who loved him not when alive assumed the virtue of joining in
the honors bestowed upon the memory of a great man." John Quincy
Adams, among those who reliably "loved him not," never broke stride.
Upon learning of the General's death he privately counted more deb-
its than credits: "Jackson was a hero, a murderer, and adulterer . . . and
slandered me before the world." He derided the Boston City Council's
decision to hold a memorial ceremony.[6]

Twenty-six thousand dollars in debt at the time of his death (about
$935,000 in current dollars), Jackson failed to evade the fate of so
many southern planters, including Jefferson. Agrarians, they rued
the speculative financial systems they devoted their presidencies to
overturning—first Hamilton's and then Biddle's banks—only to be consumed personally by the expense of subsidizing both public careers
and their own inopportune appetites. Jackson's most obvious assets,
beyond the relics and bric-a-brac, the pistols and walking canes, were
land and slaves. Combined he owned some 150 souls in the spring
of 1845, most at the Hermitage, though dozens of others were on a
plantation in Mississippi. These people appear throughout his will. To
Andrew Jackson, Jr., he left "all my negroes that I may die possessed of,"
with a few exceptions. These included "a negro boy named Ned" given
to a grandson, "one negro boy named Davy or George" bequeathed to
another grandson, and Gracey, Charlotte, Mary, and Hanna, conferred
to Sarah Yorke Jackson. Perhaps it is fitting that Alfred, a former slave
who died in 1901 was the final member of the old Hermitage circle
with living memory of the General. A house servant, he received interment in the garden near to Jackson, emblems each of the ancient days
when southern planters could be presidents.

54

Heroes and Villains

Shortly after Jackson's death, one unforgiving New York Whig damned the General as "the undisputed head of a violent, proscriptive party . . . He did more to break down the republican principles of the government and enslave the minds of the people than all the rulers who went before him." Here reigned a virtual dictator, he continued, a master of "that pernicious popular homage called *popularity*." Fifteen years later, however, in the perilous secession winter of 1860, another Yankee, a New Hampshire Democrat, thought that only an indomitable Jackson-like leader could save the nation. "Would to Heaven," he wrote, "we had another Andrew Jackson . . . at the head of this Government . . . instead of James Buchanan."[1] Both of these observers anticipated, in their divergent views, a sharp and seemingly endless debate over the meaning of power and populism in Jackson's America. The notion of the people preventing social elites and financial aristocrats from bullying, bestriding, or otherwise buying Congress is altogether attractive. And yet common man democracy's erratic energy collaterally legitimized Indian removal, slavery's expansion, and the troubling growth of presidential fiat. In important moments, as when Jackson ignored the Supreme Court in the Cherokee case or refused to honor the government's obligation to deposit public monies in the National Bank, the rule of law itself appeared imperiled.

If sides invariably divide over Jackson's record, no one can seriously question the prominence of his long public career. As both a soldier and statesman he dominated the several decades separating Jefferson and Lincoln. The Battle of New Orleans forged for Jackson an indestructible

fame sustained throughout a charged tenure in the executive office. Perhaps most enduringly, he established a precedent for future presidents
to assert vigorous executive authority. This contribution remains, like
the man himself, contested. If a Lincoln is lauded as a powerful but
responsible leader, a Lyndon Johnson stands accused in the wake of the
Vietnam War of practicing an imperial presidency. Equally ambiguous
are Jackson's contributions to partisanship. Though the product of an
emerging party system, he doubted the notion of a loyal opposition,
regarding the Democracy as the only legitimate force for reform and
good governance in the country; in turn he repeatedly and sometimes
publicly denounced Whiggery as the people's enemy. Flat and simplis-
tic, such callow name-calling hardly contributed to the development of
a healthy political pluralism in America.

In thinking over Jackson's legacy, among his defenders Jackson will always be the precocious child
of immigrants who crossed the frontier, fought his nation's wars, and
extended its republican form of government. The argument made by
the prominent historian Frederick Jackson Turner more than a century ago, "Andrew Jackson was the champion of the cause of the upland
democracy. He denounced the money power, banks and the whole
credit system and sounded a fierce tocsin of danger against the increasing influence of wealth in politics," remains for many the distinguishing
feature of the man and the democratic movement still associated, in certain circles, with his name.[2]

In thinking over Jackson's legacy, it is telling that he invites comparison to so few presidents. Unlike certain clusters—the long Virginia dynasty of Washington, Jefferson, Madison, and Monroe; the
sectionally riven failures of the 1850s: Taylor, Fillmore, Pierce, and
Buchanan; or the corporate-friendly Jazz Age trio of Harding, Coo-
lidge, and Hoover—Jackson appears more uncommon than not. Perhaps his closest compeers are Theodore Roosevelt and Richard Nixon,
considered by scholars to rank among the best and worst of the
nation's White House occupants.[3] Jackson's belief in a strongly willed
presidency, his rhetorical trust in the people, and sense that destiny
brought him to power to overcome an encrusted congressional old
guard, were articles of unshakable faith shared by TR. Nixon's remarkable assertion of executive privilege—"when the President does it, that
means it is not illegal"—and master list of political enemies, on the
other hand, evokes both Jackson's challenge to constitutional norms

and his taste for score settling. Off the presidential path, Old Hickory might also be paired with another charismatic power-seeking general, Douglas MacArthur, whom Franklin Roosevelt, sensing a wannabe Caesar, once called "the most dangerous man in America"—the same claim bandied about during the Bank War days by any number of uneasy Whigs.

In recent years some have perhaps promiscuously compared Donald Trump and Jackson. This has mainly to do with the former's public gestures, utterances, and, occasionally, his tweets. In March 2017 Trump laid a wreath at Jackson's Hermitage tomb; he displayed the General's portrait in the Oval Office (as did Lyndon Johnson, Ronald Reagan, and Bill Clinton); and he spoke against efforts to replace Jackson with Harriet Tubman on the front of the twenty-dollar bill—"Andrew Jackson had a great history, and I think it's very rough when you take somebody off the bill." In an interview with *Washington Examiner* political reporter Salena Zito shortly after the wreath laying ceremony, Trump insisted that Jackson, despite having died more than fifteen years before the assault on Fort Sumter, would have prevented the American Civil War. He subsequently tweeted, "President Andrew Jackson . . . saw it coming and was angry. Would never have let it happen!"[4]

More than admire Jackson from afar, Trump, the self-anointed candidate of the common man, the Washington outsider, actively courted comparison. "It was during the Revolution that Jackson first confronted and defied an arrogant elite," he told one group. "I wonder why they keep talking about Trump and Jackson, Jackson and Trump. Oh, I know the feeling, Andrew."[5] The conservative scholar Victor Davis Hanson seems to have felt the connection as well. His 2019 book, *The Case for Trump*, offers a heroic portrait of the forty-fifth president that sounds positively Jacksonian:

> Trump alone saw a political opportunity in defending the working people of America's interior, whom the coastal elite . . . had come to scorn. And Trump alone had the instincts and energy to pursue this opening to victory, dismantle a corrupt old order, and bring long-overdue policy changes. . . . We could not survive a series of presidencies as volatile as Trump's. But after decades of drift . . . America needed an outsider like Trump to do what normal politicians would not or could not do.[6]

Undoubtedly certain similarities do link Jackson and Trump. Both practiced a politics of disruption and populism, while fostering an anti-establishment ethos. Jackson called for rotation of office, Trump pledged to "drain the swamp"; Jackson believed slavery a viable facet of America's economic future, Trump promised to revive the coal industry; Jackson sought in the Bank War to return the nation to its "true" constitutional principles, while Trump vowed to "make America great again." Other overlaps are suggestive. Jackson's displeasure with the Marshall Court's ruling in *Worcester v. Georgia* might find some attitudinal pairing in Trump's 2017 reproach of a federal judge in Seattle (a "so-called judge," Trump declared) who had temporarily blocked enforcement of the president's travel ban, which barred people from several Muslim-majority countries from entering the U.S. Some commentators on the left, moreover, detected a trace of Jackson's Indian removal policy in Trump's efforts to round up and deport illegal immigrants. Trump seemed eager to toy with the removal tie when deriding Massachusetts senator Elizabeth Warren as "Pocahontas" for her claims to Native American ancestry. After Warren announced in 2019 her bid for the Democratic Party's presidential nomination, he replied with a provocative tweet—"See you on the campaign TRAIL, Liz!"[7]

In other respects, however, comparisons between the two men break down. Unlike Trump, Jackson mistrusted credit, speculation, and paper money. The former's 2013 pre-campaign claim on ABC News that his net worth—"probably over ten billion dollars"—made him a credible presidential candidate, appealed to the kind of economic privilege that Jackson strongly opposed. Additionally, many evangelical Christians, part of Trump's coalition, were decidedly critical of Jackson in the 1830s; some of them were missionaries and attacked his Indian policy. Interestingly, a few of the General's detractors whispered of his supposed nativity on an Irish-launched "ship at sea," thus making this alleged immigrant ineligible for the presidency—an early version of the birther hoax that Trump and others later directed against Barack Obama.[8] More broadly, Jackson's extensive public service career was unmatched by Trump. A judge, general, senator, and military governor, Jackson entered the executive mansion with a wealth of experience working with presidential administrations. And finally, there is no comparison on the question of popularity. Trump's 46.1 percent and 46.9 percent of the vote in the 2016 and 2020 presidential elections are, respectively, 9.4 percent and 7.3 percent less than what Jackson received in 1828 and 1832.

In regard to electoral affinities, Trump perhaps most closely resembles the Indiana Republican Benjamin Harrison—who captured the presidency from Grover Cleveland in 1888 despite losing the popular vote and then failed to win reelection in 1892.[9] Both men inherited partisan majorities in the House and Senate, moreover, only to lose control of these chambers upon vacating their offices.

Trump was allowed to embrace Jackson in part because Democrats have all but disowned him. In 2020 the Democratic Party's website (democrats.org) included a link both partial and incomplete to "Our History." Emphasizing four years—1920 (women's suffrage), 1935 (Social Security), 1964 (the Civil Rights Act), and 2010 (the Affordable Care Act)—it ignored the party's first century and thus airbrushed Jackson (and Jefferson) from history. But in the 1910s progressives praised Jackson's attack on special interests and in the 1930s Depression-era Democrats extolled his efforts on behalf of the working class. Today, however, the General is more often associated with slavery and Indian removal, embodying, so his critics argue, a savage side of the American character. When combined, such clashing portrayals reprise an old impulse—a desire to see Jackson at the center of the American experience, as either the first western populist or the last southern planter. Democrat and aristocrat, republican and racist, he challenges our fondness for making history adapt to a pattern. Such complexities underlie the perennial Jackson wars, which seem invariably to trace indelibly upon the imperfect meaning of America. It is in the shadow of these interpretive skirmishes that we come to reckon with the General's contentious times—eager, no doubt, to illuminate the uncertain arc of our own as well.

Acknowledgments

My interest in Jackson and his era goes back to graduate school when I wrote an apprentice piece on the Whig Party. Chancing about this time upon illustrator David Levine's sly caricature of an akimbo-haired Old Hickory, I began to think of history as something playful, contingent, and accessible—an argument without end. To such scattered seeds do I owe an original debt.

While pursuing various projects over the years, I remained attentive to Jackson studies and am grateful to a host of scholars, including H. W. Brands, Mark R. Cheathem, the late Donald B. Cole, David S. and Jeanne T. Heidler, Daniel Walker Howe, Paul E. Johnson, John F. Marszalek, Theda Perdue, the late Robert V. Remini, Harry L. Watson, and Sean Wilentz, who have informed my views on the early American republic.

My progress in the present work was aided considerably by colleagues at Elizabethtown College's High Library; I'm further obliged to the late Hendrik Booraem for a valuable conversation on Jackson's youth. My agent, Chris Calhoun, and editor, Colin Harrison—two talented hard c's—improved, respectively, the initial proposal and the bound book. Emily Polson helped to push this project across the finish line at Scribner, while Mark LaFlaur and Rick Willett showed remarkable care in crafting a clean copy.

Notes

Abbreviations

Papers *The Papers of Andrew Jackson*, volumes 1–11 to date, eds. Sam B. Smith, Harold D. Moser, Daniel Feller, et al. (Knoxville: University of Tennessee Press, 1980–)

Correspondence *Correspondence of Andrew Jackson*, volumes 1–6, ed. John Spencer Bassett (Washington, D.C.: Carnegie Institution of Washington, 1926–1933)

Memoirs *Memoirs of John Quincy Adams*, volumes 1–12, ed. Charles Francis Adams (Philadelphia: J. B. Lippincott & Co., 1874–1877)

Papers of the Presidents *A Compilation of the Messages and Papers of the Presidents*, volumes 1–4 (New York: Bureau of National Literature, Inc., 1897)

Parton James Parton, *Life of Jackson*, volumes 1–3 (New York: Mason Brothers, 1860)

Introduction

1 In 1834 Jackson called the national bank a "monster" before a group of Philadelphians critical of his fiscal policies. See *Niles' Weekly Register* (March 1, 1834), 9. Referencing the General's monster motif a century later amid the Great Depression, John Steinbeck wrote in *The Grapes of Wrath*, "The bank—the monster has to have profits all the time. It can't wait. It'll die." John Steinbeck, *The Grapes of Wrath* (New York: Viking Press, 1939), 44.

2 Harriet Martineau, *Retrospect of Western Travel*, vol. 1 (New York: Charles Lohman, 1838), 116.

3 Frances Anne Butler (Miss Fanny Kemble), *Journal of a Residence in America* (Brussels: A.D. Wahlen, Bookseller, 1835), 242–43.

4 Deirdre David, *Fanny Kemble: A Performed Life* (Philadelphia: University of Pennsylvania Press, 2007), 286.

5 Robert Remini, *Andrew Jackson and the Course of American Empire, 1767–1821* (New York: Harper & Row, 1977), 1; Alexis de Tocqueville, *Democracy in America*, ed. J. P. Mayer, translated by George Lawrence (New York: HarperPerennial, 1988), 393; Arthur M. Schlesinger, Jr., *The Age of Jackson* (Boston: Little, Brown, 1945), 93.

6 See, for example, the fine works of Michael Kazin, *The Populist Persuasion: An American History* (New York: Basic Books, 1995) and *A Godly Hero: The Life of*

William Jennings Bryan (New York: Alfred A. Knopf, 2006). On populism prior to 1890 see Ronald P. Formisano's *For the People: American Populist Movements from the Revolution to the 1850s* (Chapel Hill: University of North Carolina Press, 2008). To my mind this work—which considers a wide range of Regulators, Workingmen's parties, Anti-Masons, and Know-Nothings, among others groups—largely scatters rather than concentrates the idea of populism as a broadly based movement shaping the country's political culture.

7   *Papers of the Presidents*, 3:1153. For a recent scholarly statement on Jackson's relationships to majoritarianism, see Harry L. Watson's "Andrew Jackson's Populism," *Tennessee Historical Quarterly* (Fall 2017), 218–239.

8   For Reagan's inaugural address see Terence Ball, Richard Dagger, and Daniel I. O'Neill, eds., *Ideals and Ideologies: A Reader* (New York: Routledge, 2014), 182; for Trump's speech see Brendan Cole, "Donald Trump on Liberal Elites: 'I'm Smarter than Them, I went to the Best Schools,' Says He Has 'A Much More Beautiful House,'" *Newsweek*, March 29, 2019. https://www.newsweek.com/donald-trump-liberal-elites-smarter-schools-beautiful-house-1379578.

9   For a trio of strong synthetic works that address the impact of expanding economic development in the 1820s see Harry L. Watson's *Liberty and Power: The Politics of Jacksonian America* (New York: Hill and Wang, 1990), Charles Sellers, *The Market Revolution: Jacksonian America, 1815–1846* (New York: Oxford University Press, 1991), and Daniel Feller's *The Jacksonian Promise: America, 1815–1840* (Baltimore: Johns Hopkins University Press, 1995).

1: *Ulster to America*

1   *The Life of Mr. Robert Blair, Minister of St Andrews, Containing His Autobiography, from 1593 to 1636*, ed. Thomas M'Crie (Edinburgh: James Walker, Printer, 1848), 57.

2   Parton, 1:47, 1:42.

3   R. J. Dickson, *Ulster Emigration to Colonial America, 1718–1775* (London: Routledge, 1966), 55; Marquis James, *The Life of Andrew Jackson: Complete in One Volume* (Indianapolis: Bobbs-Merrill, 1938), 3; material on Betty Hutchinson Jackson and her sisters can be found in a private document—Mary Frances and Thomas Veach, "Sorting the Waxhaw Crawfords" (Elverta, CA, 1993), 133. There is an Andrew Jackson Centre in the village of Boneybefore in County Antrim. It features a refurbished farmhouse built in the 1750s and briefly home to Jackson's parents. The structure doubles as a period-piece museum and Jackson interpretive site.

4   Robert M. Weir, *Colonial South Carolina: A History* (Columbia: University of South Carolina Press, 1997), 178; Peter Kolchin, *American Slavery: 1619–1877* (New York: Hill and Wang, 1993), 240.

5   Dickson, *Ulster Emigration to Colonial America*, 58; John Reid and John Henry Eaton, *The Life of Andrew Jackson*, ed. Frank L. Owsley, Jr. (Tuscaloosa: University of Alabama Press, 1974), 9; James, *Life of Andrew Jackson*, 789.

6   Hendrik Booraem, *Young Hickory: the Making of Andrew Jackson* (Dallas: Taylor Trade Publishing, 2001), 215, n2.

7   Hendrik Booraem to author, July 21, 2017.

8 See chapter six, "Harmless and Friendly: The Catawba Trail of Tears," in James H. Merrell, *The Indians' New World: Catawbas and Their Neighbors from European Contact Through the Era of Removal* (Chapel Hill: University of North Carolina Press, 1989).

9 Amos Kendall, *Life of Andrew Jackson: Private, Military, and Civil* (New York: Harper & Brothers, 1843), 11.

10 *Papers*, 5:438; S. G. Heiskell, ed., *Andrew Jackson and Early Tennessee History* (Nashville: Ambrose Printing Company, 1918), 289.

11 Reid and Eaton, *Life of Andrew Jackson*, lxxix.

12 Parton, 1:64.

13 Robert Pierce Forbes, *The Missouri Compromise and Its Aftermath: Slavery and the Meaning of America* (Chapel Hill: University of North Carolina Press, 2007), 328, n42.

14 Parton, 1:64.

2: *Forged in War*

1 *Correspondence*, 5:194.

2 Reid and Eaton, *Life of Andrew Jackson*, 10.

3 Parton, 1:83.

4 Ibid.; *Papers*, 1:5.

5 Blackwell P. Robinson, ed., *The Revolutionary War Sketches of William R. Davie* (Raleigh: North Carolina Department of Cultural Resources, Division of the Archives, 1976), 15.

6 Reid and Eaton, *Life of Andrew Jackson*, 12. In fact, Jackson received two wounds that day, including a deep gash to his head, which glancingly caught the blow that his left hand slowed but could not still.

7 *Papers*, 5:431, 1:7.

8 Ibid., 5:438. A stone marker on the campus of the College of Charleston commemorates Betty Jackson, who "Near This Spot is Buried." A second tablet in the city's Washington Square park, put up by the local chapter of the Daughters of the American Revolution, honors Betty for giving "her life in the cause of independence while nursing Revolutionary soldiers." Yet another monument was installed at the Andrew Jackson State Park in the Waxhaws, while a statue of Betty, put up in 1949, resides in the cemetery of the Waxhaw Presbyterian Church.

9 Kendall, *Life of Andrew Jackson*, 44–45.

3: *But a Raw Lad*

1 *Papers*, 1:7.

2 Booraem, *Young Hickory*, 116.

3 *Papers*, 1:7.

4 Arda Walker, "The Educational Training and Views of Andrew Jackson," *The East Tennessee Historical Society's Publications*, no. 16 (1944), 23, 22; Parton, 1:98.

5 *Papers*, 4:91.

6 Parton, 1:161. Documentation is sketchy, though Booraem notes that "one tradition has it" that Jackson first read law with Charles Bruce, a neighbor of Jackson's uncle Robert McCamie, who lived near Guilford Courthouse. Booraem, *Young Hickory*, 141.

7   Parton, 1:104–07.
8   Ibid., 1:105.

4: *Western Apprentice*

1   Carl S. Driver, *John Sevier: Pioneer of the Old Southwest* (Chapel Hill: University of North Carolina Press, 1932), 1.
2   In June 1784 North Carolina had ceded its lands west of the Appalachians to the federal government, which, moving slowly, failed to promptly and officially accept this territory. That October, with Sevier making a claim for Franklin statehood, North Carolina rescinded its earlier cession and asserted control over Tennessee.
3   Peter Force, ed., *A Documentary History of the English Colonies in North America, from the King's Message to Parliament, of March 7, 1774, to the Declaration of Independence by the United States,* vol. 3 (Washington, D.C.: M. St. Clair Clarke and Peter Force, 1840), 847.
4   Parton, 1:161–62.
5   *Papers*, 1:12.
6   Parton, 1:162.
7   Avery County, North Carolina, formed in 1911, is named after Waightstill Avery.
8   Known as Avery's Trace, the trail had been directed, along a route used by the Cherokee Indians, by Peter Avery, a hunter in the Cumberland region. Augustus C. Buell, *History of Andrew Jackson: Pioneer, Patriot, Soldier, Politician, President,* vol. 1 (New York: Charles Scribner's Sons, 1904), 72.
9   Francis Baily, *Journal of a Tour in Unsettled Parts of North America in 1796 & 1797* (London: Baily Brothers, 1856), 415–16.
10 Reid and Eaton, *Life of Andrew Jackson,* 15; Parton, 1:125.
11 Francis Paul Prucha, *American Indian Treaties: The History of a Political Anomaly* (Berkeley: University of California Press, 1994), 64.
12 Christina Mune, "Rachel Donelson Robards Jackson: A Reluctant First Lady," in Katherine A. S. Sibley, ed., *A Companion to First Ladies* (West Sussex, UK: John Wiley & Sons, Inc., 2016), 112–14; Laura Carter Holloway, *The Ladies of the White House* (New York: U.S. Publishing, Co., 1870), 287.
13 Parton, 1:133; Remini, *Andrew Jackson and the Course of American Empire,* 43.
14 Parton, 1:137–38, 136.
15 J. W. M. Breazeale, *Life as It Is: or Matters and Things in General* (Knoxville: James Williams, 1842), 73.

5: *The Conspiracy Game*

1   Julian P. Boyd, ed., *The Papers of Thomas Jefferson,* vol. 17 (Princeton: Princeton University Press, 1965), 111.
2   Robert Remini, "Andrew Jackson Takes an Oath of Allegiance to Spain," *Tennessee Historical Quarterly* (Spring, 1995), 5, 8, 9.
3   J. M. Opal, *Avenging the People: Andrew Jackson, the Rule of Law, and the American Nation* (New York: Oxford University Press, 2017), 80.
4   William H. Masterson, *William Blount* (Baton Rouge: Louisiana State University Press, 1954), 193; Remini, *Andrew Jackson and the Course of American Empire,* 53.

5 "The Correspondence of Gen. James Robertson," *American Historical Magazine* 1 (July 1896), 280.

6 Opal, *Avenging the People*, 80.

6: *Marriage(s)*

1 Parton, 1:146.

2 Ibid., 1:147. When Jackson later pursued the presidency, his political opponents sometimes reprinted the divorce decree. See, for example, By An Association of Individuals, *Truth's Advocate and Monthly Anti-Jackson Expositor* (Cincinnati: Lodge, L'Hommedieu, and Hammond, Printers, 1828), 17.

3 *Journal of the Senate of the United States of America: Being the Second Session of the Twenty-Fourth Congress* (Washington, D.C.: Gales and Seaton, 1836), 81.

4 *Papers*, 1:91. In 1833 Jackson pragmatically advised a nephew to desire in a spouse something more than romance: "One word to you as to matrimony—seek a wife, one who will aid you in your exertions in making a competency and will take care of it when made. . . . Look at the economy of the mother and if you find it in her you will find it in the daughter." *Correspondence*, 5:60.

7: *Nashville Nabob*

1 *Papers*, 1:48.

2 Remini, *Andrew Jackson and the Course of American Empire*, 77; *Papers*, 1:82.

3 *Papers*, 1:54. It is unclear which Rice Overton referred to. Jackson was dealing with both Elisha and Joel Rice, brothers of the departed John, at the time.

4 According to Parton, Jackson "sent on his goods by wagons to Pittsburg, by flatboat down the Ohio to Louisville, by wagons again, or pack horses, across the country to the neighborhood of Nashville." Parton, 1:242.

5 *Papers*, 1:64.

6 Amos Kendall, *Life of Andrew Jackson*, 109.

8: *The Outsider*

1 Remini, *Andrew Jackson and the Course of American Empire*, 84; *Papers*, 1:75. In his famous 1806 duel with Charles Dickinson, Jackson was, in fact, reputed to have worn "a big coat" that may have presented to his opponent a slightly altered target.

2 Parton, 1:196; Henry Adams, *The Life of Albert Gallatin* (Philadelphia: J. B. Lippincott, 1880), 4–5. The prejudice against western men in Congress continued into the next century. In 1812 Tennessee congressman Felix Grundy wrote to a daughter of his Washington arrival, "I was claimed as a Virginian, I say no, I am a Western man altogether. . . . They formerly thought, that everything west of the mountains was done in a wild, savage manner." Grundy to My Dear Daughter, December 19, 1812, folder 1, Felix Grundy Papers, Southern Historical Collection at the Louis Round Wilson Special Collections Library, the University of North Carolina at Chapel Hill.

3 Remini, *Andrew Jackson and the Course of American Empire*, 94; *Papers*, 1:74.

4 *Papers*, 1:107.

5 Thomas Perkins Abernathy, *From Frontier to Plantation in Tennessee: A Study in Frontier Democracy* (Chapel Hill: University of North Carolina Press, 1932), 167.

6 Remini, *Andrew Jackson and the Course of American Empire*, 104–5; Sara Martin et al., eds., *The Adams Papers: Adams Family Correspondence*, vol. 12 (Cambridge, MA: Belknap Press of Harvard University Press, 2015), x, xi.

7 *Papers*, 1:78, n1.

9: Justice Jackson

1 Parton, 1:227.

2 Ibid.

3 *Papers*, 1:252; Jackson's jurisdiction can be found in Edward Scott, *Laws of the State of Tennessee, 1715–1820*, vol. 1 (Knoxville, 1821), 457, as quoted in James W. Ely, Jr., "Andrew Jackson as Tennessee State Court Judge, 1798–1804" *Tennessee Historical Quarterly* (Summer 1981), 145.

4 Ely, Jr., "Andrew Jackson," 147–49.

5 *Papers*, 1:138, 1:343; James Lee McDonough, "Archibald Roane," in Charles W. Crawford, ed., *Governors of Tennessee*, vol. 3 (Memphis State University Press, 1979), 74.

6 George W. Harris, *Sut Lovingood Yarns Spun by a Nat'ral Born Durn'd Fool* (New York: Dick & Fitzgerald, Publishers, 1867), 114; Parton, 1:164.

7 *Papers*, 1:367–68.

8 Ibid., 1:368, 1:369.

9 Ibid., 1:376.

10 Ibid., 1:377.

11 Ibid., 1:379, 1:505.

12 Driver, *John Sevier*, 187.

13 *Papers*, 2:19.

14 H. A. Washington, ed., *The Writings of Thomas Jefferson*, vol. 5 (New York: Riker, Thorne & Co., 1854), 30.

15 *Papers*, 1:252–53.

10: Befriending Burr

1 Stanley Elkins and Eric McKitrick, *The Age of Federalism: The Early American Republic, 1788–1800* (New York: Oxford University Press, 1993), 743.

2 David O. Stewart, *American Emperor: Aaron Burr's Challenge to Jefferson's America* (New York: Simon & Schuster, 2011), 295.

3 Henry Adams, *History of the United States of America During the Administrations of Thomas Jefferson* (New York: Library of America, 1986), 571.

4 Ibid., 576. For a defense of Burr see Nancy Isenberg, *Fallen Founder: The Life of Aaron Burr* (New York: Penguin Books, 2007).

5 *Papers*, 2:110; Stewart, *American Emperor*, 102.

6 Parton, 1:311.

7 Remini, *Andrew Jackson and the Course of American Empire*, 147–48.

8 Dumas Malone, *Jefferson the President: Second Term, 1805–1809* (Boston: Little, Brown, 1974), 247–48.

9 *Papers*, 2:116, 2:114; Washington, ed., *The Writings of Thomas Jefferson*, 25.

10 Merrill D. Peterson, *The Great Triumvirate: Webster, Clay, and Calhoun* (New York: Oxford University Press, 1987), 51; The Author of the Thirty Years' View [Thomas

Hart Benton], *Abridgement of the Debates of Congress, from 1789 to 1856*, vol. 3 (New York: D. Appleton & Company, 1857), 579.

11 *Papers*, 2:149.
12 For Jefferson's proclamation see Thomas Jefferson Papers, November 27, 1806, Library of Congress; Isenberg, *Fallen Founder*, 320, 321; James Parton, *The Life and Times of Aaron Burr*, vol. 2 (Boston: Ticknor and Fields, 1867), 93.
13 *Papers*, 1:353. "The Butler-Wilkinson quarrel was immortalized in *Knickerbocker's History of New York* by Washington Irving, who met Wilkinson at the Burr trial in Richmond in 1807, took an immediate and passionate dislike of him, and carica-tured him as General Jacobus Von Poffenburgh, the martinet enemy of Old Kelder-meester's queue." From *Papers*, 2:65.
14 Fred L. Borch III, "The True Story of a Colonel's Pigtail and a Court-Martial" in *The Army Lawyer: Headquarters Department of the Army* (March, 2012), 2.
15 *Papers*, 2:164.
16 Ibid., 2:175–76.

11: *The Duelist*

1 Parton, 1:268.
2 *Papers*, 2:56–57; Colonel Robert Butler to Jackson, April 20, 1817, in Andrew Jackson Papers, Library of Congress, Series 1, General Correspondence and Related Items, 1775–1885, MSS 27532, vol. 44. https://www.loc.gov/resource/maj.01044_0183_0186/?st=text.
3 *Papers*, 2:78.
4 Ibid., 2:80, 2:82.
5 Ibid., 2:87, 2:88; Parton, 1:286, 1:288.
6 Parton, 1:269. The local gossip in this case was Sam Houston, later president of the Republic of Texas. Only thirteen in 1806 when the Jackson-Dickinson duel occurred, he must have acquired his information secondhand.
7 *Papers*, 2:82.
8 Ibid., 2:90, 2:94.
9 Ibid., 2:88, 2:97–98.
10 Parton, 1:295, 1:297.
11 Ibid., 1:299.
12 Ibid., 1:300. Over time Dickinson's gravesite on Erwin's estate a few miles west of Nashville disappeared, enveloped in development. Researchers discovered it in the summer of 2009, and nearly a year later the remains were laid to rest in the Nashville City Cemetery. According to one source, descendants of both Dickinson and Jackson attended the ceremony. http://www.civicscope.org/nashville-tn/CharlesDickinson.
13 *Papers*, 4:319.
14 Ibid., 2:101.
15 Ibid., 2:104, 2:107 n3, 2:106.
16 Ibid., 1:109.

12: *Erratic Rehabilitation*

1 Reid and Eaton, *Life of Andrew Jackson*, 17.
2 *Papers*, 2:234.

3   Ibid., 2:284, 2:290, 2:291.

4   Ibid., 2:312, 2:317, 2:319.

5   Ibid., 2:358, 2:359–60.

6   Ibid., 2:361, 2:385, 2:387.

7   Ibid., 3:384. Though Jackson complained of being dismissed "eight hundred miles from home," Natchez is about five hundred miles from Nashville.

8   Ibid., 2:385.

9   Ibid., 2:403–4. In fact, officers from the regular army did, as Jackson predicted, enter "my encampment for this purpose" of recruiting. Ibid., 2:403.

10   Parton, 1:386–87.

11   *Papers*, 2:414, 2:415.

12   Ibid., 2:422.

13   Parton, 1:392–93.

14   William M. Meigs, *The Life of Thomas Hart Benton* (Philadelphia: J. B. Lippincott, 1904), 78, 79.

13: *The Creek War*

1   Donald R. Hickey, *The War of 1812: A Forgotten Conflict* (Urbana: University of Illinois Press, 2012), 22–24; 145–48.

2   *Papers*, 2:428–29, 2:441.

3   Herbert J. Doherty, Jr., *Richard Keith Call: Southern Unionist* (Gainesville: University of Florida Press, 1961), 6.

4   *A Narrative of the Life of David Crockett* (Philadelphia: E. L. Carey and A. Hart, 1834), 88–90.

5   *Papers*, 2:444; Michael Paul Rogin, *Fathers and Children: Andrew Jackson and the Subjugation of the American Indian* (New York: Alfred A. Knopf, 1975), 350, n74. On the question of adopting Indians in the early republic, see Dawn Peterson's *Indians in the Family: Adoption and the Politics of Antebellum Expansion* (Cambridge, MA: Harvard University Press, 2017), especially chapter five, "Adoption in Andrew Jackson's Empire."

6   Parton, 1:444–45.

7   *Papers*, 2:457.

8   Ibid., 2:467, 2:472–73; Reid and Eaton, *Life of Andrew Jackson*, 84.

9   *Papers*, 2:515.

10   Donald Hickey, ed., *The War of 1812: Writings from America's Second War of Independence* (New York: Library of America, 2013), 406; *Papers*, 3:42; Tom Kanon, "Glories in the Field: John Cocke vs. Andrew Jackson During the War of 1812," *Journal of East Tennessee History* 71 (1999): 47–65; Parton, 1:455.

11   *Papers*, 3:49. In March 1815, a few weeks after the Senate ratified the Treaty of Ghent, thus ending the War of 1812, Jackson released a sergeant and a private sentenced to be executed for "disobedience of orders, mutiny, desertion and using contemptuous and abusive language to their captain." His decision to spare their lives might strengthen the notion that Woods, convicted of lesser sins, was sacrificed for Jackson's notion of reasserting command over his soldiers during wartime and in light of the enlistment terms dispute. *Papers*, 3:291, n1.

12   *Papers*, 3:54–55.

13   Ibid., 3:28–29.

14: *Sharp Knife*

1   *Papers*, 3:65, 3:71; Remini, *Andrew Jackson and the Course of American Empire*, 221.

2   Ibid., 3:76; Henry Adams, *History of the United States of America During the Administrations of James Madison* (New York: Library of America, 1986), 593; J. C. A. Stagg, *Mr. Madison's War: Politics, Diplomacy and Warfare in the Early American Republic, 1783–1830* (Princeton University Press, 1983), 398–99.

3   Madison to Armstrong, May 20, 1814, retrieved from the Library of Congress, https://www.loc.gov/item/mjm022751/.

4   *Papers*, 3:74–75.

5   Ibid., 3:104, 3:113.

6   Statement by Commissioners of Indian Affairs on Distribution of Judgment Funds to Creek Indians in "United States Department of the Interior News Release," December 2, 1966, (88771–66), 1, U.S. Department of the Interior: Bureau of Indian Affairs.

15: *Optional Invasion*

1   *Papers*, 3:83, 3:90.

2   Ibid., 3:91.

3   *Papers of the Presidents*, 2:530.

4   Ibid., 3:123.

5   Ibid., 3:127; 3:170–71; Robert Allen Rutland, *The Presidency of James Madison* (Lawrence: University Press of Kansas, 1990), 169–70. Armstrong later condemned Jackson's advance into Pensacola. "The general's attack and capture of the town on the 7th of November, 1814," he wrote, "was to say the least of it decidedly ill-judged, involving at once an offence to a neutral power, and a probable misapplication of both time and force as regarded the defence of New Orleans," as quoted in Adams, *History of the United States During the Administrations of James Madison*, 1139.

6   *Papers*, 3:179–80.

7   Ibid., 3:200.

8   Ibid., 3:194, 3:187. Jalap is a purgative, while calomel was thought to cure any number of ailments, including gout, cholera, syphilis, and cancer.

9   James, *Life of Andrew Jackson*, 201.

16: *To New Orleans*

1   Parton, 1:547. According to Winfield Scott, who first entered military service in 1808 and is remembered as the longest serving general in American history, the Jeffersonians invariably elevated their favorites. "Many of the appointments were positively bad," he recalled, "and a majority of the remainder indifferent. Party spirit of that day knew no bounds, and, of course, was blind to policy. . . . How infinitely unwise then, in a republic, to trust its safety and honor in battles, in a critical war like that impending over us in 1808, to imbeciles and ignoramuses!" Lieutenant-General Winfield Scott, *Memoirs of Lieut.-General Scott, LL.D.* (New York: Sheldon & Company Publishers, 1864), 34–36.

2   On the German Coast slave rebellion see Daniel Rasmussen, *American Uprising: The Untold Story of America's Largest Slave Revolt* (New York: HarperCollins, 2011).

3 *Papers*, 3:144.
4 Ibid., 3:206–7.
5 Ibid., 3:205.
6 Ibid., 3:219.
7 Adams, *History of the United States During the Administrations of James Madison*, 1157–58. Actually Pakenham was only thirty-six when he fought and died at New Orleans.
8 *Papers*, 3:226–27.
9 Vincent Nolte, *Fifty Years in Both Hemispheres: Or, Reminiscences of the Life of a Former Merchant* (New York: Redfield, 1854), 218–19.
10 Sir Harry Smith, *The Autobiography of Lieutenant General Sir Harry Smith*, ed. G. C. Moore Smith (London: John Murray, 1902), 231–32.

17: A Victory More Complete

1 Stagg, *Mr. Madison's War*, 395. Some in England, reported London's *Cobbett's Weekly Register*, "talk with delight of the sending of Lord Wellington's army to the United States; they revel at the idea of burning the cities and towns, the mills and manufactories of that country; at the very least, they talk of forcing Mr. Madison from his seat, and new-modelling the government." Irving Brant, *James Madison: Commander in Chief, 1812–1836* (Indianapolis: Bobbs-Merrill, 1961), 268.
2 Smith, *Autobiography of Lieutenant General Sir Harry Smith*, 236; Alexander Walker, *Jackson and New Orleans: An Authentic Narrative of the Memorable Achievements of the American Army Under Andrew Jackson Before New Orleans in the Winter of 1814, '15* (Cincinnati: J. C. Derby, 1856), 327; George Robert Glieg, *The Campaigns of the British Army at Washington and New Orleans, in the Years 1814–1815* (London: John Murray, 1842), 335.
3 Daniel Walker Howe, *What Hath God Wrought: The Transformation of America, 1815–1848* (New York: Oxford University Press, 2007), 12.
4 Major A. Lacarriere Latour, *Historical Memoir of the War in West Florida and Louisiana* (Philadelphia: John Conrad and Co., 1816), cli.
5 *Papers*, 3:240.
6 Remini, *Andrew Jackson and the Course of American Empire*, 284.
7 *Correspondence*, 2:135–36.
8 Casualty estimates come from "American Battlefield Trust," https://www.battlefields.org/learn/war-1812/battles/new-orleans.
9 Charles Cist, ed., *The Cincinnati Miscellany or Antiquities of the West: And Pioneer History and General and Local Statistics Compiled from the* Western General Advertiser (Cincinnati: Robinson & Jones, 1846), 356.
10 *Papers*, 3:242, 3:251.
11 Ibid., 3:285.
12 Rutland, *The Presidency of James Madison*, 185.
13 Tocqueville, *Democracy in America*, 278; Fred Kaplan, *John Quincy Adams: American Visionary* (New York: Harper Perennial, 2014), 478.

18: Defend or Endanger

1 *Papers*, 3:241.
2 Ibid., 3:291, n1, 3:291, 3:250.

3 Parton, 2:311.
4 Ibid.
5 *Papers*, 3:306.
6 Ibid., 3:322, 3:324, 3:28.
7 Parton, 2:319; Donald R. Hickey, *Glorious Victory: Andrew Jackson and the Battle of New Orleans* (Baltimore: Johns Hopkins University Press, 2015), 120. For Hall's response to Jackson's statement see "A Note to General Jackson's Answer," in *Niles' Weekly Register* (June 17, 1815), 272–74.
8 *Papers*, 3:344–46.
9 Ibid., 3:359.
10 Ibid., 3:376–77.
11 Ibid., 3:385.
12 Abraham Lincoln, *Selected Speeches and Writings* (New York: Vintage/Library of America, 1992), 373, 381.

19: *Removal by Another Name*

1 Steve Inskeep, *Jacksonland: President Andrew Jackson, Cherokee Chief John Ross, and a Great American Land Grab* (New York: Penguin Press, 2015), 270.
2 Edward Hertslet, C. B., *The Map of Europe by Treaty*, vol. 1 (London: Harrison and Sons, 1875), 58; Remini, *Andrew Jackson and the Course of American Empire*, 302; *Papers*, 3:383.
3 *Papers*, 4:62.
4 Mary Stockwell, *The Other Trail of Tears: The Removal of the Ohio Indians* (Yardley, PA: Westholme, 2016), 61; *Papers*, 4:96.
5 *Papers*, 4:285 n4; 4:12.

20: *The Chieftain*

1 *Papers*, 4:87, 4:97.
2 Ibid., 4:113.
3 *Correspondence*, 2:319.
4 *Papers*, 4:135.
5 Ibid., 4:145–46.
6 Ibid., 4:148.
7 Parton, 2:376.
8 *Correspondence*, 2:325; *Papers*, 4:142–43.
9 *Papers*, 4:156–58.
10 *Correspondence*, 2:344; *Papers*, 4:223; Scott, *Memoirs of Lieut.-General Scott*, 199–200.
11 *Papers*, 4:155, 4:162.
12 John Quincy Adams, *The Lives of James Madison and James Monroe: Fourth and Fifth Presidents of the United States* (Buffalo: Geo. H. Derby and Co., 1850), 293.

21: *Phantom Letter, Full Invasion*

1 W. Edwin Hemphill, ed., *Papers of John C. Calhoun*, vol. 2, 1817–1818 (Columbia: University of South Carolina Press, 1963), 20.

2   *Papers*, 4:163; Hemphill, ed., *Papers of John C. Calhoun*, vol. 2, 291.

3   Howe, *What Hath God Wrought*, 99; Stephen F. Knott, *Secret and Sanctioned: Covert Operations and the American Presidency* (New York: Oxford University Press, 1996), 98.

4   *Papers*, 4:167.

5   Hemphill, ed., *Papers of John C. Calhoun*, vol. 2, 104; Harry Ammon, *James Monroe: The Quest for National Identity* (New York: McGraw-Hill, 1971), 417.

6   Remini, *Andrew Jackson and the Course of American Empire*, 348. Some years after Jackson's Florida invasion, Monroe drafted the following cautious statement: "Hearing afterwards, that an understanding was imputed to me, I asked Mr Rhea, if any thing had ever pass'd between him and me. He declar'd that he had never heard of the subject before. I knew the suggestion to be false, but having not read the letter, and it being possible, that Mr Rhea might have been written to, and have spoken to me by distant allusion, to the object, to which I might have innocently given, from a desire to acquire Florida, a reply, from which he might have inferred, a sanction, not contemplated, I was glad to find, that nothing of the kind, had occurred." *Correspondence*, 2:346. In the early 1830s, at Jackson's insistence, Rhea, then in his late seventies, produced a letter (in accordance with a draft crafted by Jackson) insisting that he *had* served as a conduit between the General and Monroe, delivering up the latter's permission for Jackson to attack Spanish forts. *Papers*, 4:165–66.

7   *Papers*, 4:186–87.

8   Ibid., 4:188–90.

9   Frank L. Owsley, Jr., "Ambrister and Arbuthnot: Adventurers or Martyrs for British Honor?," *Journal of the Early Republic* (Autumn 1985): 294, 308.

10 Remini, *Andrew Jackson and the Course of American Empire*, 358; *Niles' Weekly Register*, December 12, 1818, 281.

11 *Papers*, 4:199.

12 Ibid., 4:205–9.

13 *Memoirs*, 4:107, 4:87; Irving H. Bartlett, *John C. Calhoun: A Biography* (Norton: W. W. Norton, 1993), 101–2.

14 David Waldstreicher, ed., *The Diaries of John Quincy Adams*, vol. 1 (New York: Library of America, 2017), 452.

15 Stanislaus Murray Hamilton, ed., *The Writings of James Monroe*, vol. 6 (New York: G. P. Putnam's Sons, 1902), 54, 61; Hemphill, ed., *Papers of John C. Calhoun*, vol. 2, 408.

16 Waldstreicher, ed., *Diaries of John Quincy Adams*, vol. 1, 445, 450.

17 One could, of course, turn this construction on its head and say that the raid demonstrated conclusively the United States' inability to keep its citizens from entering Indian country. On a different note, historian Lynn Parsons makes a strong case that Quincy Adams proved to be a more earnest continentalist than Jackson. Author of the Monroe Doctrine—a policy warning off future European colonization in the Western Hemisphere—Adams believed that "the United States and North America are identical" and defended U.S. interests aggressively as secretary of state on both its northern (Canadian) and southern (Spanish) borders. "Adams's expansionism in the early 1820s," writes Hudson, "was, if anything, more robust than that of Jackson, who was mainly concerned with ridding the southwestern frontier of Spaniards and Indians." Lynn Hudson Parsons, *The Birth of*

Modern Politics: Andrew Jackson, John Quincy Adams, and the Election of 1828
(New York: Oxford University Press, 2009), 66.

18 J. Jefferson Looney et al., eds., *The Papers of Thomas Jefferson: Retirement Series*, vol.
14 (Princeton: Princeton University Press, 2017), 23, 92; *Letters and Other Writings
of James Madison*, vol. 3 (Philadelphia: J. B. Lippincott & Co., 1867), 127.

22: Congressional Qualms

1 Waldstreicher, ed., *Diaries of John Quincy Adams*, vol. 1, 443.
2 Adams to Onís, July 23, 1818, retrieved from the Library of Congress, https://www
.loc.gov/resource/maj.01049_0288_0297/?st=gallery.
3 *Papers*, 4:225–27.
4 Ibid., 4:236–37; 4:163.
5 Ibid., 4:167.
6 Hamilton, ed., *Writings of James Monroe*, 74; *Papers of the Presidents*, 2:609, 2:610,
2:612. Jackson informed Monroe on December 7 that he had read the president's
annual message "with great attention and satisfaction." *Correspondence*, 2:402.
7 James F. Hopkins, ed., *The Papers of Henry Clay*, vol. 2 (Lexington: University of
Kentucky Press, 1961), 655–57.
8 Ibid., 659.
9 Remini, *Andrew Jackson and the Course of American Empire*, 374.
10 Parton, 2:567; *American State Papers: Documents, Legislative and Executive, of the
Congress of the United States*, "Military Affairs," vol. 1 (Washington, D.C.: Gales and
Seaton, 1832), 741, 743, 740.
11 *The Debates and Proceedings in the Congress of the United States: Fifteenth Congress—
Second Session, Comprising the Period from November 16, 1818, to March 3, 1819*
(Washington, D.C.: Gales and Seaton, 1855), 264.
12 Ibid., 268.
13 Judith S. Graham et al., eds., *Diary and Autobiographical Writings of Louisa Catherine Adams*, vol. 2 (Cambridge, MA: Belknap Press of Harvard University Press,
2013), 411.

23: Florida's Revenge

1 Allan R. Millett, Peter Maslowski, and William B. Feis, *For the Common Defense:
A Military History of the United States from 1607 to 2012* (New York: Free Press,
2012), 111–13.
2 Donald E. Graves, "Forward," in John D. Morris, *Sword of the Border: Major General Jacob Jennings Brown, 1775–1828* (Kent, OH: Kent State University Press,
2000), xi.
3 *Correspondence*, 2:439; *Papers*, 4:343, 5:9; *Memoirs*, 5:321–22.
4 *Papers*, 5:10, 5:15, 5:24.
5 Ibid., 5:69–70.
6 Ibid., 5:79–80.
7 Ibid., 5:80–81, 5:99.
8 Parton, 2:617–18; Remini, *Andrew Jackson and the Course of American Empire*, 412.
9 Clarence E. Carter, ed., *The Territorial Papers of the United States*, vol. 22 (Washington, D.C.: United States Government Printing Office, 1956), 242, 255.

10 *Memoirs*, 5:375.
11 *Correspondence*, 3:129.
12 Francis Tomlinson Gardner, "The Gentleman from Tennessee," *Surgery, Gynecology and Obstetrics with International Abstracts of Surgery* (March 1949): 404–11.

24: *Ebbing Old Republic*

1 On the Panic and its impact on American politics, see Sean Wilentz's *The Rise of American Democracy: Jefferson to Lincoln* (New York: W. W. Norton, 2005), 202–17.
2 On Clay's economic nationalism see Maurice G. Baxter, *Henry Clay and the American System* (Lexington: University Press of Kentucky, 1995).
3 The second Bank of the United States established a Nashville branch in 1827. When asked as a prominent citizen of that city to sign a petition in favor of the branch, Jackson refused. Several of his friends and colleagues, including John Eaton and William B. Lewis, were bank boosters. *Papers*, 4:378, 4:304, 4:307, 4:323; Bray Hammond, *Banks and Politics in America: From the Revolution to the Civil War* (Princeton: Princeton University Press, 1957), 259.
4 Lester J. Cappon, *The Adams-Jefferson Letters: The Complete Correspondence Between Thomas Jefferson and Abigail and John Adams* (Chapel Hill: University of North Carolina Press, 1959), 548–49, 551.
5 *Correspondence*, 3:157.
6 Ibid., n3.
7 *Papers*, 4:367.
8 Ibid., 5:4.

25: *Call of the People*

1 Thomas Jefferson, *Notes on the State of Virginia*, in *The Portable Thomas Jefferson*, ed. Merrill D. Peterson (New York: Penguin Books, 1975), 217.
2 *Correspondence*, 2:220; James, *Life of Andrew Jackson*, 271.
3 Parsons, *The Birth of Modern Politics*, 75.
4 *Papers*, 5:208, 5:210–11.
5 James F. Hopkins, ed., *The Papers of Henry Clay*, vol. 3 (Lexington: University of Kentucky Press, 1963), 274.
6 David Waldstreicher, ed., *The Diaries of John Quincy Adams*, vol. 2 (New York: Library of America, 2017), 37–38.
7 *Correspondence*, 3:192.
8 *Papers*, 5:252–53.
9 Ibid., 5:281, 5:296.
10 Ibid., 5:299; Robert Remini, *Andrew Jackson and the Course of American Freedom* (New York: Harper & Row, Publishers, 1981), 51-2; Parton, 3:23.
11 *Papers*, 5:321.
12 Ibid., 5:320.
13 Chase C. Mooney, *William H. Crawford, 1772–1834* (Lexington: University Press of Kentucky, 1974), 252.
14 David S. Heidler and Jeanne T. Heidler, *Henry Clay: The Essential American* (New York: Random House, 2010), 163.
15 Historians David S. Heidler and Jeanne T. Heidler contend that Jackson owed his

presidency more to an emerging political system that produced fawning campaign biographies, flattering newspaper coverage, and backroom deals than to popular democracy. See their study, *The Rise of Andrew Jackson: Myth, Manipulation, and the Making of Modern Politics* (New York: Basic Books, 2018).

16 Martin Van Buren, *The Autobiography of Martin Van Buren*, ed. John C. Fitzpatrick, in *Annual Report of the American Historical Association for the Year 1918*, vol. 2 (Washington, D.C.: Government Printing Office, 1920), 139–40; Parton, 3:26.

17 Mooney, *William H. Crawford*, 258; James, *Life of Jackson*, 389.

18 James, *Life of Andrew Jackson*, 393.

19 *Papers*, 5:426.

20 Ibid., 5:334.

21 James, *Life of Jackson*, 390.

22 *Papers*, 5:372.

26: To Make a Myth: The Election of 1824

1 The states referred to are the coastal southern swing of Alabama, Georgia, Louisiana, and Mississippi, and the western unit of Indiana, Kentucky, Ohio, and Tennessee.

2 *The Letters of Wyoming: To the People of the United States on the Presidential Election, and in Favour of Andrew Jackson* (Philadelphia: S. Simpson & J. Conrad, 1824), 10, 12.

3 Albert Gallatin, *The Writings of Albert Gallatin*, vol. 2, ed. Henry Adams (Philadelphia: J. B. Lippincott & Co., 1879), 289–90.

4 Graham, et al., eds., *Diary and Autobiographical Writings of Louisa Catherine Adams*, 680; *Papers*, 5:341; Betty Boyd Caroli, *First Ladies: From Martha Washington to Michelle Obama* (New York: Oxford University Press, 2010), 21; James, *The Life of Andrew Jackson*, 383.

5 Remini, *Andrew Jackson and the Course of American Freedom*, 84.

6 James F. Hopkins, ed., *The Papers of Henry Clay*, vol. 4 (Lexington: University Press of Kentucky, 1972), 9–10.

7 Waldstreicher, ed., *Diaries of John Quincy Adams*, vol. 2, 86.

8 Hopkins, ed., *The Papers of Henry Clay*, vol. 4, 47.

9 Waldstreicher, ed., *Diaries of John Quincy Adams*, vol. 1, 308.

10 *Papers*, 6:26; 6:28; Waldstreicher, ed., *Diaries of John Quincy Adams*, vol. 2, 92.

11 Remini, *Andrew Jackson and the Course of American Freedom*, 95.

12 E. S. Thomas, *Reminiscences of the Last Sixty-Five Years*, vol. 2 (Hartford: Tiffany and Burnham, 1840), 91; James, *Life of Andrew Jackson*, 443; *Papers*, 6:21.

13 *Papers*, 5:121.

27: In Slavery's Shadow

1 *Papers*, 6:111.

2 Ibid., 6:124.

3 H. W. Brands, *Andrew Jackson: His Life and Times* (New York: Anchor Books, 2005), 152; Julie Aronson, "Ralph E. W. Earl," in Deborah Chotner, *American Naive Paintings* (Cambridge, England: Cambridge University Press, 1992), 103–4. For a recent study that interprets Earl as an effective Jackson propagandist, see Rachel

Stephens's *Selling Andrew Jackson: Ralph E. W. Earl and the Politics of Portraiture* (Columbia: University of South Carolina Press, 2018).

4 Remini, *Andrew Jackson and the Course of American Freedom*, 7; *Reminiscences of James A. Hamilton: Or, Men and Events, at Home and Abroad, During Three Quarters of a Century* (New York: Charles Scribner & Co., 1869), 70.

5 Parton, 3:160–61.

6 Juliana Margaret Courtney Conner Diary (1827), 49, 50, 52, #174-z, Southern Historical Collection at the Louis Round Wilson Special Collections Library, University of North Carolina at Chapel Hill.

7 *Papers*, 6:536.

8 Remini, *Andrew Jackson and the Course of American Empire*, 133; Mark R. Cheathem, *Andrew Jackson: Southerner* (Baton Rouge: Louisiana State University Press, 2013), 91; *Papers*, 2:248; 2:261–62.

9 *Papers*, 2:40–41; Cheathem, *Andrew Jackson*. 93.

28: Jacksonians

1 Remini, *Andrew Jackson and the Course of American Freedom*, 101.

2 *Papers of the Presidents*, 2:882, 2:877, 2:879.

3 *Register of Debates in Congress, Comprising the Leading Debates and Incidents of the First Session of the Nineteenth Congress*, vol. 2 (Washington, D.C.: Gales & Seaton, 1826), 387.

4 *Papers*, 6:228, 6:240, n1, 6:248.

5 Ibid., 6:177–178; on South Carolina's planter-dominated politics, see William W. Freehling's *Prelude to Civil War: The Nullification Controversy in South Carolina: 1816–1836* (New York: Harper & Row, 1965), especially chapters one and four.

6 *Papers*, 6:187–88.

7 Samuel Flagg Bemis, *John Quincy Adams and the Union* (New York: Alfred A. Knopf, 1956), 139; *Memoirs*, 7:163.

8 *Papers of the Presidents*, 1:310, 2:862–63.

9 Major L. Wilson, *The Presidency of Martin Van Buren* (Lawrence: University Press of Kansas, 1984), 27. On Van Buren's pro-party thinking, see Richard Hofstadter's *The Idea of a Party System: The Rise of Legitimate Opposition in the United States, 1780–1840* (Berkeley: University of California Press, 1969), 212–71. For an overview of the new campaigning culture in America, see Mark R. Cheathem's *The Coming of Democracy: Presidential Campaigning in the Age of Jackson* (Baltimore: Johns Hopkins University Press, 2018).

10 Van Buren, *Autobiography of Martin Van Buren*, 193, 197.

11 *Papers*, 6:392.

29: First from the West

1 An iteration of Claypoole's creation, an 1848 political cartoon portraying a military figure, presumably either Zachary Taylor or Winfield Scott, clasping a bloody sword and sitting atop a pyramid of skulls, played to the new campaigning culture. Both men, military heroes of the recent Mexican War, were potential Whig Party presidential candidates—Taylor secured the nomination that year and Scott followed in 1852. The image can be seen at: https://www.loc.gov/pictures/item/90708859/.

2 *Papers*, 6:371.
3 Thurlow Weed, *Life of Thurlow Weed: Including His Autobiography and a Memoir*, vol. 1, ed. Harriet A. Weed (Boston: Houghton Mifflin, 1884), 307–9.
4 *Papers*, 6:384.
5 Ibid., 6:385–87.
6 Ibid., 6:385.
7 Ibid: 5:398–99.
8 Richard B. Latner, *The Presidency of Andrew Jackson: White House Politics, 1829–1837* (Athens: University of Georgia Press, 1979), 25; *Papers*, 5:208.
9 Charles F. Hobson, ed., *The Papers of John Marshall*, vol. 11 (Chapel Hill: University of North Carolina Press, 2002), 173.
10 Donald B. Cole, *Vindicating Andrew Jackson: The 1828 Election and the Rise of the Two-Party System* (Lawrence: University Press of Kansas, 2009), 179, 187.
11 Svend Peterson, *A Statistical History of American Presidential Elections* (New York: Frederick Ungar, 1963), 308–9.
12 Cole, *Vindicating Andrew Jackson*, 187; Waldstreicher, ed., *Diaries of John Quincy Adams*, vol. 2, 188.
13 Rachel's death apparently took Jackson by surprise. Hours before she expired, he wrote to a colleague, "I trust in a kind providence, that he will restore her to her usual health in due time to set out for washington." *Papers*, 6:546.
14 Henry Wise, *Seven Decades of the Union* (Philadelphia: J. B. Lippincott, 1872), 114–15.
15 William Seale, *The President's House: A History*, vol. 1 (Washington, D.C.: White House Association, 1986), 175.

30: *The People's Pell-Mell*

1 Donald B. Cole, *The Presidency of Andrew Jackson* (Lawrence, University Press of Kansas, 1993), 23; Parton, 3:165.
2 Cole, *Presidency of Andrew Jackson*, 6–7.
3 Waldstreicher, ed., *Diaries of John Quincy Adams*, vol. 2, 197; James Grant, *John Adams: Party of One* (New York: Farrar, Straus and Giroux, 2005), 429; Ammon, *James Monroe*, 544.
4 Gaillard Hunt, ed., *The First Forty Years of Washington Society: Portrayed by the Family Letters of Mrs. Samuel Harrison Smith (Margaret Bayard), from the Collection of Her Grandson J. Henley Smith* (London: T. Fisher Unwin, 1906), 291; Remini, *Andrew Jackson and the Course of American Freedom*, 173.
5 *Papers of the Presidents*, 3:999–1001.
6 Albert J. Beveridge, *The Life of John Marshall*, vol. 4 (Boston: Houghton Mifflin, 1919), 466; Charles M. Wiltse, ed., *The Papers of Daniel Webster, Correspondence*, vol. 2 (Hanover, NH: University Press of New England, 1976), 405.
7 Hunt, ed., *First Forty Years of Washington Society*, 295.
8 Seale, *The President's House*, 179.
9 Ibid., 253.

31: *New Politics, New Men*

1 Waldstreicher, ed., *Diaries of John Quincy Adams*, vol. 2, 197; *Memoirs*, 6:474.
2 Howe, *What Hath God Wrought*, 333.

3 Barbara B. Oberg, ed., *The Papers of Thomas Jefferson*, vol. 34 (Princeton: Princeton University Press, 2007), 556.
4 *Papers of the Presidents*, 3:1011–12.
5 Howe, *What Hath God Wrought*, 334; Sean Wilentz, *Andrew Jackson* (New York: Time Books, 2005), 57; *Papers*: 7:249. In the 1950s Columbia University sociologist C. Wright Mills penned the classic study *The Power Elite*, a critique of the country's potent military, corporate, and political entities; the book questioned the degree of democracy in a post–World War II America dominated, so Mills insisted, by entrenched interests.
6 *Papers*, 7:193, 7:249.
7 Philip Hone, *The Diary of Philip Hone, 1828–1851*, vol. 1, ed. Allan Nevins (New York: Dodd, Mead, 1927), 357.
8 Van Buren, *Autobiography of Martin Van Buren*, 268–69.
9 Robert Seager II, ed., *The Papers of Henry Clay*, vol. 8 (Lexington: University Press of Kentucky, 1984), 79.
10 Henry Adams, *The Great Secession Winter of 1860–61: And Other Essays*, ed. George Hochfield (New York: Sagamore Press, 1958), 111–12.

32: *Peggy vs. the Moral Party*

1 Van Buren, *Autobiography of Martin Van Buren*, 339.
2 Peggy Eaton, *The Autobiography of Peggy Eaton* (New York: Charles Scribner's Sons, 1932), 11. My discussion on Margaret Eaton and the Eaton Affair is informed by John F. Marszalek's perceptive study, *The Petticoat Affair: Manners, Mutiny, and Sex in Andrew Jackson's White House* (New York: Free Press, 1997).
3 Marszalek, *Petticoat Affair*, 36–38.
4 *Papers*, 5:330; Remini, *Andrew Jackson and the Course of American Freedom*, 62.
5 *Papers*, 6:541–42; Parton, 3:185.
6 Waldstreicher, ed., *Diaries of John Quincy Adams*, vol. 2, 216; Catherine Allgor, *Parlor Politics: In Which the Ladies of Washington Help Build a City and a Government* (Charlottesville: University Press of Virginia, 2000), 200.
7 Van Buren, *Autobiography of Martin Van Buren*, 352; Remini, *Andrew Jackson and the Course of American Freedom*, 161.
8 Marszalek, *Petticoat Affair*, 73; Kirsten E. Wood, "'One Woman So Dangerous to Public Morals': Gender and Power in the Eaton Affair" *Journal of the Early Republic* (Summer 1997): 256, 252; Hunt, ed., *First Forty Years of Washington Society*, 318.
9 *Papers*, 7:184.
10 Waldstreicher, ed., *Diaries of John Quincy Adams*, vol. 2, 218; *Papers*, 8:57.
11 *Papers*, 8:57–58.
12 Seager II, ed., *Papers of Henry Clay*, 8:138.
13 *Memoirs*, 8:184; *Papers*, 7:101–4.
14 *Papers*, 7:113–18.
15 Parton, 3:204.
16 Jon Meacham, *American Lion: Andrew Jackson in the White House* (New York: Random House, 2008), 78; Pauline Wilcox Burke, *Emily Donelson of Tennessee*, vol. 1 (Richmond: Garrett and Massie, Incorporated, 1941), 178.
17 Meacham, *American Lion*, 79.
18 Wilcox Burke, *Emily Donelson*, 250; *Papers*, 8:357.

19 Meacham, *American Lion*, 79.
20 *Papers*, 8:580.
21 Bartlett, *John C. Calhoun*, 164; *Memoirs*, 8:185; *Papers*, 7:655–56.
22 Van Buren, *Autobiography of Martin Van Buren*, 403.
23 Marszalek, *Petticoat Affair*, 190; Eaton, *Autobiography of Peggy Eaton*, 87.
24 Van Buren, *Autobiography of Martin Van Buren*, 407–8.
25 *Correspondence*, 5:489; Marszalek, *Petticoat Affair*, 220.
26 Van Buren, *Autobiography of Martin Van Buren*, 365.

33: *Economy and Expansion*

1 *Papers*, 8:224.
2 Ibid., 8:224, 8:225.
3 Van Buren, *Autobiography of Martin Van Buren*, 326.
4 *Papers of the Presidents*, 3:1046–56.
5 Ibid., 3:1165; Van Buren, *Autobiography of Martin Van Buren*, 326. In total, Jackson approved some $10 million in public works during his eight years in office—more than all previous administrations combined. This suggests a president eager to employ federal funds, though considering the nation's rapid growth in population, increasing from 9.6 million in 1820 to 17 million in 1840, the expenditures were by no means extravagant. Cole, *Presidency of Andrew Jackson*, 67.
6 *Papers*, 8:332.
7 Waldstreicher, ed., *Diaries of John Quincy Adams*, vol. 2, 231.
8 *Papers*, 7:366.
9 Remini, *Andrew Jackson and the Course of American Freedom*, 219; Russell D. James, "Anthony Wayne Butler," in Spencer C. Tucker, ed., *The Encyclopedia of the Mexican-American War: A Political, Social, and Military History*, vol. 1 (Santa Barbara: ABC-CLIO, 2013), 100.
10 *Papers*, 9:518.
11 Ibid.
12 *Correspondence*, 6:291.

34: *The Graves of Their Fathers*

1 For state populations of Native Americans in 1830 see, http://www.teachushistory.org/indian-removal/resources/indian-populations-1830.
2 *Papers of the Presidents*, 3:1020, 3:1021–22.
3 John C. Fitzpatrick, ed., *The Writings of George Washington*, vol. 27 (Washington, D.C.: United States Government Printing Office, 1938), 140; Theda Perdue and Michael D. Green, *The Cherokee Nation and the Trail of Tears* (New York: Viking, 2007), 26–27; Colin G. Calloway, *The Indian World of George Washington: The First President, the First Americans, and the Birth of the Nation* (New York: Oxford University Press, 2018), 477.
4 Barbara B. Oberg, ed., *The Papers of Thomas Jefferson*, vol. 39 (Princeton, N.J.: Princeton University Press, 2012), 590.
5 Cappon, ed., *Adams-Jefferson Letters*, 308.
6 Richard K. Crallé, ed., *Reports and Public Letters of John C. Calhoun*, vol. 5 (New York: D. Appleton and Company, 1855), 18; *Papers of the Presidents*, 2:649.

7   Waldstreicher, ed., *Diaries of John Quincy Adams*, vol. 2, 164.

8   Michael D. Green, *The Politics of Indian Removal: Creek Government and Society in Crisis* (Lincoln: University of Nebraska Press, 1985), 116; Remini, *Andrew Jackson and the Course of American Freedom*, 258; David S. Reynolds, *Waking Giant: America in the Age of Jackson* (New York: HarperCollins, 2008), 60.

9   The civilization argument hardly crested with Jackson; rather it persisted into the next century. In 1900 Theodore Roosevelt, then candidate for vice president, wrote, "There are now in the United States communities of Indians which have advanced so far that it has just been possible to embody them as a whole in our political system, all the members of the tribe becoming United States citizens. There are other communities where the bulk of the tribes are still too wild for it to be possible to take such a step. There are individuals among the Apaches, Pawnees, Iroquois, Sioux and other tribes who are now United States citizens, and who are entitled to stand, and do stand, on an absolute equality with all our citizens of pure white blood." Elting Morison, ed., *The Letters of Theodore Roosevelt*, vol. 2 (Cambridge, MA: Harvard University Press, 1951), 1405.

10 *Governor's Message to the General Assembly of the State of Georgia at the Opening of the Extra Session* (Milledgeville, GA: Camak & Ragland, Printer, 1825), 122.

11 *Papers of the Presidents*, 3:1021. There are currently some twenty-eight thousand Iroquois living in New York State and perhaps another thirty thousand in Canada.

12 Ibid.

13 Perdue and Green, *The Cherokee Nation*, 71; Robert V. Remini, *John Quincy Adams* (New York: Times Books, 2002), 91.

14 Perdue and Green, *The Cherokee Nation*, 57.

15 A. J. Langguth, *Andrew Jackson and the Trail of Tears to the Civil War* (New York: Simon & Schuster, 2010), 141.

16 Cole, *Presidency of Andrew Jackson*, 74; Alfred A. Cave, "Abuse of Power: Andrew Jackson and the Indian Removal Act of 1830," *The Historian* (December 2003), 1334. For a discerning assessment of removal studies see Regan A. Lutz, "West of Eden: The Historiography of the Trail of Tears," Ph.D. Dissertation (University of Toledo, 1995).

17 Perdue and Green, *The Cherokee Nation*, 61–62.

18 Ronald N. Satz, *American Indian Policy in the Jacksonian Era* (Lincoln: University of Nebraska Press, 1975), 22.

19 Beveridge, *Life of John Marshall*, vol. 4, 546; Inskeep, *Jacksonland*, 250.

20 Charles Warren, *The Supreme Court in United States History*, vol. 2 (Boston: Little, Brown, 1923), 217.

21 *Papers*, 10:226; Jill Norgren, *The Cherokee Cases: The Confrontation of Law and Politics* (New York: McGraw-Hill, 1992), 122. Nearly 160 years later a second amnesty was issued. In November 1992 the Georgia State Board of Pardons and Paroles "unconditionally and fully" absolved the two missionaries, citing both the refusal of Georgia officials "to obey the U.S. Supreme Court" and Jackson's unwillingness "to use federal troops to enforce the order of the U.S. Supreme Court." Norgren, *The Cherokee Cases*, 2.

22 Tocqueville, *Democracy in America*, 324.

35: *Cornering Calhoun*

1 Jackson today stands as the ninth oldest president to be sworn in. Until Eisenhower in 1953 only three presidents—William Henry Harrison (68), Zachary Taylor (64), and James Buchanan (65)—exceeded Jackson in age; the first two died in office. *Papers*, 6:38.
2 Parton, 3:284.
3 Van Buren, *Autobiography of Martin Van Buren*, 414–16.
4 *Papers*, 8:577, 8:585.
5 Latner, *Presidency of Andrew Jackson*, 80; *Memoirs*, 8:222.
6 Remini, *Andrew Jackson and the Course of American Freedom*, 237.
7 Richard Hofstadter, *The American Political Tradition: And the Men Who Made It* (New York: Alfred A. Knopf, 1948), 72.
8 Hemphill, ed., *Papers of John C. Calhoun*, vol. 3 (Columbia: University of South Carolina Press, 1967), 114; *Papers*, 6:442.
9 *Papers*, 8:258, n1, 8:257.
10 Ibid., 8:256, 8:260.
11 Ibid., 8:305, 8:307.
12 Ibid., 8:322.
13 *Correspondence Between Gen. Andrew Jackson and John C. Calhoun, President and Vice-President of the U. States, On the Subject of the Course of the Latter, In the Deliberation of the Cabinet of Mr. Monroe, on the Occurrences In the Seminole War* (Washington, D.C.: Duff Green, 1831), 4.
14 *Papers*, 9:68.

36: *Kitchen Politics*

1 Si Sheppard, *The Partisan Press: A History of Media Bias in the United States* (Jefferson, North Carolina: McFarland & Company, Inc., 2008), 95.
2 William Ernest Smith, *The Francis Preston Blair Family in Politics*, vol. 1 (New York: Macmillan, 1933), 62.
3 Remini, *Andrew Jackson and the Course of American Freedom*, 293.
4 Marc Friedlaender and L. H. Butterfield, eds., *Diary of Charles Francis Adams*, vol. 4 (Cambridge, MA: Belknap Press of Harvard University Press, 1968), 34; *Papers*, 9:200, 9:214.
5 Hone, *Diary of Philip Hone*, vol. 1, 143.
6 Thomas Hart Benton, *Thirty Years' View: Or, a History of the Working of the American Government for Thirty Years, from 1820 to 1850*, vol. 1 (New York: D. Appleton and Company, 1858), 215.
7 George Ticknor Curtis, *Life of Daniel Webster*, vol. 1 (New York: D. Appleton and Company, 1870), 375.
8 *Papers*, 9:346.

37: *Breaking the Bank*

1   Cappon, ed., *Adams-Jefferson Letters*, 424.
2   Reginald C. McGrane, ed., *The Correspondence of Nicholas Biddle: Dealings with National Affairs, 1807–1844* (Boston: Houghton Mifflin, 1919), 93.
3   *Papers of the Presidents*, 3:1025.
4   McGrane, ed., *Correspondence of Nicholas Biddle*, 92.
5   *Papers*, 9:158.
6   Ibid., 7:568; *Papers of the Presidents*, 3:1121.
7   McGrane, ed., *Correspondence of Nicholas Biddle*, 112.
8   *Papers*, 10:161.
9   Cole, *Presidency of Andrew Jackson*, 103.
10 *Papers of the Presidents*, 3:1140, 3:1144, 3:1145.
11 Ibid., 3:1140, 3:1153.
12 Ibid., 3:1153.
13 McGrane, ed., *Correspondence of Nicholas Biddle*, 195–96.
14 *Papers of the Presidents*, 3:1145, emphasis added. During the sixth Lincoln-(Stephen) Douglas Debate, held in Quincy, Illinois, in October 1858, Lincoln made use of Jackson's "as he understands" it quote when opposing the controversial Dred Scott decision (1857), in which the Supreme Court declared that Congress could not keep slavery out of the nation's western territories. Lincoln observed: "General Jackson once said each man was bound to support the Constitution 'as he understood it.' Now, Judge Douglas understands the Constitution according to the Dred Scott decision, and he is bound to support it as he understands it. I understand it another way, and therefore I am bound to support it in the way in which I understand it." This line received prolonged applause. *Lincoln: Selected Speeches and Writings* (New York: Library of America, 1992), 188.
15 *The Works of Daniel Webster*, vol. 3 (Boston: Little, Brown, 1853), 446–47; McGrane, ed., *Correspondence of Nicholas Biddle*, 196; Latner, *Presidency of Andrew Jackson*, 119.
16 On the Jacksonian appeal to the past, see Lawrence Frederick Kohl, *The Politics of Individualism: Parties and the American Character in the Jacksonian Era* (New York: Oxford University Press, 1989), 22–61, and Marvin Meyers, *The Jacksonian Persuasion: Politics and Belief* (Palo Alto: Stanford University Press, 1957), 16–32.

38: *More Popular than a Party*

1   Melba Porter Hay, ed., *The Papers of Henry Clay*, vol. 10 (Lexington: University Press of Kentucky, 1991), 504.
2   Cole, *Presidency of Andrew Jackson*, 151.
3   In Theodore Roosevelt's case I use the term "reelection" loosely, and in respect to his incumbency, as he came to power in 1901 following the assassination of President William McKinley.
4   Friedlaender and Butterfield, eds., *Diary of Charles Francis Adams*, 394; Seager II, ed., *Papers of Henry Clay*, 8:537; Herbert Weaver, ed., *Correspondence of James K. Polk*, vol. 1 (Nashville, Tenn.: Vanderbilt University Press, 1969), 537.
5   Three other Democrats served multiple terms, but failed to crack 50 percent of the popular vote. These were Grover Cleveland (48 percent in 1884 and 46 percent

in 1892), Woodrow Wilson (41 percent in 1912 and 49 percent in 1916), and Bill Clinton (43 percent in 1992 and 49 percent in 1996). Though various coalitions—Populists, Socialists, and Ross Perot's Reform Party—took support away from these candidates, Jackson too faced third-party competition in 1832, from both the Nullifiers and the Anti-Masons.

39: The Nullification Crisis

1 Waldstreicher, ed., *Diaries of John Quincy Adams,* vol. 2, 239.
2 *Papers,* 6:476.
3 Ibid., 6:481.
4 Cole, *Presidency of Andrew Jackson,* 153.
5 "Exposition and Protest, Reported by the Special Committee of the House of Representatives, on the Tariff" (Columbia: D. W. Sims, State Printer, 1829), 11; Davy Crockett, *An Account of Col. Crockett's Tour to the North and Down East* (Philadelphia: Carey, Hart, and Co., 1835), 67.
6 Freehling, *Prelude to Civil War,* 11.
7 *Papers of the Presidents,* 3:1119; *Papers,* 10:422.
8 *Papers,* 10:477.
9 Freehling, *Prelude to Civil War,* 255.
10 *Papers,* 10:678.
11 Ibid., 10:506, 10:630, 10:558; Asbury Dickins, ed., *American State Papers: Documents, Legislative and Executive, of the Congress of the United States; Military Affairs,* vol. 5 (Washington, D.C.: Gales & Seaton, 1860), 161.
12 *Papers of the Presidents,* 3:1161.
13 Ibid., 3:1204.
14 Ibid., 3:1205.
15 Ibid., 3:1206, 3:1207.
16 Ibid., 3:1211.
17 Ibid., 3:1215, 3:1216, 3:1217.
18 Friedlaender and Butterfield, eds., *Diary of Charles Francis Adams,* vol. 4, 419; Hone, *Diary of Philip Hone,* vol. 1, 84. Hone's intimation of infantilization more generally underscored Jackson's response to the recalcitrant. Often in his dealings with soldiers and Indians did Jackson, the "Great Father," adopt some variation of the "wayward children" theme.
19 Seager II, ed., *Papers of Henry Clay,* vol. 8, 613.
20 *Papers,* 10:730.
21 Freehling, *Prelude to Civil War,* 288.
22 Merrill D. Peterson, *Olive Branch and Sword: The Compromise of 1833* (Baton Rouge: Louisiana State University Press, 1982), 55.
23 William J. Cooper, Jr., *The South and the Politics of Slavery, 1828–1856* (Baton Rouge: Louisiana State University Press, 1978), 44–45; Richard E. Ellis, *The Union at Risk: Jacksonian Democracy, States' Rights, and the Nullification Crisis* (New York: Oxford University Press, 1987), 85.
24 Eric Foner, *The Fiery Trial: Abraham Lincoln and American Slavery* (New York: W. W. Norton, 2010), 145; William E. Gienapp, ed., *This Fiery Trial: The Speeches and Writings of Abraham Lincoln* (New York: Oxford University Press, 2002), 91.

40: *New England Swing*

1   Josiah Quincy, *Figures of the Past: From the Leaves of Old Journals* (Boston: Robert Brother, 1883), 354–55; Fletcher M. Green, "On Tour with President Andrew Jackson," *New England Quarterly* (June 1963): 212.

2   Hone, *Diary of Philip Hone*, vol. 1, 96; *Correspondence*, 5:109. Cupping is a technique used to facilitate healing by placing cups on the skin and creating suction, which is said in some cases to aid blood circulation and relieve muscle tension. Among "watering places," Jackson enjoyed during his presidential years retreating to Rip Raps, an artificial island created in 1817 at the mouth of the Hampton Roads harbor in Virginia.

3   *Correspondence*, 5:109.

4   Benjamin Drake, *The Life and Adventures of Black Hawk: With Sketches of Keokuk, the Sac and Fox Indians, and the Late Black Hawk War* (Cincinnati: George Conclin, 1838), 218; Charles Richard Tuttle, *History of the Border Wars of Two Centuries: Embracing a Narrative of the Wars with the Indians from 1750 to 1874* (Chicago: C. A. Wall & Company, 1874), 318; J. B. Patterson, ed., *Black Hawk's Autobiography* (Rock Island, IL: American Publishing Company, 1912), 123.

5   Robert Remini, *Andrew Jackson and the Course of American Democracy* (New York: Harper & Row, 1984), 73; *Correspondence*, 5:110.

6   Donald B. Cole and John J. McDonough, eds., *Benjamin Brown French, Witness to the Young Republic: A Yankee's Journal, 1828–1870* (Hanover, NH: University Press of New England, 1989), 30.

7   *Correspondence*, 5:110.

8   Cole and McDonough, eds., *Benjamin Brown French*, 31; *Memoirs*, 9:5.

9   The politics of conferring academic titles on presidents persisted at Harvard. In 1901 anti-imperialist sentiment on the university's Board of Overseers—stemming from the recent Spanish-American War—kept William McKinley from receiving an honorary degree that spring. A few months later he was assassinated.

10 Maureen T. Moore, "Andrew Jackson: 'Pretty Near a "Treason" to call him Doctor!,'" *New England Quarterly* (September 1989): 427–28; Quincy, *Figures of the Past*, 352.

11 *Memoirs*, 8:546–47.

12 Marc Friedlaender and L. H. Butterfield, eds., *Diary of Charles Francis Adams*, vol. 5 (Cambridge, MA: Belknap Press of Harvard University Press, 1974), 115, 116; Louisa Catherine Johnson Adams to Mary Catherine Hellen Adams, Adams Papers microfilm, reel 497, July 6, 1833, Massachusetts Historical Society. I'm grateful to Gwen Fries for passing along Louisa Catherine's deflating salute to both Jackson and Harvard.

13 *Correspondence*, 6:416.

14 Remini, *Andrew Jackson and the Course of American Democracy*, 81; Quincy, *Figures of the Past*, 374.

15 Cole and McDonough, eds., *Benjamin Brown French*, 32; *Memoirs*, 9:4. As mentioned, Adams thought Jackson shamming illness, noting in his diary, "He is one of our tribe of great men who turn disease to commodity, like John Randolph, who for forty years was always dying." *Memoirs*, 9:5.

16 Friedlaender and Butterfield, eds., *Diary of Charles Francis Adams*, vol. 5, 110.

41: *Shades of Caesar*

1 Wilentz, *Andrew Jackson*, 105.
2 *Correspondence*, 5:46.
3 Ibid., 5:77, 5:86, 5:87, 5:99.
4 Ibid., 5:101.
5 William J. Duane, *Narrative and Correspondence Concerning the Removal of the Deposits and Occurrences Connected Therewith* (Philadelphia, 1838), 40, 42, 43.
6 Remini, *Andrew Jackson and the Course of American Democracy*, 88.
7 *Correspondence*, 5:159.
8 Duane, *Narrative and Correspondence*, 96. *Correspondence*, 5:187. Another member of Jackson's cabinet, Postmaster William Barry, was not in Washington during these discussions.
9 Duane, *Narrative and Correspondence*, 102; *Correspondence*, 5:207.
10 William W. Story, ed., *Life and Letters of Joseph Story*, vol. 2 (Boston: Charles C. Little and James Brown, 1851), 154.

42: *Censure*

1 Robert V. Remini, *Henry Clay: Statesman for the Union* (New York: W. W. Norton, 1991), 444–45; *Correspondence*, 5:216–17.
2 Calvin Colton, ed., *Works of Henry Clay: Comprising His Life, Correspondence and Speeches*, vol. 2 (New York: Henry Clay Publishing Company, 1896), 76.
3 Colton, ed., *Works of Henry Clay*, 78.
4 Seager II, ed., *Papers of Henry Clay*, vol. 8, 683.
5 Remini, *Andrew Jackson and the Course of American Democracy*, 235.
6 Benton, *Thirty Years' View*, 423.
7 *Correspondence*, 5:261.
8 *Papers of the Presidents*, 3:1289, 3:1290, 3:1291.
9 Ibid., 1301; Cole, *The Presidency of Andrew Jackson*, 208.
10 *Papers of the Presidents*, 3:1309.
11 Daniel Webster, *The Writings and Speeches of Daniel Webster*, vol. 7 (Boston: Little, Brown, 1903), 143, 137.
12 Two years later, with a Democratic majority in the Senate, Jackson again nominated Stevenson to serve as the nation's minister to the United Kingdom. He was confirmed 26–19.
13 Weed, *Life of Thurlow Weed*, 431.
14 Cole, *Presidency of Andrew Jackson*, 213–14.

43: *Facing Europe*

1 The five are James Hamilton, Martin Van Buren, Edward Livingston, Louis McLane, and John Forsyth. Hamilton served for less than a month as secretary pro tem until then New York governor Van Buren could resign his post and arrive in Washington. At two years and eight months, Forsyth served the longest.
2 *Papers of the Presidents*, 3:1066; Cole, *Presidency of Andrew Jackson*, 124.

3   *Papers*, 9:562; John M. Belohlavek, *"Let the Eagle Soar!": The Foreign Policy of Andrew Jackson* (Lincoln: University of Nebraska Press, 1985), 109; *Correspondence*, 5:272.

4   *Papers of the Presidents*, 3:1321–22, 3:1324.

5   Ibid., 3:1325.

6   Ibid.; Marc Friedlaender and L. H. Butterfield, eds., *Diary of Charles Francis Adams*, vol. 6 (Cambridge, MA: Belknap Press of Harvard University Press, 1974), 82.

7   George C. Herring, *From Colony to Superpower: U.S. Foreign Relations Since 1776* (New York: Oxford University Press, 2008), 166–67; Remini, *Andrew Jackson and the Course of American Democracy*, 236.

8   *Papers of the Presidents*, 4:1379, 4:1377, 4:1378.

9   Belohlavek, *"Let the Eagle Soar!,"* 123; *Papers of the Presidents*, 4:1446.

10 Reynolds, *Waking Giant*, 115.

44: Jackson and the Abolitionists

1   Remini, *Andrew Jackson and the Course of American Democracy*, 259. For an overview of the abolitionists' postal campaign see Richard R. John's *Spreading the News: The American Postal System from Franklin to Morse* (Cambridge, MA: Harvard University Press, 1995), 257–80.

2   Bertram Wyatt-Brown, "The Abolitionists' Postal Campaign of 1835," *Journal of Negro History* (October 1965): 227–28; *William Lloyd Garrison, 1805–1879: The Story of His Life Told by His Children*, vol. 1 (New York: Century Co., 1885), 123.

3   Wyatt-Brown, "The Abolitionists' Postal Campaign of 1835," 229, 230.

4   Ibid.

5   *Correspondence*, 5:360–61.

6   Remini, Jackson's most sympathetic biographer, calls the president's actions during this episode a "hands-off policy," though it is difficult to reconcile that sentiment with Jackson's active encouragement to Kendall—and disseminated through the *Globe*—to identify and punish men such as Tappan. Remini, *Andrew Jackson and the Course of American Democracy*, 261, 271.

7   Leonard L. Richards, "The Jacksonians and Slavery," in Lewis Perry and Michael Fellman, eds., *Antislavery Reconsidered: New Perspectives on the Abolitionists* (Baton Rouge: Louisiana State University Press, 1979), 109.

8   *Papers of the Presidents*, 4:1394–95.

9   Ivor D. Spencer, "William L. Marcy Goes Conservative," *Mississippi Valley Historical Review* (September 1944), 217; Howard Alexander Morrison, "Gentlemen of Proper Understanding: A Closer Look at Utica's Anti-Abolitionist Mob," *New York History* (January 1981), 61–82.

10 Richard Robert Madden, *The Memoirs (Chiefly autobiographical) from 1798 to 1896 of Richard Robert Madden* (London: Ward & Downey, 1891), 96.

45: Removal Redux

1   Cave, "Abuse of Power," 209.

2   Langguth, *Andrew Jackson and the Trail of Tears to the Civil War*, 232–35.

3   Perdue and Green, *The Cherokee Nation*, 113.

4 Anthony F. C. Wallace, *The Long, Bitter Trail: Andrew Jackson and the American Indians* (New York: Hill and Wang, 93), 1993.
5 James Elliot Cabot, ed., *A Memoir of Ralph Waldo Emerson*, vol. 2 (Boston: Houghton, Mifflin, 1888), 698, 700, 699, 701.
6 *Papers*, 7:494; Stockwell, *The Other Trail of Tears*, 323–25.

46: To Kill a President

1 Steven Mintz, *Moralists and Modernizers: America's Pre–Civil War Reformers* (Baltimore: Johns Hopkins University Press, 1995), 3.
2 One of the bullets referred to, lodged in Jackson's left arm since 1813 but having moved over the years closer to the skin, was removed in January 1832 by Dr. Thomas Harris, second chief of the navy's Bureau of Medicine. Kenneth S. Greenberg, *Honor & Slavery: Lies, Duels, Noses, Masks, Dressing as a Woman, Gifts, Strangers, Humanitarianism, Death, Slave Rebellions, the Proslavery Argument, Baseball, Hunting, and Gambling in the Old South* (Princeton, N.J.: Princeton University Press, 1996), 20–22.
3 Parton, 3:487.
4 Ibid.; *Correspondence*, 5:74; Waldstreicher, ed., *Diaries of John Quincy Adams*, vol. 2, 305.
5 Waldstreicher, ed., *Diaries of John Quincy Adams*, vol. 2, 349; Benton, *Thirty Years' View*, 521; Martineau, *Retrospect of Western Travel*, 122. Police later tested Lawrence's pistols, at which time they fired perfectly.
6 *Washington Globe*, January 31, 1835, as quoted in Meacham, *American Lion*, 434, n299; Charles M. Wiltse, ed., *The Papers of Daniel Webster: Correspondence*, vol. 4, (Hanover, NH: University Press of New England, 1980), 25.
7 Benton, *Thirty Years' View*, 523.
8 Carlton Jackson, "Another Time, Another Place—The Attempted Assassination of President Andrew Jackson," *Tennessee Historical Quarterly* (Summer 1967): 187–90.
9 Martineau, *Retrospect of Western Travel*, 123; Richard C. Rohrs, "Partisan Politics and the Attempted Assassination of Andrew Jackson," *Journal of the Early Republic* (Summer 1981), 152.

47: Texas Again

1 Waldstreicher, ed., *Diaries of John Quincy Adams*, vol. 2, 600–601. On the theme of "reannexation" see Amy S. Greenberg's *A Wicked War: Polk, Clay, Lincoln, and the 1846 U.S. Invasion of Mexico* (New York: Alfred A. Knopf, 2012), 33.
2 *Correspondence*, 5:214–15.
3 Ibid., 5:221, 5:229, 5:219, 5:228, 4:81.
4 Ibid., 5:222.
5 Michael A. Morrison, *Slavery and the American West: the Eclipse of Manifest Destiny and the Coming of the Civil War* (Chapel Hill: University of North Carolina Press, 1997), 14; Herring, *From Colony to Superpower*, 175.

48: The Jackson Court

1 William Howard Taft also appointed six justices—and did so in a single term. Seager II, ed., *Papers of Henry Clay*, vol. 8, 757. In the Judiciary Act of 1801 a

lame duck Federalist Congress voted to reduce the size of the Supreme Court from six justices to five—a move designed in part to prevent the incoming executive, Thomas Jefferson, from reshaping the court. The following year a Republican Congress repealed the act.

2 *Correspondence*, 5:390.

3 John Gregory Jacobsen, "Jackson's Judges: Six Appointments Who Shaped a Nation," Ph.D. Dissertation, the University of Nebraska, 2004, 57. Legal scholar Kermit Hall wrote that Jackson occasionally "ignored other Democratic candidates with more distinguished records of judicial service" to tab loyalists. Kermit L. Hall, *The Politics of Justice: Lower Federal Judicial Selection and the Second Party System, 1829–1861* (Lincoln: University of Nebraska Press, 1980), 6.

4 Waldstreicher, ed., *Diaries of John Quincy Adams*, vol. 2, 360–61.

5 John McLean to Felix Grundy, March 24, 1837, folder 1, Felix Grundy Papers, Southern Historical Collection at the Louis Round Wilson Special Collections Library, the University of North Carolina at Chapel Hill.

49: *The Politics of Succession*

1 Josiah Quincy, *Figures of the Past*, 355.

2 *Papers*, 10:176.

3 Seager II, ed., *Papers of Henry Clay*, vol. 8, 792, 794.

4 *The Works of Daniel Webster*, vol. 4 (Boston: Little, Brown, 1853), 280; *Correspondence*, 5:463.

5 Waldstreicher, ed., *Diaries of John Quincy Adams*, vol. 2, 393; Wilson, *Presidency of Martin Van Buren*, 19; Richards, "The Jacksonians and Slavery," 102.

6 Benton, *Thirty Years' View*, 718.

7 Ibid., 719.

8 Ibid., 730–31.

50: *Administration's End*

1 *Correspondence*, 5:462–63; Parton, 3:628; John Niven, *Martin Van Buren: The Romantic Age of American Politics* (New York: Oxford University Press, 1983), 409–11; Benton, *Thirty Years' View*, 735. Emerson doubtlessly agreed with Benton's assessment of the rising and setting presidential suns. In an 1840 journal entry he wrote, "The Democratic party in this country is more magnetic than the Whig. Andrew Jackson is an eminent example of it. Van Buren is not." *Ralph Waldo Emerson: Selected Journals, 1820–1842*, ed. Lawrence Rosenwald (New York: Library of America, 2010), 750.

2 *Papers of the Presidents*, 4:1512; *Correspondence*, 5:465.

3 *Papers of the Presidents*, 4:1524.

4 Ibid., 4:1517.

5 Edward Pessen, *Jacksonian Panorama* (Indianapolis: Bobbs-Merrill, 1976), 159; Hone, *Diary of Philip Hone*, vol. 1, 245.

6 Parton, 3:627.

51: *Unquiet Retirement*

1   The economist Jane Knodell has written, "From 1834 to 1836 the money supply grew at an average annual rate of 30 percent, compared to 2.7 percent between 1831 and 1834." Jane Knodell, "Rethinking the Jacksonian Economy: The Impact of the 1832 Bank Veto on Commercial Banking," *Journal of Economic History* (September 2006): 542.

2   Story, ed., *Life and Letters of Joseph Story*, 273; McGrane, ed., *Correspondence of Nicholas Biddle*, 272; *Correspondence*, 5:478.

3   *Correspondence*, 5:546. Under the direction of Jackson's Tennessee protégé James K. Polk, an Independent Treasury Act passed through Congress in 1846. Designed to be independent of the private banking system, the Treasury would only accept payments in specie or Treasury notes. And yet as specie payments both to and from the government impacted the money supply, the Treasury's influence was never really divorced from the broader economy. The Civil War demonstrated the inadequacy of such a restricted system in a time of financial duress, leading to the National Banking Acts of 1863 and 1864, which established a regime of nationally chartered banks and permitted government funds to be deposited in some private banks. These modifications to the Independent Treasury were accompanied in the decades after the war by other adjustments. The Panic of 1907 led to the Federal Reserve Act of 1913 and the end of the Independent Treasury idea.

4   Remini, *Andrew Jackson and the Course of American Democracy*, 189–90. For an inventory of Hermitage furniture, see Heiskell, ed., *Andrew Jackson and Early Tennessee History*, 554–578.

5   *Correspondence*, 6:77.

6   Nancy N. Scott, ed., *A Memoir of Hugh Lawson White: With Selections from His Speeches and Correspondence* (Philadelphia: J. B. Lippincott & Co., 1856), 325.

7   Correspondence, 6:83, 6:80; Donald B. Cole, *Martin Van Buren: And the American Political System* (Princeton, NJ: Princeton University Press, 1984), 344.

8   *Niles' National Register*, November 7, 1840, 155.

9   *Correspondence*, 6:82.

10   Ibid., 6:105, 6:128, 6:131.

11   Ibid., 6:275.

12   Ibid., 6:148–49; Jean-Marc Serme, "Stormy Weather at Andrew Jackson's Halcyon Plantation in Coahoma County, Mississippi, 1838–1845," *Revue Française d'Études Américaines* 4 (2003): 32–47. Andrew Jackson, Jr., failed in the 1850s to honor Blair's note. This, and other debts—totaling some $48,000, about $1.7 million in current dollars—threatened to put him into bankruptcy. In 1856 the state of Tennessee purchased the Hermitage's remaining five hundred acres—Jackson, Jr. had from time to time sold off portions of the estate—on the condition that the Jackson family could remain in residence. Andrew Jackson, Jr., died in April 1865 and is buried at the Hermitage. His wife remained on the property until her death in 1887.

13   *Correspondence*, 6:177.

52: *The Last Push*

1   *Correspondence*, 6:286, 6:202. Post–Indian removal, Jackson was concerned that "the numerous hords of savages within the limits of Texas and on her borders

would be easily excited to make war upon our defenceless frontier." Ibid., 6:291. Eager as president to separate the Indians from their eastern homes, he now suggested that the lands west of the Mississippi formerly allotted to them by the government offered launching points for attacks on the United States.

2 Niven, *Martin Van Buren*, 525; The "Hammett Letter" can be found at http://van burenpapers.org/document-mvb03868; *Correspondence*, 6:284–85.

3 Wayne Cutler, ed., *Correspondence of James K. Polk*, vol. 7 (Nashville, TN: Vanderbilt University Press, 1989), 137.

4 Joel H. Silbey, *Storm Over Texas: The Annexation Controversy and the Road to Civil War* (New York: Oxford University Press, 2005), 50.

5 *Correspondence*, 6:283.

6 Ibid., 6:303, 6:304, 6:305, 6:315; Christopher J. Leahy, *President Without a Party: The Life of John Tyler* (Baton Rouge: Louisiana State University Press, 2020), 338.

7 Ibid., 6:313, 6:330.

8 Ibid., 6:320; Wayne Cutler, ed., *Correspondence of James K. Polk*, vol. 8, (Knoxville: University of Tennessee Press, 1993), 324.

9 *Correspondence*, 6:339–40.

53: *No Terrors*

1 For a description of Jackson's bedroom see Heiskell, *Andrew Jackson and Early Tennessee History*, 560–61; Remini, *Andrew Jackson and the Course of American Democracy*, 519; *Correspondence*, 6:378.

2 Parton, 3:672–76.

3 Hannah's narrative was recorded by William G. Terrell in 1880. He used parts of it for an article in the June 22, 1880, (Cincinnati) *Commercial*, "Old Hannah: Reminisces of the Hermitage." I quote from *Correspondence*, 6:415; Wayne Cutler, ed., *Correspondence of James K. Polk*, vol. 9 (Knoxville: University of Tennessee Press, 1996), 436.

4 Ludwig M. Deppisch, Jose A. Centeno, David J. Gemmel, and Norca L. Torres, "Andrew Jackson's Exposure to Mercury and Lead," *Journal of the American Medical Association* (August 11, 1999): 570–71; *Correspondence*, 6:411.

5 Cutler, ed., *Correspondence of James K. Polk*, vol. 9, 439.

6 Philip Hone, *The Diary of Philip Hone, 1828–1851*, vol. 2, ed. Allan Nevins (New York: Dodd, Mead, 1927), 734; Lynn Hudson Parsons, "In Which the Political Becomes the Personal, and Vice Versa: The Last Ten Years of John Quincy Adams and Andrew Jackson," *Journal of the Early Republic* (Autumn, 2003), 443.

54: *Heroes and Villains*

1 Hone, *Diary of Philip Hone*, vol. 2, 732; Cole and McDonough, eds., *Benjamin Brown French*, 338. Jackson remained a model for the martially inclined into the twentieth century. "The United States would stand like a unit if we had in the Presidency a man of the stamp of Andrew Jackson," wrote former president Theodore Roosevelt following the 1915 sinking of the RMS *Lusitania*. "Think of Old Hickory letting our citizens be constantly murdered on the high seas by the Germans." Elting E. Morison, ed., *The Letters of Theodore Roosevelt*, vol. 8 (Cambridge, MA: Harvard University Press, 1954), 964.

2   Frederick Jackson Turner, *The Frontier in American History* (New York: Henry Holt, 1920), 173. In 1922 Turner wrote of his family's vicarious connection to Jackson: "My father was named Andrew Jackson Turner at his birth in 1832 by my Democratic grandfather, and I still rise and go to bed to the striking of the old clock that was brought into the house the day that he was born, at the edge of the Adirondack forest." Wilbur R. Jacobs, *The Historical World of Frederick Jackson Turner: With Selections from His Correspondence* (New Haven: Yale University Press, 1968), 62. Like most historians of his era, the Wisconsin-born Turner regarded Jackson as more western pioneer than southern slaveholder.

3   Jackson biographer Augustus C. Buell dedicated his three-volume *History of Andrew Jackson* (1904) to Roosevelt for being "The Embodiment in Our Times of the Jacksonian Spirit."

4   Trump, calling Jackson the "people's president," visited the Hermitage to mark the 250th anniversary of the General's birth. He did not visit Massachusetts four months later to honor the 250th anniversary of John Quincy Adams's birth. On Trump's interview with Zito see Louis Jacobson and Sarah Waychoff, "What's Up with Donald Trump and Andrew Jackson?," PolitiFact, May 2, 2017, at https://www.politifact.com/truth-o-meter/article/2017/may/02/whats-up-with-donald-trump-andrew-jackson/; Trump's May 1, 2017, tweet on Jackson and the Civil War can be accessed at https://twitter.com/realDonaldTrump/status/859209801175269376.

5   "Remarks by the President on 250th Anniversary of the Birth of President Andrew Jackson," March 15, 2017, at https://www.whitehouse.gov/briefings-statements/remarks-president-250th-anniversary-birth-president-andrew-jackson/.

6   Victor Davis Hanson, *The Case for Trump* (New York: Basic Books, 2019). The quote is taken from the dust jacket's front flap.

7   See, for example, Jamelle Bouie, "Trump's Trail of Fears," *New York Times*, February 11, 2019, https://www.nytimes.com/2019/02/11/opinion/trump-warren-trail-tears.html, and Cathy Norris, "On Immigration, President Trump Channels Andrew Jackson," *San Angelo Standard-Times*, February 1, 2018, https://www.gosanangelo.com/story/opinion/readers/2018/02/01/opinion-immigration-president-trump-channels-andrew-jackson/1089347001/. On Trump and Warren see Sarah Mervosh's "Trump Mocks Warren with Apparent Reference to Trail of Tears, Which Killed Thousands," February 10, 2019, https://www.nytimes.com/2019/02/10/us/trump-trail-of-tears.html.

8   Trump interview with ABC News's Jonathan Karl at the Iowa State Fair, https://www.youtube.com/watch?v=FC_wapgQLxw. "Birtherism" proved decidedly fringe in the 1820s, perhaps because of the constitutional clause, "No Person except a natural born Citizen, *or a Citizen of the United States, at the time of the Adoption of this Constitution*, shall be eligible to the office of President" (emphasis added). Jackson was born in 1767, twenty years before the Constitution's ratification.

9   John Quincy Adams also won the presidency with less than 50 percent of the popular vote before losing to Jackson four years later with, again, less than half of the popular tally. His case is complicated by the fact that four major candidates vied for the presidency in 1824 and thus divided the vote in an election that ultimately went to the House of Representatives. The outcomes of Grover Cleveland's several candidacies are interesting. He captured the presidency in two of three elections between 1884 and 1892, outpolling his opponents in the popular vote each time, though never cracking 48.9 percent.

Illustration Credits

4. Courtesy of the Library of Congress
5. Courtesy of the Library of Congress
6. Courtesy of the Library of Congress
7. Courtesy of the Library of Congress
8. Courtesy of the Library of Congress
9. Courtesy of the Library of Congress
10. Andrew Jackson's Hermitage, Nashville, Tennessee
11. Courtesy of the Library of Congress
12. Courtesy of the Library of Congress
13. Courtesy of the Library of Congress
14. Courtesy of the Library of Congress
15. Courtesy of the Library of Congress
16. Courtesy of the Tennessee State Library and Archives
17. Courtesy of the Library of Congress
18. Andrew Jackson's Hermitage, Nashville, Tennessee

Index

About the Author

David S. Brown teaches history at Elizabethtown College in Pennsylvania. He is the author of several previous books, including *The Last American Aristocrat: The Brilliant Life and Improbable Education of Henry Adams, Paradise Lost: A Life of F. Scott Fitzgerald,* and *Richard Hofstadter: An Intellectual Biography.*